Contemporary Jewelry in Perspective.

Contemporary Jewelry in Perspective.

Edited by Damian Skinner

in association with Art Jewelry Forum

LARK JEWELRY
& BEADING

This book is dedicated to Mike Holmes, who opened the door, and
Susan Cummins, who invited me in.

**LARK JEWELRY
& BEADING**

An Imprint of Sterling Publishing
387 Park Avenue South
New York, NY 10016

ISBN 978-1-4547-0277-1

Library of Congress Cataloging-in-Publication Data

Contemporary jewelry in perspective / edited by Damian Skinner.
     pages cm
  Includes index.
  ISBN 978-1-4547-0277-1 (hardcover)
  1. Artist-designed jewelry--20th century. 2. Artist-designed
jewelry--21st century. I. Skinner, Damian, editor of compilation. II. Art
Jewelry Forum (Mill Valley, Calif.)
  NK7310.C66 2013
  739.2709'051--dc23

                                  2013002468

Distributed in Canada by Sterling Publishing
c/o Canadian Manda Group, 165 Dufferin Street
Toronto, Ontario, Canada M6K 3H6
Distributed in the United Kingdom by GMC Distribution Services
Castle Place, 166 High Street, Lewes, East Sussex, England BN7 1XU
Distributed in Australia by Capricorn Link (Australia) Pty. Ltd.
P.O. Box 704, Windsor, NSW 2756, Australia

For information about custom editions, special sales, and premium and
corporate purchases, please contact Sterling Special Sales at 800-805-5489 or
specialsales@sterlingpublishing.com.

Email academic@larkbooks.com for information about desk and examination copies.
The complete policy can be found at larkbooks.com.

Every effort has been made to ensure that all the information in this book is accurate.
However, due to differing conditions, tools, and individual skills, the publisher cannot be
responsible for any injuries, losses, and other damages that may result from the use of the
information in this book.

Manufactured in China

10 9 8 7 6 5 4 3 2 1

larkbooks.com

FRONT COVER
Karl Fritsch, *Ring*, 2007

BACK COVER
Left column, top to bottom
Otto Künzli, *Gold Makes Blind*, 1980
Robert W. Ebendorf, *Man and His Pet Bee*, 1968
Taweesak Molsawat, *This Is Thailand*, 2011
Art Smith, *Modern Cuff*, ca. 1948

Right column, top to bottom
Maria Constanza Ochoa, *Soft Black and White*, 2007
Reny Golcman, *Mandibula*, 1966
Kang Youn-mi, *Bouncing Lesson*, 2008
Louis Aucoc, *Brooch*, ca. 1900

What Is Contemporary Jewelry?

Damian Skinner

Quite early on, when this book was just an idea rather than a manuscript, I had a clear idea of who it was for. I would imagine someone who had just graduated from a jewelry course, facing the inevitable questions from people about why their work didn't look like the jewelry found in the local shopping center or in the pages of glossy magazines—in other words, facing the question of defining or explaining the term *contemporary jewelry*. I imagined a book that would address the kinds of objects and practices that are named by the term *contemporary jewelry*, explain how these objects and practices have developed in different countries around the world, and talk about some of the challenges and opportunities that contemporary jewelry has to face in the present moment.

As anyone familiar with contemporary jewelry will know, it's surprising how many kinds of objects and practices can fit under that term. Take, for example, three works by Otto Künzli, a well-known jeweler who teaches at the prestigious Akademie der Bildenden Künste München (Academy of Fine Arts, Munich). Künzli's jewelry is a great example of the conceptual tendency that makes contemporary jewelry distinctive, in which materials and skills are placed in the service of ideas, rather than being celebrated as ends in themselves. The eminently wearable *Gold Makes Blind* (1980) asks us to consider the way we ascribe value to materials like gold by hiding the "precious" substance underneath a covering of "non-precious" rubber. Indeed, the buyer/wearer is initially asked to take the presence of gold on faith, since it will only become visible when the rubber wears away during regular use. (The purchase of the piece includes a guarantee to replace the rubber tube for free.) Ultimately, Künzli sets two kinds of value against each other: the value of precious materials, which underpins conventional jewelry, and the value of artistic expression and the maker's conceptual work, which underpins the value of contemporary jewelry.

Gold as a marker or guarantor of value also makes an appearance in Künzli's *Beauty Gallery* series (1984), which consists of Cibachrome photographs of people wearing elaborate picture frames, including one covered with gold leaf, around their necks. When a sign of preciousness is shifted from one world (fine art) into another (jewelry), a shift that also involves a kind of creative misuse in terms of function, the sign is no longer taken for granted and thus becomes visible as conventional and arbitrary rather than natural. But the *Beauty Gallery* series is also notable for another reason: the necklace here disappears into the photograph, into the world of images.

These aren't images of people wearing jewelry; rather, the photograph *is* the work, which exists in no other form. Outside of the image, all you have is a picture frame and a person, not a piece of jewelry. The field of contemporary jewelry, as Künzli demonstrates, is open to experimentation that can leave jewelry behind, including works that don't have to be something you can wear or even a three-dimensional object at all.

The final work by Künzli I want to mention here is *Cozticteocuitlatl 1995-1998 B.M.* (1995–1998), a series of gold and silver pendants of various dimensions. Cozticteocuitlatl, an Aztec word that translates as the yellow feces of the gods, shows that Künzli is again tackling mythic dimensions and cultural notions of value that many human cultures attach to gold. These pendants—which, like the bangle of *Gold Makes Blind*, are a common genre or type of jewelry—investigate the possibility of contemporary jewelry as signs, motifs and images that are meaningful as part of the system of visual representation. What's curious here, and what makes this work so dynamic, is that these particular signs aren't easily interpreted. The title might suggest archaeological origins, as though Künzli is translating elements from Mesoamerican art into contemporary jewelry. But then the story shifts when we realize that *B.M.* at the end of the title stands for *Before Mouse*. The silhouette of some of the pendants is revealed as pointing to a very different, much more modern, magic kingdom. But even while gesturing in part to Mickey Mouse, Künzli keeps the visual references open-ended, mixing up modern popular culture and ancient art forms and celebrating the mutated, hybrid results. Contemporary jewelry shows its potential as a kind of visual art, commenting on the nature of images in our highly mediated society.

You'll find lots of definitions of what in this book is called contemporary jewelry, and they won't always agree with each other. It isn't easy dealing with ambiguity, but it's precisely the contradictory, in-between nature of contemporary jewelry objects and practices that makes them interesting. Certainly, this is where contemporary craft theory is heading. As art historian Glenn Adamson puts it in his book *Thinking Through Craft* (2007), "Rather than presenting craft as a fixed set of things—pots, rather than paintings—this book will analyze it as an approach, an attitude, or a habit of action. Craft only exists in motion. It is a way of doing things, not a classification of objects, institutions, or people."[1] Craft, he suggests, should be conceived as an unstable category, changing when it encounters other

Otto Künzli
Gold Makes Blind, 1980
8.3 x 7.9 x 1.3 cm
Rubber, gold ball
Courtesy of the artist

Otto Künzli
Susy from *Beauty Gallery Series,* 1984
75 x 62.5 cm
Cibachrome SB
Courtesy of the artist

Otto Künzli
Cozticteocuitlatl 1995–1998
B.M., 1995–98
Dimensions vary
Gold, silver
Courtesy of the artist

fields like fine art or design, rather than containing some kind of fixed meaning inside itself.

This point of view runs counter to how craft, including contemporary jewelry, has usually been defined. As art historian Maria Elena Buszek suggests, writing about craft has drawn strength from the various functions that craft media have historically provided, and focuses on what distinguishes the applied arts from the fine arts. Most writing, she says, "not only tends to take for granted historical tendencies to associate them with a 'crafts culture' separate from fine arts traditions but also proudly discusses and dissects this distinction as a badge of honor."[2] Increasingly, this approach has come to look like a conceptual dead-end. It certainly hasn't resulted in the outcomes that supporters of contemporary jewelry have historically wished for—the elevation of contemporary jewelry from craft to fine art. And it has tended to result in the kind of discussions about contemporary jewelry that are all about celebration and validation. The most visible model in contemporary jewelry publications consists of beautiful monographs in which jewelers are written about by their colleagues and friends, who of course only have nice things to say. Or at least, this used to be true. A steady stream of books is proving that there are robust, exciting and conceptually rigorous discussions to be had about contemporary jewelry.

But let's get back to the question of definitions. In doing research for this book, I came across this definition of craft by jeweler Bruce Metcalf, which I like very much.

Craft, he suggests, is multivalent, by which he means has more than one dimension or aspect. He offers five ways to identify a craft object. One, it must be an object. Two, it will usually be made by hand. Three, it will usually be made from "traditional craft material" using "traditional craft techniques"— although it doesn't have to be. Four, it will often "address traditional craft functional contexts"—Metcalf provides the examples of furniture and clothing. And five, it will usually make some kind of reference to what he calls "the vast histories of craft." As he concludes, "the craft identity is incremental: the more of these aspects that are embodied in an object, the more craft it is. There is no simple black-and-white here, only matters of degree."[3]

Metcalf's definition is flexible, but it also describes a series of tendencies or histories that craft practices like contemporary jewelry will engage with. Most often, contemporary jewelry is an object which has been substantially made by hand, and it also tends to be—although it isn't always—made from traditional craft materials, by traditional craft techniques. And lots of contemporary jewelry demonstrates an interest in history—its own history (the 70-plus years of contemporary jewelry) as well as the much larger histories of jewelry and adornment.

As Metcalf puts it in another essay, "craft is a series of limitations suggested by tradition."[4] This phrase is important because it captures something of the backwards-looking nature of contemporary jewelry as a kind of craft, a quality that is both a gift and a curse. The point of defining contemporary jewelry is not to fix its nature, or to identify a kind of essential identity that will include or exclude certain objects, but rather to identify a series of conditions that make contemporary jewelry possible and meaningful.

At this point I would like to offer the definition that has shaped my thinking in putting this book together: Contemporary jewelry is a self-reflexive studio craft practice that is oriented to the body.[5] Let me unpack what this means.

Contemporary jewelry: There are many names used to refer to the objects and practices I am calling contemporary jewelry. In her book *On Jewellery: A Compendium of International Contemporary Art Jewellery*, art historian Liesbeth den Besten identifies six different names for the type of jewelry she's interested in: contemporary jewelry, studio jewelry, art jewelry, research jewelry, design jewelry, and author jewelry.[6] These names are complicated in terms of how they relate to each other, and how they relate to different time periods and regions. Some, for example, are chronological, and some are specific to certain countries, while some involve terms also used in the fine arts or other forms of visual culture. Names are important because they shape what we see, as much as they identify and bring into focus something that already exists. This is why den Besten spends time in her book thinking through the limitations of each term. To paraphrase her conclusions, *contemporary* indicates the present and "of our time," yet describes a practice that includes 70 years of objects and some dramatic shifts in framework. The term *studio* places too much emphasis on where and how and thus is too limited. *Art* implies an acceptance by the fine art world that just isn't true, as well as overlooking the true potential of jewelry as a specific kind of object with its own history that's different from fine art. *Research* points to something interesting about the artistic process but the term is limited to Italy. *Design* is a term that arose as part of specific debates in the Netherlands, and the distinction between concept and handwork has been theoretically dismantled, as well as not seeming like such a big issue in the present. *Author* invokes a sense of isolation and pride, and is also limited to the object and thus overlooks conceptual practices. Ultimately, den Besten settles on *contemporary jewelry, art jewelry* and *author jewelry*, moving between these three terms because they represent the status quo in the field.

Names do reflect a variety of preoccupations and ideas about what these objects and practices are, and they have histories, so in using one or the other of these terms, certain characteristics will be emphasized or downplayed. Art historian Mònica Gaspar suggests that the different names of contemporary jewelry have a temporal dimension: "If traditional jewellery aspires to eternity and passing between generations, contemporary jewellery is obstinately anchored in the present, as a creation linked to the 'here and now' of its creator."[7] And we can track this temporal dimension in the different names: avant-garde jewelry, which positions itself as radically ahead of mainstream ideas; modern or modernist jewelry, which claims to reflect the spirit of the times in which it is made; studio jewelry, which emphasizes the artist studio over the craft workshop; new jewelry, which takes an ironic stance to the past; and finally contemporary jewelry, a term that represents "a perfect balance between innovation, personal languages and recognition by an established circuit of galleries, museums and collectors."[8] I like *contemporary jewelry* precisely because it's general and can refer to all of the qualities emphasized by the other names, and also because it represents the temporal desire of jewelers to be of their time. It's also been in use since the 1970s, which gives it a certain historical weight.

Self-reflexive: Contemporary jewelry is a self-reflexive practice, which means that it's concerned with reflecting on itself and the conditions in which it takes place. In general, contemporary jewelers work in a critical or conscious relationship to the history of the practice, and to the wider field of jewelry and adornment. This is what makes contemporary jewelry different from other forms of body adornment, and it isn't found just in the way contemporary jewelry objects and practices engage with the history of jewelry, or the relationship to the body and wearing. Contemporary jewelry is shaped by a distinct awareness of the situations in which it exists, meaning that jewelers engage directly with the spaces in which their work circulates—the gallery or museum, for example, or books and catalogs. Some contemporary jewelers make work that's precisely about what it means for jewelry to exist in such sites, and in which an awareness of the relationship between object and location is effectively their subject. Not all contemporary jewelry is equally self-reflexive, but as a field, this is one of its notable characteristics.

Interestingly, while contemporary jewelry as a term includes modernist jewelry (and to a lesser extent, art jewelry from the late nineteenth and early twentieth centuries), I would argue that these types of jewelry are not the same thing, precisely because modernist jewelry is not necessarily self-reflexive. Both modernist and art jewelry did begin the work of freeing jewelry from the restrictive idea that its value was tied to the precious materials from which it was made, which in turn allowed jewelry to become a form of artistic expression. Yet the avant-garde status of modernist jewelry tends to come from its adoption of modernist styles from fine art, whereas contemporary jewelry's avant-garde status tends to relate to its investigation of jewelry's traditions and functions, and the jewelers' willingness to assume a critical relationship to the history within which they are working. Modernist jewelry didn't, as a movement, call into question its own nature and history, whereas contemporary jewelry, as a movement, does. Modernist jewelry broke with its history, but didn't treat this break as a subject.

Art historian Maribel Königer offers an interesting perspective on these issues in her discussion of why contemporary jewelry is so vigorously distinguished by name from other jewelry practices. Talking about the idea of "conceptual" jewelry, which is a strong tendency within the field of contemporary jewelry, she writes: "What is usually meant by such terms is that basically an idea is inherent in a piece of jewellery, that the choice of materials, colours, forms, techniques of execution, functions and determination of a particular way to wear it can be, and are intended to be, *legible*."[9] Contemporary jewelry is not so much being distinguished from jewelry per se; instead, this is an "attempt to detach oneself through terminology from the products of the commercial jewellery industry that reproduce clichés and are oriented towards the tastes of mass consumption, on the one hand, and, on the other, the individualistic, subjectively aestheticising designs of pure crafts."[10]

Studio craft practice: While many different kinds of objects and practices belong to the term contemporary jewelry, the field has been deeply shaped by the values and history of the studio craft movement. As curator Kelly Hays L'Ecuyer writes in *Jewelry by Artists in the Studio 1940–2000*, studio craft is not defined by

Lisa Gralnick
The Gold Standard, Part I: #11 Tiffany Ring, 2005
101.6 x 40.6 x 5.1 cm
Gold, acrylic
Photo by Jim Escalante
Collection of Rotasa Foundation

Mah Rana
*Have you ever dreamt your
teeth have fallen out?,* 1997
Hairbrush, 12.2 x 2.5 x 0.2 cm
Reworked gold wedding ring,
table, hairbrush, wallpaper
Photo by artist

particular artistic styles or even particular philosophies, but rather by the circumstances in which the work is produced. "Studio jewelers are independent artists who handle their chosen materials directly to make one-of-a-kind or limited-production jewelry. . . . The studio jeweler is both the designer and fabricator of each piece (although assistants or apprentices may help with technical tasks), and the work is created in a small, private studio, not a factory."[11] Built on the platform of studio jewelry, contemporary jewelers favor the unique or one-off, or limited production model, and tend to shy away from the idea of the multiple or mass-production; skill and an investment in the special qualities of materials are central to the idea of the contemporary jeweler (as demonstrated by the fact that many jewelers choose to represent themselves sitting at their bench); individuality and artistic expression are the priority, for both the maker and the wearer/owner; and contemporary jewelers follow the model of the art world, rather than mainstream commercial jewelry production, in distributing their work through dealer galleries, accompanied by artist statements, catalogs, etc.[12]

Contemporary jewelry as a kind of visual art practice keeps breaking the limits of what it can be, so studio jewelry doesn't describe everything that's important about the objects and practices referred to in this book. But a great deal of contemporary jewelry does share strongly the values of studio jewelry, which extend right back to the nineteenth century, and the ways in which the Arts and Crafts Movement promoted an ideal of craft, including art jewelry, as an antidote to the evils of the industrial revolution. And this is important, since studio jewelry represents a series of values and historical relationships that contemporary jewelry needs to deal with in order to embrace its potential in the present.

In the introduction to *Extra/Ordinary: Craft and Contemporary Art*, Buszek suggests that the romantic associations attached to materials such as clay, fiber, glass, wood and metal—which boil down to the idea that handicraft is an antidote to the tyrannical pressures of technology—are a real dilemma for contemporary craftspeople. The crafts world insists on maintaining this material romance as much as the art world insists on its romance with the conceptual. The craftsperson using these materials in a conceptual way gets caught in the middle—not romantic enough, or romantic by association—and belongs nowhere.

The most common solution to this problem has been essentialist, which means, as Buszek puts it, "to encourage artists working in craft media to draw strength from the various functions that those media have historically provided and to focus on that which has historically differentiated the 'applied arts' from the 'fine arts' . . ."[13] The problem is that this approach has been entirely inward looking. It turns away from the possibilities of craft as something embedded in everyday life, and focuses on the preciousness of materials as expressed in objects made by craftspeople in the studio. After World War II, craft entered into an unholy alliance with modernist art theory, concerning itself with concepts like honesty or truth to materials and dismissing the world in favor of autonomous objects that didn't need to be used, or in the case of contemporary jewelry, worn.

At the same time this was happening, there was a shift in the wider visual arts scene, in which life and popular culture— dismissed by high modernism—came flooding back into fine art. Artists began to adopt a wide palette of materials and approaches. In turn this has led, as Buszek puts it, "to a view that craft media are simply among many that may or may not serve any artist's purpose in our contemporary art world. For artists working today media, naturally, still matter—but they are generally chosen with regard to the sociohistorical underpinnings of a medium, rather than any essential regard for or desire to plumb its unique material properties."[14]

And so you get all manner of artists working in materials of great relevance to the crafts world, but you don't get the craft world engaging with these artists or acknowledging what they're doing. And this is because craft writing and crafts institutions find it difficult to leave behind a focus on materials and their romantic associations—even though these block any connection with the contemporary moment. It is the legacy of studio craft that remains one of contemporary jewelry's greatest problems, precisely because it also sustains and informs the field.

Oriented to the body: This is essentially the "jewelry" part of the term *contemporary jewelry*, and it's important because most, even if not all, contemporary jewelry is designed to be worn, or can be worn. When it can't be worn, or wearability is suspended, the body is still invoked as an important subject or limit. The wearer is often forgotten: the contemporary jewelry field spends much more energy thinking about being *contemporary* (e.g. a form of artistic expression, all about the ideas of the maker) than it does on the idea and possibilities of *jewelry* (one of the oldest forms of human creativity, which is a rich archive of object types, materials and relationships to the body and to wearers).

Indeed, art historian Linda Sandino has argued that some contemporary jewelry has an antagonistic relationship to the body, as its claims to being a kind of fine art are grounded in modernism, "wherein attitudes to female corporeality were fundamentally controlling and repressive, or at least veiled. Moreover, the Western Enlightenment privileging of the mind created an ideology of an idealised body that shuns corporeal realities such as dirt and sex."[15] But the cluster of ideas around the wearer, wearing and the body remain the key way in which the objects and practices of contemporary jewelry distinguish themselves from other kinds of craft and art practices. And jewelry is a cultural symbol that links the private and public body, allowing contemporary jewelers to engage, as Sandino writes, "with definitions and critiques of the body which reinvigorates the possibility of the applied arts as a critical practice, rather than merely a supplementary, decorative one."[16]

The term *contemporary jewelry* balances a number of approaches: for example, practices that emphasize the artistic agency of the maker, and place all the focus on the object as an autonomous work of art; and practices that treat contemporary jewelry as an opportunity to create interactions between people, or to intervene in contemporary life from what we might call a jewelry point of view. As a term, contemporary jewelry allows that all of these approaches belong to the field being discussed in this book, even if they contradict each other.

This book is divided into three sections. Part 1 offers some ways to think about what makes contemporary jewelry a distinctive kind of visual art practice. It does this by exploring seven spaces in which contemporary jewelry circulates, and how the meanings and possibilities of contemporary jewelry change as objects and practices move from one situation to another. Part 2 provides an introduction to contemporary jewelry as an international practice that has now existed for the better part of 70 years. There are many challenges in properly accounting for contemporary jewelry in different parts of the world, and these essays are a contribution to developing a truly global history of contemporary jewelry. Finally, Part 3 offers a series of perspectives about the issues that are currently impacting the way contemporary jewelry is made, circulated and discussed. Much has changed in the way we think about the contemporary jewelry field, and new developments in related fields can inspire different ways to think about contemporary jewelry and its possibilities in the present and future.

Notes

1. Glenn Adamson, *Thinking Through Craft*. Oxford & New York: Berg, 2007, pp.3-4.

2. Maria Elena Buszek, 'Introduction: The ordinary made extra/ordinary', in Maria Elena Buszek (ed.), *Extra/Ordinary: Craft and Contemporary Art*. Durham & London: Duke University Press, 2011, p.3.

3. Bruce Metcalf, 'Evolutionary biology and its implications for craft,' in M. Anna Fariello and Paula Owen (eds.), *Objects and Meaning: New Perspectives on Art and Craft*. Maryland & London: The Scarecrow Press, 2004, p.217.

4. Bruce Metcalf, 'Replacing the myth of modernism', in Sandra Alfoldy (ed.), *NeoCraft: Modernity and the Crafts*. Nova Scotia: The Press of the Nova Scotia College of Art and Design, 2007, p.6.

5. I'd like to acknowledge New Zealand jeweler Areta Wilkinson, who first proposed a version of this definition of contemporary jewelry in a talk she gave in 2011.

6. Liesbeth den Besten, *On Jewellery: A Compendium of International Contemporary Art Jewellery*. Stuttgart: Arnoldsche, 2011, pp.9-10.

7. Mònica Gaspar. "Contemporary Jewellery in Post-Historical Times." In *Time Tales*, by Maria Cristina Bergesio. Lucca, Italy: Preziosa, 2007, p.12.

8. Gaspar, 14.

9. Maribel Königer, 'A class of its own', in Florian Hufnagl (ed.), *The Fat Booty of Madness*. Stuttgart: Arnoldsche, 2008, p.32.

10. Königer, p.32.

11. Kelly L'Ecuyer, 'Introduction: Defining the field', in Kelly L'Ecuyer (ed.), *Jewelry by Artists in the Studio*. Boston: MFA Publications, 2010, p.17.

12. L'Ecuyer, pp.17-18.

13. Buszek, p.3.

14. Buszek, p.5.

15. Linda Sandino, 'Studio jewellery: Mapping the Absent Body', in Paul Greenhalgh (ed.), *The Persistence of Craft: The Applied Arts Today*. London: A&C Black, 2002, p.108.

16. Sandino, p.107.

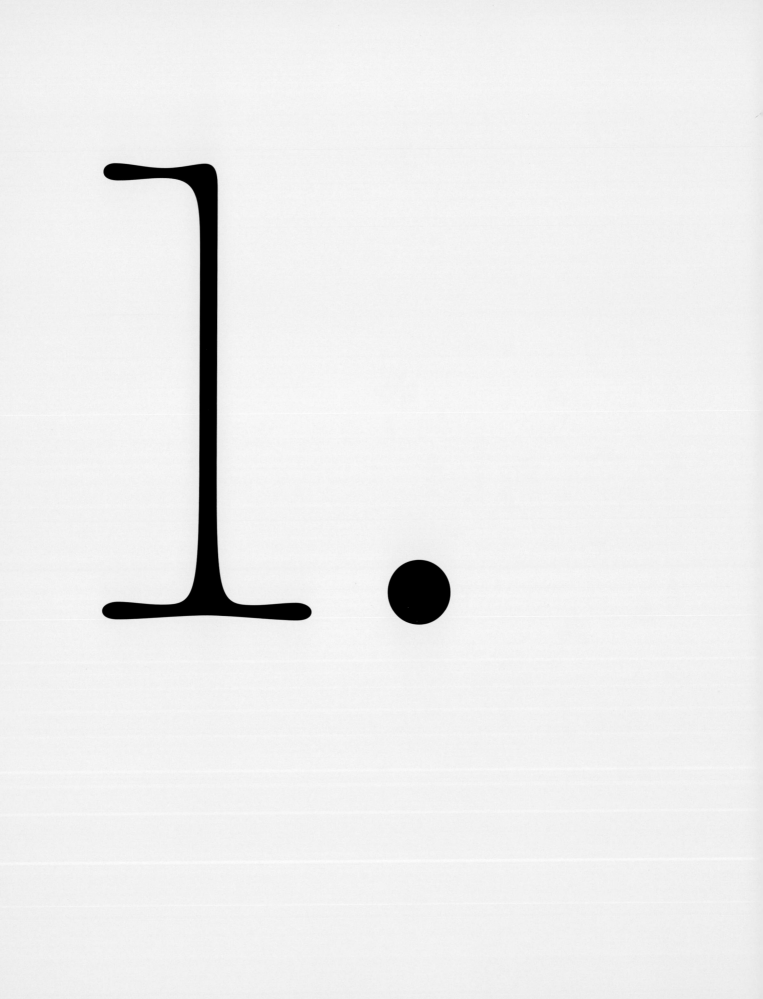

Thinking about Contemporary Jewelry.

Damian Skinner

Part 1 of this book identifies what kinds of objects and practices come under the term contemporary jewelry. Most people working in the contemporary jewelry field would probably agree with the following statements. It's a kind of jewelry, and so it shares things in common with conventional jewelry and also with the wider category of adornment. It's oriented to the body, is often worn, and belongs to a category of objects that are involved in different ways with wearing. It's a kind of craft practice, and it's affected by contact with art on the one hand, and design on the other. It belongs to the wider category of visual arts.

But what makes contemporary jewelry unique? What are the singular characteristics that distinguish these objects and practices from other visual arts? In 2011, five writers met in the United States to discuss these questions and to decide how to write about them in this book. The group, consisting of Mònica Gaspar, Benjamin Lignel, Kevin Murray, Namita Gupta Wiggers and myself, started by trying to identify contemporary jewelry's particular characteristics. To explore the diversity of contemporary jewelry objects and practices, we began to identify and describe the spaces in which contemporary jewelry is found—the situations, places and events in which it is encountered, discussed, made, presented.

In contrast with art forms such as painting, contemporary jewelry circulates through a more diverse range of situations. It inhabits not only the walls and plinths of museums, but also the private spaces of collectors' drawers and the body as it moves through the public spaces of the street. Much of the energy in discussions about contemporary jewelry come from having to take these different contexts into account. While contemporary jewelry isn't entirely determined by the spaces in which it circulates, it's sensitive to these spaces, and many contemporary jewelers have decided that actively thinking about the spaces in which their objects circulate is an interesting and productive experiment.

By describing the conditions of possibility that shape contemporary jewelry and make it possible for it to exist, it's possible to create a nuanced, open-ended and complex account of the objects and practices that are the subject of this book. The authors of Part 1 have attempted to create a new theoretical approach to contemporary jewelry— to apply new methods, and to hopefully open a platform for deeper theoretical engagement, a new space for conversation and new thinking to emerge.

There's a tradition of writing about contemporary jewelry that is serious, critical and theoretical, and this literature is growing all the time. But it's also true that, as a field, contemporary jewelry lacks sufficient serious, critical and theoretical analysis of itself. Too often, fundamental concepts and values are not thought through, and the forces that affect the meanings of contemporary jewelry are not identified. At the heart of Part 1, then, is an attempt to show that contemporary jewelry is not a stable category, but rather a term that stands for a multitude of different objects and ways of thinking about objects. In Part 1, the five authors involved in this part of the book argue that what contemporary jewelry appears to be will be significantly shaped by the different spaces—page, bench, plinth, drawer, street, body, world—in which it's encountered.

As you'll see, these aren't "real" or literal spaces. They are discourses, a term that refers to a kind of larger category created from values, ideas, conversations, texts, images, institutions, events and ways of behaving. All of these things combine to create a discourse. There's a discourse about contemporary jewelry that this book, and Part 1, is keen to both challenge and extend.

The page, made up of digital and printed pages, is a space governed by the values of art history, notably originality and innovation, and it's deeply concerned with legitimacy and authority. The bench, a piece of furniture used in the production of jewelry, is also a changing and evolving discourse about the makers of contemporary jewelry and their activities, as well as a key site

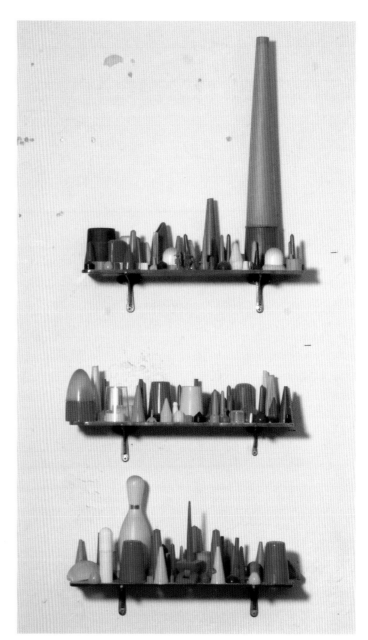

The vertical drawer—a library of forms
Marc Monzó's workshop, Barcelona, 2012
Photo by Marc Monzó

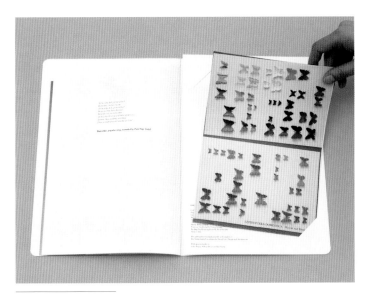

The artist's book as an
extension of practice
Manon van Kouswijk
Lepidoptera Domestica, 2007
Artist book by Manon van
Kouswijk in close collaboration
with Esther de Vries (graphic
design), Uta Eisenreich (photog-
raphy) and Mònica Gaspar (text)
Photo by Richard Niessen and
Esther de Vries

in which values like authenticity and mastery are confirmed (and challenged). The display device of the plinth brings contemporary jewelry into contact with the histories and ideologies of the museum as well as contemporary strategies of display. The drawer, in turn, is a discourse that concerns classification, collecting and preservation, as contemporary jewelry is shaped by all the different drawers (private and public) in which it is stored.

The street, related to the world, represents questions about use and the process of creating meaning, as contemporary jewelry circulates beyond the jeweler's studio, the "white cube" of the gallery and museum, or the private spaces of the collector's drawers. The body is, like the bench, one of the privileged spaces that shapes contemporary jewelry's meanings, as the jewelry object encounters both a fleshy home and a complex set of social and cultural ideas. Finally, the world, signifying spaces beyond those usually taken into account by the contemporary jewelry field, brings into play questions about politics and ethics. Together, these spaces—or discourses—provide a way to identify the conditions of possibility within which contemporary jewelry can exist.

The order of these spaces isn't supposed to suggest a hierarchy, with some spaces being "better" or "worse" than others—and certainly not the idea of a life cycle, a series of stages that contemporary jewelry passes through. The page comes first because the five of us responsible for Part 1 have written a text that goes inside a book. Because our text is published on a printed page, it's subject to all the ideas and values that make up the discourse of the page, and it made sense to acknowledge up front which conditions of possibility are shaping this particular representation of contemporary jewelry. But what follows is not a linear progression, from the bench to the plinth to the body to the street, but different— and sometimes simultaneous—frameworks through which contemporary jewelry objects and practices are made visible and meaningful.

Page.

The glossy page, or
expanding the vocabulary
of contemporary jewelry
through the complicity of
fashion photography
Noon Passama
*A compilation of necklaces
and brooches,* 2009–2010
Dimensions vary
Mixed media
Photo by Stu Stu Studio de Joode /
www.studio.racheldejoode.com
Published in *Surface Magazine,*
issue 92, February 2012

The page as a record

Books, catalogs, artists' monographs, press releases, invitations, articles in newspapers and magazines … and also websites, blogs and all the pictures, texts and event announcements spread over social networks—all of these make up the space of the page.

The overall logic of the page is that of art history, which is concerned with origins and innovation, a history of avant-garde gestures that break with the past and set in play new possibilities for contemporary jewelry. The page is a field of action in which certain achievements are noted and celebrated. Creating an original move in contemporary jewelry guarantees a place in history, the ongoing presentation of the work as iconic and important within the many types of pages that make up the space of the page. This is the prize that stimulates activity within the contemporary jewelry scene, and it can be achieved by disruptive strategies (creating something new) or iterative strategies (revisiting an old proposition in a new way). In both cases, the goal—and the key to success—is innovation.

The page is also, in the form of all the individual pages, a record of what happened. The succession of printed evidence is the foundation on which the history of contemporary jewelry is written. It's possible to know that the first European exhibition of contemporary jewelry was held in 1961 at the Goldsmiths' Hall in London, and the first forum on contemporary jewelry was held in Jablonec, Czech Republic, in 1968, because both left behind evidence in the form of catalogs, invitations, reviews and so on. This is a limited form of evidence, however, because these documents rarely provide information about the dynamics, the content or the context of such crucial events.

The printed page and the digital page

Until a decade ago, the page as a space was defined by the printed page: a blank white space upon which text and image reside. Navigation in this format is linear, with individual pages following one another. The reader encounters information in the order determined by the author and designer.

Today, however, the page refers also to digital formats, where navigation is nonlinear and information can be manipulated in various ways by the reader/user. The digital page seems almost entirely without restriction—in terms of both format and authority. The page now includes videos posted on YouTube, an album on Flickr, a Facebook page and a Twitter feed as much as it does the high production values and elegant white space of a monograph produced by a prestigious publishing house.

Internet publishing has changed the contemporary jewelry scene dramatically, with the sheer quantity of websites eclipsing printed formats, and online publishing opening up unparalleled opportunities for individuals to present their work. All sectors of the contemporary jewelry field have migrated online, which has resulted in a flattening of authority. The primacy of the printed page as the main location of legitimate practice and privileged discourse has been challenged, and the publisher is no longer a powerful gatekeeper, deciding who will and will not be visible by appearing on the page. And yet the issues of legitimacy and power haven't disappeared; they've merely moved from one realm—print—to the many realms that make up the page.

The page of contemporary jewelry

There are many different kinds of printed pages that present contemporary jewelry, and therefore many different ways that contemporary jewelry is positioned as a kind of art practice. Quite commonly, the printed page in contemporary jewelry is modeled after the values of contemporary art. The white page is usually handled like the "white cube" of the gallery space. The photography employed tends to treat contemporary jewelry as an object to be gazed upon, more in keeping with a sculpture. Text is introduced as another element on the page, emphasizing the conceptual ambitions of the contemporary jewelry object and exploring the nature of its difference from other forms of jewelry and adornment.

Sometimes there's a tension between textual and visual representations found on the pages of contemporary jewelry. For example, images showing people wearing contemporary jewelry disrupt the idea of the autonomous, isolated object that emerged from modernism, and insinuate a more complex narrative. Theories of consumption, which argue that use is critical to interpreting objects, come into play as alternative approaches to creating meaning and articulating what's at stake with contemporary jewelry as a specific kind of cultural practice and object.

The page is a space of making

Although it's tempting to think of the page as the domain of those who work with contemporary jewelry after it's been made, this isn't true. Many contemporary jewelers are directly concerned with what takes place on the page, whether printed or digital. The page is not external to the concerns of the maker, but becomes a space in which they attend— directly or indirectly—to the definition and dissemination of their work.

The page functions as a running commentary decoding and appraising the work, as well as an arena where makers shape their relationship to the heritage of contemporary jewelry. The page allows them to demonstrate their affinity with craft, sculpture, design or performance by variously invoking the other spaces of the bench, the plinth, the street and the body through visual and textual clues.

The way contemporary jewelers use the digital and printed page is strategic: the choice of a particular kind of photography, or the selection of one kind of writer (and one kind of narrative) over another, allows the maker to construct and frame the object as much as simply present it. Because of limited infrastructure and lack of resources, contemporary jewelers have often had to act as their own publishers.

As much as the bench, the page is a space of making. Thinking about the page in this way leads to a reconsideration of what the work of contemporary jewelry actually is. For many jewelers, the production of discourse is as important as making the objects themselves. This is partly driven by the fact that the contemporary jewelry object doesn't travel as widely as the various kinds of pages that together form the space of the page.

The power of individual examples of contemporary jewelry is directly related to the way these objects circulate within the page. The currency of contemporary jewelry is generated by the number—and quality—of pages on which it appears.

Contemporary Jewelry Publications

Printed publications such as monographs and exhibition catalogs have served to trace a particular history of contemporary jewelry until the mid-'90s, a time before the coexistence of digital and analog formats led to the current complexity and simultaneity of discourses. In the '90s, several jewelry artist monographs were published. Often they looked like an artist's diary or the pages of a sketchbook. Drawings and expressive handwriting were combined with images of jewelry to scale, as if the object were lying on the page. These publications created a genre where the myth of the (male) jewelry artist as sculptor was perpetuated. It was probably the monograph on Onno Boekhoudt, *Why Not Jewellery?*, that prompted a change of paradigm. With its half-empty pages, populated by scattered images of ambiguous objects, halfway between (un)finished pieces of jewelry and fragments from nature, the book exuded an antiheroic feeling and a calculated casualness. The use of the printed page as an invitation to glimpse into artistic processes even in their most chaotic and uncertain facets inaugurated a new aesthetic for the jewelry monograph.

At the turn of the twenty-first century, publications also showed bench tops and images revealing inspiration sources, which reinforced a sense of research and a conceptual approach to jewelry. The virtual pages on the Internet were increasingly receptive to engaged and critical writing. Authors coming from disciplines like philosophy, art and design theory, or material culture widened the discussion, bringing their opinion to the field, where artists themselves were also composing and writing their own pages. At the same time, due to more accessible channels to print publications, paper often seemed to neutralize critical discourse. The publication of the colossal *The Compendium Finale of Contemporary Jewelry* is an example of that. This exciting and novel multilayered project, where a thousand artists got involved via self-directed curatorial mechanisms taking place online, was narrowed down from its innovative approach to a conventional hardcover book. Its hefty weight of roughly 30 pounds (13.6 kg) transformed the book into a caricature of the light, flexible and transversal nature of its initial purpose. Today, in tacit agreement, printed publications document artistic careers in luxurious formats, where the sensitive use of images and intelligent writing seems to serve as a palliative for the meager impact of contemporary jewelry as cultural player.

Mònica Gaspar

Babetto, Giampaolo. *Artisti Orafi Contemporanei: Giampaolo Babetto*. Zurich: Aurum, 1991.

Britton, Helen, and Julie Ewington. *Helen Britton: Second Nature*. Perth: Form Contemporary Craft and Design, 2004.

den Besten, Liesbeth, Robert Kurvers, and Marie-Jose van den Hout. *Change*. Amsterdam: Voetnoot, 2002. An exhibition catalog of Ruudt Peters' Change.

Lim, Andy, ed. *Compendium Finale of Contemporary Jewellery*. Cologne: Darling, 2010.

Staal, Gert. *Robert Smit: Empty House*. Stuttgart: Arnoldsche Art Publishers, 1999.

Van der Lugt, Rein, ed. *Onno Boeckhoudt. Why Not Jewellery?* Groningen, The Netherlands: Groninger Museum, 1997.

The Compendium Finale of Contemporary Jewellery, 2008
22 x 27 x 26 cm
Munken & Profisilk 200 gr. paper, Bamberg Kaliko last edition techno fabric
Photo by Andy Lim
Pforzheim Jewellery Museum, Germany; Coda Museum, Apeldoorn, The Netherlands

Legitimacy

Contemporary jewelry begs for critical attention. Its ambition to renovate the jewelry genre or assert itself as a discipline of its own, and the difficulties of breaking out of cultural insularity, make it extremely dependent on discourse.

"I wish you well." The problem of discourse on contemporary jewelry starts with those four words. It's a problem of attitude: with the task of evaluating a body of work hijacked by the field's insecurity about its legitimacy, reviewers forgo critical evaluation in favor of justification; they defend when they should criticize. This form of critical thumbs-up, one step up from the "like" function on Facebook, lives (and reproduces) in exhibition press kits, blogs, monographs and magazines alike. It's often authored by those from the community with a vested interest in the field's survival, their pen caught between the need to report and the fear that criticism might undermine one of their own. The problem isn't that most reviews are positive. They have good reasons to be, for contemporary jewelers are very often extremely good at what they do. The problem is that reviews forget to state why they're worth talking about, and against what criteria success is defined.

Meanwhile, the photographic strategies favored by makers often fall prey to or capture the visual conventions of the creative fields nearest to contemporary jewelry:

- performance arts in the '70s, with pictures of bodies in motion (Susanna Heron, Gijs Bakker, Emmy van Leersum)
- the fine arts from the '80s onward, with flattering drop-shadow shots on a white background. Scaleless and totemic, these inevitably encourage a sculptural reading of contemporary jewelry, while erasing references to context of use
- fashion, which allows contemporary jewelry to accessorize a motley cast of stranger-than-life personae (Noon Passama, Pia Aleborg, Nanna Melland).

The sheer range of these visual strategies—whether cogent or tentative—points to the divided allegiances of the field as a whole, but also to the makers' sensitivity to the page as production site. By emulating (or distancing themselves from) fine arts publications, commercial glossies or artist ephemera, contemporary makers stake different claims and manufacture evidences of their practice.

It's unclear whether these documents and the artist statements that accompany them will help us locate the unique role of contemporary jewelry as an art form. It mostly informs us about the way artists (re)present themselves and the various narratives they court in words and images.

Benjamin Lignel

Heinich, Nathalie. *Le triple jeu de l'art contemporain [The triple game of contemporary art]*. Paris: Éditions de Minuit, "Paradoxe" collection, 1998.

O'Doherty, Brian. *Inside the White Cube: The Ideology of the Gallery Space*. Santa Monica: The Lapis Press, 1976.

Fabrizio Tridenti
Lo Stato delle Cose, 2008
4.5 x 10.5 x 4 cm
Silver, iron, brass, acrylic paint
Photo by artist
Collection of Pinakothek der
Moderne, Munich, Germany

Photography

Photography is the most common way in which contemporary jewelry is experienced today. The lack of galleries, exhibition venues and museums in which such works are regularly on public view heightens the value and power of the photograph for jewelers. The photograph is more than a record or document; it's a tool by which the experience of contemporary jewelry becomes known, fictionalized and expanded.

A photograph offers constructive fictional experiences with the jewelry object. For example, both sides of a brooch can be viewed simultaneously on a single page—an experience that's impossible in real life. Through the photograph, jewelers can communicate and enhance understanding of how a piece functions cohesively in the round, as well as reveal how it disrupts expectations or jewelry traditions. This contrast is evident in a comparison of Karen Pontoppidan's *Brooch* (2006), in which a minimalist approach and attention to line is carried through from front to back, versus Lisa Walker's *Brooches* (2005–2007), which appear hodgepodge from the front but are clearly carefully constructed if one looks at the back.

Manipulation of scale works to the jeweler's advantage through the photograph's ability to falsify the dimensions of the actual object. A small, intimate work can be enlarged, monumentalized so that details take on attributes of other art forms—Melanie Bilenker's tiny drawings made from hair grow to page-sized illustrations in enlarged photographs. This manipulation offers jewelry a critical opportunity to function differently in print than in exhibition formats. For example, an image of an Anish Kapoor sculpture on a printed page is miniaturized, brought down to the scale of an image of enlarged jewelry. Within a single page spread, the Kapoor and a piece of jewelry can have equal status and spatial strength, which couldn't happen with the actual works.

The ability to disseminate a photograph via the Internet not only allows jewelers to expand beyond their regions and the confines of printed matter, but it also opens avenues to further explore how jewelry is presented through both fixed and moving image platforms. While how-to videos prevail on YouTube and images can be "collected" through Flickr and Pinterest, the use of digital video to communicate the experience of wearing jewelry has yet to be fully explored. Rather than limit themselves to working with image options that currently exist, jewelers could create new ways of using such media to better convey the specificities of the field.

Namita Gupta Wiggers

Edwards, Elizabeth. "Photographs as Objects of Memory." In *The Object Reader*, edited by Fiona Candlin and Raiford Guins, 331–342. New York: Routledge, 2009.

Lupton, Ellen. "Framing*The Art of Jewelry." *Metalsmith* 27, no. 4 (2007).

Stewart, Susan. *On Longing: Narratives of the Miniature, the Gigantic, the Souvenir, the Collection*. Durham, NC: Duke University Press, 1993.

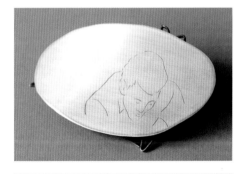

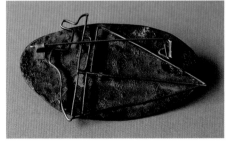

Karen Pontoppidan
Untitled, 2006
4.5 x 7.7 x 0.8 cm
Silver, niello, steel
Photos by artist

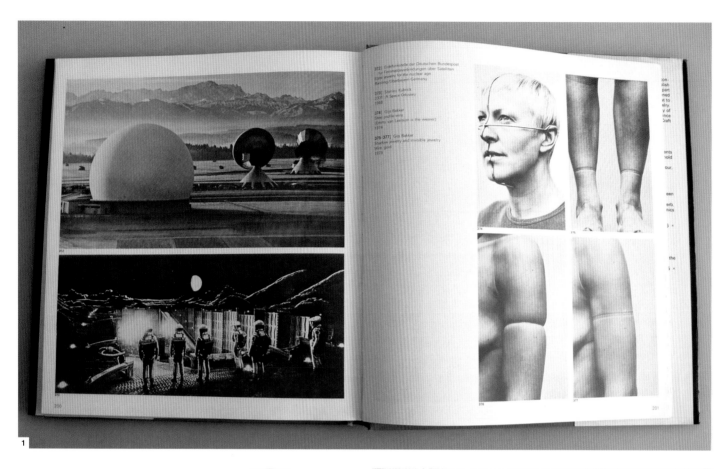

1 The page as landmark, or the role of the publication in understanding the history of contemporary jewelry
Ralph Turner, *Contemporary Jewelry: A Critical Assessment, 1945–1975*
London: Studio Vista, 1976
Photo by Mònica Gaspar

2 The digital page—new technologies enable the distribution of old forms of knowledge in new ways
Kajsa Lindberg and Daniela Hedman
Jewellery Talk, 2006
DVD with interviews
© Adellab / Metallformgivning, Konstfack, Sweden; Kajsa Lindberg and Daniela Hedman

3 The ephemeral page; presentations and artist's talks constitute fleeting pages for contemporary jewelry
Marc Monzó, artist's talk with Power Point, 2010
Taller Peril, Barcelona
Photo by Tanja Fontane

4

5

7

6

4 The page as a source of inspiration—
an imaginary archive of books on
contemporary jewelry
Lin Cheung
Jewellery Library, 2007
40 x 200 x 30 cm
Installation of 200 books
Photo by artist

5 Borrowing the pop culture conventions
of the graphic novel or fanzine
Tin Years: Workshop 6, 2003
15 x 20 cm, pages 8 and 9
Ink on paper, illustration by Jane Dodd
Courtesy of Workshop 6

6 Documenting what is happening—the
nomadic page of invitations and notices
Notice board, Sydney College of the Arts, Sydney,
September 2012
Photo by Karin Findeis

7 The digital page; or how social media
contributes to the dissemination of
contemporary jewelry
Youtube screen shot, Naomi Filmer makes
breathing visible, 2009
http://www.youtube.com/watch?v=z7M-7k2vJjI
Created for Art Tube, The Boijmans Van Beuningen
Museum, Rotterdam, September 2009

Bench.

The bench as a space
for assembling things
Lisa Walker Studio,
Munich, 2007
Photo by Markus Maria Molthoff

Physicality

Unlike the easel or computer monitor, the bench is a horizontal surface. Given the nature of gravity, objects come to rest on the horizontal plane. If the vertical dimension provides a space from which we can stand back and view the world, as with a map, a landscape or a window, then the horizontal surface is in the world. The horizontal is the natural domain of craft, which involves things in themselves rather than their representations.

The peg on a jeweler's bench offers a niche on which the jeweler can file a piece of metal. As it wears with use, this toothy extrusion becomes a signature of its resident jeweler, a physical index of individuality. Below the peg is a pouch, which gathers any precious dust that falls during the filing process. This cache ensures that the maker at the bench remains conscious of the material value of the craft and positions the jeweler as keeper of precious value. Finally, though it has no material function, a bulletin board beside most benches keeps visual material available to makers for inspiration or administration of their business.

Sociology

Beyond its physical properties, the bench is an important sign of authenticity for the jeweler. The photographs of contemporary jewelers featured on specialized websites or in monographs most often show the maker looking up from the bench, sometimes with tools in hand.

As a space, the bench is more or less exclusive to makers. Unlike other spaces such as the plinth or the street, the bench is under total control of the maker, and it embodies a number of values that define contemporary jewelry from the maker's perspective. For example, an important source of value in contemporary jewelry remains the skill embodied in the maker. To varying degrees, makers have invested time at the bench refining techniques for manipulating metals and other materials. Within the space of the bench, the work of jewelers is invested with a value that cannot be claimed by nonjewelers.

For contemporary jewelers, the personal engagement with making involves subjective and emotive meanings attached to materials. Certain jewelers develop a special facility with a particular material, like silver or aluminum. Their work, as much as their concepts, can seem like an articulation of the material itself. The bench privileges the personal qualities of the artist, including skill, creativity, identity, memory and pleasure in working with materials.

Despite its lasting appeal to the contemporary jewelry scene, the bench is under increasing pressure to justify its preeminence as the site of contemporary jewelry production. Firstly, skill can be substituted by various means, and labor-saving technologies such as laser cutting are increasingly used along with ready-made components. Craft making now encompasses such strategies as reproduction, outsourcing, upcycling and assemblage. Secondly, there's a tension between the modernist ideal of truth to materials, which sees skill as unlocking the essential language of the substance at hand, and conceptual approaches that treat jewelry as contemporary visual art—as an idea that's independent of the skill involved in its realization. And thirdly, the bench does not account for the meaning attached to jewelry by those who wear it after its production.

Alternative setups

The word bench routinely implies a set of assumptions about the kind of activities taking place: handmade, laborious, technically exacting, solitary, bent over—and therefore exclusive. But the space of the bench actually encompasses a huge variety of making situations that can't easily be combined. A survey of contemporary jewelry workplaces reveals that they resemble one another only in the most abstract way. They tend to feature places for arranging, shaping and fixing elements and materials into their final forms, as well as all the necessary tools.

But the workshop does not precede the practice. It grows by accumulating equipment—sampled from passing encounters or sustained love affairs with various technologies—around a core object: an actual bench in some cases but equally a table or desk, or even a horizontal surface outside the studio.

The bench, then, is to contemporary jewelry what the easel is to contemporary art: a practical, if outdated, misrepresentation of the practice, favoring what has remained the same over the different ways these practices have moved on.

Deconstructing the bench

While the bench simplifies the nature and the range of activities of contemporary jewelers, its currency as a space has remained more or less intact despite significant changes in practice. Why does it survive?

One reason is craft's willful antagonism toward the industrial machine and the designer's desk/ computer. This ideological position doesn't describe craft practice: it merely frames the way practice represents itself in opposition to other practices— design, mass production—despite the fact that many contemporary jewelers rely on machines and design ideals to make their work. Here, the bench articulates a context against which contemporary jewelry practices evolve, digress and forget themselves.

Another reason is that the bench is a way to connect two narratives: what the bench means for an internal contemporary jewelry audience, and what it means for the wider public. Contemporary jewelers see the bench as a multipurpose—and very personalized—territory where their creative intentions are transformed into singular objects through iterative experimentation, in which the discoveries of each experiment are incorporated into the next as a new point of departure. The public, in contrast, sees the bench as the common denominator between different kinds of objects and practices, onto which they project assumptions of skill, secrecy, collaborative or workshop production, repetitive forms, etc.

As a space, the bench suggests that the two narratives have enough in common to be regarded as merely needing adjustments, when in fact they stake different claims. In both cases, the seductive image of crafting matter has penetrated the collective consciousness at the expense of the many other activities that mobilize the jeweler's time, such as captioning, photographing, curating or cataloging.

The bench as the place where things are made continues to play a leading role in the narrative of contemporary jewelry and the definition of its value. The bench prevails particularly in the page and the plinth, where artistic profiling is often anchored on personal qualities including skill and creativity. But while the bench can be a productive source of meaning, it can also close off other spaces, such as the street, the body and the world, that generate alternative creative strategies.

Materials

While conceptualism has become an important framework for contemporary jewelry, materials continue to play a critical role in setting the creative agenda. Materiality helps define most of the contexts in which jewelry has artistic value. The enduring quality of metal contrasts with the impermanence of flesh, for example, charging it with a strong emotional resonance related to experiences such as mourning. The value of craftsmanship is defined by the mastery over materials gained through the acquisition of technical skills. Unlike technologies such as video, the capacity to work with metals requires a specialized dedication.

Conventional jewelry approaches materials in terms of hierarchy, ordering precious metals and stones above all other substances. The art critic Peter Fuller saw this order as grounded in nature, and therefore an authentic language for expression. By contrast, German philosopher Karl Marx viewed it as a social construct: the value of gold and gems is derived from their relative rarity. Contemporary jewelry is defined by a material relativism. Gold and silver can be valued purely by their aesthetic qualities, and this opens up the possibility of using other materials less common in conventional jewelry, such as aluminum and acrylic. There's also the potential to invert this hierarchy to include materials that are at the bottom of the value chain, such as those defined as rubbish. This evokes the alchemic quest to turn base metal into gold, which is the ultimate mystery of classical goldsmithing. In a modern context, this use of poor materials functions as a political symbolism.

Beyond the hierarchical value of materials, there's a context for their use as a language of expression. The "truth to materials" modernist credo reads the work in terms of the qualities of the substances used—ductility and color, for example. The evocative nature of certain materials, such as the relation of stone to nature, can be handled poetically. And materials can be associated with place, as when artists use an indigenous plant or shell as a way of identifying their place in the world.

Thus, in contemporary jewelry, one of the first questions to ask is, "What's it made of?" This is at odds with conceptual art, where the message overrides the material. Recently, the core value of materiality has also been challenged by relational jewelry, in which objects function primarily to connect people together rather than to stand alone as examples of artistic expression or material investigation.

Kevin Murray

Bennett, Jane. *Vibrant Matter: A Political Ecology of Things*. Durham, NC: Duke University Press, 2009.

Bourriaud, Nicolas. *Relational Aesthetics*. Translated by Simon Pleasance and Fronza Woods. Paris: Les presses du réel, 2002.

Fuller, Peter. "Modern Jewellery." In *Images of God: The Consolations of Lost Illusions*, 269-273. London: Chatto & Windus, 1985.

Renee Bevan
The World is a Giant Pearl pendant, 2012
1,275,620,000 x 1,275,620,000 x 1,275,620,000 cm
(the dimensions of the Earth)
9-karat gold, planet Earth; worn by the artist
Photo by Caryline Boreham
Courtesy of the artist

The Skill Trap

Skill is part of the magic of craft: an affirmation of virtuosity and an appeal to myth. When embarking on a new project, makers enter a deliberation with available techniques. They throw questions at the work in progress and modify their plan of attack according to its responses. Skill thus describes a maker's technical repertoire as well as her capacity to successfully overcome unexpected and unknown technical obstacles. It's part ruse, part accumulated knowledge.

The rebuttal of a skill-based definition of craft in the 1990s prolonged the critique of preciousness leveled at conventional jewelry three decades before. Its point was to distance contemporary craft from the time-intensive techniques that once defined it. Producing low-tech (or no-tech) work meant leveraging the tension between conventional forms and unconventional methods in order to expand the definition of artistic skill and encompass new forms of competence: transgressive appropriation, assemblage, co-production, conceptual work. A ring by Karl Fritsch using a claw setting but cast from barely shaped putty is thus both technically coherent with the tradition and completely at odds with its ambition. It's at once radical and reactionary.

Often called upon to describe a meaningful difference between those who make with their own hands and those who do not, between the intentional and the formless, skill has become a rallying call for a certain branch of craft. It's a refuge not only because it makes good on the promise that craft objects and practices are fundamentally tied up with manufacturing competence, but also because its evaluation appeals to our sense of wonderment rather than the arbitration of specialized critics. Skill is simply a more accessible quality than is artistic merit.

Skill is also a form of expression, with its own internal logic—where form is the expression of method and method is defined by the pursuit of increasing technical challenges. In its most spectacular forms, excess skill— or hypermaking—has given the field of contemporary jewelry a means to reconnect, as if after a long break, with what it once rejected: preciousness.

De-skilling and hypermaking bracket the ongoing debate about the relationship of craft to transmissible knowledge. Both approaches make a case for developing one's own skills and point to the rather more usual scenario, whereby a jeweler acquires specialized skills on the go, through schooling or effort, as and when needed. This last approach suggests that contemporary jewelers' relationship to skill isn't so much post-disciplinary as opportunistic, project-driven.

Benjamin Lignel

den Besten, Liesbeth, and Mònica Gaspar, eds. *Think Tank Edition05, Skill.* Gmunden, Austria: Think Tank, A European Initiative for the Applied Arts, 2009.

Hesse, Herman. *Narcisse et Goldmund.* Paris: Le Livre de Poche, 1975.

Roberts, John. *The Intangibilities of Form: Skill and Deskilling in Art after the Readymade.* London: Verso, 2007.

Karl Fritsch
Ring, 2007
3.5 x 3.5 x 2 cm
Silver, rubies
Photo courtesy of the artist

Self-Reflexive

One of the most notable characteristics of contemporary jewelry is that it's a self-reflexive or self-aware practice. Contemporary jewelers critically investigate the idea of jewelry in the objects that they make, using different techniques to consciously explore how their new work fits into a heritage of jewelry (potentially all the different kinds of jewelry and adornment made by human cultures) and jewelry-related concerns (the body, wearing, materials, preciousness, types of objects and so on).

While not all contemporary jewelry is created to explore the nature and possibilities of jewelry as a practice, the contemporary in the name precisely indicates the prevalence of strategies that do seek to make the wearer, owner or viewer of contemporary jewelry aware of the conditions of possibility in which such objects exist. A diamond solitaire ring is about value, skill, status and tradition, but it takes all these things as givens, seeking to extend or, more commonly, comfortably inhabit the conventions that have developed around such rings. A contemporary jewelry version of a diamond solitaire ring is different precisely because it will tackle the conventions—of value, skill, status and tradition—that make such rings meaningful, usually by choosing forms or materials that disrupt expectations and raise questions.

The mechanism that led to the self-reflexive character of contemporary jewelry is the critique of preciousness, which emerged in the 1950s and '60s as a challenge to the prevalent notion that jewelry's value emerged from, and was equivalent to, the preciousness of its materials. Freed from a limited and tyrannical notion of value, contemporary jewelry was born, and a number of jewelers over the next 30 years made a multitude of arguments (verbally and in the objects themselves) about where the value of the jewelry object could and should be located. Generally, most proposals favored artistic expression, novel engagements with the body or the social possibilities of contemporary jewelry as a democratic practice as the best way to evaluate the worth of this new kind of jewelry.

The critique of preciousness established a critical attitude to jewelry conventions and traditions, and the field of contemporary jewelry has maintained a sense of questioning and taking nothing for granted as the most productive way of inhabiting the visual arts and contributing to new thinking around objects and the body.

Damian Skinner

Bernabei, Roberta. *Contemporary Jewellers: Interviews with European Artists*. London: Berg, 2011. See 24–37.

den Besten, Liesbeth. *On Jewellery: A Compendium of International Contemporary Art Jewellery*. Stuttgart: Arnoldsche Art Publishers, 2011.

Koniger, Maribel. "A Class of Its Own." In *The Fat Booty of Madness*, edited by Florian Hufnagl, 30–35. Stuttgart: Arnoldsche Art Publishers, 2008.

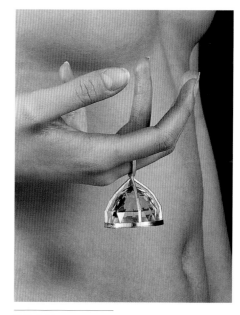

Philip Sajet
The Great Mogul, 1999
2.2 x 5.5 x 2.2 cm
Replica of precious stone, rock crystal, gold
Photo by Beate Klockmann
Courtesy of Stedelijk Museum's-Hertogenbosch

Workshops and Symposia

International workshops and symposia have proved important sites for knowledge transfer, acting as extended benches for practice, whether in the format of discussions, working sessions or lectures.

It's widely stated that the first forum on contemporary jewelry was held in Jablonec, Czech Republic, in 1968, where artists like Bruno Martinazzi, Anton Cepka, Elisabeth Kodré-Defner and Hermann Jünger came together to make jewelry and discuss their work. The jewelry symposium in Zimmerhof, Germany, has taken place since the mid-'60s as well, making it the oldest European meeting of contemporary jewelry makers. In the United States, the Society of North American Goldsmiths (SNAG, founded in 1969) has been organizing annual conferences since 1970. The Schmucksymposium in Erfurt, which began in 1984, aims, according to its website, to "foster creativity when working in a shared space, share know-how, progress the field, and widen the understanding of jewelry in society."

During the 1990s symposia and conferences in Europe were mainly organized by nonprofit associations and collectives of jewelry makers. The most serious and regular meeting, which acted as a network of networks, was the Ars Ornata Europeana (1993–2007), organized by the German Forum für Schmuck und Design (founded in 1984 in Cologne) in collaboration with international contemporary jewelry platforms like the Association for Contemporary Jewellery (UK), Orfebres-FAD (Spain), Corpus (France), VES (The Netherlands), STFZ (Poland) and PIN (Portugal). These platforms relied on personal initiatives, altruistic work and favorable circumstances. While some of these associations still exist, increasingly colleges and academies are taking over and organizing these events themselves.

Examples include the international symposium and publication Nocturnus, initiated by the Eesti Kunstiakadeemia (Estonian Academy of Arts), and the international exhibition, workshops and conference called Koru, organized by the Saimaan ammattikorkeakoulu (Saimaa University of Applied Sciences) in Finland. The Gray Area Symposium, organized in Mexico, has set a milestone for cultural exchange among jewelry artists from Latin America and Europe.

In such meetings the working sessions have the same weight as the time dedicated to eating, drinking and socializing. In the undefined space between work and leisure, one exercises emotional intelligence and social talent, soft skills that are sometimes as valuable as technical and conceptual ones.

Mònica Gaspar

Feiler, Uta, and Bernhard A. Früh, eds. *Experiment Schmuck. Das Erfurter Symposium 1984–2002.* Erfurt, Germany: Landeshauptstadt Erfurt, 2002.

KORU4: International Jewellery Event 2012. www.saimia.fi/koru4.

Vallarta, Valeria. *Gray Area Gris. Contemporary Jewellery and Cultural Diversity.* Mexico: Biblioteca de Mexico and Otro Diseño Foundation, 2010.

Zimmerhof Jewellery Symposium. www.schmucksymposium.de.

Schmuck Tisch (jewelry table) at the annual Zimmerhof symposium, 2006
Photo by Mònica Gaspar

Someone's, Everyone's, No One's

There's no doubt that the body gives jewelry its measure and defines its range: not too big and preferably up close. These constraints delineate the arena in which jewelry is tested and inform the way we move from the body to somebody.

The body imagined and referred to by makers is a trial site on which the work comes alive—plugged in, as it were, to the organic. The body moves in the public domain, and makers hope their work will piggyback on this mobility in order to engage with reality, be relevant, modern, activated. This body is an environment, invented to provide the work with a sound box. Sometimes featured in exhibition catalogs, it defines a target population and can serve as a user's manual. Its main purpose is to create and advertise a good match between an object and a carrier. It is where contemporary jewelry hopes to go when it leaves the workshop.

Somebody is a more difficult client. His or her emotional investment in jewelry takes its cue from our deep-rooted propensity to incorporate generic ornaments into private fictions. It's dependent on ownership and built upon routine use. This individual may like to deal with contemporary jewelry at close range but will find, firstly, that its authorial ambitions make it resilient to appropriation and, secondly, that the market value of this smaller sort of artwork is indexed on preservation rather than wear. In short, the individualized body operates like a boundary switch: being on and off the body alternatively grants contemporary jewelry the status of personal effects or private asset and underlines its affiliation to contradictory value systems.

It may be best, then, to switch to a system of collective ownership and remove the body altogether. In the museum, where no body can inhabit the showcases, jewelry is everybody's. It's there at its most immaterial. The distance that separates us from it hasn't changed, though, and we peer into vitrines as we would at someone's brooch pinned to her coat: not too big and never too far.

The divide that runs between the body and somebody, no body and everybody, duplicates other sets of contiguous notions, such as the corporeal and the personal, the public and the client. It's tempting to think that contemporary jewelry derives its pervasive arguments from disregarding their differences and finding its inspiration in their uneasy overlap.

Benjamin Lignel

Ciambelli, Patrizia. *Bijoux à Secrets*. Paris: Editions de la Maison des Sciences de l'Homme, 2002.

Martin Parr
Fashion shoot for
Citizen K International, 1999
© Martin Parr/Magnum Photos

1 **The bench as a space for shaping things**
Gabriel Craig's studio
Detroit, 2012
Photo by Gabriel Craig

2 **The bench as place of rebirth**
Jewelers sorting through donated jewelry
at Ethical Metalsmith's Radical Jewelry
Makeover, Richmond, Virginia, 2007
Photo by Christina Miller

Representing the traditional tools of the goldsmith
trade—five (self-)portraits posted on KLIMT02 by
the makers themselves

3 Kellie Riggs (USA / IT) Photo RISD Yearbook Staff, 2011
4 Esther Brinkmann (CH) Photo by Werner Nievergelt, 2010
5 Christiane Köhne (DE) Photo by Mike Siegel
8 Timothy McMahon (USA)
9 Helen Britton (Aus/Ger) Photo by David Bielander, 2004

6 **The bench as testing area**
Walka studio's atelier
Santiago, 2012
Photo by walka studio

7 **Instant customisation–
group space as bench**
Yuka Oyama's *Schmuck Quickies*
set up at the Echigo-Tsumari Art
Triennial in Japan, 2003
Photo by Chika Yasuma

10 **The ad-hoc bench, and
the nomadic jeweler
Roseanne Bartley**
Working the Intersection
The Mall, West Heidelberg,
Melbourne (Australia)
Photo by Caz Guiney

Plinth.

Sculpted body versus real body as plinth
Sigurd Bronger
Turbine Neckpiece, 2007
Fine gold plated brass, enamel paint
on silver, steel and rubber cord;
from Romancing the Stone, a 2007
exhibition at Manchester Town Hall,
curated by Jo Bloxham
Photo by Jonathan Keenan
Private collection, UK

Presenting

A plinth is the primary space on and within which an object is placed on view, typically with a protective transparent cover or vitrine. It doesn't just refer to the traditional raised pedestal, but includes a range of forms of visual or physical demarcation. The plinth is to sculpture what the wall is to painting—an architectural and display device that presents objects within a gallery or museum environment. It functions like quotation marks, encouraging the viewer to look attentively at objects that have been relocated into the gallery, separated from the visual noise and chatter of everyday life, the mess of the studio or workshop, or the wearer's body.

Within the museum or gallery setting, the term plinth refers to the tool kit of devices employed by curators for the display of objects, craft and non-craft alike. This kit includes covered pedestals, wall cases, plinths and shelves or casework, all modified to set a particular stage and choreograph movement through an exhibition setting. Curators work with space and may choose to emulate the display conventions of high-end jewelry shops (the closed horizontal showcase), natural history museums (the glass cabinet), modern art galleries (the plinth as backdrop in the form of a vertical wall), and contemporary art spaces (installation and site-determined displays).

Staging

The environment matters. Contemporary jewelry enshrined in a series of brightly lit cases within a darkened room mimics the experience and sensation of viewing ancient artifacts in the tradition of cabinets of curiosities or *Wunderkammer*, defining the objects within a broad category of human-made wonders. Museological approaches, in turn, present jewelry as anthropological artifacts, portraying contemporary objects as ethnographic sculptures-in-miniature. Finally, the evenly lit "white cube," the acknowledged primary cultural space for the presentation of conceptually driven contemporary art, presents contemporary jewelry as autonomous art objects divorced from their socio-historical and use-related contexts.

Distancing

To place anything behind glass intensifies the act of looking: it temporarily suspends some of the properties of jewelry and shifts the use value of contemporary jewelry to that of an object of contemplation. Like the space of the page, the space of the plinth privileges sight and textual interpretation above other ways of understanding an object and favors the sculptural rather than functional qualities of jewelry.

This denial of phenomenological experience and kinesthetic knowledge ultimately fails to communicate the specific qualities of contemporary jewelry as a unique type of object within the world of human-made objects. The plinth shifts jewelry into a class of autonomous objects that don't require being worn to be complete. As contemporary jewelry belongs to a class of objects where understanding is contingent on touch, this results in a double distancing.

Firstly, within the museum setting, an interpreter or docent who hasn't been able to handle or put on the object must rely upon a curator's verbal or textual observations; but even the curator hasn't been able to fully handle work loaned from private collectors or housed in public collections. Within the space of the plinth, the desire to protect the object from damage or theft conflicts with the way particular understandings of contemporary jewelry emerge from direct contact. The plinth presents and distances at the same time.

Secondly, to the extent that contemporary jewelry is wearable, curators must contend with the absence of a real or imagined body in their exhibitions. As a result the practice of jewelry display, or scenography, is shaped by the notion that, fundamentally, displays lie or at best are incomplete since they transform the "natural" perception of the object by removing the body. The plinth both shows too much (a clasp, for example, that would never be seen when a necklace is worn), and, in preventing direct access to the object, denies complete knowledge of it. Certainly, conventional displays of jewelry provide mediated experiences that look for meaning in qualities other than use: the form or composition, technical aspects, materials, narrative elements, and so on.

Strategies of display

Quite often institutions inhabit old buildings that aren't necessarily suitable for displaying art of whatever kind. Curators must manage the presentation of objects—from collections and temporary exhibitions—within the spatial constraints, equipment restrictions, and bureaucratic limitations of the institutions in which they work. However, as a primary element in scenography, the plinth can reinforce or subvert institutional perspectives. The plinth can be the space where curators rework heritage and subvert the spatial limitations of display strategies determined by the values of the museum as a physical and conceptual site.

Alternative display strategies redress the problem of "inherited plinths" and allow the jargon of the new to make itself heard over the inertia of the old. Some curators have, for example, tried to overcome the double-distancing inherent in the space of the plinth and engage a disenfranchised public by providing hands-on experiences, effectively promoting encounters between people and objects that may not happen elsewhere. The fact that meanings are made and lost in the display of jewelry has also encouraged some makers to reshape their practices around the questions of display itself. Experiments with formats, media, and processes have led some makers to create objects deliberately adapted to the plinth. Previously a transitory place of exile, the space of the plinth becomes a permanent and targeted destination. The object's relationship with use, and with the wearer, becomes purely referential. Other contemporary jewelers have locked down the installation protocol and made display—rather than objects—the subject of

their investigation. Through such alternative scenographic approaches as site-specific installation and experiential environments, contemporary jewelry reworks its heritage as commodity, technical specimen, historical document, or sculptural object.

These transformations satisfy several aspirations. On the one hand, they satisfy the maker's need to assert the autonomy of the practice from the value system and ergonomic constraints of conventional jewelry, and they bolster the desire to find cultural legitimacy by emulating, in form if not in name, the art market. On the other hand, they have given curators the opportunities to act as mediators or co-producers of the site/situation, to develop practices that revolve around site-specificity, and to resist the habitual display strategies of cultural institutions. In the wake of these new developments, the plinth is being transformed from something given to something produced, and from a destination to a means of expression.

The Catalog

When given the task of composing a catalog essay, the writer begins by visiting the artist's studio. While there, the writer learns what inspired the artist to make the work. The writer looks at source materials, including books and photographs. She gathers information about previous shows and tries to discern a sequence of creative development. Sometimes there's already a prefabricated artist statement that can be quoted from. The writer then takes all this material away and looks for some rhetorical hook around which she can fashion an essay. The hook will usually reference something outside the particular artist's studio and be familiar to most people who visit the gallery, creating a bridge between the public and the work. The aim is to give the works in the exhibition a voice.

The catalog essay is a rather formal device. The few people who read it will use it to gather some background information on the artist. What's more important is the cultural capital that the writer represents— how her name and the number of words she has written reflect on the worth of the exhibition. But more important still, this catalog essay provides a framework for her relationship with the artist. In the process of writing the essay, she'll have the chance to learn about the artist's work in some depth. This knowledge will be available for future use in the writer's other projects, and if the writer is a significant gatekeeper within the scene, the encounter will perhaps open up other opportunities for the artist.

The catalog essay is a modest venture that produces text and engages the reader. But in terms of understanding the work, it does have limitations. It often seals the meaning of the work at the point of exhibition. The trajectory begins at the bench and ends at the plinth.

The limits of this arrangement are particularly apparent in the case of contemporary jewelry. Unlike art objects, which are designed to circulate in the "white cube" of the gallery (replicated on domestic walls), jewelry objects have an implicit life in the wearing. A catalog essay can only speculate on this state of existence. The writer has no means of knowing what happens when one of the pieces on display is worn over time. In the conventional studio model, this isn't relevant to the artistic project of the work because it's outside the control of the maker.

Kevin Murray

Pascale Casanova *The World Republic of Letters* (trans. M.B. Bevoise) Cambridge, Mass: Harvard University Press, 2004.

Karl Fritsch
The Baby Brick: The LIM Collection
Cologne: Darling Publications, 2007
10.5 x 12.5 cm
Photo courtesy of the artist

Scenography

Methods used to display jewelry are consistent with the tools or devices employed in the visual display of nearly all art forms: stands, lighting, color and wall labels. The ways in which these elements come together, along with the architectural space of the room, affect how contemporary jewelry is perceived, received and understood in a broader cultural context, and highlights the specificities of this particular art form.

The Museum of Fine Arts, Boston's installation of Daphne Farago's collection, for example, mirrors display strategies frequently employed in larger encyclopedic museums. Enshrined within a series of spotlit cases lining the walls of a darkened room, the mood is theatrical. All design elements converge to heighten a sense of wonder, awe and preciousness regarding the works behind glass. Here, Farago's gifts to the museum are presented for public consumption in the same way as Egyptian or Roman jewelry is displayed at the Met. This locates Farago's collection within a logical linear historic trajectory; however, this presentation denies the ruptures with tradition upon which contemporary work is contingent by presenting work in a manner typically reserved for ancient or ethnographic artifacts.

The exhibition relegates much of the work to the wall through the use of recessed and protruding wall cases. Peering into such boxes, however, flattens objects and shifts the experience of three-dimensional work into that more akin to a two-dimensional screen. By contrast, more modern installations are illuminated with an evenly toned bright light, influenced more by the "white cube" of the contemporary art world than by the *Wunderkammer*. The large free-standing plinth in the Museum of Arts and Design in New York, for example, offers a perambulatory experience; visitors may walk around the case and fully view the dimensional qualities of the displayed works. The location of this large plinth within a special collection area, however, isolates the work physically, conceptually and ideologically.

Such scenographic approaches are common, and replicate the art museum's emphasis on visual analysis and textural interpretation. Institutional alternatives such as *Equilibrium: Body as Site, Metalsmith* magazine's 2008 exhibition-in-print turned into an exhibition-on-view at the Rubin Center, The University of Texas at El Paso, and Touching Warms the Art, exhibited at the Museum of Contemporary Craft in Portland, Oregon, offer alternatives to traditional plinths, lighting and interpretive opportunities. These include performances, strategic use of color, plinths constructed from heavy duty corrugated cardboard, a makeshift photo booth using a Mac computer, and Flickr for documentation and dissemination of photos of visitors wearing artist-made jewelry. Ultimately, all of these examples highlight unfulfilled opportunities to develop new devices, and approaches that address the complexities of displaying jewelry. This is exhibition design that acknowledges the history of jewelry, its rupture with tradition and its conceptual, visual and haptic qualities at the same time.

Namita Gupta Wiggers

Howard, Pamela. *What Is Scenography?* London: Routledge, 2002.

Karp, Ivan, and Steven D. Lavine, eds. *Exhibiting Cultures: The Poetics and Politics of Museum Display.* Washington, DC: Smithsonian Institution, 1991.

Marincola, Paula, ed. *What Makes a Great Exhibition?* Philadelphia: Philadelphia Exhibitions Initiative, 2006.

Wiggers, Namita Gupta. "Curatorial Conundrums: Exhibiting Contemporary Art Jewelry in a Museum." *Art Jewelry Forum*, October 2010. www.artjewelryforum.org/articles/curatorial-conundrums-exhibiting-contemporary-art-jewelry-museum.

1 20th century museum display following
  the anthropological tradition
  Installation view of *Ornament as Art: Avant-Garde
  Jewelry from the Helen Williams Drutt Collection*
  RG 36-989-039, 1/19/2008
  Photo by Thomas R. DuBrock / Museum of Fine Arts,
  Houston Archives

2 Me looking at you looking at me (or celebrity
  shows)—when institutions publicize the well-known
  *Madeleine Albright Introduces Exhibition of Her Famous
  Pin Collection,* September 29, 2009
  Getty Images/Spencer Platt

1 Worn and then hung—
   referencing the (absent) body
   Ruudt Peters
   Interno, 1992
   Exhibition at Galerie Spectrum, Munich
   Curated by the artist
   Photo by Jürgen Eickhoff

2 Body as portable display
   Gésine Hackenberg
   *Tableau Vivant with Kitchen Glass
   Brooches*, 2009
   Dimensions variable, 7–16 x 6–8 x 2–3 cm
   Glass jars, ruthenium-plated nickel silver;
   cut and ground
   Photo by Karin Nussbaumer

3 Adorning public spaces—exposing
   the building as plinth
   Suska Mackert
   Plüschow, site-specific intervention, 2004
   Gold leaf
   Photo by Valentina Seidel, from the series
   Exchange: Portraits with Artists

4 Challenging institutional uniformity with a motley herd of (borrowed) plinths
Des Wahnsinns fette Beute (The Fat Booty of Madness), with curation, concept and design by Otto Künzli, was shown at Die Neue Sammlung—The International Design Museum, Pinakothek der Moderne in Munich in 2008.
Photo by Mirei Takeuchi

5 Cultural campfire—the low, covered plinth as site of collective Show-and-Tell
Visitors at the Jakob Bengel Foundation's Villa Bengel in Germany view Guten Tag—Bijou Gigi by artist and curator Volker Atrops. The show was on exhibit from October 11–November 23, 2011.
Photo by Judith Hosser-Schulz

6 Up and across—activating the tension between things to handle and things to look at
Lisa Walker
Diploma final exam exhibition, Academy of Fine Arts, Munich, Germany, 2004
Photo by Karl Fritsch

7 Adorning public spaces—the pastoral as plinth and media
Cristina Filipe
…il est tout plat, et il a une émeraude, la plus belle que j'ai jamais vu… (after Tristan and Isolde), 1996
Site-specific work in Jazenuille, France
Photo by artist

8 Techno-plinth—between carrier and object
Gisbert Stach
Transformation, 2011
11 x 6 x 1 cm
iPod touch, video loop 7 minutes 31 seconds, steel cable
Photo by artist

Drawer.

Summary — Materials

Metal

Draw an arrow to things in the pict are made out ot

the picture draw a ring and some living wood thing that is made

wood

There are many kinds of drawers

The drawer is a form of storage that offers an efficient use of space as well as a means of protecting whatever is placed within it. Contemporary jewelry inhabits a number of different drawers. It exists in the drawers of museum collections, along with many other kinds of objects. (Most commonly, museums collect contemporary jewelry as a subset of studio craft.) It's found in the drawers of collectors/owners, which can tend toward either the domestic (a collection of regularly worn contemporary jewelry that lives in the bedroom or dressing room) or the institutional (specially designed drawers to house the collection in an archivally sound manner, and as a form of display). Contemporary jewelry also fills drawers in dealer galleries and the galleries of some museums, which will be opened and closed by the buyer/viewer.

Often multiple pieces of jewelry are placed together in a single drawer, making this space a contextual scenario. A single term, written on the outside of the drawer, represents and identifies the contents, the many within. In this sense, the drawer as a space involves classification: at times accidental, it can also be strategic, as when collectors reorganize their drawers based on who's coming to research the works in their collection.

The drawer oscillates between private and public. A drawer can be a way to hide from view or a way to present objects to an audience. Both of these possibilities make the most of the drawer as storage and protection. More than the plinth, which as a space grapples with the implications of use, the drawer seems to offer a form of suspension. Placed in certain kinds of drawers, jewelry is not simply denied use but is taken out of circulation altogether, decommissioned.

And yet suspension isn't quite the right word, because really the contemporary jewelry object shifts from one system to another. For example, tucked in the drawer of a collector or a museum, the jewelry still performs as part of the collection—whether in the mind of the collector or in the online database of the institution. Placed in the drawer of a dealer gallery, the object is available to be seen and purchased while acting as evidence of a practice, supporting the featured contemporary jewelry displayed on the plinth. As a space, the drawer offers what might be called intermediate forms of exhibition, but it can also indicate potential: objects-in-waiting in a drawer.

More about storage

Owners/collectors store their contemporary jewelry in drawers. These can be dedicated spaces, in the case of serious collectors, or multipurpose, in the case of owners who may put their contemporary jewelry in drawers that also house other kinds of objects, such as socks. Owned—parked?—by a collector or buyer, the contemporary jewelry object is in conversation with the rest of the collection and becomes an asset. (One of the prerogatives of ownership is that the owner can remove the piece from circulation.)

However, storage of this kind neither deactivates nor disables the emotional attachment the owner feels for the contemporary jewelry object. Wearing and display aren't the only ways to enjoy contemporary jewelry, because a collection is as much a conceptual idea as a group of physical objects. The inventory list documents a collector's emotional investment in a set of invisible holdings: as accumulated worth ("I have all of this") and the very personal history of the collection ("I bought this in Nijmegen in 1984" or "I was given this by so-and-so on our anniversary").

Display

Dealer galleries and museums sometimes store their contemporary jewelry in drawers, in the same gallery space but separated from the objects on display. In such situations, the drawer houses objects that aren't receiving immediate attention.

In the drawer, and therefore subject to the logic of the drawer rather than the plinth, jewelry is contextual, evidential, part of a backlist or collection, stock or objects made of materials that require special protection. There, the singular aspects of the contemporary jewelry object are subsumed to other elements—such as typologies (here are lots of different rings), or collection status (this jewelry is owned by the Louvre or the Museum of Arts and Design) or an artist's oeuvre (here's older or other work by this maker that positions or explains the featured work).

And yet, although it's not on display in the same way, the space of the drawer, unlike the plinth, offers the possibility of active participation. Viewers have to physically open the drawer, make decisions about what to look at and develop their own narratives and meanings around what they see—and it's sometimes a richer experience precisely because it's less proscribed.

Stock and work in progress

In some drawers, notably those in the maker's studio and to a lesser extent the dealer gallery, contemporary jewelry becomes stock, a kind of asset that hasn't yet been successfully commodified. While contemporary jewelry that's part of an inventory is complete and therefore won't be altered or modified, such objects demonstrate that the drawer is part of the space of production and thus connected, in certain situations, with the bench. The drawer is the space where a finished piece goes while the maker decides whether it's successful, and what its future life will be. The drawer represents the point at which contemporary jewelry is finished but not yet complete.

Jewelers rely on drawers to house their jewelry: not just finished work waiting to be sent out—stock—but also old work—archives, personal collection—as well as unfinished jewelry and the raw materials from which new work will be fabricated. This last category encompasses all the stuff of the working process: notes, drawings, half-finished pieces, objects that may include an interesting element, things to be cast and so on.

Placing them in the studio drawer means preserving them from oblivion, locating them

both at bay and within reach. Such things are speculative and still have a foot in the realm of the formless. Because they're inchoate, these loose ends are less possessions than presences: hyperlinks to contemporary jewelry envisaged.

The Collector's Drawers

American Chara Schreyer collects art and design, and the conceptual frameworks of these two fields structure the way she thinks about—and stores—her collection in her home. Within the logic of Schreyer's collection, contemporary jewelry features as a subset of design, which also includes fashion that tends to be conceptual and intellectual—designers such as Commes des Garçons or Junya Watanabe. The jewelry follows this trend. However, its requirement to be wearable, to reside on the body, pulls it away from conceptual jewelry as practiced in the field of contemporary jewelry—which often discards objects or functionality in favor of other concerns.

Schreyer uses the same system of classification for her fashion and contemporary jewelry collections, with items from each collection connected by information sheets, indicating how different pieces can be worn and the possible combinations of garments, jewelry and other accessories. A manual holds all these sheets, one for each object relating to the body, recording them and the permutations of wearing. The information sheets relating to the clothes also accompany each garment, attached to the hanger, thus indicating that the decision of what to wear is generated by the fashion rather than the jewelry, which takes on the status of accessories.

The drawers in which the jewelry resides are in the dressing room off the master bedroom, and they're organized according to type—earrings, necklaces, bracelets and so on. Schreyer also owns fine jewelry, inherited from her mother, but this isn't classified by the system, because its value is in spectacle rather than conceptual or artistic exploration. Interestingly, the fine jewelry is stored in a wall safe, which is a spatial recognition that these objects are subject to the systems of value of conventional jewelry: the heirloom, with its appeal of sentimental and personal history, rather than the collection; and the market, which still values precious materials over artistic expression. The drawer, like the safe, is a form of storage, but the drawer is also oriented to the body, and to wearing.

The fashion and the jewelry both go into storage, but the fine art does not. The art is displayed all around the house, which also doubles as a kind of gallery, and is staged as a series of conversations, like an exhibition. This isn't so for the fashion and jewelry, which is staged when Schreyer wears it, for discrete periods of time. But mostly the collections that belong to the category of design exist in storage in drawers and wardrobes, something that never happens to the art.

Damian Skinner

Chara Schreyer's
jewelry drawers, 2012
Photo by Curtis Grindahl

The Fair

A number of fairs promote contemporary jewelry. Some of them, such as COLLECT in London, and SOFA in the United States, are craft fairs that show ceramics, furniture, glass and textiles alongside contemporary jewelry. Others, like SIERRAD in the Netherlands or INHORGENTA MUNICH in Germany, are jewelry-specific, showing contemporary alongside conventional or fine jewelry. There are different kinds of fairs. Most prominent is the COLLECT or SOFA model, in which an organization (the British Crafts Council in the case of COLLECT; the private Art Fair Company, Inc., in the case of SOFA) rents out space to dealer galleries and nonprofit organizations to show the objects and, to a lesser extent, the makers they represent. Another kind of fair, such as Craftboston or the American Craft Council shows in Baltimore, San Francisco, St. Paul and Atlanta, provide an opportunity for individual makers to sell their work directly to the public, promoting the studio craftspersons as much as the objects they make. A third model is provided by the SCHMUCK and TALENTE competitions in Munich, at which, although they're part of the commercial Internationale Handwerksmesse (International Trade Fair for the Skilled Trades), nothing is sold.

The most prestigious fair in the contemporary jewelry field is SCHMUCK, held each March in Munich. Actually an exhibition located—ironically, considering contemporary jewelry's artistic aspirations—within the Internationale Handwerksmesse, a massive fair focusing on the craft trades, SCHMUCK is a curated exhibition that, in the absence of any other contenders, stands as a presentation of international jewelry trends—and thus as a kind of symbol of the contemporary jewelry scene and its various systems of legitimation. No doubt its importance is connected to its noncommercial nature and its association with prestigious awards like the Hoffmann Prize, given each year to three jewelers featured in the exhibition.

SCHMUCK is a center of gravity around which elements of the contemporary jewelry scene cohere for a week. In 2012, for example, more than 500 people from all over the world gathered in Munich, including makers, dealers, collectors, curators and writers, providing unparalleled networking opportunities. SCHMUCK week includes, along with TALENTE (an exhibition of aspiring craftspeople under 30 years old), myriad exhibitions at local dealer galleries and Die Neue Sammlung (The International Design Museum in Munich). In addition, various alternative exhibitions by the full spectrum of contemporary jewelers, from students to established professionals, take place in venues all over the city. The 2012 official guide listed more than 30 different events. While commercial considerations are certainly in play as part of the framework of SCHMUCK week, the fundamental lack of commercial activity at the heart of this event demonstrates how important fairs are as networking opportunities, allowing key players in a globally dispersed scene to easily connect and reestablish a sense of being part of a field.

Damian Skinner

American Craft Council.
www.craftcouncil.org/shows.

Bucci, Doug. "Schmuck 2010: A Report," *Art Jewelry Forum*. April 13, 2010. www.artjewelryforum.org/conference-fair-reviews/schmuck-2010-report.

International Handwerksmesse.
www.ihm.de.

SOFA. www.sofaexpo.com.

Inheritance

Jewelry has long served as primary evidence of wealth and status throughout global cultures. From a dowry delivered by a father to secure his daughter's future to polite Victorian-era references to male genitalia as the "family jewels," connections between jewelry and inheritance are gendered and familial. Each successive generation bears the responsibility of stewardship, as proclaimed in recent ads by a luxury watch company: "You never actually own a Patek Philippe. You merely take care of it for the next generation."

Contemporary jewelry challenges long-held traditions of intergenerational transfers of wealth through jewelry. Contemporary jewelry isn't necessarily created with traditional luxury materials, and collecting such work can be highly subjective. "Investment" in such works is contingent on the artist's status and reputation, which is developed and maintained through specialized galleries and art fairs, modeled after contemporary art markets. The value of private collections, therefore, isn't necessarily apparent from generation to generation. If the next generation doesn't appreciate the work for its aesthetic qualities and can't justify caring for it for sentimental reasons, where will it go? As a relatively young form of jewelry—and of visual production—there is no secondary market for contemporary jewelry, as there is for contemporary art, decorative arts or even mid-century design. This leaves current jewelry collections at risk of being lost as collections scatter between generations.

Ideally, for jewelers, museums would be the primary target for long-term storage and care of such works. Although most contemporary jewelry is created with the "white cube" of the contemporary art museum and gallery in mind, the transfer from home to institution isn't as easy as one might think. If the works are intended to be, and actually are, worn, then visible signs or marks of use run the risk of devaluing the works as less-than-perfect art objects. Few museums intentionally collect contemporary jewelry. If an institution cannot classify the work within its established categories of decorative arts or contemporary art, then contemporary jewelry will not find a place in the collection. Until the value for such work is extended beyond the confines of a small, deeply invested community, the current situation in which neither family nor institution stakes claim on the work will place such work in peril of neglect, obsolescence and homelessness.

Namita Gupta Wiggers

Appadurai, Arjun, ed. *The Social Life of Things: Commodities in Cultural Perspective*. Cambridge: Cambridge University Press, 1988.

Crafts Council. Video of jeweler Mah Rana. www.youtube.com/watch?v=0or46gKQRIY.

Riedel, Mija. "Susan Beech." *Metalsmith* 31, no. 1 (2011): 22.

Sudjic, Deyan. *The Language of Things: Design, Luxury, Fashion, Art: How We Are Seduced by the Objects Around Us*. New York: Penguin, 2009.

Constanze Schreiber
Untitled, 2009
Silver, copper, electroforming
Photo by Mirei Takeuchi
Courtesy of the artist

Redefining Use

The notion of "use," in traditional jewelry, describes the range of interactions between an object and its owner: a mix of emotional investment and public display grounded on social conventions that tell us "how" and "when" to use the object.

Contemporary jewelry has repeatedly challenged this. Lin Cheung's *Wear Again* series and Manon van Kouswijk's *Soap* can all be used, but they're also about use. Cheung dredges sentimental jewelry trinkets out of the silt of commercial storefronts, and re-injects them— now permafrosted under their plastic wrapping—into the contemporary market. The melancholy results acknowledge traditional jewelry's greater dependency on use, and questions whether those objects in waiting can be reconfigured and re-activated through contemporary practice. Manon van Kouswijk's *Soap* (a pearl necklace encased in a bar of translucent soap) follows an opposite strategy. The impact of the object—which suspends use indefinitely, while inviting it—depends on our capacity to imagine, but not implement, washing our hands to release the necklace. While wearability still brackets the form of these two works, physical interaction is neither essential nor necessary to them. "Use" is a useful metaphor of "old jewelry" and a discursive opportunity for the new one.

While the remittance of use, and its transformation into a motif, is one of contemporary jewelry's defining elements, it's also one of its most problematic aspects. Challenging use is how contemporary jewelry can expect to become more "like art": this reduces its dependence on physical interaction—when it enters the museum— but also threatens its currency as cultural good. Makers who have sought to address the problem have typically chosen one of the following two options: either to (re)turn to jewelry's roots by involving the user physically and/or emotionally; or to exit the museum and re-engage with the public.

The first option taps into jewelry's "natural" propensity to invite appropriation: either by appealing to the magical—as in the case of modern-day talismans, ex-votos or sentimental jewelry—or by integrating the wearer into the making process—as in the case of DIY, modular and evolutive designs. In both cases, the object provides the means of its transformation and isn't "complete" unless it has been activated by use.

The second option, which draws its inspiration from social studies and performance art, seeks to reframe the applied arts notion of "use" into the contemporary art notion of "participation." It's human resourced rather than object-based, and encompasses practices that involve the active participation of the visitor, or of the spectator in an event stage-directed by the artist: walks, performances, site-specific community projects and awareness-building events. This approach is particularly strong in Australia (as for example in the work of Caz Guiney, Roseanne Bartley, Bin Dixon-Ward, Melissa Cameron and Jacqui Chan), with some isolated advocates elsewhere.

However different in format and inspiration, the two options outlined above share the hypothesis that use and interaction are a form of proof, and a similar purpose: to breach the gap between contemporary jewelry and its disenfranchised public/users.

Benjamin Lignel

Bishop, Claire, ed. *Participation*. London: Whitechapel; Cambridge, MA: MIT Press, 2006.

Cummings, Neil. "Reading Things: The Alibi of Use." In *Sight Works: Reading Things v. 3*, 13–28. London: Chance Books, 1993.

Staal, Gert. "In Celebration of the Street: Manifesto of the New Jewellery." In **Noten, Ted.** *CH2=C(CH3)C(=O)OCH3 enclosures and other TN's*, edited by Ted Noten, see the Manifesto Section, 114. Rotterdam: 010 Publishers, 2006.

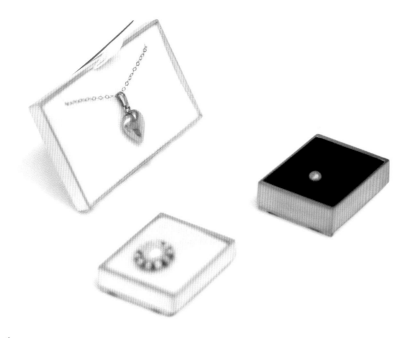

1 Unused jewelry relegated to the drawer
  circulates again through the intervention
  of the jeweler
  Lin Cheung
  Wear Again (3 brooches), 2008
  Smallest, 4 x 3 x 1 cm; largest, 10 x 3 x 1 cm
  Gold, silver, mixed media, found objects, stain-
  less steel
  Photo by artist

2 **Lin Cheung**
  Wear Again (26 brooches), 2011
  Smallest 4 x 3 x 1 cm; largest, 10 x 3 x 1 cm
  Nylon flocked acrylic and brass, faux leather,
  stainless steel
  Photo by artist

3 Use suspended between the promise of liberation
  and the threat of destruction
  Manon van Kouswijk
  Soap, 1995
  Edition of 50, each 8 x 5.5 x 2.5 cm
  Glycerine soap, freshwater pearls, thread
  Photo by artist

1 **The drawer as user-activated display**
Drawers of stock at Galerie Marzee in Nijmegen, The Netherlands, 2012
Photo by Michiel Heffels
Courtesy of Galerie Marzee

2 **The drawer as temporary storage in a rotational display system**
Art Deco-inspired steel and glass cabinet by Jonathon Maxwell housing part of Susan Beech's contemporary jewelry collection, Tiburon, California, 2008
1.8 m x 1.8 m x 50.8 cm
Photo by John White

3 **Using the drawer to store and classify ready parts**
Peter Hoogeboom's atelier in Amsterdam, 2012
Photo by artist

4 **The drawer as user-activated display**
Stock drawers, Galerie Marzee, Nijmegen, The Netherlands, 2012
Photo by Michiel Heffels
Courtesy of Galerie Marzee

5 **Storing knowledge—the reference library**
Near the workbench in Volker Atrops's workshop in Rheurdt, Germany, 2009
Photo by artist

6 **The drawer as static display**
Stock drawers at Lure, Dunedin, New Zealand, 2012
Photo by Neil Satori Brand

7 The vertical drawer—the material library
Leonor Hipólito's atelier in Lisbon,
Portugal, 2012
Photo by artist

8 Using the drawer as inventory place—
finished pieces
Drawer of stock in Warwick Freeman's studio
in Auckland,
New Zealand, 2012
Photo by Warwick Freeman

9 Using the drawer to store and
classify—tests and mock-ups
Drawers, Karin Johansson's studio,
Göteborg, Sweden, 2012
Photo by Johan Hörnestam

Street.

The street as author—involving the public to participate in creative processes
Yuka Oyama
From the Schmuck Quickies: "I would like to have an amulet for shooting many goals in my basketball games" and "I am Philippino-Japanese. There aren't many who are like me in this town. I would like to feel strong. Something for the shoulders," Performance, Echigo-Tsumari Art Triennial, Niigata, 2003
Photo by Shiho Kito

Between high and popular culture

Jewelry accompanies the individual onto the street and into the crowd. It's in the space of the street that jewelry operates in the tension between the personal and the public, at once an object of private use, not necessarily shared, and an object with an immense capacity to interact and seduce.

As a space, the street has both negative and positive connotations. The street is where objects leave social life, to be thrown into bins or washed down gutters. To live on the street is to occupy the lowest rank of society. But the street is also a positive field of social interaction, where individuals emerge from their private spaces to mingle, parade and connect with each other. The street is the home of popular culture, the place where people can shape and display their identity through acts of consumption, affiliation, activism or leisure.

Jewelry plays a key role in these acts of identification, from the piercings of youth cultures to the showing off of bling and luxury jewelry by rappers and bankers alike.

The street can be a carnivalesque space where existing order is upturned: beggars become kings, underdogs defeat champions and thieves uphold honor. Unlike the tightly controlled and copyrighted clothing brands found in shopping malls, street fashion is largely unauthored, just like stencil art or graffiti. The street is also home to a gift economy, where objects such as braided friendship bracelets can circulate as part of a purely sentimental exchange. The domain of street jewelry extends from cheap objects like badges to so-called ethnic souvenirs, the simplified versions of traditional, non-Western jewelry that are sold in street markets.

The street hosts both amateur and professional practices in a nonhierarchical manner. Contemporary jewelry does circulate in this space to a limited degree when it's discreetly displayed in gallery windows or worn by members of the contemporary jewelry scene. However, the street is directly at odds with the plinth. Though objects like ready-mades might be sourced from the street,

in the gallery they become art objects through a strict separation from their roles in the world outside. The gallery or museum as "white cube" frames the art inside as distinct from street life beyond its walls.

The street as catalyst for aesthetic experiences

At different times, artists have sought to cross the border between everyday life and the art world by bringing street activities such as dining or partying into the art gallery. The recently developed relational aesthetics movement sees the value of art in how it connects people together rather than in the object isolated from its social context. But contemporary art must eventually locate itself in the gallery in order to gain recognition as art. It can do so through photography and video documentation of performances and events that have happened "outside." Some artists even draw from the street vocabulary, evoking urban tribalism or guerrilla politics.

Unlike art, contemporary jewelry is a conduit for art objects to move out of the gallery or museum and into the street precisely because, as a subset of craft, it doesn't require institutional validation. When making use of performances, relational situations, pop-up stores and other ephemeral events, contemporary jewelry relocates itself in the street while exploring alternative ways to connect to new, changing and unexpected audiences. Given the nature of contemporary jewelry as a form of body ornament, it can circulate more easily than other art objects, which depend on fixed structures such as walls or plinths.

Street as a generator of value

Although the use of wearable currency has been largely abandoned, jewelry continues to have an association with money. To some extent, the cultural insistence on sentimental gifts encourages the production of expensive jewelry that can communicate its value through more or less sophisticated channels: the professional certificate of purity at one end, the simple authority of bling at the other.

Contemporary jewelry was born, in part, out of a reaction against ostentation and specifically set out to offer an alternative to luxury jewelry. At the root of this territorial expansion is a challenge to the wider public to reassess its assumptions about the value of jewelry and its role as a form of currency. One answer has been to emphasize contemporary jewelry as a kind of artistic expression. But aware of the privilege of circulation, scale and closeness to the individual, the makers of contemporary jewelry have invested no less effort in the question "What does jewelry mean to you?" Especially since the mid-1990s, the emphasis has shifted from material and formal research, which constitutes the maker's statement, toward the narrative created around the object and the impact of its use. New technology facilitates this shift. For example, jewelers take advantage of blogs to include comments that capture the experience of wearing the object on the street.

More than the other spaces, the street privileges the agency of the object as a device for engaging with the social and physical environment. Contemporary jewelry has been endowed with the aura and values of an art piece, and this exerts significant control over the way it's worn and used. Within the values established by the street as a space, contemporary jewelry means little until it's incorporated into the life of the wearer.

There are calls for contemporary jewelry to abandon the plinth and embrace the street. But the question remains as to how the narratives that have gathered around the plinth can extend into a space that claims immediacy and ephemerality among its values. There are also other questions about what might be lost. Unlike the plinth, which has been a space of criticism and self-reflection, the street doesn't facilitate the same level of consciousness and reflection about its own operations. One of the creative challenges facing the contemporary jewelry field is therefore to articulate the relationship between the plinth and the street in a way that productively engages their historical tensions. How can we find a space to reflect on the street without reducing its immediacy? This promises to open a new set of possibilities that unlock the potential of both spaces.

The Shop

The jewelry store is less committed to art than a gallery is, but a store is easier to navigate for that reason. According to Cummings and Lewandowska, the store holds "the promise of a semiotic democracy." Its wares are organized so as to muffle cross-competition and encourage the consumer to browse, manipulate, try out things. The items in the store are "things"—often organized by use category rather than authorship—before they are artworks. The point is to shorten the distance between that original product and this potential user.

The concept store, on the contrary, increases that distance and makes the most of the alleged opposition between the cultural and the commercial. "Value," according to Moss founder Murray Moss, "should be inferred from inaccessibility." The museum-like environment of the concept store helps spike the price point of its collection precisely because, in this case, "collection" derives its power from being intensely fastidious and specific—a creation in its own right, staged to suggest that the selection makes the value of the object, rather than the other way around.

The pioneer contemporary jewelry pop-up store Op Voorraad (which translates as In Stock) sells work made in editions of five in temporary spaces around the world. The name of its game is mobility and low infrastructure: the store resembles modular hardware stores, and the "multiples" sell on average for 250 euros. Pop-ups question the division between makers and sellers. This is to some extent about jewelers taking control of sale profits, like an alternative business plan to the gallery network. But it's also about alternative offerings: most of the work presented in pop-ups is conceived for that platform, following batch production methods that are unusual in the field of contemporary jewelry. In short, this is also about reaching a younger public and shifting the conventional product placement of contemporary jewelry toward the realm of design products.

The same object might travel from shop to pop-up, then from pop-up to concept store. Each gives a particular flavor to the encounter with jewelry, depending on the quality and strength of the curatorial force fields that surround and protect the object. More important, perhaps, these various setups give form to jewelry practice as they pull it toward different types of commodification and their attendant narratives. These spaces encourage particular types of relationships with objects, and inform our perception of what we are looking at.

Benjamin Lignel

Cummings, Neil, and Marysia Lewandowska. *The Value of Things*. London / Berlin: August / Birkhaüser, 2000. See 69.

Op Voorraad pop-up store, Munich, March 12–16, 2009
Curated by Ineke Heerkens, Jeannette Jansen and Jantje Fleischhut
Courtesy of Op Voorraad

Use and Meaning

According to the conventions of contemporary jewelry, the work is complete at the time of exhibition. Although the jeweler may change it at any time prior to exhibition, there's an expectation that, as with a published book or a released film, the form will remain fixed from its point of dissemination. This standard freezes the creative process, enabling us to focus on artistic intention independently of the work's use. But there's an obvious loss. In the case of jewelry, this closure elides the way the work can take on meaning as it becomes part of the wearer's life. It's like exhibiting a blackboard and chalk while prohibiting anyone from writing on it.

This raises the issue of activation in contemporary jewelry. Activation is the process whereby the object is brought to life and able to be used. Activation is particularly important in design, where objects need to be evaluated against the history of use. In technology, for example, many fine devices such as the Apple Newton failed because they weren't embraced by users.

Beyond practical use, activation also refers to ritual processes that charge the object with meaning. In the art gallery, this rite of passage is the opening, where dignitaries herald the appearance of the artwork. The opening can sometimes influence the meaning of the work, particularly if it's given a particular spin by a distinguished speaker. However, this is a relatively controlled process.

Some artists have attempted to incorporate use into the final work. Ted Noten's *Chew Your Own Brooch* (1998) asked users to masticate a piece of gum, which became the form that was cast into the brooch. Susan Cohn's *Black Intentions* (2003) sent out rings to be worn by identifiable individuals, and the final rings were exhibited with scratches caused by use.

By contrast, Vicki Mason's *Broaching Change* (2009) sent an object into the world with a covenant, specifying that whoever wore it had to give it to the first person who made a positive statement about it. The brooch carried a message about the desire for Australia to become a republic. Whenever it changed hands, the recipient was encouraged to leave a comment about the process on a blog site. The Internet now opens up the potential for activation as a part of the artistic project.

Kevin Murray

Appadurai, Arjun, ed. "Introduction: Commodities and the Politics of Value." In *The Social Life of Things: Commodities in Cultural Perspective*, 3–63. Cambridge: Cambridge University Press, 1988.

Mason, Vicki. *Broaching Change Project*. http://broachingchangeproject.wordpress.com.

Atelier Ted Noten
Chew Your Own Brooch,
1998
Dimensions vary
Chewed gum; cast in gold,
silver, or bronze
Courtesy Atelier Ted Noten

Impermanence

A diamond may last forever, but jewelry doesn't have to. As a wearable currency made out of precious metals and gems, jewelry could be transformed into money anytime by being melted and therefore destroyed, by being successively taken apart into smaller bits or by removing its gems. Even though contemporary jewelry makers have rejected the issue of pure monetary exchange and have replaced it with artistic and intellectual value, the compulsion toward banishment and transformation has remained a fascinating topic and a source of inspiration.

Ephemeral materials like paper were introduced in jewelry in the early '60s. One example is the *Something Special* collection by David Watkins and Wendy Ramshaw. Fragility becomes a physical attribute as much as a conceptual frame in the dust necklace by Teruo Akatsu (2001) or the latex and surgical steel *Chain* by Christoph Zellweger (1998). The latter, bought by the British Crafts Council, became a central piece for discussing the role of institutions that collect contemporary jewelry, when facing the preservation of this kind of work, in accepting or avoiding their unexpected transformations over time.

The aspect of wearing as an activity fatal to the jewelry, which transforms it and precipitates its decay, has been explored in a number of jewelry projects: Ruudt Peters' pigmented *Ouroboros* objects for the hand lose color when worn, and Naomi Filmer's ice jewelry is transformed by the body temperature of the wearer. Peter Bauhuis's gallium jewelry is made out of a metal that melts at 85.5°F (29.7°C), making it practically unwearable unless one is ready to accept its sudden loss. Daily rituals related to sensuality and hygiene serve as the inspiration for ephemeral jewelry like the soap skull by Constanze Schreiber.

The transgressive gesture of destroying value seems to resist commodification and escape history, but at the same time such gestures often survive in other media such as photography and video. Such alternative media play a central role when it comes to recording jewelry as pure experience, without actual objects involved. This is the case of *Shadow Jewelry* (1973) by Gijs Bakker, which marked the skin on arms and legs with tight gold bracelets and rubber bands. Another example is *Green Jewelry* (1987) by Johanna Dahm, a fleeting optical effect achieved by irritating the eye after staring intently at the picture of a red square. Recent examples include a site-specific work by Suska Mackert, who painted a sentence with gold leaf in front of a jewelry store window. Passersby inadvertently trapped gold particles in their soles and spread them all over the city.

Mònica Gaspar

Cassel Oliver, Valerie, ed. *Hand + Made: The Performative Impulse in Art and Craft.* Houston: Contemporary Arts Museum Houston, 2010.

Crafts Council. *Object in Focus: Chain & Red Chain by Christoph Zellweger.* Online curatorial discussion. www.craftscouncil.org.uk/collection-and-exhibitions/exhibitions/online-exhibitions/view/object-in-focus-chain-amp-red-by-christoph-zellweger/discussions.

Teruo Akatsu
Illusion Dust Necklace, 1993
96 cm long
Dust, stainless steel wire
Collection of Powerhouse Museum, Sydney, purchased with funds from the Yasuko Myer Bequest, 2005
Photo courtesy of the artist

The Portable Bench

The desire to connect directly with people and environments continues to lead jewelers to explore ways to shift the locus of making from the private studio to the public sphere. Equally enmeshed in romanticism of past centuries and the current zeitgeist for social art making, Gabriel Craig and Roseanne Bartley offer two examples of performative and publicly engaging practices today.

Gabriel Craig manipulates the romantic idealism of the pre-industrial-era craftsman, adding a contemporary twist that emphasizes the self-reliance promoted by the early twenty-first-century DIY movements. Craig's *Pro Bono Jeweler* (2007–present) relocates the traditional jeweler's bench from the privacy of the studio into picturesque, public urban settings. Through carefully choreographed attire, demeanor and actions, Craig offers an image of the young jeweler immersed in the pleasure of physical labor to passersby. Inviting engagement, Craig shares the process of fabricating a silver ring, pulling observers into the activity by revealing the tools and process and concluding with the presentation of the completed ring as a gift. A deceptively simple project, Craig's performance establishes a story of fabrication in the consciousness of every observer. The gift of the ring expands a residual object beyond a mere souvenir. The whole experience is a storytelling trigger for the newly initiated to learn how a ring is made and potentially become involved in the process themselves.

Bartley's work, such as *Seeding the Cloud: A Walking Work in Process* (2010–present), taps into the urban and industrial-era ethos of the flâneur. However, where Baudelaire's flâneur is a distracted, self-possessed stroller, Bartley is a purposeful pilgrim deliberately connecting herself to her environment through her tools and training as a jeweler. As she moves through the urban streets of Melbourne, Australia, any potential surface becomes a makeshift portable bench where the detritus she finds are modified through her tools, thereby marking her travels. Through her hands, tools, materials and conversations, Bartley shifts the detached aesthetic observations associated with the flâneur to create engaged cartographic markers in the form of jewelry. The resulting works reveal jewelry as a vehicle to redefine the flâneur from observer to observer *and* participant by moving the site of production into the public sphere.

What remains to be seen is how artists might shift away from traditional practices and modes of making to develop new performative strategies that take jewelry making into the broader art arena and, potentially, forge new strategies for crossing the private/public divide.

Namita Gupta Wiggers

Adamson, Glenn. "Pastoral." In *Thinking Through Craft*, 103–137. London: Berg, 2007.

Baudelaire, Charles. *The Painter of Modern Life and Other Essays*. New York: Da Capo Press, 1964.

De Certeau, Michel. *The Practice of Everyday Life*. Berkeley, CA: University of California Press, 1984.

Lefebvre, Henri. "The Knowledge of Everyday Life." In *Critique of Everyday Life (Volume I)*, 130–137. New York: Verso, 1992.

Gabriel Craig
The Pro Bono Jeweler,
Houston, 2010
Photo by Amy Weiks

The Critique of Preciousness

In their 1985 book *The New Jewelry: Trends + Traditions*, Peter Dormer and Ralph Turner described the characteristics of the movement they termed "the new jewelry" as "a desire to avoid clichés in design; a desire to make exciting, robust and, where possible, cheap ornament; a desire to make adornment that can be worn by either sex; a frequently expressed distaste for jewelry which is vulgar and merely status-seeking; and always an interest in ensuring that the ornament works with and complements the wearer's body." An outcome of the energy and experimentation produced by the meeting of Dutch and British contemporary jewelers in the late 1970s, the new jewelry movement was concerned with artistic expression and experimentation, a deeper engagement with society and a new awareness of the body and the wearer.

The new jewelry is the high point in what we might call the critique of preciousness, a critical moment in the development of contemporary jewelry as we know it today, and, as Dormer and Turner's book demonstrates, a central narrative in the shaping of contemporary jewelry history. At its core, the critique of preciousness is, as the name suggests, a desire to put into question the idea of preciousness—particularly the idea that the value of jewelry is intimately tied to the precious materials from which it's made. Beginning with German goldsmiths, who in the '50s continued to use precious materials such as gold but who emphasized the central role of artistic expression (thus introducing the division between conventional and contemporary jewelry), the critique of preciousness was fed by Dutch jewelry experiments in the '60s that introduced culturally relevant materials and a new willingness to explore the body as a site and to align jewelry with contemporaneous visual arts movements. The critical project encapsulated by the term critique of preciousness is the conceptual platform on which all subsequent contemporary jewelry has been produced.

Of course, at different moments contemporary jewelry has engaged with this heritage in more or less interesting ways. At its weakest, the critique of preciousness becomes a search for novel materials, as though a justification for contemporary jewelry can be established by making the jewelry object from a substance never before used in jewelry. (This dead end is closely related to the emphasis on contemporary jewelry as a form of artistic expression and the focus on the actions and desires of the maker.) At its most productive, the critique of preciousness encourages contemporary jewelers to continually question the field itself, to renew the arguments about value that sit close to the heart of jewelry's legacy, and to draw on the techniques of art and craft to explore how the jewelry object can propose new conclusions about the body and society.

Damian Skinner

Dormer, Peter, and Ralph Turner. *The New Jewelry: Trends + Traditions*. London: Thames & Hudson, 1985.

Heron, Susanna, and David Ward. *The Jewellery Project: New Departures in British and European Work, 1980–83*. London: Crafts Council Gallery, 1983.

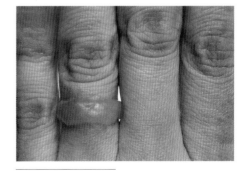

Tiffany Parbs
blister-ring, 2005
33 x 47 x 4 cm
Skin; digital print
Photo by Terence Bogue
Courtesy of the artist

1 Seeing jewelry everywhere—subverting
 the normative codes of the urban space
 Liesbet Bussche
 Urban Jewelry, 2009
 Photo by artist

2 Jewelry as a metaphor
 for creating community
 Roseanne Bartley
 *Human Necklace: Pendant, (Bar-
 celona Residency, 2005–06),* 2007
 Edition of six digital photos, each 54
 x 38 cm
 Photo by Christian Shallert

3 Jewelry that draws on the street as a site
 of continuing technological adaption
 Susan Cohn
 HubHead, 2002–2003
 Headpiece with attachments
 26.5 x 17.5 x 18.5 cm; ring, 9 x 2 cm; digital Lambda print, 150 x 70 cm
 Anodized aluminum, 18-karat gold, 9-karat gold, Monel, acrylic, thermoplastic,
 steel wire, lacquered copper wire, rubber (or alternative mixed media)
 Photo by Greg Harris
 Collection of Anna Schwartz

4 **The street as a meeting point—bringing contemporary jewellery to new audiences**
Zoe Brand during her *Yes / No / Maybe*
performance at the Melbourne Central Swanston
railway station entrance on September 2, 2011
Photo by Benjamin Lignel

5 **A jewelry intervention that reflects on the role of body ornament in everyday life**
Mah Rana
Meanings and Attachments, 2003
Performance at the Year of Design Festival,
Barcelona, 2003
Photo by Xavier Padrós

6 **Wearing the city—ornament as carrier of information**
Ulrike Solbrig for Schmuck2
Subway Map / New York City from the
What do you wear? Jewellery! project, 2000
Knotted colored thread
Photo by Alan Marsik

7 **Street culture inspiring contemporary jewelry**
Frank Tjepkema
Bling Bling, 2003
2 x 8 x 8 cm
Gold-plated silver alloy;
commissioned by Chi ha paura …?
Photo courtesy of Tjep

Body.

The sites of jewelry

As a physical space and an environment, the body encompasses everything from the head to the toes. Depending on cultural or historical factors, different locations or subspaces of the body are addressed by forms of adornment, including contemporary jewelry.

Specific arenas on the body are brought into focus through archetypal forms of jewelry commonly found across the globe: ears, jaw and face by earrings; the face and the region from collarbone to waist by necklaces; hands and digits by rings; waist and genital regions by chatelaines or belts; shoulder and chest by brooches. The acceptance of previously marginal or ancient traditions of adorning the body in a more invasive way, such as piercing, tattooing or scarification, has emphasized previously obscure and less obvious sites for jewelry: nose, ear tops, eyebrows, nipples, genitalia and cheeks.

The quest for originality is an important focus of contemporary jewelry practice and leads to the exploration of new parts of the body that can host jewelry, such as the teeth.

Jewelry as an embodied practice

Some forms of traditional jewelry are able to fuse with the wearer's body. Consider the wedding ring, tiny button earrings, or a religious medal hanging from a thin chain. These objects tend to disappear; they become flesh. The ubiquity of such objects makes their connections to the body easily understood and even assumed when they're not being worn. The hand is understood to be the destination for objects that look like rings, and the ears for pairs of objects that have some element that fits into tiny holes.

The body itself, as a critical and essential factor within the fabrication process, is frequently overlooked largely because of the longstanding hierarchy that places the conceptual above the corporeal, the mind over the body. For the studio jeweler who fabricates an object from start to finish, making contemporary jewelry is an embodied practice. The body is a tool, the means by which the jewelry is produced.

But once completed, the body of the maker disappears from view as the focus shifts instead to the made object and its relationship to the body of the wearer. On a plinth, the body is physically absent but present as an abstracted ideal. When jewelry is worn, the wearer's body takes on the role of portable display. The body involved in the physical act of fabrication disappears as the completed jewelry object moves into the public realm.

The body as a living display

In terms of contemporary jewelry, the space of the body is not so much a physical destination as it is a reference point and a vehicle. The body functions simultaneously as a platform or a vacancy poised for adornment, a space and an environment in which pieces of contemporary jewelry deliberately do not blend into the wearer's body. The history of contemporary jewelry can be summarized as a sequence of movements that swing, pendulum-like, between embracing and rejecting the possibility of wearing the jewelry object, and thus challenging the collective understanding of how jewelry has to relate to the body.

Arguably the body is the most challenging site in and on which to appreciate any artistic object, because on a living display there's little ability to control the conditions of presentation and reception. The space of the body complicates perception but activates objects in a transformative way. Considered from the point of view of the body, contemporary jewelry becomes something that's not merely an image or a three-dimensional sculpture but a conceptually driven artwork that can move fluidly between spaces and both carry and create meaning through such travels.

The invisible body, the banished body

When worn, jewelry adorns and socializes the body, mediating its encounter with society. The body itself—whether actual or abstractly referenced—

is frequently treated as an idealized form. Both conventional and contemporary jewelry is typically photographed on a young, female body, perpetuating an ideal of contemporary practice as fresh, youthful and fashion-forward. However, the bodies of the vast majority of those choosing to wear contemporary jewelry don't conform to the idealistic perfections of the fashion industry or to photographic images created by artists within the field; the opportunity to reevaluate such representations from a critical and gendered perspective remains untapped.

If the object is intended to be collected but not worn—which is increasingly a major aspiration for contemporary jewelry practice—it becomes effectively beyond wearing once accessioned into a museum collection. Here, the objects are placed beyond the body, quarantined by museum ethics and stewardship protocols, and relegated to handling with white gloves, the eyes and the imagination—never worn again except in extenuating circumstances.

The body as a contested site

The body as a site for jewelry raises a number of questions about adequacy (or the relationship with the tradition of body adornment), dependence (or the possibility of use and personal meaning) and even incompatibility (the tension between autonomous or applied object). Because it's a critical, questioning practice, contemporary jewelry puts the body in question, both as the "natural" site for jewelry and as a problematic, portable host.

The body is a contested but irreducible site where individuals can make statements about their identity. Not only jewelry makers but also fine artists and fashion designers are aware of the existential, aesthetic and political dimensions of the body as a theme. One could ask which body is the subject of contemporary jewelry, as well as suggesting that the body is a space that remains indispensable to the field precisely because it represents the intersection of the physical body and various conceptual and social forces. When worn,

jewelry adorns and socializes the body, mediating its encounter with society. Questions regarding whose body, which body and from where the body originates are open arenas for contemporary jewelry to explore in the next decades.

Pleasure

It's significant that the title chosen by Susan Cohn for her 2012 survey exhibition of contemporary jewelry at the National Gallery of Victoria, Australia, and the Design Museum, London, was Unexpected Pleasures. This situates jewelry outside of place, politics or concepts. It takes a surrealist approach to art that touches on the vein of experience that exists below official order, particularly on the level of personal experience. Pleasure is a form of aesthetics that is particular to the subject. Unlike the beautiful, what gives pleasure affects the senses at a direct level. For Freud, pleasure was the psychological basic currency to which most conscious life, even moral indignation, could be reduced.

Jewelry affords many pleasures. Its contact with the body provides it with a strong erotic potential. There's the convention of the pearl necklace to draw the gaze down the female torso. Contemporary jewelry can include more original pleasures, as generated by fetish devices. Publications frequently contain the naked body as a site for contemporary jewelry. But off the page, pleasure isn't limited to the eye. The contact of jewelry on skin offers a tactile pleasure, which includes the polished surface that is smooth to rub, metal that retains body heat and haptic pressures on sensitive areas like the wrist or neck. Beyond the erotic, there's the pleasure of enchantment. Jewelry can suggest a fantastic world redolent with nostalgia that offers an escape from the restrictions of normal existence.

From a critical perspective, the reference to pleasure has potential to consign contemporary jewelry to a frivolous art form. There are various moves to resist the imposition of more utilitarian values. Critiquing ethical jewelry, Bruce Metcalf writes, "Pleasure, if allowed in to the equation at all, is a means, a delivery system that makes the social activism more effective." He implies that pleasure is intrinsic to the meaning of contemporary jewelry.

Pleasure can still complement critical values such as originality and craftsmanship. On its own terms, it can have a variety of critical purposes. Social theorists like Herbert Marcuse attempt to combine Freud with Marxism to identify sexual and social liberation. For the Lacanian Slavoj Žižek, the road to critical engagement is to follow your desire to its logical end. Critical approaches certainly don't preclude pleasure as a valid dimension. But there's a distinction between the type of pleasure that unsettles, and the comfort zone of familiar diversions.

Kevin Murray

Freud, Sigmund. "Beyond the Pleasure Principle." In *On Metapsychology: The Theory of Psychoanalysis.* Translated by James Strachey, edited by Angela Richards. Vol. 11 of The Pelican Freud Library. Harmondsworth, UK: Penguin, 1984.

Marcuse, Herbert. *Eros and Civilization: A Philosophical Inquiry into Freud.* 2nd edition. London: Routledge, 1987.

Metcalf, Bruce. "Concerning Ethics in Jewelry." CraftGadfly. www.brucemetcalf.com/blog/?p=97.

Žižek, Slavoj. *For They Know Not What They Do: Enjoyment as a Political Factor.* London: Verso, 1991.

Alidra Alić
Haute Jewelry—Hyacinth, 2008
11 x 8 x 8 cm
Sterling silver, plastic, strawberry quartz
Photo by Katrine Rohberg
Courtesy of the artist

Gender

Which body is the subject of contemporary jewelry? Extricating jewelry from its feminine associations is nearly impossible. Despite the numbers of men involved in contemporary jewelry—from artists to gallerists to critics—jewelry forms remain largely conceptually and aesthetically connected to a woman's body. With the exception of hip-hop culture's masculine embrace of the dookie chain, most jewelry today references an idealized or actual female body. Although the body as considered in jewelry shifts from any body (idea) to some body (projected) to somebody (actual), gender is a relatively unexplored aspect.

Women are inculcated from childhood to equate jewelry as a marker of coming of age, of being "a lady." Even today, boys are encouraged to role-play, and young girls to play "dress up" with their mothers' and grandmothers' jewelry boxes. The Opulent Project's *Costume, Costume* (2011) brought together works by artists who share a conceptual and material interest in costume jewelry. This grouping of bricolaged creations reveals how the performance of costuming oneself shifts as women age. Moving through the acts of "dress up" through mass-produced jewelry from the mall to the punk aesthetics of teenagers, and through the developing tastes of young women to the refined aesthetic of contemporary jewelry as most commonly found on older women, the project uncovers important connections between the acculturation of jewelry as feminine and the performance of feminine identity over time.

The older woman who chooses to collect and wear conceptual jewelry works against the social indoctrination and gender bias that claims women of a certain age shouldn't call visible attention to themselves or wear things that aren't "tasteful." She will stand out in a homogenous crowd, and her jewelry choices will indicate she belongs to a specific group of collectors and aficionados of contemporary jewelry. Today, when wearability operates as a dimension rather than an assumed goal of practice, conceptual considerations need to extend beyond the idea of the wearer as portable plinth. Critical attention needs to shift from what is being worn to where, how and why this body is the body that is the most common public platform for the performance of contemporary jewelry in public.

Namita Gupta Wiggers

Blau, Herbert. "Rhetorics of the Body: Do You Smell a Fault?" In *Cultural Artifacts and the Production of Meaning: The Page, the Image, and the Body*, edited by Margaret J. M. Ezell and Katherine O'Brien O'Keeffe, 223–239. Ann Arbor: University of Michigan, 1994.

Butler, Cornelia, and Lisa Gabrielle Mark. *Wack! Art and the Feminist Revolution*. Los Angeles / Cambridge, MA: Museum of Contemporary Art / MIT Press, 2007.

Lola Brooks
bloodgarnetheart, 2009
10.2 x 10.2 x 4.4 cm
Vintage rose-cut garnets, stainless steel, 18-karat gold solder
Photo by Tatsuro Nishimura

The Body in Jewelry

Making and wearing jewelry that resembles body parts has a long history. Such objects are thought to have therapeutic and protective effects for the wearer. From superstition to pleasure and expression, the body as a theme, and even as a material, has reached contemporary jewelry. Witness the hair drawings in jewelry by Melanie Bilenker and the pearls made of mother's milk by Stefan Heuser.

Since the '70s, body artists such as Orlan, Ana Mendieta and Valie Export have developed practices that use the human body as a theme and as a medium. In jewelry, Gijs Bakker represented the body through photography sealed in laminated PVC. Bruno Martinazzi was inspired by classical sculptural representations of the body, while Gerd Rothmann developed work resembling ritual and funerary jewelry, taking molds of body parts or using skin imprints to constitute the ornament itself. In the '90s, Iris Eichenberg and Christoph Zellweger focused on the body in a way that had not been done previously. Eichenberg deals with aspects of sexual and social identity through organic forms, vaguely resembling body parts, using materials such as wool, porcelain and wax to suggest warmth as much as fragility. Zellweger stated that in society's quest for beauty, the body has become a luxury item in itself and therefore a matter of design. He made use of a clinical aesthetics to reflect on issues of (bodily) identity and the limits between nature and artifice. The Lingam international exhibition initiated by Ruudt Peters in 2010 invited several makers to get inspired by ancient phallic amulets and design a fertility symbol that would help reconcile contemporary living with the most essential life-driving forces.

The body as a theme favors exploration and complicity among different media, such as performance, video and photography. Lauren Kalman transforms undesirable afflictions of the body, such as skin diseases, into powerful ornaments, their splendor manifested through photography. Jewelry, like clothing, inhabits the liminal space at the boundary of the body, yet the skin becomes an interface as well as a limit that eventually can be trespassed, breaking the taboo of exposing the interiority of the body, as Nanna Melland's *Charm* (2000), a bracelet made of a pig heart, exemplifies. Frédéric Braham actually intrudes the human body and makes a case for designing inner beauty. In his *Therapeutic Attitude* series (since 2000), he offers potions that contain particles of precious metals to be experienced as drinkable jewelry, the ultimate fusion of body and ornament.

Mònica Gaspar

Bergesio, Maria Cristina. "No Body Decoration!" *No Body Decoration: Research Jewellery as a Redefinition of the Human Body*, edited by Maria Pacini Fazzi. Florence: Le Arti Orafe, 2006. An exhibition catalog.

Broadhead, Caroline. "A Part/Apart." In *New Directions in Jewellery*, edited by Catherine Grant, 25–35. London: Black Dog Publishers, 2005.

Finessi, Beppe. *Ultrabody: 208 Works from Art to Design*. Milan: Corraini, 2012.

Morandi, Pietro. "Body Design in Bio-political Discourse." In *Christoph Zellweger: Foreign Bodies*, edited by Mònica Gaspar, 42–59. Barcelona: Actar, 2007.

Pieter T'Jonck. *SuperBodies: 3rd Triennial of Contemporary Art, Fashion and Design*. Hasselt, Belgium: Lido, 2012.

Ruudt Peters
Lingam Pendant, 2009
20 x 14 x 30 cm
Glass, silver, wood
Photo by Rob Versluys, Amsterdam
Courtesy of the artist

1 Seeing jewelry everywhere—
subverting the normative
codes of the urban space
Tord Boontje
Cut Here, 2003
Dimensions vary
Acrylic multipolymer temporary tattoo
Commissioned by Chi ha Paura …?

2 Turning the body inside out
Nanna Melland
Heart Charm, 2000
Photo by artist

3 Gestural repetition—using
the body to determine form
Jennifer Crupi
Power Gesture, 2009
Fabricated, riveted, and die-formed
aluminum, laser print on cotton
vellum, acrylic
Photo by Christian Luis
Courtesy of the artist

4 A public tattooing performance fus-
ing experience with mark-making
Emmanuel Lacoste
*Share—When Sharing the Private
Space Makes It Larger*, June 9, 2012
A two-hour performance presented as
part of the 44th Zimmerhof symposium,
Bad Rappenau, Germany
Photo by Benjamin Lignel

5 The body uncensored—jewelry as
a threshold between private and
public domains
Carole Deltenre
Nymphes brooches, 2008
Left to right, 6.5 cm in diameter, 6 x 6
cm, and 9.5 x 6.5 cm
Silver, porcelain
Photo by artist

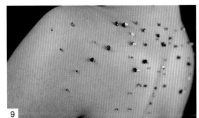

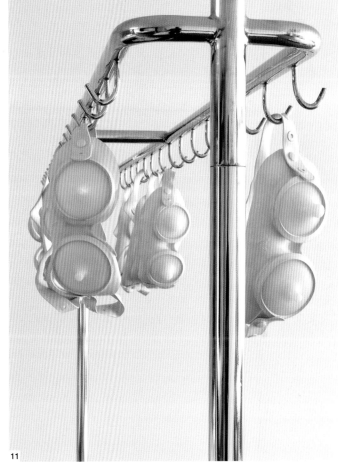

6 Body as a site for the carnivalesque—jewelry as invitation to fantastical mutations
Rachel Timmins
Elvira Snow, 2012
76.2 x 91.4 x 61 cm
Spandex, thread, polyester stuffing, rubber, lace, woven fabric, grommets, flax seeds; machine and hand sewn
Photo by Joseph Hyde

7 Body as plinth
Marie Pendariès
La Dot (The Dowry), 2008
Dimensions vary
Porcelain
Photo by artist

8 Family jewels—borrowing gender and wearing heirlooms
Sophie Hanagarth
Bijoux de Famille (Family Jewels), 1999
80 x 7 x 3.5 cm
Silicone, stainless steel
Photo by artist

9 & 10 Abnormal versus idealized body—medical maladies made ornamental
Lauren Kalman
Blooms, Efflorescence, and Other Dermatological Embellishments (Cystic Acne, Back), 2009
20.3 x 20.3 cm and 66 x 66 cm
Inkjet print and object: acupuncture needles, silver, gold, garnet, ruby, pearls, diamond
Courtesy of the artist

11 Jewelry and medical surgery intersect around the body as ultimate luxury artefact
Christoph Zellweger
From the Incredibles series (detail), 2010
Dimensions vary
Wax, rubber
Photo © artist

World.

Dealing directly with the
economic structures
through which mainstream
jewelry is given value
Lisa Gralnick
*The Gold Standard Part 1:
#7 (Starbucks Coffee)*, 2004
60 x 50 x 50 cm
Two months supply of Starbucks
coffee. Eight pounds of French
roast @ $10.99/lb. Total cost
$87.92. London PM fixed rate
on gold. 12/06/03 $399/0z.
Value in pure (24K) gold: .22 oz.
Value in 18K gold: .30 oz.
Weight of gold in artwork: .30 oz.
Plaster of paris, gold
Photo by Jim Escalante, 2009

The world is invisible

Spaces such as the page, the plinth, the bench, the drawer, the body—and to a lesser extent the Street—are understood to be connected to each other. The values and possibilities of one space are negotiated in the others. The body, for example, haunts the page, the plinth, the bench, the drawer and the street; each space exerts a kind of gravitational pull on the other spaces, helping to shape the sense of what's at stake in each context.

If the street has a complex relationship to the other spaces because it introduces issues that sit uncomfortably with the artistic aspirations of the contemporary jewelry scene, then the world is effectively invisible even as it maintains an intimate relationship with each of these spaces.

While the world is a distant space, beyond the street, on the horizon, it's also close at hand, encountered when the jeweler leaves the bench and reads the newspaper or turns on the TV. The world represents the implications, responsibilities and possibilities of contemporary jewelry in the space beyond the contemporary jewelry scene.

The world brings into play questions that don't find a ready or easy home within the stories that contemporary jewelry usually attracts. As a space, it encourages a number of questions. Has the world become a better place because of contemporary jewelry? Has contemporary jewelry strengthened communities, helped people escape poverty or enjoy better health? The very strangeness and irrelevancy of these questions tells us something important about the values that underpin contemporary jewelry.

These will be strange questions as long as the desire to be a kind of fine art remains the dominant framework for evaluating contemporary jewelry. How can the world help us approach contemporary jewelry in other ways?

Jewelry is made from the world

In the twentieth century, art became self-reflexive, seeking to uncover the very conditions that make the practice of art possible. The framing spaces, like the white-walled gallery, which set art apart from everyday life, as well as the semiotic structures that make meaning possible, have themselves become the subject of art.

The same critical turn has affected contemporary jewelry. And yet, as a subset of studio craft, contemporary jewelry remains interestingly—stubbornly?—attached to materiality, which continues to define the conditions of possibility within which the practice can take place.

The materials of jewelry can lead to an engagement with world politics in a way that's different from most visual art, which doesn't have the same investment in materials—or materials with such a complex legacy. Mining for precious metals, for example, can involve disrupting people's lives, damaging the environment and supporting illegal arms trade and political corruption. The transformation into glittering commodities obscures the "dirty" sources of gold and diamonds. The elegant vitrines of high-end jewelry boutiques seem a world away from the mines of the Congo. The world provides the opportunity to reconnect them, and to find ways to disrupt the system that keeps them separated.

The politics of contemporary jewelry

Increasing global awareness has encouraged an ethical approach to many cultural pursuits. There's growing sensitivity to the appropriation of indigenous culture by Western artists. Global justice campaigns such as Make Poverty History and Kony 2012 have been widely successful thanks partly to mass-produced bracelets. In design, the focus has shifted from an elite form of consumption to accepting responsibility for global change. The Philippe Starck lemon squeezer, an icon of design intended for stylish, First World kitchens, has been replaced as a signifier of contemporary design's values by the mobile water filtration device and other socially engaged answers to world problems in exhibitions such as Design for the Other 90%.

Contemporary jewelry might seem irrelevant to larger world problems partly because it's underpinned by a belief in autonomy and artistic freedom, an idea that's an outcome of modernism. The narrative surrounding contemporary jewelry privileges the internal demands of the practice, particularly artistic freedom, over the perceived moral responsibility of the maker. Contemporary jewelry needs to be protected as an autonomous aesthetic pursuit. This contrasts with the obligation to effectiveness, which sits at the core of social activism.

An alternative way of looking at this situation is to argue that politics is at the heart of contemporary jewelry. The critique of preciousness, in which contemporary jewelry's value was established as being different from the value of the (precious) materials from which it was made, began as a democratic project seeking to counter the elite hierarchy of diamonds and gold. The meaning of jewelry extends beyond the personal. As a way of connecting people, jewelry can be a powerful means for mobilizing change. The challenge is to find a way of connecting this potential to the creative values that have marked contemporary jewelry most powerfully so far.

Design opens contemporary jewelry to the world

Design is a framework that contributes other ways of identifying the opportunities of contemporary jewelry in the world. It holds the engagement with everyday life as a critical value, as important as originality, innovation and artistic expression. Design leads us to ask, "How does this object transform the world of the wearer?" This can be an ethical reform, as in the increased use of recycled gold, for instance, or the rejection of blood diamonds. It can also entail a democratic transformation that opens up new connections among people, renewing the relationship between the critique of preciousness and contemporary jewelry.

The combination of innovation and effectiveness explored within design offers an opportunity to refocus discussions about contemporary jewelry.

The emphasis moves from the form of the material used by the maker (the artistic statement) to the narratives created around the object and the impact of its use (the wearer/owner statement). The question shifts from "What is contemporary jewelry?" to "What does contemporary jewelry do?"

Contemporary jewelry has an extraordinary ability to materialize social and political relationships, to symbolize power and belief, to originate and accompany rituals in different stages of life, to tell stories and extend cross-generational bonds and to symbolize psychological states or encode messages. In the space of the world, contemporary jewelry concerns itself with precisely these issues.

Awareness Bracelets

Gel or jelly bracelets are made from silicone in a variety of colors. A subgenre called awareness bracelets carries words or phrases to demonstrate support for a cause or charity. Their current popularity began with the yellow Livestrong bracelet, which raises money for cancer research as part of the Lance Armstrong Foundation. (Yellow is the color of the Tour de France leader's jersey, which Armstrong wore seven times.) Launched in 2004, the Livestrong campaign has been followed by many others, the best known perhaps being Make Poverty History, which is represented by a white bracelet.

The form referenced by gel bracelets is very ancient, and it has been manufactured from a huge variety of other materials since its invention as a form of adornment. Bracelets can have religious or cultural significance—think of charm bracelets—but they're also a kind of generic adornment. While bangles are a symbol of matrimony in India, for example, the bangle and the bracelet in Western societies are less symbolically loaded than the ring. Gel bracelets don't become meaningful as political statements of allegiance because they're bracelets, but rather because they're jewelry and therefore worn on the body. Badges, for example, have at different times been popular for precisely the same reasons as gel bracelets, and performed the same function.

A rumor emerged around 2004 that the bracelets were being subverted from their original causes, their colors being used in code to signal sexual availability. A teenage girl would wear bands in different colors to advertise the sexual acts she was willing to perform or engage in. (Yellow = hug; orange = kiss; black = intercourse; red = lap dance.) A boy would try to snap the color bracelet that represented the sexual act he desired and if successful would redeem that particular act. This demonstrates the appealing cultural and social potential of gel bracelets. The joy of

this particular set of meanings—apart from their probable status as an urban myth and thus a sign of the gullibility of adults—is that it represents excorporation, a term from sociology that refers to the way in which mass commodities are remade to reflect the consumer's cultural preferences. Jewelry, in the sense of worn objects that stimulate stories for the wearer and mediate social relationships, asserts itself.

Damian Skinner

---

www.en.wikipedia.org/wiki/Gel_bracelet.

www.urbanlegends.about.com/library/bl_jelly_bracelets.htm.

Make Poverty History.
www.makepovertyhistory.org/whiteband.

Fuck Cancer Bracelets, 2009
Photo by Fuzzy Gerdes, fuzzyco.com

Craft
Knowledge

According to Mike Press, professor of design policy in the UK and an influential author, "Craft knowledge is too important and too unique to be limited to the domain of the handcrafted object. A focus on craft knowledge—as opposed to craft products—opens up new opportunities to demonstrate the relevance of craft in the twenty-first century." This statement invites testing in the field of jewelry. What does jewelry have to offer beyond objects? Which kind of knowledge is embedded in its practice? A jewelry designer and an artist, both understood as authors, master technical and aesthetic skills at a high level and in a very specific scale, the human scale. They also have a deep understanding of how personal objects "vehiculate" and materialize identity. A jeweler must be a privileged observer of human nature if he/she wants to succeed in giving shape to thoughts, emotions, events or memories. This professional is an expert in creating and transmitting value, aware of the political, social and cultural implications of such activity, and still cultivates a privileged sense for beauty, wonder and preciousness.

Few artists and designers are able to think out of the box and define their practice beyond the dominant expectation based on creating new objects for a specialized circuit. Some of them are already exploring the possibilities of the knowledge embedded in jewelry making. Yuka Oyama has a deep understanding of how ornament can lend visibility to local communities. She initiates projects where, through the strategies of the carnavalesque, she bejewels buildings, environments and people to reinforce their identity. Hazel White collaborates with multimedia artists, health care professionals, craft makers, computer programmers, forensic scientists and designers to explore how engagement with personal objects can translate into products and systems that have meaning in people's lives. Her work *Hamefarers Kist*, a wooden sewing box full of little knitted pillows, hides a sophisticated technology that facilitates intergenerational communication. And in the context of film and fashion industry, Pia Aleborg arranges full environments where objects play a crucial role in telling a story.

People trained in jewelry are already working in the fields of medicine and health care, psychology and social projects involving communities and scientific visualization, to mention just a few. Expanding the understanding of practice will not only affect views on what jewelry is but will also inspire unseen prospects for what jewelry can do.

Mònica Gaspar

Aleborg, Pia. www.piaaleborg.com.

Press, Mike. *Handmade Knowledge: The New Challenge for Craft*. 2011. http://mikepress.wordpress.com/2011/03/04/handmade-knowledge-the-new-challenge-for-craft.

White, Hazel. *Telling Tales: Hamefarers kist*. www.youtube.com/watch?v=T8O14EcZO10.

Hazel White
Hamefarer's Kist (in use), 2010
Dimensions vary
Radio Frequency Identity (RFID) tagged knitting, Knitted Remotes app, iPod Touch, Mac Mini, found box, laser cutting, photography
Photo by Hazel White / Paul McKinnon (programming), Shetland Arts, AHRC Past, Present, Future Craft

Class

Contemporary jewelry is often positioned as an extension of the decorative arts. The kind of premodern jewelry collected by museums is usually associated with aristocracy. Great feats of gold- and silversmithing were promoted by elites to create objects (and dispays) of ultimate wealth. With crown jewels at the apex, typical decorative art collections of jewelry are founded on diamond necklaces, tiaras and rings worn by those who inherited status, displayed alongside their dignified portraits in oil. To an extent, the gallery inherits the legacy of the court as a rare space in society for displaying the best in jewelry. The key difference is that contemporary jewelry is in principle for enjoyment by anyone, compared to the strict rules associated with access to aristocratic society.

The philosophy of the Bauhaus school of design was to develop products that could be afforded by the masses. The bourgeois resurgence after World War II harbored democratic aspirations to render culture accessible to all. This egalitarian design philosophy has echoes in the Dutch school of contemporary jewelry, particularly through Droog. Gijs Bakker's use of laminated images offered jewelry an egalitarianism that paralleled what photography in art offered over painting.

One association of jewelry and class—costume jewelry—is particularly problematic for contemporary jewelry. This jewelry provides the appearance of preciousness for less wealthy people, but it carries with it a sense of deception. Associated particularly with rap culture, bling emerged in the late twentieth century as a form of pride in imitation. The value of bling is in its visual sparkle rather than in any conceptual meaning or association with craft. It's often produced using industrial methods, such as casting or laser cutting. Its natural home is the street, where display means more than authenticity. Underdogs can dress like aristocrats, array themselves in diamantinas, gold tooth caps and platinum pendants, and hire stretch limousines for the night. Bling is the antithesis of contemporary jewelry. While the contemporary jeweler seeks to embrace the nonprecious in a democratic spirit, the working class moves in precisely the opposite direction. It's rare even in popular jewelry shops to find reference to bling.

Tjep's *Bling Bling* (2003) uses bling culture to satirize contemporary society. The jewelry highlights the superficiality of logos. By contrast, Ted Noten's *Lady K* (2004) takes a Nietzschean interest in popular culture, through which he exercises wit and compelling design.

Kevin Murray

Bourdieu, Pierre. *Distinction: A Social Critique of the Judgement of Taste.* Translated by Richard Nice. Cambridge, MA: Harvard University Press, 1984.

Sennett, Richard. *Flesh and Stone: The Body and the City in Western Civilization.* New York: Norton, 1994.

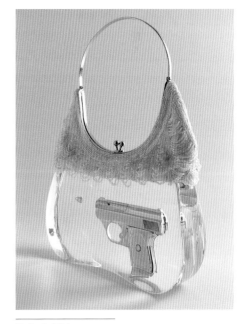

Atelier Ted Noten
Lady K, 2004
30 x 22 x 8 cm
Engraved and heavily gold-plated gun and bullet, textile, chrome, steel
Photo courtesy of Atelier Ted Noten

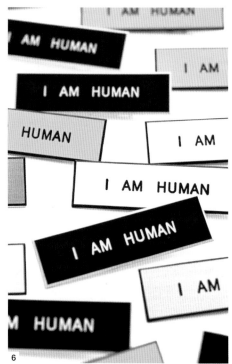

1 Reflecting elusively on the aesthetics of commodification
Suska Mackert
Wrappinghood site-specific intervention, 2005
20 x 180 cm
Gold leaf
Photo by Valentina Seidel, from the series *Exchange: Portraits with Artists*

2 The ruins of Beirut during the Lebanese civil war set the scene for the subject of the human tendency toward self-destruction
Bruce Metcalf
Wood Pin #103, 1995
Brooch, 10.2 x 6.4 cm; landscape, 40.6 x 25.4 cm
Carved and painted wood, brass

3, 4 & 5 Jewelry forms created out of the ground on which we stand
Liesbet Bussche
Urban Jewellery (sand necklace), 2009
Installation, Amsterdam
Photos by artist
Collection Françoise van den Bosch Foundation

6 Brooches that counter jewelry's capacity to elevate the wearer above others
Auli Laitinen
I Am Human, 2001
Each, 6.5 x 2 cm
Plastic
Photo by Gunnar Bergkrantz

7 Brooches as material agents, actively engaging with events in the world around them
Jacqui Chan
Host A Brooch, wearing project, Christchurch, New Zealand, 2011
Dimensions vary
Demolition materials (aluminium joinery), brass tube, stainless steel pin (riveted)
Photo taken by participant
Project presented in collaboration with The National, Christchurch

8 An installation/performance that counters the divide between private and public space
Yuka Oyama
Invasion of Privacy Projects: Christmas (Tokyo, Japan), 2004
40 square meters
Recycled materials
Photo by Beck Yee
Courtesy of the artist

9 Engaging with the earth's resources, otherwise invisible in the refined products from which they're produced
Katrin Spranger
Best Before, 2011
Dimensions vary
Crude oil and its products, silver, gold; cast and assembled; fashion by Thomas Stoess
Photo by Gerrit Meier

2.

The History of Contemporary Jewelry.

Damian Skinner

Part 2 of this book examines the history of contemporary jewelry. It asks: How has contemporary jewelry developed in various parts of the world? In what ways do differences in history, culture and society affect and transform contemporary jewelry? What does it mean to claim that contemporary jewelry is an international, or global, practice? Should we be talking about contemporary *jewelry* or contemporary *jewelries*?

Very few contemporary jewelry books are actually histories. The most common model presents a selection of jewelry grouped thematically, perhaps according to materials, subject matter, or the type of jewelry (rings, necklaces, etc.). These books contain an opening essay that offers a short historical introduction saying how contemporary jewelry got to the particular point the book then explores through its chosen categories. This approach sidesteps the issues of writing history, because you don't need to rank or order the categories or think about causal relationships, and you can create as many categories as you wish so that everything fits. Such books create a kind of space that floats free of history, context, place or relationships.

When a history of contemporary jewelry is presented, it's usually organized around the critique of preciousness, which challenges the idea that the value of jewelry is tied to the precious materials from which it's made. By transforming the conventional idea of value, jewelers liberated contemporary jewelry for artistic expression and experimentation, a deeper engagement with society, and a new awareness of the body and the wearer. While the critique of preciousness is a good way to organize a history of contemporary jewelry, because it captures precisely what makes contemporary jewelry different from other forms of jewelry, it also sets up a hierarchy. European contemporary jewelry, where the critique of preciousness emerged first, becomes the standard against which all other regional forms of contemporary jewelry are compared.

There are, I believe, some good reasons for trying to write a history of contemporary jewelry in every part of the world, or at least taking seriously the idea that contemporary jewelry is an international, and possibly a global, practice. One is that it challenges the provincial ideas of the contemporary jewelry field, which tends to know very little about anything that happens outside the major centers. Another reason is that contemporary jewelry is already international; as the essays in Part 2 clearly show, contemporary jewelry takes place in different countries all around the world. Even though we mostly hear about what's going on in Europe or, depending on where you live, the United States, contemporary jewelers are working away in all corners of the globe, and histories of contemporary jewelry should take this into account.

By looking at what happens in a wide range of practices from different places, we can avoid setting up the major jewelry centers as the arbiters of the official or most correct forms of contemporary jewelry, which then spread to other places, where jewelers will copy or emulate what they see going on in the powerful centers. The story isn't complete by understanding only how, say, modernism developed in American jewelry, or how the critique of preciousness was worked out in European jewelry. Although these might be the earliest examples of these ideas, it also matters what happens to the ideas when they travel to other places. By looking only at the centers, we miss important discoveries about these ideas made by jewelers in other countries. We mistakenly assume that part of the story is the whole story.

The essays in Part 2 explore the ways in which contemporary jewelry has developed across the globe. Six essays by different authors provide a general introduction to the history of contemporary jewelry in Europe (written by Liesbeth den Besten), North America (Kelly Hays L'Ecuyer), Latin America (Valeria Vallarta Siemelink), Australasia (myself), East Asia (Chang Dong-kwang) and Southern Africa (Sarah Rhodes), while the seventh essay (by Elyse Zorn Karlin) surveys art jewelry at the beginning of the twentieth century. The purpose of this essay, which comes first, is to show that contemporary jewelry has much in common with the movements that preceded the development of modernist jewelry in the middle of the twentieth century.

Each of the authors has been asked to keep the focus on contemporary jewelry, by which I mean a self-reflexive studio craft practice that is oriented to the body. This means imposing a kind of sameness onto the very thing these essays are trying to describe, and

Kadri Mälk
Journey Carpet Brooch,
1990
3.5 x 6.2 cm
Silver, enamel (cloisonné)
Photo by Rauno Träskelin
Collection of Helena and Lars
Pahlman, Finland

Taweesak Molsawat
*This Is Thailand: Article No.
8: 11-23-2011 (ring),* 2011
3.2 x 7.3 x 2.1 cm
Found plastic buoy from fishing
net, scrap sterling silver
Photo by artist
ATTA Gallery, Private collection
of Atinuj Tantivit

a more open perspective—looking at jewelry, say, or adornment—would result in a lot more variation. There are advantages and disadvantages to both strategies, but this tight focus was chosen so as to enable the essays in Part 2 to try to identify which factors are required for contemporary jewelry to exist as a specific kind of jewelry.

The authors were commissioned not to write comprehensive histories of their respective parts of the world, but rather regional summaries that sketch out general tendencies and historical patterns. The struggles in doing this vary enormously. Contemporary jewelry, as opposed to jewelry or adornment, is an international practice, but it doesn't exist everywhere, and it isn't the same thing in each place. If adorning oneself is a universal human activity, then making contemporary jewelry is not. As a specialized activity, it needs an infrastructure to survive: schools, dealers, collectors, museums, writers, curators, international networks that allow exchanges of information and so on. Not all parts of the world have these resources—something that also affects this book's attempt to tell the history of contemporary jewelry—because some regions don't have the same number of art historians and institutions creating and publishing the history of contemporary jewelry.

For example, it's obviously impossible to account for all the contemporary jewelry made in Europe over the past 70 years in 5,000 words, while it's equally difficult to talk about contemporary jewelry in Africa, because what we define by this term is not something that exists in all African countries. This creates an uneven quality in this section of the book, both in terms of the subject matter and in terms of how these histories are written. But this difference, which I believe is critical to our understanding of contemporary jewelry as an international or global phenomenon, is precisely what this section is designed to show. It's time to assert that the model of contemporary jewelry found in Europe or North America, while important, isn't the only way to judge contemporary jewelry as a world practice.

Early Twentieth-Century Art Jewelry.

Elyse Zorn Karlin

Introduction

In the last quarter of the nineteenth century, or the late Victorian period, jewelry was heavy and ornate. A woman might wear a pair of wide bracelets on her wrists, dangling earrings, a large brooch at her throat, as well as long chains and rings. In the final years of the century, a new aesthetic emerged as antithetical to this style: art jewelry. It appeared in many countries around the world, although the forces that drove it, and the forms that it took, varied from one country to another. It was both a reaction against stuffy Victorian taste, which had further deteriorated with the rise of machine-made jewelry, and a hopeful look forward to the beginning of a new century. Paradoxically, in looking forward, it often mirrored the past by reusing stylistic elements from earlier periods.

Best known to us are the artistic movements in jewelry and the decorative arts that took place at the beginning of the twentieth century in England, Scotland, Germany, Austria, France, Belgium and the United States. Additionally, Denmark, Norway, Italy, Spain, Canada, Ireland, Australia and New Zealand produced art jewelry. Even Israel and Russia, to a small extent, had their own versions. For most jewelers, art jewelry was a personal artistic quest as well as a search for a new national identity. Based on a combination of historical references, reactions to regional and world events, newly available materials and other factors, art jewelry reflected a country's identity while at the same time being part of a larger international movement of design reform.

New styles and ideas disseminated quickly. In fact, we can trace to a certain degree how artists from one country influenced the work of those of another—even crossing the ocean. This was accomplished through widely distributed publications like *Studio* magazine and *Jugend* magazine, published in England and Germany, respectively. In addition, artists traveled to other countries to study—for example, many American jewelers went to study with the famed English enamelist Alexander Fisher, who himself had studied in Limoges, France. With today's availability of instant information and the ease of international travel, the interchange of ideas has become more global but has also made the national identity of an artist's work less distinct than that of work made circa 1900.

Art jewelry provided the opportunity for exploration and experimentation and developed outside the boundaries of

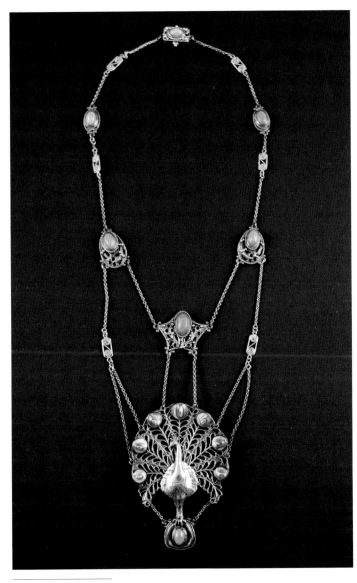

Charles Robert Ashbee
*Peacock Necklace Designed
for the Guild of Handicraft,*
ca. 1900–1905
8.3 x 4.8 cm
Silver, gold, coral, abalone
Private collection

mainstream design. The "new art jewelry," for the most part, was initially meant to be worn and appreciated by a select group of people with artistic tastes, but as its popularity grew, commercial firms produced versions that increased its availability. Today, collectors recognize and covet even the more commercial output for its elegant design.

English Origins

The Arts and Crafts Movement flourished in Great Britain between 1860 and 1920. A reaction against the mass production of jewelry and other goods, the movement railed against the low quality of such products and took a socialist view about the poor conditions under which factory workers toiled. Designer and social reformer William Morris, one of the movement's leaders, wrote, "Art is a man's embodied expression of interest in the life of man; it springs from man's pleasure in his life . . . and as it is the expression of pleasure in life generally, in the memory of the deeds of the past, and the hope of those in the future, so it is especially the expression of man's pleasure in the deeds of the present: in his work."[1] Morris's example as a designer of furniture, textiles and embroideries was coupled with the artistic tenets of art critic John Ruskin, who believed that art should be based on nature and reflect the virtues of a simpler, earlier time.

As Alan Crawford writes of English architect and designer Charles Robert Ashbee, one of the first to make jewelry in the Arts and Crafts style, "From Ruskin he learned to see art, architecture and the decorative arts as the reflection of the social condition in which they are made, and to bring them within the scope of its morality."[2] Ashbee founded a craft class and then the Guild and School of Handicraft for young, untrained men to learn to make jewelry, metalwork and furniture. Both can be credited with producing the earliest Arts and Crafts jewelry in a guild setting, a place where the workers lived in a community and all of the artisans were equal. An example of the early work of the Guild and Ashbee is a silver, gold, coral and abalone pendant necklace featuring a peacock with a spread tail, circa 1900. This is by no means fine jewelry, but it exhibits a rather appealing handmade quality, having most likely been wrought by a craftsman who was still learning metalsmithing skills.

Ashbee and other artisans of the movement viewed their jewelry as an antidote to the production of the industrial revolution. A jeweler, they believed, should both design and make a piece of jewelry by his or her own hand. The first generation of Arts and Crafts jewelers in Great Britain had no professional silversmithing or goldsmithing skills, and many, including such notables as Henry Wilson and John Paul Cooper, were trained as painters and architects. The second generation of Arts and Crafts jewelers was more skilled, with some receiving formal training in art schools.

Women jewelers played a significant role within the Arts and Crafts Movement. Because the early movement was one of untrained craftsmen, women had as much chance for success as men did. Up until this time, it wasn't acceptable for women to enter such a career. But many factors led to this change during the Arts and Crafts Movement.

Women were glorified in Pre-Raphaelite paintings and some women even painted in this style. The relationship between the Pre-Raphaelites and the Arts and Crafts circles was strong and therefore brought women into the mix— some began to make jewelry either as partners with their husbands or on their own. Craft classes were organized for working-class women on a scale never before seen, and there was a new class of woman—the "destitute gentle-women"—who needed a means of support. Jewelry making was acceptable because it was done in the home and within the domestic sphere.

At the same time, women were agitating for the right to vote. The artists of the Arts and Crafts Movement were liberal minded and supported this movement, even creating jewels that were specifically suffragist-themed. Magazines and craft exhibitions allowed women jewelers' names to become known for the first time. Charlotte Newman, for example, became well known in the late Victorian period. She began as an assistant to renowned revivalist goldsmith John Brogden and went on to have a solo career after his death. She opened the door for those who came after her.[3] Among the many British female jewelry artists who remain well known today are Georgie Gaskin, Edith Dawson, Ernestine Mills, Phoebe Traquair and Jessie Marion King.[4]

Unidentified English maker
Suffragette Necklace, ca. 1900
14 x 26.7 cm
Silver, pearl, amethyst, enamel
Photo by J. Gold & Co., New York
Private collection

Attributed to Arthur and Georgina Gaskin
Necklace, n.d.
Necklace, 24 cm; pendant,
2.5 x 1.3 cm
Silver, opal, enamel
Photo by J. Gold & Co., New York
Talia Roland-Kalb Collection

Materials and Motifs

Victorian jewelry was often designed as a parure or demi-parure (a large or small set of matching jewelry) or worn in pairs, such as several bracelets together, or a brooch with

Frank Gardner Hale
Necklace, ca. 1915
Pendant, 9.5 x 5.7 cm; necklace,
51.4 cm
Gold, moonstone, Montana
sapphire
Courtesy of Siegelson, New York

matching earrings. Arts and Crafts jewels were usually worn solo. Pendants, necklaces, brooches, belt buckles, cloak clasps and hair combs were favored, while bracelets (never in pairs) and rings can be found in lesser quantities, with earrings uncommon due to hairstyles that covered the lobes. The new silk tea gowns worn by artistic women often featured a matching cape, so the Arts and Crafts cloak clip was the perfect accessory. Many of these dresses featured smocking or embroidery around the neck; too much jewelry would have clashed with the new fashions. Artistic belt buckles perfectly suited the more tailored clothing style liberated women were wearing—a slimmer skirt with a blouse or jacket rather than a tight-fighting dress with a bustle. The more enlightened class of society, supportive of women's new roles, were the same people who patronized the Arts and Crafts jewelers. The Pre-Raphaelite influence is seen in the shapes of necklaces adorned with chains and festoons, the motif of the girandole (a central piece with several drops at the end of it) and the heavy use of enamel. Later pieces have very beautiful and intricate gold work. Chains were also wrought with detail and care and are sometimes of the form we today refer to as paper clip style. The movement also responded to the ancient Celtic jewelry and metalwork being discovered in Great Britain in the nineteenth century, and the opening of Japan to the West, which made Oriental designs all the rage.[5]

For the most part, Arts and Crafts jewelers intentionally chose materials of little intrinsic value as a statement about the purpose of their jewelry. The work was meant to delight the eye with color and texture rather than be assessed by the worth of its components. It was also meant to be affordable to anyone who desired it. Base metals were frequently employed, and a low grade of silver was common. Silver was favored because it was softer and easier to work for self-taught metalsmiths, and it held the hammer marks that were often left unplanished as a sign of being handmade. Later pieces were more likely to utilize precious materials such as gold, although this was never the focal point of Arts and Crafts jewelry at any time. In the United States, many of the noted jewelers were well-trained goldsmiths who adopted the Arts and Crafts style. They had an established following of clients who could afford (and required) gold and precious stones but liked the new style. The work of these more experienced jewelers is therefore more expertly rendered than that of their English counterparts. This group includes Frank

Gardner Hale, Edward Everett Oakes and Josephine Hartwell Shaw in New England, and Madeline Wynn, Matthias Hanck, James Winn and Horace Potter in the Midwest.

Gemstones were for the most part used as accents in Arts and Crafts jewelry, not as the main event. Diamonds were most likely to be found in commissioned pieces and had previously belonged to the person who ordered the jewelry. Semiprecious stones were usually used en cabochon (unfaceted) following Ruskin's belief that this was their proper use.[6] Most were put into simple collet settings or even affixed to a piece of jewelry by simply winding wire around them. Moonstones and opals were particularly favored in Britain and America because they looked opaque and mysterious and were inexpensive. Pearls were also ubiquitous, but not the creamy colored spherical type found in mainstream jewelry. They were likely to be misshapen Baroque pearls or elongated river pearls (also called dog teeth) with casts of gray or yellow, chosen to add color and shape rather than for their perfection. Turquoise was used in its raw state for a more natural, hand-hewn look, and was of a less deep color than that normally found in Victorian jewelry. Also popular were unconventional and valueless materials, including abalone, coconut shell, mother-of-pearl, Connemara marble (serpentine) and glass.

Enamel was integral to Arts and Crafts jewelry as both the center "stone" in some jewelry and as the accent in others. Most often it was done in the Limoges style that allows an artist to paint a miniature image or even a landscape that's then framed in metalwork. Nature themes abounded in these enamel works, while images of people were found infrequently. The same enamels were set in boxes, in covered metal bowls and as inserts in picture and mirror frames.

Materials can be a clue to the origin of Arts and Crafts jewelry produced in different countries, although Ireland, Scotland, New Zealand and Australia tended to be similar because these jewelers, for the most part, studied with English Arts and Crafts jewelers.[7] Some American jewelry is clearly recognizable through its use of materials and motifs. For example, American jewelers used Montana sapphires, Mississippi River pearls and other American stones extensively. Flowers depicted on a number of English pieces aren't common in American gardens, including love-in-a-mist, a favorite of Nelson and Edith Gaskin. While British artists often chose a Renaissance style for their jewels, American

Edward Everett Oakes
Ring, early twentieth century
2.1 x 2.4 x 1.3 cm
18-karat yellow gold, blue
faceted zircons, pearls
Courtesy of ChicagoSilver

James Winn
Bar Pin, early twentieth century
7.4 x 1.4 cm
Gold, amethysts, bezel-set
faceted diamonds
Courtesy of ChicagoSilver

Krementz & Co.
Pendant, ca. 1900
5.7 x 6.6 x 2.2 cm
Gold, enamel, pearl
© Photo courtesy of The Three
Graces Gallery

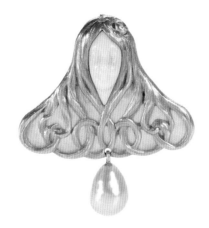

René Foy
Brooch, ca. 1900
8 x 3.3 cm
Gold, plique-à-jour enamel,
coral, freshwater pearl
Photo by Antonio Virardi
Courtesy of Macklowe Gallery

Louis Aucoc
Brooch, ca. 1900
5.1 x 3.8 x 1.3 cm
Gold, enamel, diamond, pearl
Private collection

jewelers and metalworkers looked back to the simple lines of colonial metalwork and at times used indigenous motifs, such as an image of the head of a Native American chief in full headdress. Americans embraced the handmade concept intellectually but weren't as stringent in practice, using mechanical processes to work their jewelry.

Art Nouveau

Art Nouveau jewelry, originating in France and Belgium, was created for a very different market: it was meant to appeal to a wealthy but artistically aware stratum of society. This included, most famously, the notorious women of the Paris demimonde—the courtesans kept by wealthy men. Many of these women, including Sarah Bernhardt and actress/courtesan Liane de Pougy, helped make the work of Art Nouveau jewelers such as René Lalique and Alphonse Mucha well known by wearing their work in public when other women dared not do so because the jewelry was so avant-garde.[8]

Art Nouveau jewelry had its roots in the symbolist movement's dream-based art, literature and music, in which obscure, hard-to-decipher symbols stood for ideas known mostly only to the artist, and in a revival of the rococo period of design in architecture and the decorative arts, with its curvilinear forms. Additionally, Lalique, who had studied in England, was familiar with the curving forms in William Morris's textiles, which bore a relationship to the rococo style.[9] The result was jewels of staggering beauty and imagination, sensual, sexual and beguiling, and at times even frightening. These jewels were a far cry from the symmetrical and somewhat placid designs of Arts and Crafts jewelry, which more closely resembled Renaissance jewels.

Art Nouveau jewelry also differed from Arts and Crafts jewelry in the choice of materials. French makers more often used precious metals and precious gemstones, sometimes mixing them with unusual materials such as horn. Their clientele was both artistically minded and financially well-off and could afford this more expensive jewelry. In addition to the plique-à-jour enamel work that set Art Nouveau jewelry apart from that of the Arts and Crafts style, another unusual technique, cabochonné enamel, was used. It consisted of building up enamel to mimic a rounded cabochon-cut stone.

The last half of the nineteenth century had not been kind to France. Military defeat and political imbroglios polarized and demoralized French citizens.[10] The government made a decision to support the new art style as a means to elevate France as a world leader in the production of luxury goods, as well as to instill a greater sense of self-esteem in the population. Looking back to the eighteenth century, a glorious period in France's history, helped accomplish that goal. The curvilinear line of Art Nouveau can be seen in rococo designs of the eighteenth century but reinterpreted more sensuously in the later style.

Art Nouveau design also reflected a strong conflict in the French psyche regarding the role of women as they fought for the right to higher education and to work outside the home. An early twentieth-century cartoon in a French newspaper depicts the femme fatale. The woman is illustrated wearing the newly invented bloomers, her hands are placed on the handlebars of her bicycle and she smokes a cigarette— all very scandalous for its time and signifying the fear of French men for the *nouvelle femme*. With French birth rates decreasing as Germany's rose, it was deemed even more important for woman to stay in the home and have children, producing a future army should it become necessary.

Thus we see the schizophrenic view of women that pervades Art Nouveau jewelry, which was all designed by men. (We know the name of only one female Art Nouveau jeweler, Elizabeth Bonté, who made insect pendants carved from horn.) In all cases we see an eroticized portrayal of the female form, some more outrageous than others. The fantasies displayed on the jewelry illustrate the fact that French men were uncertain whether to revere women or be frightened by their changing role in society. Until this time, even the image of a woman's face or body on jewelry was considered improper. In the Art Nouveau genre we consistently see women in every form. Lalique's *Brooch with a Female Figure* is a good example. The unclothed body on this sensual brooch was considered scandalous. The woman kneels so we see both the glorification of her eroticism and the need to bring her to her knees. The intertwining enamel forms a depiction of her hair, which reminds us of the mythical Medusa (a frequent subject for Lalique), a woman who turned men to stone when they gazed upon her. The female figure often appeared in Art Nouveau jewelry as a fantastic creature, a half-woman, half-insect hybrid, or with a mermaid's tail or

René Lalique
Brooch with a Female Figure, ca. 1903
3.8 x 6.9 x 1 cm
Gold, enamel, diamond, sapphire
Photo © 2013 Museum of Fine Arts, Boston
Private collection
© 2013 Artists Rights Society (ARS), New York / ADAGP, Paris

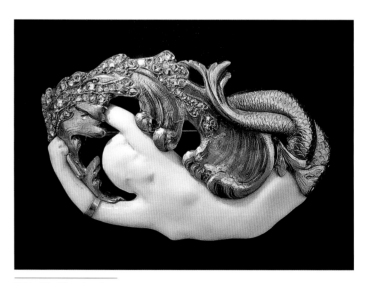

Unidentified French maker
Sea Nymph Brooch, ca. 1900
5.7 x 3.8 cm
Ivory, yellow gold, rose-cut diamonds
Photo by Cole Bybee
Courtesy of Lang Antiques

Elizabeth Bonté
*Wind Blown
Chrysanthemum,* ca. 1900
9.5 x 5.7 cm
Carved horn, colored beads,
wooden beads, silk cord
Photo by Antonio Virardi
Courtesy of Macklowe Gallery

Charles Desrosiers, for
Georges Fouquet
Orchid Brooch, ca.
1898–1901
8.5 x 11.3 x 2 cm
Gold, enamel, diamond, pearl
Photo © 2013 Museum of Fine
Arts, Boston
Private collection
© 2013 Artists Rights Society
(ARS), New York / ADAGP, Paris

fairy's wings grafted onto her human form. Women were at times portrayed as Medusa with snakes or bats for hair, or as the biblical Salome, who cut off John the Baptist's head and served it on a platter. These women represented men's deepest fears and their eyes were often set with stones, such as opals, that appeared to be pools of evil. When American jewelers adopted the Art Nouveau style, the woman as a symbol simply became a young woman with curls wreathing her pretty face. The American public did not warm to the unique French designs.[11]

Nature was also an equally important subject. In Arts and Crafts jewelry, nature was depicted in a rather realistic and straightforward way, in line with Ruskin's and Morris's belief that art should follow nature. French Art Nouveau jewelers took a decidedly different approach. They incorporated all of nature, real and mythical, and with great sensuality. The seasons are seen both in their decaying cycle as well as blooming, and animals can evoke fear. There's strong evidence of the awareness of Japanese art in these jewels, specifically in the style of Japanese woodcuts that depict nature in flat planes. Plique-à-jour enamel, a technique almost exclusively used by the Art Nouveau jewelers (light passes through it like a small stained glass window), served perfectly to imitate the transparent features of an insect's wings.

The Rest of Europe

Art jewelry on the Continent often melded influences of both the English and the French movements. In Germany and Austria, a number of jewelers worked in a restrained form of the curvilinear French Art Nouveau. Others followed the highly original and inventive, more geometric Austrian secessionist style that was pared down and more abstract than the French art jewelry. Artists of the Wiener Werkstätte (Vienna Workshops) knew and were influenced by Charles Rennie Mackintosh and his wife Margaret MacDonald. This is an excellent example of how ideas were constantly exchanged or assimilated by jewelers across borders. In some cases, style was transplanted from one country to another; in other cases, it was more theoretical. In each country nationalism played a certain role, affecting the outcome of the design and how much it borrowed from another country's oeuvre. In Germany it was acceptable to use some machinery to create jewelry, while in England it wasn't. Sometimes we can see a direct relationship from the work of one country to another, sometimes not. But we can always understand immediately that this jewelry was very different from what came before it, and this impulse to break with the past was the thread that connected art jewelry in this period.

The Wiener Werkstätte was modeled after the Guild of Handicraft in England. It was run as a cooperative workshop producing beautiful objects for the home as well as for personal adornment. One of its founders, architect Josef Hoffmann, had visited several British guilds in 1902 and what he saw no doubt had an impact. Hoffmann and fellow architect Koloman Moser created many of the designs that were executed by others. They approached jewelry as they did other design projects—good craftsmanship and design were more important than the materials. They tended to work with silver more often than gold, alone or set with semiprecious stones, and often took advantage of the colored patterns of variegated stones. The Wiener Werkstätte also had an ivory workshop and created beautiful beaded necklaces. Some of the jewelry was designed to be worn specifically with clothing created by the workshop. An example of a simple item made by the workshop is a circular all-silver brooch designed by Josef Hofmann. The repoussé work is no doubt based on floral design, but one highly stylized to the point of becoming almost abstract. While exhibiting the more geometric elegance of the workshop's jewelry, it also has a sense of movement and sensuousness related to French Art Nouveau.

Art jewelry was also being made in Scandinavia. One of the first to make it was Mogens Ballin of Denmark, who trained as a painter in Paris, where he was likely exposed to the works of the symbolists. Ballin, who like his British counterparts had no formal training, opened a workshop and made beautiful everyday objects in metalwork based on the ideals of Morris and Ruskin. His work was somewhat abstract and organic in nature. The young aspiring sculptor Georg Jensen went to work in Ballin's shop, where he had his first opportunity to use his art training to create highly sculptural jewelry.[12] Although Jensen is the most recognized name of the Danish *Skonvirke* (aesthetic work) movement today, we cannot ignore Ballin's contribution and the work of other Danish art jewelry artists.

Danish art jewelers imitated the British Arts and Crafts Movement in their desire to create affordable, high-quality jewelry, but they sometimes tooled their pieces by machine. The handmade aspect was not as critical to them. Danish

Josef Hoffmann
Brooch/Pendant Designed for Wiener Werkstätte,
ca. 1910
Diameter, 5.6 cm
Silver
Private collection

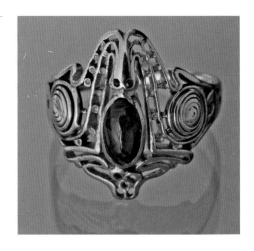

Karl Rothmüller
Octopus Ring, 1904
Height, 1.9 cm
Gold, sapphire, ruby
Courtesy of Tadema Gallery

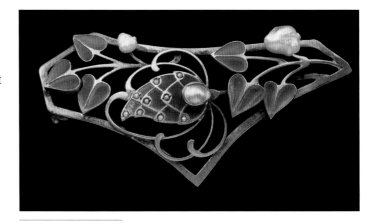

Attributed to Levinger & Bissinger
Jugendstil Brooch, ca. 1900
2.9 x 6.6 cm
Gilded silver, plique-à-jour enamel, pearl
Courtesy of Tadema Gallery

Mogens Ballin
Belt Buckle, n.d.
9 x 7.5 cm
Silver, malachite
Photo by J. Gold & Co.
Private collection

pieces were almost always made in silver, featured little enamel work and used native Scandinavian stones. They are larger, heavier and more abstract than Arts and Crafts and Art Nouveau jewelry but are clearly in the art jewelry genre. Jensen was well aware of both English Arts and Crafts and the work of Lalique, and some of his earliest pieces show his interest. A bird brooch by Jensen circa 1904–10 is an early example of the sculptural quality of his jewelry. The brooch has almost a three-dimensional quality, as if we can actually see the bird perching on a branch. Foliage swirls around it, a slightly Art Nouveau suggestion, and, following the tenets of the Arts and Crafts style, the semiprecious stones, chosen for color, are collet set.

Other important Danish designers included Erik Magnussen, who immigrated to the United States in 1924 and became artistic director for the Gorham Manufacturing Company; Evald Nielsen, whose jewelry shows the influence of both German and Arts and Crafts design; Harald Slott-Moller; and Thorvald Bindesboll. And as with the British Arts and Crafts Movement, women jewelers made a name for themselves, including Inger Moller; Thyra Marie Vieth, who had her own workshop and chasing school; and Marie Christiansen, who studied horn and ivory carving in France and worked in a style related to that of Lalique.

By the 1890s, the ideals of William Morris and John Ruskin had reached Finland. At least one metalsmith, Erik O.W. Ehrstrom, became well known as an art jeweler, and his work foreshadowed the Art Deco style. In Sweden, the best-known silversmith influenced by British Arts and Crafts was Jacob Angmann, who began working around 1900 in a "new art" style.

Norway, after breaking away from Swedish rule in 1905, entered into a period of Viking revival to celebrate its freedom. The best-known firm to work in an early twentieth-century art style that incorporated this revival, especially the dragon heads that appeared on Viking ships, was that of David Anderson, still in business today. J. Tostrup made items decorated in the French-style plique-à-jour enamel, and Marius Hammer and Thorvald Olsen were known to make silver items in the Art Nouveau style. Scandinavian artists used semiprecious stones, including coral and amber (known as Nordic gold), and indigenous stones, including quartz, garnets, labradorite, smoky quartz and iolite. Native plants, birch leaves and pine twigs are prevalent design motifs.

Georg Jensen
Moonlight Blossom Brooch,
ca. 1904–1910
6 x 6 cm
Silver, blue stones
Photo courtesy of Georg Jensen

In Spain, the new art style was known as *modernisme* and was largely a movement in architecture. Prominent among jewelers was the firm of Masriera, already well established by this time. Luis Masriera, son of the firm's founder, created his own form of Art Nouveau jewelry. It was beautifully executed but more restrained in design than that of its French counterparts. The firm is still in business today, recreating pieces from Luis Masriera's original designs.

Stile liberty or *stile floreale* referred to the new art jewelry in Italy. The former is related to the commercial version of Arts and Crafts that was made and sold by Liberty & Co. in London. Few jewelers who worked in Italy are known today and examples are rare to find. A small craft community known as Aemilia Ars worked in Bologna. Its craftsmen had a small output of jewelry that was almost a direct replication of fourteenth-century ecclesiastical pieces.

Only a small quantity of art style jewelry can be attributed to Russian artists. What is found appears as a tighter, more stylized version of French Art Nouveau. The famed House of Fabergé produced a few pieces that were in an Art Nouveau style. The physical isolation of Russia may partly explain this, but the majority of jewelry at this time was made for the royal family and it favored highly classical styles. Although the Netherlands is physically closer to Great Britain and France, Dutch Art Nouveau took on other influences, such as that of Indonesian architecture (the country had ties with Indonesia through the spice trade). Frans Zwollo, Sr., a Dutch artisan who was a theosophist, was a follower of Rudolf Steiner. (Steiner was an Austrian-trained scientist who lived in Germany and preached a relationship between scientific study and spiritual knowledge.) Zwollo's jewelry shows evidence of his philosophies, as the colors he used represent the highest spiritual aura. In yet another expression of art jewelry, in Hungary, Art Nouveau was blended with a popular historic style to produce a unique manifestation. It's often difficult to identify, because much of the Budapest-made jewelry that survives is often marked as Viennese, there being one standard set of marks for the Austro-Hungarian Empire. The empire was dissolved after World War I and the marks retired in 1922.

Although some aspects of design and technique were more common in a particular movement or country, there was significant cross-pollination of ideas. Whereas French and Belgian jewelers most often used the technique of plique-à-jour enamel, Englishman Fred Partridge created plique-à-jour pieces akin to Lalique's, and additional English examples can be found. The

Unidentified Italian artist
Belt Buckle, ca. 1900
5.7 x 8.3 cm
Enamel on metal
Private collection

Marcus & Co.
Morning Glory Brooch/
Pendant, ca. 1900
10.2 x 7.6 cm
Gold, plique-à-jour enamel
Courtesy of Siegelson, New York

Museum of Fine Arts, Boston recently acquired an important plique-à-jour brooch, converted from a hair comb, designed by the Guild of Handicraft. This piece, though atypical for the Guild, demonstrates the crosscurrents among movements and countries. Another important enamel jewel, a brooch convertible to a pendant depicting three-dimensional morning glories, made by renowned American firm Marcus & Co., also demonstrates unusual skill with plique-à-jour and shows how American makers were looking to Europe to learn new techniques.

The Decline of Art Jewelry

In the later 1920s and '30s, the flapper era and the new, waistless style of dress, new forms of transportation like planes and trains and the first skyscrapers all helped create a rectilinear and bold style that overshadowed the early art jewelry movements. During this period jewelers such as Gérard Sandoz and Raymond Templier created one-of-a-kind Art Deco art jewels, sometimes made with unusual materials like eggshell embedded in lacquer, to continue the art jewelry tradition. Although World War I and changing tastes were the primary reasons for the cessation of the work of the early twentieth-century art jewelers, there were other factors as well. Art Nouveau jewelry was functionally and aesthetically challenging—the extensive use of fragile enamel made it easy to break, and perhaps it was just too outrageous for most people—so much of it was simply admired by its owners but never worn in public. In the 1940s, the modern studio jewelry movement had its beginnings with famed educator Margret Craver teaching craft classes to returning GIs, much as Ashbee had created classes for young boys who needed a trade. However, it wasn't until the 1960s that the work of the early twentieth-century art jewelry movements began to be rediscovered and valued for their radical break with the past.

Art jewelry valued the handmade and prized innovative thinking and creative expression. These jewelers were the first to use materials that didn't have the intrinsic value expected in jewelry, and they rejected mainstream jewelry tastes. They thought of their work as an artistic pursuit and made it for a small audience that shared their aesthetic and conceptual values. This is much like the work of many studio jewelers working internationally today, jewelers who take risks with new materials and unusual forms and who blur the boundaries between jewelry and art.

Notes

1. William Morris, *The Worker's Share of Art* (London: Commonweal, 1885).

2. Alan Crawford, *C. R. Ashbee, Architect, Designer and Romantic Socialist* (New Haven, CT: Yale University Press, 1985).

3. Charlotte Gere, *American & European Jewelry, 1830–1914* (New York: Crown, 1975).

4. Vivienne Becker, *Art Nouveau Jewelry* (New York: E. P. Dutton, 1985).

5. Ibid.

6. Becker, *Art Nouveau Jewelry*.

7. Anne Schofield and Kevin Fahy, *Australian Jewellery: 19th and Early 20th Century* (Woodbridge, UK: Antique Collectors' Club, 1991).

8. Yvonne Brunhammer, *The Jewels of Lalique* (Paris: Flammarion, 1999).

9. Ibid.

10. Stephen Escritt, *Art Nouveau* (London: Phaidon, 2000).

11. Yvonne Markowitz and Elyse Zorn Karlin, *Imperishable Beauty: Art Nouveau Jewelry* (Boston: Museum of Fine Arts, Boston, 2008).

12. Ibid.

Further Readings

Becker, Vivienne. *Art Nouveau Jewelry.* New York: E.P. Dutton, 1985.

Crawford, Alan. *C. R. Ashbee, Architect, Designer and Romantic Socialist.* New Haven, CT: Yale University Press, 1985.

Darling, Sharon. *Chicago Metalsmiths.* Chicago: Chicago Historical Society, 1977.

Dietz, Ulysses Grant, and Janet Zapata. *The Glitter & The Gold: Fashioning America's Jewelry.* Woodbridge, UK: Antique Collectors' Club, 1977.

Drucker, Janet. *Georg Jensen: A Tradition of Splendid Silver.* Atglen, PA: Schiffer, 2001.

Falino, Jeannine, and Yvonne Markowitz. *Jewels from the House of Tiffany.* Woodbridge, UK: Antique Collectors' Club, 2008.

Harrison, Stephen, Emmanuel Ducamp, Christie Mayer, and Jeannine Falino. *Artistic Luxury: Fabergé, Tiffany, Lalique.* Cleveland / New Haven, CT: Cleveland Museum of Art / Yale University Press, 2008.

Karlin, Elyse Zorn. *Jewelry & Metalwork in the Arts & Crafts Tradition.* Atlgen, PA: Schiffer, 2007.

Markowitz, Yvonne, and Elyse Zorn Karlin. *Imperishable Beauty: Art Nouveau Jewelry.* Boston: Museum of Fine Arts, Boston, 2008.

Sataloff, Joseph. *Art Nouveau Jewelry.* Bryn Mawr, PA: Dorrance & Co., 1984.

Staggs, Janet. *Wiener Werkstätte Jewelry.* Ostfildern, Germany: Hatje Cantz, 2008.

Taylor, David, ed. *Georg Jensen Jewelry.* New York: Bard Graduate Center for Studies in the Decorative Arts, Design, and Culture, 2005.

Von Hase-Schmundt, Christianne Weber, and Ingeborg Becker. *Theodor Fahrner Jewelry: Between Avant-Garde and Tradition.* Atglen, PA: Schiffer, 2007.

Zapata, Janet. *The Jewelry and Enamels of Louis Comfort Tiffany.* New York: Harry N. Abrams, 1993.

Europe.

Liesbeth den Besten

Introduction

Europe is a patchwork quilt of countries and cultures. On this continent, about 750 million inhabitants live in 51 countries and speak about 70 different languages. The former communist countries, hidden until the 1990s behind the Iron Curtain, are only slowly developing economically. Spain, Portugal and Greece suffered under fascist regimes and were closed to the rest of Europe until the early '80s. We can hardly talk about a union in a practical sense. In jewelry the differences among countries are equally big; some encountered radical changes in jewelry, while others remained silent until now because traditional goldsmithing set the tone there. Therefore, we can't stipulate that there's a particular European history of contemporary jewelry. Instead, there are many.

At the turn of the nineteenth century, conventional ideas about values in jewelry—and the value of jewelry—were turned upside down for the benefit of artistic creativity. The new thinking and artistic productions of this period were the motor for the later movements in twentieth-century jewelry. Radical changes only became apparent in the course of the 1960s due to a combination of factors. The growing prosperity of European countries resulted in an increased number of jewelry schools and students. Some important traveling exhibitions provided for an exchange of ideas. And finally, a growing awareness of the creative individuality in the arts was underscored by the ideology of the avant-garde.

In the early 1950s, a growing group of jewelers established their own small workshops, claiming artistic independence. They worked on commission for private clients while striving for self-expression. This generation of jewelers (born around 1920 or earlier) was well educated. Ebbe Weiss-Weingart in Germany and Mario Pinton in Italy studied painting and sculpture in art school, then became important goldsmiths. Others studied at arts and crafts schools with excellent teachers who themselves were often part of the important arts and crafts movements of the early twentieth century. Chris Steenbergen in the Netherlands and Max Fröhlich in Switzerland studied at applied art schools based on Bauhaus principles. Vivianna Torun Bülow-Hübe, a Swedish jeweler known simply as Torun, opened her own workshops, first in Stockholm and later in France in the 1950s, after studying at Konstfack (Konstfack University College of Arts, Crafts and Design). She impressed Pablo Picasso with her unconventional attitude. Her early jewelry designs were elegant mobiles that might move over the shoulder or hang down the back of the body. The elements were made from simple found materials such as wood and pebbles.

Rough Surfaces and Exploding Forms

Generally, *art informel* was predominant in central and southern Europe and in England during the 1950s and '60s. Informal art, abstract expressionism or tachism (all names for roughly the same artistic attitude) in jewelry was characterized by splendor (an emphasis on yellow gold and exploding forms), color (preferably through stones), sparkle (diamonds) and the rough finishing of surfaces. This style of working was slowly abandoned during the '60s and '70s in favor of a controlled way of working based on a geometric vocabulary.

In Germany and Austria in the 1950s, the *informal* attitude was predominant, often combined with figuration. Reinhold Reiling, teacher and professor at the Kunst + Werkschule in Pforzheim from 1954 to 1983, injected new life into postwar German jewelry. His early work, influenced by tachism, was made of warm gold combined with colorful stones and a lively surface treatment. At the end of the '60s his work became graphic, applying geometry in a free and nonrational, compositional way. Another important postwar German jeweler was Hermann Jünger. His work in the '50s and '60s was strongly related to abstract expressionism. He used enamel and stones to add color to his pieces as if he were using paint, liberating precious stones from their economic value and generating criticism in traditional goldsmith circles. From 1972 to 1990, Jünger was a professor at the Akademie der Bildenden Künste München (Academy of Fine Arts, Munich), where his teaching gave a new energy to contemporary jewelry. In Germany, he's considered the one who "redefined the art of the goldsmith."[1]

The important contribution of fine artists to the renewal of jewelry design is what sets apart Italy from the other European countries. The Milan Triennial became an important platform for international jewelry during the 1950s. Italian jewelry of this period is characterized by an informal mentality as expressed in the work of fine artists such as the brothers Arnaldo and Giò Pomodoro. Also, sculptor Bruno Martinazzi created Informal jewelry pieces characterized by a refined and sculptural surface treatment. Toward the end of the 1960s, inspired by the human body, his forms became plastic and organic. He used white gold as a contrasting and defining element in his body jewels. This naturalism was new in contemporary jewelry, and it

Ebbe Weiss-Weingart
Brooch, 1961
3.4 x 4.8 cm
Gold
Photo by Günther Meyer
© Schmuckmuseum Pforzheim

Vivianna Torun Bülow-Hübe
Vivianna, 1956
Photo courtesy of Georg Jensen

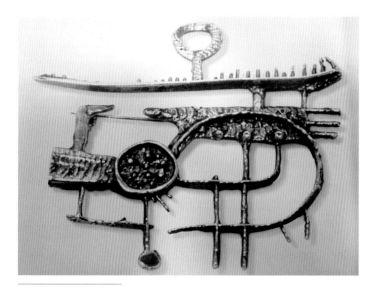

"3P" (Giorgio Perfetti and
Giò and Arnaldo Pomodoro)
Brooch, 1954
Dimensions unknown
Silver, cuttlefish casting
Photographer unknown
Photo reproduced in
*Contemporary Jewellery, The
Padua School*
Courtesy of Graziella Folchini
Grassetto

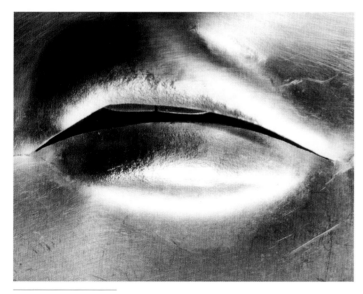

Bruno Martinazzi
Economic Growth—Mouth,
1968
3.4 x 4 cm
20-karat gold, 18-karat white
gold; repoussé, chiseled
Photo by Pucci Giardina
Collection of the Montreal
Museum of Fine Arts / Musée
des Beaux-Arts de Montréal
Photo courtesy of the artist

emphasized jewelry's autonomy as a wearable piece of art.

Mario Pinton, educated as a jeweler and a sculptor, regenerated the old and respected Istituto Statale d'Art Pietro Selvatico Padova (Pietro Selvatico State Institute of Art in Padua), where he began teaching in 1944 and which he directed from 1969 to 1976. Two of his students, Francesco Pavan and Giampaolo Babetto, began teaching at the school in the 1960s, and gave the jewelry course a new and abstract direction, geometrical and minimalist in form. Gold and excellent craftsmanship formed the core of the jewelry course. In the 1960s the kinetic movement in the visual arts influenced Pavan, whose jewelry was shown at the 1964 Venice Biennale alongside the kinetic work of the famous Gruppo Enne. Pavan's creative research in jewelry was directed in a formal, rather minimal and mathematical approach, which became the hallmark of the so-called "school of Padova." In Italy, gold remained the standard until the 1990s, when artists such as Annamaria Zanella started subverting ideas about preciousness with the help of oxides, iron and acrylic enamels.[2]

Barcelona, in Catalonia, was the only center for jewelry in Spain. In the 1960s through to the '80s, Catalan jewelry stood quite on its own, its style sometimes described as Mediterranean and associated with lively colors, rounded forms, undulating lines and a painterly abstraction. Its inspiration was found in the early twentieth-century avant-garde Catalan *Noucentista* jewelry, and in *informal* art.[3]

Roughly speaking, some kind of division can be observed between central and southern *informal Europe* on the one hand, and northwest and northern *concrete Europe* on the other. England, however, is the exception. Its jewelry was more related to the central and southern European mentality. John Donald's and David Thomas' compositions, made in England in the 1950s and early '60s, fit into an international expressionist tendency with an emphasis on forms that seemed to explode from the center with rough and undulating surfaces combined with colorful stones, diamonds and pearls. Other important jewelers in the UK originated from central and southern Europe: Gerda Flöckinger, who taught briefly at Hornsey College of Art, where she introduced a new modern jewelry course in the 1960s; Andrew Grima, who founded a company in the same decade and counted royals and socialites among his clientele; and Helga Zahn, who revitalized British jewelry through her uninhibited choice of pebbles and colored stones as compositional elements.

A new wind started blowing in British jewelry with the couple David Watkins and Wendy Ramshaw. Neither was trained as a jeweler, but Ramshaw was already interested in jewelry as a sculpture student. Their 1964 line of screen-printed Perspex fashion jewelry, *Optik Art Jewelry*, was followed by their *Something Special* screen-printed jewelry (1966–67). This commercial project brought in much-needed earnings. It was industrially produced and became quite popular, on par with the paper fashion trend and with op art. Their acrylic and paper jewelry sold in department stores, fashion icon Mary Quant's shop and other boutiques. They could make around 2,000 earrings a day, and they sold tens of thousands of pieces. Watkins and Ramshaw's path to contemporary jewelry was quite peculiar and inspired by the currents and flows of their time: op art, fashion, design, music and film (Watkins worked in the music and film industries). By the early 1970s, they were both designing and making on the lathe. Ramshaw turned jewelry from bars of silver combined with inlays of colored enamel (and later with mounted colored stones), while Watkins turned acrylic that was then dyed. In the early 1970s, they were the first to use computer designing and programming in jewelry. Their work expressed a machine aesthetic and meant a breach with the prevailing British *informal* approach. Yet because of their explicit use of color and their loose abstraction, Watkins and Ramshaw's jewelry stood apart from Scandinavian and Dutch jewelry.[4]

Wendy Ramshaw and David Watkins
"Something Special" paper jewellery, 1966–1967
Dimensions vary, between 12 x 6 cm and 3.5 x 3.5 cm
Printed lightweight card, wire, ceramic and wooden beads, adhesive tape, metal findings
Photo by Bob Cramp

The Economy of Form and Construction

The Nordic countries are known for their modernist design culture during the twentieth century and modernist design set the tone in jewelry, too. The name and fame of the Georg Jensen company for jewelry, cutlery and silverware, a typical result of the arts and crafts movements of the late nineteenth and early twentieth centuries, has spread worldwide. From 1946 onward, the Georg Jensen company collaborated with designers such as Nanna and Jørgen Ditzel, Henning Koppel and Torun, who designed jewelry in an organic modernist style. In Sweden, Sigurd Persson was known for approaching jewelry as a rational design problem, while in Finland Björn Weckström (one of the founders of Lapponia Jewelry) embraced a more informal design aesthetic. The dogma of modernist design finally became an obstacle in setting off new

Sigurd Persson
Ring, 1963
No dimensions given
Gold, almandine garnets
Photo by Rüdiger Flöter
Photo © Schmuckmuseum
Pforzheim
© 2013 Artists Rights Society
(ARS), New York / BUS,
Stockholm

ideas and concepts. A case in point is the work of Norwegian Tone Vigeland. She first had to go through a modernist phase before she was able to liberate herself and find her own style and way of working around 1980. It was only at the end of the 1980s that more Scandinavians started entering the European jewelry scene.

Formal or concrete art, and a cool and restrained attitude, also prevailed in countries that had a history of constructivist, abstract and concrete art. In the Netherlands, individual goldsmiths, such as Archibald Dumbar and Chris Steenbergen, seldom applied precious metals to abstract linear compositions. This generation of Dutch jewelers was strongly influenced by the constructivist sculpture of Naum Gabo and Antoine Pevsner and other modernists such as Henry Moore. Their style of working, characterized by a preference for rounded forms, line compositions and transparency, was so recognizable that it became known under the name of *spijltjesstijl*, or sticks or spills style.[5]

In the early 1960s, the modernist industrial jewelry design of Persson and other Scandinavians appealed to young Dutch jewelers. Gijs Bakker moved to Stockholm in 1962 to finish his education in the center of modernist design. At the Konstfack School he learned to think as a designer, which was a step beyond the crafts education he had had in Amsterdam. After returning to the Netherlands, Bakker worked as an assistant designer for Van Kempen and Begeer, makers of fine cutlery. During this period Bakker and his wife, Emmy van Leersum, managed a jewelry studio in the center of Utrecht. In 1967 they were invited to an exhibition showcasing young jewelers in the Stedelijk Museum in Amsterdam. They proposed to do a catwalk show. The jewelry, mainly head and neck ornaments, was big, like a manifesto. It was their coming out as contemporary jewelry designers.[6]

The next generation of Dutch jewelers broke radically with the modesty and transparency of their predecessors. They turned to cheap and light industrial materials like stainless steel and aluminum to make large abstract forms that confronted the body intellectually and physically. The jewelry was made by hand, often departing from prefab material (such as tubes), and had to be finished elaborately until it gained the proper "industrial" look. The result had contemporary appeal and attracted both attention and a following. Their criticism of the use of precious materials as a safe-seeming investment that corrupted the freedom of creation was widely noted in the many newspaper articles and magazines that featured their work.

At the end of the 1960s, the foundations were laid for the work of independent designers who had a strong vision to express in jewelry. The advocates of this way of working, Bakker and Van Leersum, had connections with artists in the fine art world creating geometric abstraction. They and their contemporaries aimed at industrial production and claimed to be "jewelry designers." They also discovered other approaches. Bakker soon started making conceptual jewelry, questioning jewelry as a status symbol and investment. Van Leersum was interested in integrating jewelry and fashion by conceiving them as an entity, eventually leading to clothing designs. The zest for the formal and rational approach was so strong in the Netherlands that everything else was simply dismissed. Those jewelers who worked in the *informal* style, most of them educated and based in the south of the country, were completely overruled by the then-predominant and internationally recognized style of the jewelers based in Amsterdam and Arnhem. In the Netherlands, *art informel* was a no-go zone.

An important figure in European postwar *concrete* art was the Swiss designer, architect, painter and sculptor Max Bill. Trained as a silversmith in Zurich, he studied two years at the Bauhaus in Dessau. He stood for "good form," with its emphasis on abstract and neutral forms that found their logic in design principles instead of in sentimentality or romanticism. Bill designed some jewelry, but was more important as an artist, designer and theorist. The principle of the Möbius strip, worked out by Bill in his sculptures, was widely known and also applied by jewelry designers like Persson, Torun and Bakker in the 1960s.

Bill's contemporary and countryman Max Fröhlich was a true craftsman. He led the jewelry and metal class at the Kunstgewerbeschule in Zurich for almost 30 years. Otto Künzli, Therese Hilbert and Johanna Dahm were among his students. The school was known for its rational style inspired by Bill's theories. Yet Fröhlich worked in a rather *informal*, expressionist and organic style, as well as in a reduced and more geometric way, for instance using prefab metal wire covered with plastic. In fact, like Fröhlich, many postwar European designers, artists and architects switched easily from one style to the other, although this fact is often neglected in official histories of this period. In his early work, around 1970, Swiss artist Bernhard Schobinger showed that *concrete*, rational art could be

Gijs Bakker
Neckpiece Ornament: Shoulder Piece/Halskraag, 1967
33.7 x 23 x 36 cm
Aluminum
Photo by Matthijs Schrofer
Courtesy of the artist

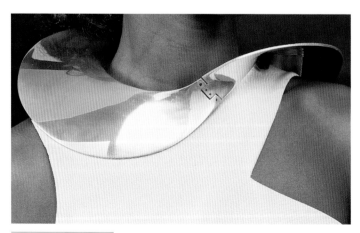

Emmy van Leersum
Collar with Fastenings and Dress, 1967
Collar, 33 x 16.5 x 10 cm
Aluminum, textile
Courtesy of Stedelijik
Museum's-Hertogenbosch

obscured by "irrationalism." His *Lipstick Ring* merged concrete and pop art. In the 1970s and '80s, Schobinger's jewelry became radical, combining precious materials like diamonds and gold with the detritus of consumer society.[7]

Czechoslovakia enjoyed a relatively supportive climate toward the arts in the 1960s. In 1968 (the year of the Prague Spring), Václav Cigler created head ornaments that consisted of circles and disks framing the face, establishing a personal safe environment for the wearer. Around 1970, glass artist Svatopluk Kasalý started making large wearable body objects of metal and glass disks. In the early 1980s, Vratislav Karel Novák applied glass chips directly to the face, fastened with rubber and stainless steel strips. Czech jewelry was quite radical, but it remained isolated; there was hardly any contact between Western and Eastern Europe, although in the 1980s Novak's performative body pieces were included in international exhibitions in Barcelona and Linz. Anton Cepka's abstract constructivist jewelry was shown abroad on many occasions during the 1970s and '80s, thanks to his recognition in Germany. Roughly sketched, from 1945 to 1970, abstraction prevailed in all of Europe. Around the year 1970, the victory of *concrete* jewelry (smooth and geometrical) over *informal* jewelry (rough and expressionist) was a fait accompli.

The Exhibition as a Catalyst

Big exhibitions catalyze; they attract attention to the field and stimulate discourse. Yet important exhibitions are also organized in the wake of things going on. The increase in international jewelry exhibitions during the 1960s and '70s points to the growing importance of contemporary jewelry.

In 1965 Museum Boijmans van Beuningen in Rotterdam presented an international jewelry exhibition organized by the Hessisches Landesmuseum in Darmstadt in 1964. The show was supplemented by a collection of contemporary Dutch jewelry.[8] The exhibition received good press coverage, but for some it represented exactly what to rebel against. Bakker, Van Leersum, Klaas van Beek and other young jewelry students decided that the emphasis on craftsmanship and splendor was not what they aimed for.[9]

During the 1960s, Pforzheim, with its Kunst + Werkschule, developed into a center of contemporary jewelry. In the Schmuckmuseum, Fritz Falk organized the Tendenzen exhibitions. Focusing on the newest work, these five exhibitions put on between 1967 and 1982 brought together jewelry from many different countries as well as from outside Europe. The exhibitions also demonstrated that the German approach was rather one-sided: the emphasis was on small and wearable objects of beauty. There was no room for the new wearable object trend that was developing quickly during the 1970s in the Netherlands and England.

Ralph Turner's groundbreaking Jewellery in Europe: An Exhibition of Progressive Work, held in Scotland and England at different venues in 1975 and 1976, presented jewelry as an art form.[10] It was a statement, probably the first exhibition that focused on international contemporary jewelry in its own right, without any historical justification. It included all the young and innovative jewelers who mattered—most of them born in the 1940s. Was it because of Turner's claim of jewelry as a new art form that this exhibition stressed sculptural tendencies and also included many drawings, collages and photography? Or was this indeed the state of jewelry at that time, uncertain of what was to come, which direction to take, in a context characterized by "a constant blurring of boundaries between the various arts"?[11] The exhibition also showed the influence of Pop Art and popular culture in the use of acrylic, resin, bright colors and graphic patterns. Of additional interest were the shimmering new contours of a conceptual and self-reflexive approach in jewelry, represented in the work of Bakker, Claus Bury, Robert Smit and Zahn.

Within seven years, two new exhibitions, both organized by the British Crafts Center, marked important new trends in contemporary jewelry: easy-to-wear multiple jewelry, and the wearable object. Jewellery Redefined, the 1st International Exhibition of Multi-Media Non-Precious Jewellery in 1982 marked the new interest in making jewelry out of cheap, nonprecious, ready-made and discarded materials. This trend was popular in many countries, but Britain rivaled them all, with artists such as Nora Fok, Alison Baxter, Rowena Park and Ros Perry. The influence of Studio Alchimia's post-modernist decorative schemes is visible in the colorful patterns applied on plastics, paper and other cheap materials. Dutch jewelry was introduced to the playfulness of British jewelry through different exhibitions in the first half of the 1980s. In this period new impulses in Dutch jewelry came from artists with a textile background, such as LAM de Wolf, Mecky van den Brink and Beppe Kessler. Other artists adopted paper and flexible materials. In 1979, textile artist

Robert Smit
Brooch, 1985
18 x 17 x 2.5 cm
Gold
Courtesy of Stedelijik
Museum's-Hertogenbosch

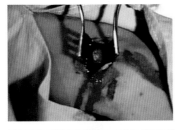

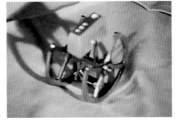

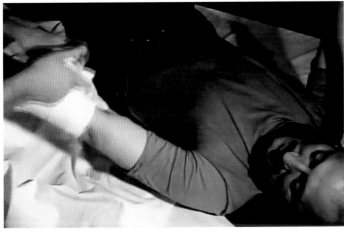

Peter Skubic
Jewellery Under the Skin,
1975
Film stills by Rainer
Schmitzberger, from a video by
Harry Ertl
Courtesy of Die Neue
Sammelung—The International
Design Museum Munich

Henriëtte Wiessing and Marion Herbst, a goldsmith who fought against the prevailing style of "Dutch smooth," as she called it, made brooches woven from colorful embroidery silk in sequences that were based on sheer coincidence—it was a bold statement in the world of rationalism and conceptuality.[12]

The exhibition New Tradition, the Evolution of Jewellery, 1966–1985, curated by Caroline Broadhead, showed under the heading "Extensions" how the body became a source of inspiration to many young jewelers in this period. Wearables, a term first used by Susanna Heron in 1981 and subsequently adopted by writers and curators, tried to bridge either the gap between clothing and jewelry or that between the body and jewelry. Various artists, especially in Britain, the Netherlands and Belgium, created soft ornaments that surrounded the body. In this period, photography gained importance, documenting the objects worn on static or moving models.

Objects, Signs and Concepts

Around the mid-1980s, a tendency toward sculpture became visible. Most of the British artists who made body-related wearable objects moved away from jewelry. In the Netherlands, an interest in the small object became apparent, especially under the influence of Onno Boekhoudt, the head of the jewelry department at the Gerrit Rietveld Academie. In Germany, jewelry had moved away from the informal to rather formal design, often in nonprecious materials, as seen in the early work of Georg Dobler, Manfred Bischoff, Therese Hilbert, Gabi Dziuba and Daniel Kruger.[13]

Underneath all these tendencies was a strong conceptual current that became an important source. Otto Künzli and Gijs Bakker were the main protagonists, while Peter Skubic and Manfred Nisslmüller, both working in Austria, also explicitly engaged with jewelry as an intellectual artistic discipline. This resulted in pieces challenging to wear, such as Nisslmüller's two-finger rings and Skubic's early sculptural between-finger rings, which had a monumental and phallic character. Later in the 1970s, Nisslmüller substituted texts for jewelry, while Skubic moved on to performance and event, such as his radical *Jewellery Under the Skin* (1975), a steel plate implanted in his left forearm.[14] The 1970s and '80s were a period in which jewelry was explicitly questioned and in which the foundation was laid for the research of jewelry as a social phenomenon by younger generations of artists in different countries.

Photography, printed matter, video and audience participation became additional media in jewelry.

In the second half of the 1980s, jewelry was discovered as a sign on the body. Three exhibitions in Austria, Spain and Germany bore witness to this new development. The 1987 exhibition SCHMUCK, Zeichen am Körper in Linz, Austria, focused on jewelry's social meanings, and its function as a sign.[15] Jewelry was considered from different perspectives—historically, socially, emotionally and artistically. It was not only observed as decoration or as an aesthetic object, but also as a sign that is worn on the body and that generates meaning. The exhaustive catalog sheds light on every aspect of jewelry, including power, mythology, and even robbery. A new aspect was the involvement of fine artists, architects and designers, who were invited to design a piece that was then executed by Austrian goldsmiths. The reason for doing so, in the words of curator Helmuth Gsöllpointner, was that all applied art is rooted in fine art and that real impulses come from the fine arts, where forms and ideas are formulated at least 10 to 20 years earlier.[16] This touched on a heated debate that had just started in the Netherlands, when in an article Robert Smit blamed Gijs Bakker for sponging off the fine arts.[17] In contrast, Christoph Blase in Switzerland claimed that while only a few jewelry artists were really original, they were actually responsible for artistic innovations that only became apparent in the fine arts some time later.[18]

The 1987 exhibition Joieria Europea Contemporània was held in the Fundacio Caixa de Pensions in Barcelona. It was state of the art, showcasing about 100 artists from 13 European countries. The exhibition's catalog emphasized the importance of wearing by showing the jewelry on models in a series of color illustrations (an expensive novelty in those days). By choosing prominent artists (actors, writers, fashion designers, dancers, musicians, etc.) to model the jewelry, connections were made among jewelry, art and society.

It was no coincidence that the name of the first biennial for jewelry, Ornamenta, organized by the Schmuckmuseum in Pforzheim in 1989, resembled the title of the famous Documenta art bienniale in Kassel.[19] The question of whether jewelry was art was a huge issue. The subtitle Internationale Schmuckkunst (International Jewelry Art) was a clear statement, dismissed by many as too pretentious. The central exhibition showed how a conceptual attitude alongside an object-orientated one ruled in the international contemporary jewelry of the late 1980s. The emphasis was on abstraction, not

Caroline Broadhead
Neckpiece/Veil, 1983
45 x 25 cm
Finger-woven monofilament
Photo by David Ward © 2013
Artists Rights Society (ARS),
New York / DACS, London

Onno Boekhoudt
Object with Bracelet, 1984
55 x 35 x 3 cm
Lead, silver, copper
Photo by the artist
Courtesy of Museum CODA
Apeldoorn, Holland

Otto Künzli
Dieter V. with Centifolia, 1983
Brooch, 13 x 8.8 x 6 cm
Wallpaper, hard foam
Photo courtesy of the artist

necessarily of a geometric or rational nature, and objecthood, which might be expressed in monumentality (of wearables) or in series of connected pieces. There was hardly any figuration involved in the exhibition. One part, the Treasure Trove, was heavily criticized. In this room, stars from sports, fashion, art and society showed their most beloved objects, while jewelry artists were invited to design a piece of jewelry especially for them. This attempt to establish a connection between person and object can be seen as a necessary strategy in a period of contemporary jewelry characterized by an emphasis on the status of the autonomous object. At the same time, the scene was struggling with the question of what contemporary jewelry actually stood for. It was controversial because it brought to mind the loathed practice of commissioned jewelry, which had been abolished so successfully in the previous 20 years.

The Return to the Jewel

The 1990s witnessed a return to the jewel and a new sophistication in the choice and use of materials—often, though not always, combined with some sort of narrative. Symbols and figuration were reintroduced, while gold and precious stones were slowly liberated from their condemned status as investment objects. Jewelry was rediscovered as ornament.

Around the mid-1990s, an organic, rather anti-aesthetic style became apparent. Pieces were now loaded with content. The main protagonists of this approach were Christoph Zellweger (from Switzerland) and Iris Eichenberg (from Germany, based in the Netherlands), both rather influential as teachers. Zellweger's steel *Finds and Fakes*, his polystyrene *Body Pieces*, and Eichenberg's knitted wool necklaces were not about beauty as such, nor about decoration or symbols. Instead, this work made the viewer aware of the body and its processes of decay and deterioration.[20]

In the 1990s, German jeweler Karl Fritsch and New Zealander Lisa Walker, who both studied at the Akademie der Bildenden Künste München (Academy of Fine Arts, Munich), became the champions of a new brutalism. Whether using precious metals and stones or discarded materials and wool, their aim was not to make graceful, pleasing ornaments but to challenge our ideas about beauty. In their work, they crossed traditional crafts borders that seemed inviolable, such as leaving bare obvious traces of the making in the material, drilling holes in (semi)precious stones, and using glue lavishly as a substantial material. Eventually, a "sloppy jewelry" trend became popular all over Europe in the first decade of the new century, with pieces assembled from different elements rather than formed out of one or a few materials.

New Centers

At the beginning of the twenty-first century, in a period of economic boom with cheap airfares, the Internet, political change and the efforts of individual teachers who regenerated existing schools, new centers for the teaching and dissemination of contemporary jewelry emerged. A list of schools and teachers might run something like this: Lisbon, Portugal (Cristina Filipe); Finland (Eija Mustonen); Stockholm, Sweden (Ruudt Peters and Karen Pontoppidan); Paris and Strasbourg, France (Monika Brugger and Sophie Hanagarth); Prague, Czech Republic (Eva Eisler); and Bratislava, Slovakia (Karol Weisslechner). Today these new centers organize international exhibitions, as well as conferences and competitions—opening up the jewelry scene and attracting young students from other countries. These developments are dependent on individuals. A case in point is the highly appreciated Klimt02 website, created in Barcelona by Leo Caballero and Amador Bertomeu in 2002, the first worldwide Internet network for information on contemporary jewelry.

It goes without saying that interesting, internationally known artists worked in these countries before the year 2000, among them Tone Vigeland and Sigurd Bronger in Norway, Joaquim Capdevila and Ramón Puig Cuyàs in Spain, the Finn Helena Lehtinen, Ana Campos and Tereza Seabra of Portugal, Kim Buck in Denmark and Monika Brugger of Germany/France. Some of them studied abroad because their homelands had no good jewelry education, while others came from a traditional goldsmith's background. The language problem can't be underestimated: in many European countries English wasn't a common second language. The exchange between the countries in the "periphery" and those in the "center" was ponderous. The center—Germany, Holland and initially the UK—can be understood as having a contemporary jewelry infrastructure with specialized galleries, an interested audience, a stimulating government, exhibitions and art academies with jewelry departments that guaranteed a constant flow of young jewelry artists. The center attracted students from many other countries, while the periphery kept to itself.

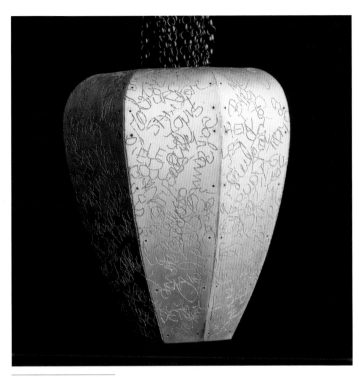

Ruudt Peters
Passio Alexis, 1992
6.5 x 6.5 x 8 cm
Silver, jade
Photo by Rob Versluys
Courtesy of the artist

Within Germany, a shift in centers took place. For a long time Pforzheim had attracted many promising, ambitious young artists and was the only place in Europe where international jewelry was exhibited on a regular basis in the Schmuckmuseum. But gradually, during the 1970s, Munich overtook Pforzheim for a number of reasons: education (a school with an excellent reputation), recurring exhibitions (SCHMUCK), commerce (the international trade fair that enables this show), a museum focused on contemporary jewelry (the Die Neue Sammlung), an educated, art-minded audience and the presence of private and institutional art collectors. Thanks to Jünger and Künzli, Munich attracted (and still does) many international students. In the 1990s the Handwerkskammer in Munich succeeded in transforming the large SCHMUCK show at the Internationale Handwerksmesse into a prominent yearly event. Taking place in March, it attracts thousands of visitors. It has outgrown the borders of the international trade fair and expanded into the city, where many small presentations are put on by international artists, groups of artists and organizations. The fusion of Die Neue Sammlung and the Pinakothek der Moderne in a new building with an independent permanent jewelry display in the Danner-Rotunde also played a key role.

Halle is a local German center that has been rather isolated. Only after the fall of the communist German Democratic Republic was the international public introduced to the monumental and evocative jewelry of Dorothea Prühl, who taught in the jewelry program at Burg Giebichenstein, where she became the department's head in 1991 and a professor from 1994 to 2002. Under her leadership, a recognizable school of working developed, characterized by the use of metals and enamels and an ornamental and sculptural style. Students were mostly recruited from the vicinity.

Some centers combine a mainly local function with a recognizable contemporary style. The Istituto Statale d'Art Pietro Selvatico Padova (Pietro Selvatico State Institute of Art in Padua) attracts mainly students from the region who start studying there at age 14. With classes taught in Italian, the school remains rather isolated. The art academy in Tallin, Estonia, developed into a center for jewelry after Kadri Mälk was appointed as a teacher in 1989 (she's been a professor since 1996). She studied there under Leili Kuldkepp, who was fascinated by mythological subjects and inspired by ethnographic excursions in the Nordic countries. This search for their roots was prompted by Estonia's centuries-long occupation by other countries. After World War II, a national style developed that is associated with mythology, mysticism and a love of natural materials. Independence came in 1990. Now, Estonia has developed an active contemporary jewelry scene.

The idea of the center and the periphery could be subverted as well. The idea is actually dependent on where the observer sits: Barcelona's Escola Massana, the periphery from a European point of view, is also a center that attracts many students from Latin American Spanish-speaking countries, while Centro de Arte e Comunicaçao Visual (Ar.Co) in Lisbon attracts students from Brazil. Stockholm's Konstfack draws students from all Scandinavian countries.

Inspiring international exhibitions and events are now organized far away from the usual centers in Europe. These include Nocturnus, which took place on Muhu Island in Estonia in 2001, organized by the Eesti Kunstiakadeemia (Estonian Academy of Arts) in Tallinn; the Koru exhibitions in Lappeenranta, Finland (2003, '06 and '09); the 2005 Ars Ornata Europeana symposium in Lisbon; and international symposia in Turnov (Czech Republic) and Legnica (Poland). The new centers breathe new life into jewelry, adding new foreign—not to mention exotic—ingredients in the European contemporary jewelry world, which for so long has been dominated by German and Dutch influences.

Dorothea Prühl
Titanium Chain III, 1997
Height, 28 cm
Titanium, ivory
Photo by Helga Schulze-Brinkop
Collection of Schmuckmuseum Pforzheim

Education

It's clear that education is a requirement for a flourishing jewelry scene. Many schools in Europe kept a rigorous international standard in education for decades, but only the Akademie der Bildenden Künste München (Academy of Fine Arts, Munich) and the Gerrit Rietveld Academie in Amsterdam will be discussed here. The jewelry courses at both schools have a long history. One way to estimate a standard of education is by following and judging a school's output, that is to say, the international success of its alumni and the events in which the school takes part. Of all educational institutions, the Akademie der Bildenden Künste München is the most outstanding. Its fame, begun in the 1970s under Jünger, continues under Künzli, the present head of the department. This stability differs vastly from the jewelry department at Rietveld, which had far more changes in its direction in the same period. The jewelry course in Munich is renowned for its length (five to six years), its relative freedom and its postgraduate character. Every

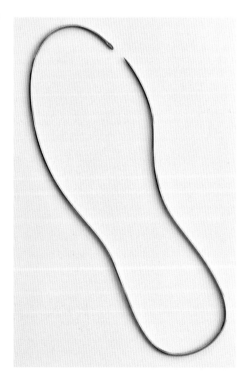

Leonor Hipólito
Beyond Emotions, 2011
22 x 7.5 x 0.2 cm
Gold-plated silver
Photo by Arne Kaiser
Courtesy of the artist

student works independently, without assignments. The total group of students is rather small, about 20, and critiques are a group process in which each student is involved.[21]

Onno Boekhoudt directed the jewelry department at Rietveld from 1974 to 1990. Under his direction the department became a clearly defined place where students were confronted with a refreshing look at jewelry and craft. Boekhoudt also attracted international students, such as Cristina Filipe, who became the head of the jewelry department at Ar.Co in Lisbon. Under Ruudt Peters, from 1990 to 2000, the department gained a truly international reputation. There have been three directors since 2000: Iris Eichenberg from 2000 to 2007, Manon van Kouswijk from 2007 to 2009, and Suska Mackert since 2009. Although this situation may seem unfavorable, that is not the case. Education at the Gerrit Rietveld Academie relies not only on the department's leader but also on the method of education, which is founded on contemporary jewelry as a valid historical and conceptual practice, and its positioning within the context of the arts and design. The first year of education is based generally on the basic Bauhaus system, where students learn about all the different artistic possibilities. It continues with an intense three-year course that delves deep into ideas and finding the right materials, techniques and ways to visualize these ideas.

The Contemporary Jewelry Scene

Internationalization is an essential characteristic of contemporary jewelry. Artists show and sell their work in galleries in many different countries and take part in international exhibitions, conferences, workshops and residencies. Teachers travel around the world to teach and students also travel, either in a temporary exchange or for a full education. Today students choose an academy because of its output. In the European patchwork quilt of countries and cultures, local centers have turned into international centers. Styles and methods of working, ideas and concepts do not hew to national borders. Internationalization has become the hallmark of contemporary jewelry. Within this context of "global jewelry," there are only a few local centers —Padua, Estonia—that succeed in somehow keeping a signature of their own while being connected with the world. It's not unthinkable that in the near future the call for a more local identification will become stronger.

Notes

1. Fritz Falk, Cornelie Holzach, *Schmuck der Moderne, 1960–1998: Bestandskatalog der modernen Sammlung des Schmuckmuseums Pforzheim* (Stuttgart: Arnoldsche Art Publishers, 1999), 104.

2. For a history of Italian contemporary jewelry, see Graziella Folchini Grassetto, *Contemporary Jewellery: The Padua School* (Stuttgart: Arnoldsche Art Publishers, 2005).

3. *Noucentista* refers to a period in the arts and literature in Catalonia ranging from about 1910 until the 1930s. It implicated a return to Catalan and Mediterranean values after the excesses of the Art Nouveau period. For a better understanding of the Catalan history of jewelry, see the exhibition catalog *Jaume Mercade i la joia d'art* (Tarragona: Caixa Tarragona 2005).

4. See Graham Hughes, *David Watkins, Wendy Ramshaw: A Life's Partnership* (London: Starcity, 2009).

5. For a history of Dutch jewelry, see M. Mokveld, "Dutch Jewelry" and L. den Besten, "Art in Precious Metals," in *Holland in vorm, Dutch design, 1945–1987*, ed. Gert Staal and Hester Wolters, 196–213 (The Hague: Stichting Holland in Vorm, 1987). Also see Marjan Unger, *Het Nederlandse sieraad in 20ste eeuw* (Bussum: Uitgeverij Thoth, 2004).

6. See Ida van Zijl, *Gijs Bakker and Jewelry* (Stuttgart: Arnoldsche Art Publishers, 2005); and Yvonne G. J. M. Joris, ed., *Broken Lines: Emmy van Leersum, 1930–1984*. ('s-Hertogenbosch, The Netherlands: Snoeck-Ducaju & Zoon, 1993).

7. For a history of Swiss contemporary jewelry, see *Art Jewellery in Switzerland in the 20th Century* (Geneva / Zurich / Ligornetto: Musée d'art et d'histoire Genève, Schweizerische Landesmuseum Zürich, and Museo Vincenzo Vela, 2002–03).

8. Schmuck, Jewellery, Bijoux: Hessisches Landesmuseum, Darmstadt, 1964, Museum Boijmans van Beuningen, Rotterdam, 1965. Nederlandse sieraden van nu: Museum Boijmans van Beuningen, 1965.

9. Monique Mokveld, "Discussion, Amersfoort, 3.10.1985," in *Sieraden Schmuck Jewellery Images* (Amsterdam: Art Book Publications, 1986), 100–101.

10. Jewellery in Europe: An Exhibition of Progressive Work, a touring exhibition organized by the Scottish Arts Council and the Crafts Advisory Committee, 1975–76.

11. Scottish Arts Council, *Jewellery in Europe: An Exhibition of Progressive Work* (Edinburgh: The Council, 1975), 4.

12. L. Crommelin, A. van Berkum, and M. van Ooststroom, *Marion Herbst Mag het ietsje meer zijn?* (Wijk en Aalburg, The Netherlands: Pictures Publishers, 1993).

13. Carin E. M. Reinders, ed., *Onno Boekhoudt—Work in Progress* (Apeldoorn, The Netherlands: CODA Museum, 2010); and Helmut Bauer, ed., *Münchner Goldschmiede Schmuck und Gerät, 1993* (Munich: Klinkhardt & Biermann, 1993).

14. Florian Hufnagl, ed., *Radical.Skubic.Jewelry* (Munich: Moderne Kunst Nürnberg, 2011).

15. Helmuth Gsöllpointner, Gerhard Knogler, et al., *Schmuck: Zeichen am Körper* (Vienna: Falter Verlag, 1987).

16. Ibid., 5.

17. Godert van Colmjon, "Een onpersoonlijk lijf tegenover de borst van Rob van Koningsbruggen, Godert van Colmjon in gesprek met Gijs Bakker en Robert Smit."

18. Christoph Blase, "Schmuck Kunst Schmuck Kunst Schmuck Kunst Schmuck Kunst Schmuck Wo sind wir eigentlich?" in the catalog *Tragezeichen, Schmuck von Giampaolo Babetto, Manfred Bischoff, Falko Marx, Manfred Nisslmüller, Francesco Pavan, Bernhard Schobinger, Peter Skubic, Robert Smit* (Leverkusen, Germany: Museum Morsbroich, 1988), 6–13.

19. Fritz Falk, Michael Erlhoff, and Schmuckmuseum Pforzheim, *Ornamenta I, Internationale Schmuckkunst* (Munich: Prestel-Verlag, 1989).

20. See the discussion between Iris Eichenberg, Christoph Zellweger, and Ted Noten, "The Afternoon Talk," in *Christoph Zellweger: Foreign Bodies*, ed. Mònica Gaspar (Barcelona: Actar, 2007).

21. Florian Hufnagl, ed., *The Fat Booty of Madness: The Goldsmithing Class at Munich Art Academy* (Stuttgart: Arnoldsche Art Publishers, 2008).

Further Reading

Derrez, Paul, Ralph Turner, Liesbeth den Besten, and Marjan Boot. *Radiant, 30 years Ra*. Amsterdam: Ra books, 2006.

Dormer, Peter. "What Is the Future of Contemporary Jewellery?" In *Joieria Europea Contemporània*, 59–71. Barcelona: La Fundació, 1987.

English, Helen W. Drutt, and Peter Dormer. *Jewelry of Our Time: Art, Ornament and Obsession*. New York: Rizzoli, 1995.

Grassetto, Graziella Folchini. *Contemporary Jewellery: The Padua School*. Stuttgart: Arnoldsche Art Publishers, 2005.

Gsöllpointner, Helmuth, Gerhard Knogler, et al. *Schmuck: Zeichen am Körper*. Vienna: Falter, 1987.

Holder, Elisabeth, ed. *Choice: Contemporary Jewellery from Germany, a Reader*. Düsseldorf: Elisabeth Holder, Herman Hermsen, 2005.

Hufnagl, Florian, ed. *The Fat Booty of Madness: The Goldsmithing Class at Munich Art Academy*. Stuttgart: Arnoldsche Art Publishers, 2008.

Mälk, Kadri, and Tanel Veenre, eds. *Castle in the Air / õhuLoss: Jewellery from Estonia*. Stuttgart: Arnoldshche Art Publishers, 2011.

Staal, Gert, and Martina Margetts. *London Amsterdam: New Art Objects from Britain and Holland*. London / Amsterdam: Crafts Council / Galerie Ra, 1988.

Turner, Ralph. *Contemporary Jewelry: A Critical Assessment, 1945–1975*. London: Studio Vista, 1976.

Van Colmjon, Godert. "Een onpersoonlijk lijf tegenover de borst van Rob van Koningsbruggen, Godert van Colmjon in gesprek met Gijs Bakker en Robert Smit." *Museumjournaal* 3 and 4 (1986): 169–179.

North America.

Kelly Hays L'Ecuyer

Introduction

The foundations for contemporary jewelry were established at a relatively early date in North America, especially in the United States. In the 1940s and '50s, internationally recognized artists gave credibility to the concept of jewelry as a modern (even avant-garde) art form, and articulated a critique of precious jewelry as one of the enduring tenets of the field. Studio jewelers with a healthy independence from the commercial jewelry industry and a sense of free-wheeling experimentation established thriving small businesses, craft associations and informal personal networks, all of which supported makers and wearers of contemporary jewelry. A convergence of private initiatives and broad governmental support led to the creation of educational programs at dozens of institutions, perpetuating the culture of contemporary jewelry through subsequent generations. These academic programs fostered increasing internationalism in the last third of the twentieth century, connecting North American jewelers with their peers around the world.

Not all regions and cultural groups joined the international contemporary jewelry movement simultaneously, although other kinds of jewelry continued to thrive and at times overlapped with contemporary jewelry. Mexico, geographically part of North America but culturally tied to Latin America (and therefore discussed in that essay, page 131), has until recently remained largely disconnected from the kind of individualistic contemporary jewelry so avidly made and collected in the United States and Canada. Strong vernacular and regional traditions of metalsmithing and jewelry making have long existed throughout Mexico, blending indigenous and Spanish colonial influences. Today, Mexicans continue to produce handmade jewelry for local use or commercial sale, while Mexican art jewelers with a progressive outlook often embark for Europe to advance their contemporary work.

In many Native American communities in the United States and Canada, jewelry and adornment have long traditions of regional and cultural significance, and handmade jewelry has been produced for sale to tourists and collectors since the late nineteenth century. The recurrence of conventional forms and devices—more so than individual innovation—is important to Native traditions and has also been key to the success of trade-oriented production. Some Native jewelers explore original designs and modern styles, and a small number have gained recognition in the broader field of contemporary jewelry, but for the most part, their work is understood within its own framework of conventions and meanings. Many Native artists view the expression of continuity and tradition as a symbol of the survival of their culture in the present day. Thus, the idea of the "contemporary" takes on a dimension of cultural identity in most Native American jewelry that differs from mainstream Euro-American contemporary jewelry.[1]

The 1940s and 1950s: Pioneering Artists

Contemporary jewelry in North America began in the urban centers of the United States and Canada in the 1940s, where the Arts and Crafts Movement of the late nineteenth and early twentieth centuries had established essential philosophical underpinnings of modern craft: a reaction against machine-driven mass production, a belief in the aesthetic and moral benefits of handcraft and the goal of uniting the "fine" and "applied" arts. Two world wars and a major economic depression interrupted the craft revival as Americans sought slick, streamlined designs intended to evoke notions of technological progress. Nevertheless, the disruptions of war also had surprising consequences that contributed to the resurgence of contemporary jewelry afterward. One was the displacement and international movement of artists and intelligentsia. American artists, feeling rootless and disconnected from the industrial capitalism of their homeland, spent much of the 1920s and '30s in Europe, especially Paris, where they absorbed the radical ideas and experimental techniques of European modernism. By the mid-1930s, the chilling climate of European totalitarian regimes sent artists and many of their patrons (American and European) scrambling to North America. Artists, art dealers, collectors and intellectuals reestablished the leading edge of contemporary art on the other side of the Atlantic.

Amid this cosmopolitan art scene and the booming postwar economy in the United States, American contemporary jewelry flourished. Modern artists investigated a variety of media—including jewelry making—and museums and galleries showed experimental jewelry in prominent exhibitions in the 1940s. The Museum of Modern Art (MoMA), which had by then positioned itself as the principal authority on contemporary art, endorsed contemporary jewelry when it mounted its 1946

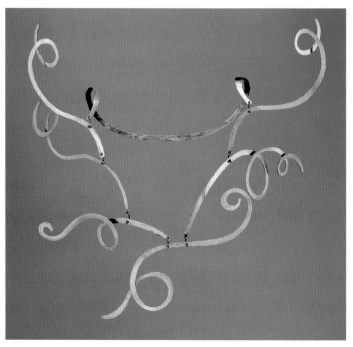

Alexander Calder
Necklace, ca. 1940
54 x 55.9 x 25.4 cm
Brass
Metropolitan Museum of Art, New York
The Muriel Kallis Steinberg Newman Collection, Gift of Muriel Kallis Newman, 2006
© 2013 Calder Foundation, New York / Artists Rights Society (ARS), New York

Anni Albers
Brooch, 1941–1946
10.8 x 7.9 x 1 cm
Aluminum strainer, paper clips,
safety pin
Museum of Fine Arts, Boston
The Daphne Farago Collection,
2006.44
Image © 2013 Museum of Fine
Arts, Boston
© 2013 The Josef and Anni
Albers Foundation / Artists
Rights Society (ARS), New York

exhibition Modern Handmade Jewelry. MoMA curator Jane Sabersky selected the work of pioneering studio jewelers Paul Lobel and Margaret De Patta, along with adornment made by painters and sculptors including Richard Pousette-Dart, Jacques Lipchitz and Alexander Calder, writing in the show's catalog that "in general it is the individual craftsman or artist, less restricted by commercial standards, who makes new contributions to the art."[2] Two years later the Walker Art Center of Minneapolis, Minnesota, mounted the first in a series of traveling exhibitions titled Modern Jewelry Under Fifty Dollars.[3] These reflected the broad spectrum of contemporary jewelry makers active from coast to coast: men and women in equal numbers, from a variety of backgrounds and levels of training, making contemporary jewelry an alternative to conventional precious adornment.

Calder's jewelry was central to many of the museum and gallery exhibitions of this period, and he continues to be viewed as the seminal figure in American contemporary jewelry. His seemingly effortless explorations of many different media established strong links between jewelry and other branches of contemporary art. Calder emphasized the improvisational and creative process, using only simple cold construction techniques. In both his crude technique and his choice of forms and motifs, he referred to the modernist interpretation of African, ancient Greek and other so-called "primitive" arts that he'd encountered in Paris in the 1920s. Most important, Calder brought to jewelry making the idea that sculpture need not consist of solid, stationary objects, but could use line and movement to describe space. His *Necklace* of about 1940 is more than an adornment for the neck: it's a mobile sculpture using the body as an armature. Each section of curled and flattened wire is riveted to the next, allowing the piece to sway freely away from the wearer's body. Radical in scale, form and conception, Calder's jewelry and his international prominence had an immediate and lasting impact on innumerable jewelers.[4]

Like Calder, Anni Albers was a restlessly creative designer and artist who explored many media, and thus connected jewelry to broader concepts and issues in contemporary art. An émigré from the German Bauhaus who brought the school's principles to the United States, she asked viewers to consider everyday objects and industrial materials from a fresh perspective. In 1946, she created a small series of jewelry objects from ordinary hardware-store supplies. They were exhibited at MoMA and widely published. Her brooch assembled from a cheap aluminum sink strainer and a handful of paper clips denies the importance of precious materials and even fine craftsmanship in favor of a starkly abstract sense of good design. Albers expanded on the idea that art depended on the inherent elegance of simple materials—rather than the skill of a particular artist—by selling do-it-yourself kits for creating similar pieces of jewelry.[5]

De Patta emerged from the tutelage of Hungarian-born Constructivist Lázló Moholy-Nagy at the New Bauhaus in Chicago. Encouraging De Patta's efforts with jewelry design, Moholy-Nagy urged her to rethink traditional settings and instead to "catch your stones in the air; make them float in space."[6] De Patta's jewelry manipulated light, space and optical perception. In her *Pendant* of 1951, she mounted a polished crystal over a piece of fine steel mesh to explore the ideas of magnification and distortion. Viewed through the transparent cabochon, the steel grid lines bend, stretch and blur, shifting with the movement of the wearer. Not only was her jewelry a consummate expression of abstract art concerns in jewelry, but De Patta also actively promoted contemporary jewelry. In 1951 she founded the Metal Arts Guild (MAG) of San Francisco (along with metalsmiths Irena Brynner, Peter Macchiarini, Bob Winston and others) to develop the work of studio metalsmiths through juried shows, a newsletter and design critique sessions based on Bauhaus models. Both De Patta's individual influence and the work of MAG created a dynamic culture of contemporary jewelry on the West Coast.[7]

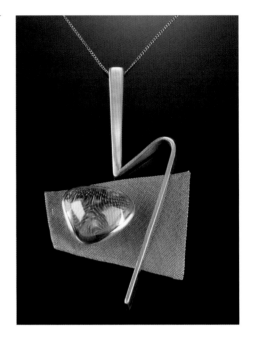

Margaret De Patta
Pendant, 1950
10.2 x 7.6 x 3.2 cm
Sterling silver, screen, stainless steel, crystal
Collection of the Oakland Museum of California
Gift of Eugene Bielawski, The Margaret De Patta Memorial Collection

Education and Institutions in the Mid-Twentieth Century

After World War II, the United States experienced an unprecedented surge in educational programs that helped make contemporary jewelry a widespread movement. Large public and private efforts were launched to help the generation of returning veterans recover from the traumas of war and reenter civilian life, and craft programs in metals played a major role. From 1944 to 1948, MoMA offered free classes in jewelry and other crafts and published jewelry made by veterans alongside works by Calder and other well-known artists.[8] In the early 1940s, Margret Craver first worked with the Army to develop jewelry classes as a form of rehabilitation for soldiers in Army hospitals. After the war, she went on to establish the seminal conference series known as the Handy and Harmon Workshops (1947–51), at which European silversmiths taught

Georges Delrue
Bracelet, 1954
6.7 x 6.6 x 4.4 cm
Silver, petrified wood, gold
Photo by Christine Guest
Courtesy of the Montreal
Museum of Fine Arts / Musée
des beaux-arts de Montréal
Liliane and David M. Stewart
Collection, gift of Georges
Delrue

intensive courses at American art schools. The participants in these workshops—among them John Paul Miller, Alma Eikerman and Earl Pardon in the United States, and Harold Stacey in Canada—went on to become leading makers and educators.[9]

Furthermore, the GI Bill, which funded college scholarships for returning veterans, led directly to the creation of degree-granting metalsmithing programs that sustained a new generation of art jewelers. The flowering of crafts education in the 1950s gave jewelers with faculty positions the resources to experiment with increasingly complex techniques such as lost-wax casting, gold granulation and niello. The School for American Craftsmen (SAC), founded in 1943 and finally housed in Rochester, New York, offered the first four-year college degree specialized in craft, with an especially strong program in metals led by Scandinavian-trained John Prip and Hans Christensen.

Scandinavian educators also played an important role in Canada, where modern metalsmiths tended to look to Europe. The Metal Arts Guilds founded in Ontario in 1946 and in Nova Scotia in 1951 were modeled on the English Worshipful Company of Goldsmiths, a medieval guild, and many in the mid-century generation of Canadian jewelers and metalsmiths were European-born or trained. Danish-born Carl Poul Petersen, for example, had apprenticed under Georg Jensen, and helped popularize Scandinavian modern style in Canada. The proximity of the SAC to Southern Ontario had a strong impact on Toronto metalsmiths, and reinforced the prevalence of Scandinavian modern design in both areas.[10]

A host of other European master jewelers arrived in Canada in the 1950s and '60s: Hero Kielman from the Netherlands, Georges Delrue from France, Karl Stittgen from Germany and Toni Cavelti from Switzerland. Many of them trained apprentices and worked to develop modern metalsmithing in Canada through juried shows and other exhibitions. They shared the ideals of their American counterparts. Delrue, for example, maintained, "Let us be contemporary … If we are really honest we will be true to the spirit of our own time."[11] Works such as Delrue's constructivist bracelet of silver, gold and petrified wood clearly correlates with the work of American artists like De Patta. However, Canadian jewelers struggled with fairly conservative conditions and a small market.[12]

In the United States, contemporary jewelry enjoyed connections with museums, university programs and the wider art world, and gradually developed a supportive network of small galleries and shops frequented by an art-loving clientele. The development of a self-conscious group of contemporary jewelry wearers in the 1940s and '50s was at least as important as the artistic advances of pioneering makers, enabling jewelry makers to support themselves independently from the commercial industry. From these beginnings emerged the specialized contemporary jewelry galleries and dedicated collectors of the 1970s and beyond. At mid-century, however, most market development was undertaken by individual makers.

Art Smith, born in Cuba but raised in New York, developed a loyal following within the African-American arts community from his small shop in Greenwich Village. His designs for body ornaments for black dance troupes led to connections with African-American musicians, writers and artists who became his friends and customers. At the same time, he developed ways to produce his work in multiples for a broader audience willing to wear the bold, large-scale works that reflected his interest in the curves of the body. One of his most popular designs, the *Modern Cuff* bracelet, wrapped the forearm with a dynamic composition of positive and negative elements, yet could be shaped quickly from inexpensive metal sheet and wire. Juggling the roles of maker and marketer, Smith made his work with only one or two assistants, and also managed to sell his work in boutiques and galleries across the United States.[13]

Sam Kramer's jewelry was rooted in Surrealism and expressed themes of unconscious fantasy, sexuality and dark humor. The *Lovers Brooch* he made with his wife Carol depicts two abstract figures constructed so that they move back and forth suggestively. His talent for appealing to the adventurous and eccentric qualities of his customers was summarized in his business card, printed with the slogan "Fantastic Jewelry for People Who Are Slightly Mad." He created an unusual gallery setting that cultivated a particular type of buyer and wearer for his jewelry. From the moment a visitor approached his shop, where they were greeted by a cast bronze hand in place of a doorknob, to their encounter with Kramer, who might appear dressed in his pajamas or an outlandish costume, to the display cases teeming with what Kramer called "things to titillate the damndest ego—utter weirdities conceived in moments of semi-madness," customers were made to feel like they were participating in an extraordinary art experience.[14]

Kramer's approach was unusually dramatic, but his appeal to the nonconformist mindset of contemporary jewelry

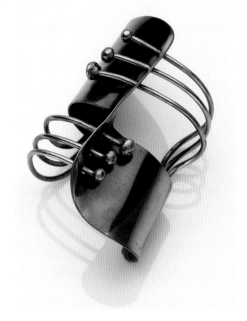

Art Smith
Modern Cuff, ca. 1948
10.8 x 6.4 x 5.7 cm; 105.7 g
Copper, brass
Museum of Fine Arts, Boston
The Daphne Farago Collection, 2006.531
Image © 2013 Museum of Fine Arts, Boston

Sam Kramer and Carol Kramer
Lovers Brooch, 1949
11.4 x 8.3 x 2.5 cm
Silver, turquoise, garnet; hinged and
riveted construction
Museum of Fine Arts, Boston
The Daphne Farago Collection,
2006.288
Image © 2013 Museum of Fine Arts,
Boston

wearers has continued to resonate to the present day, and it helped establish a strong niche market of American jewelry collectors. An oft-repeated quote from art historian Blanche Brown summarizes what American collectors valued in the mid-twentieth century: Brown recalled of a pin that "it looked great, I could afford it, and it identified me with the group of my choice—esthetically aware, intellectually inclined, and politically progressive. That pin (or one of a few others like it) was our badge and we wore it proudly. It celebrated the hand of the artist rather than the market value of the material. Diamonds were the badge of the philistine."[15] Early galleries such as Nanny's Design in Jewelry (San Francisco), America House (New York), Shop One (Rochester, New York), Bordelon Designs (Chicago) and Margaret Brown Gallery (Boston) cultivated a similar clientele. Museum exhibitions in the 1950s— especially contemporary jewelry surveys at the Walker (1948, 1952, 1955, 1959), the de Young Museum in San Francisco (1955, 1956) and national craft exhibitions such as Designer-Craftsmen U.S.A. 1953 at the Brooklyn Museum in New York and the First National Fine Crafts Exhibition at the National Gallery of Canada (1957)—also boosted contemporary jewelry's visibility and prestige among patrons.

The 1960s and '70s: Postmodernism and Diversity

By the early '60s, Abstraction, Constructivism and Surrealism, so new and radical in jewelry of the 1940s, had become homogenized under the rubric of "good design." Space Age and Scandinavian modern design began to seem limited. While their predecessors had already articulated a critique of precious metals and gems, radical American jewelers of the 1960s expanded this idea to attack the preciousness of good taste and elegant design.

The new generation of jewelers emerging from postwar university programs and art schools sought greater personal expression through the diverse possibilities of postmodernism, often using raw discarded materials, found objects and Pop Art imagery in surprising juxtapositions. Robert Ebendorf, for example, shunned the cool, elegant Scandinavian style he'd mastered while studying in Norway in the mid-1960s in favor of a highly personal form of assemblage. Combining bits of discarded photographs, toys, tin cans and other cast-offs reflected the Assemblage art of Americans Robert Rauschenberg, Ed Kienholz and others. J. Fred Woell's "anti-jewelry" used assemblage to comment on pop culture and politics, while Ken Cory and Les LePere's irreverent works reflected the drug-laced bohemianism of the West Coast Funk movement.[16]

The revolutionary changes affecting all of society in the late 1960s were felt in contemporary jewelry as well: civil rights and antiwar activism, feminism, body awareness, environmentalism and counterculture lifestyles reverberated in the concept and aesthetics of body adornment. The new generation of American jewelers explored ancient, historic and non-Western forms of adornment—rich with decorative ornament and cultural meaning. In some ways, this echoed the primitivism of early modernists like Calder, who admired African and ancient Greek jewelry for aesthetic reasons, but American jewelers of the '60s and '70s saw historic and non-Western sources as a way of liberating the body from dull bourgeois conventions and gender stereotypes. As proposed by the curators of the 1965 exhibition The Art of Personal Adornment at New York's Museum of Contemporary Crafts (now the Museum of Arts and Design), ornaments from around the globe demonstrated interpretations of the entire human body and of variations in gender roles. The exhibition catalog, with abstract images of male and female bodies on the cover, was organized by regions of the body, and included many photographs of men and women wearing elaborate regalia in a variety of cultural contexts.[17]

Rediscovering such sources and concepts had a galvanizing effect on American jewelers, who began to create experimental forms such as large neck collars, headpieces, belts and unclassifiable body sculptures. Arline Fisch, too, had grown frustrated with the constraints of Scandinavian design, and launched wild explorations such as 1968's Halter and Skirt. A hand-forged silver halter attached to a skirt, creating a unified garment with a feminist sense of transgression and body consciousness.[18]

Although radical Dutch jewelers like Gijs Bakker and Emmy van Leersum were also pursuing similar fusions of jewelry and clothing in avant-garde body sculpture, their severe modernist or minimalist aesthetic avoided any trace of historical reference or handcraftsmanship. By contrast, American jewelers were noted for their interest in richly detailed ornament and lavish display of craft techniques. The influence of Art Nouveau forms pervaded the work of many American jewelers in this period, including Mary Lee Hu, John Paul Miller and Albert Paley.

Influenced by the hippies' "back to the land" philosophy and the emerging environmental movement, natural forms

Robert W. Ebendorf
Man and His Pet Bee, 1968
17.1 x 11.1 x 1.3 cm
Copper, silver, tintype photo, stones, brass, aluminum, other found objects
Museum of Fine Arts, Boston
The Daphne Farago Collection, 2006.150
Image © 2013 Museum of Fine Arts, Boston

Arline Fisch
Halter and Skirt, 1968
35 x 35 cm
Sterling silver, printed velvet skirt (fabric by Jack Larsen); formed and fabricated
Collection of the Museum of Art and Design (MAD), New York
Photo by Ferdinand Boesch
Courtesy of the artist

Ken Cory
Squash Blossom Necklace,
1974
40 x 10.2 x 1.5 cm
Shells, light bulbs, cast bronze,
leather, sterling silver, copper,
found objects
The Museum of Fine Arts,
Houston; Helen Williams Drutt
Collection, promised gift of
Helen Williams Drutt English

and landscape imagery became increasingly prevalent in American jewelry of the 1970s. In this context, Olaf Skoogfors, John Prip and John Iversen blended metalwork with natural materials such as bone and stone to evoke the colors and textures of tree bark, pebbles and plant life. Intertwined with the broad interest in nature was a renewed focus on Native American culture, both within and without Native communities. Non-Native amateurs dabbled in making craft jewelry as part of the countercultural lifestyle of "doing your own thing," and they also wore widely available Native jewelry in a long-standing American tradition of whites "playing Indian" to signify opposition to oppression.[19] Artist Jan Brooks recalled, "It was impossible to avoid … the whole notion of Indian jewelry, because it was in every truck stop in America."[20] Ken Cory responded to the fad and his own earnest studies of Northwest Coast and Southwest jewelry designs and techniques with his playfully critical *Squash Blossom Necklace* in 1974. Substituting light bulbs and empty bullet casings for traditional silver and turquoise elements, and a cast-bronze pencil for the *naja*, or crescent-shaped pendant, Cory reflected on the violent collision between Euro-American technology and Native culture.

A few Native jewelers explored greater personal expression while maintaining traditions from their own particular cultures; several had life experiences in the non-Native world that led them to develop an individualistic approach. Bill Reid, the son of a Haida mother and a Euro-American father, and a student of the British-trained metalsmith James Green, creatively revived the bracelets customarily worn by Haida men on Canada's west coast. He drew motifs and symbolism from Haida beliefs, but used European-derived techniques—repoussé, chasing and casting—to create boldly sculptural interpretations.[21] Self-taught Hopi artist Charles Loloma developed a distinctive adaptation of the stone-inlay jewelry practiced by the nearby Zuni and Navajo Indians. Instead of flat, channel-set bands of stone, Loloma's chunks of turquoise, lapis lazuli, ivory, wood and coral project boldly above the wristband, suggesting mountainous outcroppings or modernist cityscapes. Rejected three times by the Gallup Inter-Tribal Indian Ceremonial (a white organization that ran a wholesale Indian crafts market) for not being "Indian enough," Loloma's work eventually earned praise and recognition from contemporary craft museums and collectors.[22]

Another response to environmental awareness was to examine the relationship between nature and technology. While watching a broadcast of the first moon landing, Mary Ann Scherr, who combined a background in fashion and industrial design with training in jewelry, became enthralled with the idea of jewelry that monitored bodily functions such as pulse rate or body temperature. By partnering with research scientists and engineers, she devised wearable objects fitted with cutting-edge miniaturized electronics, enclosed within ornately decorated cases.[23]

Stanley Lechtzin's exploration of electroforming and acrylics was similarly concerned with blending nature and technology. Wishing to make large sculptural forms that weren't uncomfortably heavy, Lechtzin adapted the industrial process of electroforming—which creates a thin, self-supporting shell of metal—for the studio. Later he combined electroformed metal with another industrial process, cast acrylic plastics, in a series of torques that meld advanced technology with organic shapes. For Lechtzin, the process of electroforming, in which metal molecules are pulled together in an electrolytic solution, was "analogous to numerous growth processes observed in nature … the growth of coral under the sea, and the multiplication of simple organisms as observed under the microscope."[24] Canadian Neil Carrick Aird, too, blended technology with organic forms in jewelry made from fused layers of aluminum and niobium, cut and colored to resemble abstract landscapes.[25]

By the end of the 1970s, all craft media had become increasingly professionalized and oriented to the wider art world. Academic programs in metalsmithing encouraged the refinement of technique and experimentation with conceptual objects; a critic observed in 1974 that universities had "remove[d] from the craftsman the burden of having to sell work in order to eat, so that work tends to be produced more for exhibition than for wear or use."[26] The Society of North American Goldsmiths organized exhibitions and symposia, and published the newsletter that later became *Metalsmith*. The successful exhibition Objects: USA appeared in 22 American museums from 1969 to 1970 before touring Europe, and introduced a vast new audience to the best in American contemporary craft, including jewelry. In 1973, Boston's Institute of Contemporary Art showcased the work of famous sculptors, designers and studio jewelers together in Jewelry as Sculpture as Jewelry, echoing the connections between contemporary sculpture and jewelry explored by MoMA in the '40s.[27] Specialized galleries for contemporary jewelry and craft opened

Charles Loloma
Bracelet, 1975
8.9 x 4.1 cm
14-karat gold with inlaid turquoise, lapis lazuli, coral, fossil ivory, abalone, shell, ironwood and other woods; fabricated
Photo by Craig Smith
Heard Museum, Phoenix, 4274-1
Courtesy of the Heard Museum

Mary Ann Scherr
Electronic Oxygen Belt Pendant, 1974
30.5 x 10.2 x 2.5 cm
Sterling silver, electronics, amber, oxygen cylinder, face mask, batteries; fabricated, etched
Photo by John Bigelow Taylor
Museum of Arts and Design, New York
Gift of Mary Lee Hu, through the American Craft Council, 1979

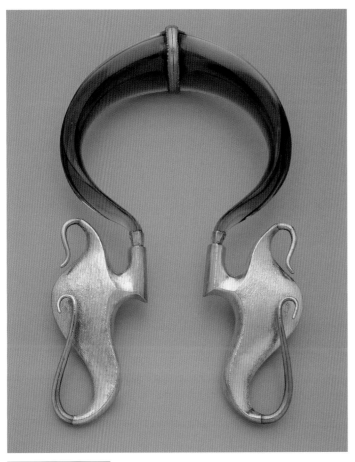

Stanley Lechtzin
Torque 33-D, 1973
Diameter, 30.5 cm
Electroformed silver, partial gold
plating, acrylic collar
Yale University Art Gallery,
American Arts Purchase Fund

in several cities, including Sculpture to Wear, Aaron Faber Gallery, and ArtWear in New York City; Helen Drutt Gallery in Philadelphia; and Mobilia in Cambridge, Massachusetts.

Although there were no comparable Canadian jewelry galleries in this period, Canadian jewelers were connected to developments in contemporary jewelry through publications, traveling exhibitions and workshops given by visiting American and European jewelers. For Canadian crafts more broadly, the 1960s and '70s represented a watershed period when organizations such as the Canadian Crafts Council and other professional groups asserted greater authority over selecting and legitimizing "experts" in the field. Influenced by Rose Slivka, editor of the American Craft Council's journal *Craft Horizons*, Canadian craft leaders downplayed amateur and hobbyist craft in favor of a late modernist approach to "fine craft." They emphasized fine art concepts, rigorous jury selection for admission to shows and guilds and the establishment of degree-granting university programs for craft media.[28] Sheridan College and Nova Scotia College of Art and Design (NSCAD) became leading centers for professionalized craft. As Canadian craft artists adopted this new professionalism, jewelers among them—such as John and Nancy Pocock, Anita Aarons and Walter Schluep—voiced their desire to have jewelry viewed as sculpture and contemporary art.[29]

The 1980s and 1990s: New Narratives

With the American economy booming and conspicuous consumption back in style, a new class of collectors emerged who were willing to pay art-gallery prices for contemporary jewelry. Jewelry in the 1980s became even bigger, brasher and more colorful, reflecting the exuberant and wildly polychrome look found in international design of the era. Jewelers explored many materials to achieve slick, colorful surfaces, including anodized aluminum and titanium, and laminates such as ColorCore, plastics, painted metal and enamels. Geometric abstraction and flattened shapes contrasted with the organic, textural forms of the preceding decade. Such vibrant jewelry had the added benefit of looking great in color photography, now widely used in the glossy exhibition catalogs, magazine covers and gallery brochures that helped define "stars" in the field. Through such professional instruments, jewelers in North America also became increasingly connected to their counterparts across the globe, yielding fertile interactions as well as a confusingly diverse array of styles and approaches.

One of the first such international exchanges was not without misconceptions on both sides. "The new jewelry" movement originating among avant-garde English, Dutch and German artists in the late '70s coincided with ongoing stylistic turnover in American jewelry and reflected the iconoclastic experimentation of young European jewelers rebelling against centuries-old goldsmithing traditions.[30] Their work, in which jewelry was reduced to anything worn on the body, regardless of scale, aesthetic or material, was introduced to American audiences to decidedly mixed reviews with the 1983 exhibition New Departures in British Jewelry at the American Craft Museum (now the Museum of Arts and Design) in New York. Malcolm and Sue Knapp, the collectors who sponsored the project, intended the New York venue to help "expand [the] horizons" of American jewelers.[31] However, for many in the United States, the alternative materials and large-scale body sculpture in New Departures came across as old hat, already explored by Americans in the 1960s.

Others, however, were in sympathy with "the new jewelry" tendencies. Marjorie Schick had been making body sculptures from papier-mâché, wire, foam rubber and other lightweight materials since the late '60s, and, like some British "new jewelry" artists, related her body jewelry to dance and performance. In the early '80s she began making large, architectural forms using painted wooden dowels. When some were included in the 1982 Jewelry Redefined exhibition at the British Crafts Centre, they immediately gained her recognition in Europe.[32] In Canada, the 1985 exhibition Body Work featured works by Canadian artists that mirrored aspects of European new jewelry: large-scale forms, lightweight and ephemeral materials, and critiques of value and preciousness. Pamela Ritchie, a leading Canadian jeweler and head of the jewelry department at NSCAD, exhibited jewelry made with canceled postage stamps, noting that "stamps are, after all, at the same time one of the most common and one of the most sought-after items."[33]

Throughout the 1980s and '90s, a large number of American and Canadian jewelers created figurative jewelry with personal and historical narratives, as conveyed in the exhibitions Tales and Traditions: Storytelling in Twentieth-Century American Craft (1988) and Brilliant Stories: American Narrative Jewelry (1992).[34] J. Fred Woell's politically charged assemblages and Richard Mawdsley's intricately constructed objects had entered this territory in the late '60s and '70s; Mawdsley's masterful Feast Bracelet, for example, is

Marjorie Schick
Dowel-Stick Brooch, 1983
36.2 x 18.4 x 2.2 cm
Wood, paint, nickel silver; riveted
Museum of Fine Arts, Boston
The Daphne Farago Collection,
2006.499
Image © 2013 Museum of Fine
Arts, Boston

Pamela Ritchie
Le Carrousel Bracelet, 1983
8 x 8 x 2.7 cm
Wood, postage stamps, paint;
constructed
Photo courtesy of the artist

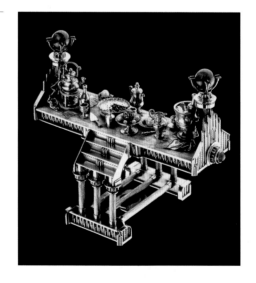

Richard Mawdsley
Feast Bracelet, 1974
9.6 x 7.0 x 11.5 cm
Sterling silver, jade, pearls;
fabricated
Smithsonian American Art
Museum, Washington, DC, gift
of the James Renwick Alliance
in honor of Lloyd E. Herman,
director emeritus
Smithsonian American Art
Museum, Washington, DC / Art
Resource, NY

reminiscent of Dutch still-life paintings using table settings as memento mori images. In the 1980s and continuing into the present, issues of race, gender and cultural identity moved to the foreground. Joyce Scott's sculptural beadwork neckpieces and installations boldly address difficult subjects such as racial prejudice and sexual violence, while Ron Ho's quieter works deal with his experience in the Chinese-American community of the Pacific Northwest. Bruce Metcalf's works often take a slyly humorous look at personal history; his large-headed cartoonlike figures inhabit strange worlds but also engage the viewer's sympathy for human foibles and absurdities. His brooch *Crushed* depicts one of these hapless figures trapped between two chunks of volcanic stone, feeling the overwhelming pressure of "an apparently insurmountable problem."[35]

In the 1990s and the early years of the twenty-first century, a plurality of styles and subject matter persisted, though narrative and conceptual work remained at the forefront. Many jewelers returned to the history of adornment itself and its associations with social and cultural ideals such as protection, spirituality, love, remembrance—aspects of jewelry's identity that had been stripped away in the mid-twentieth century by modernist disdain for "sentimental" or "old-fashioned" conventions. Kiff Slemmons' 1994 necklace *Luck* is composed of found objects and handmade silver elements symbolizing both good and bad luck. With these conflicting tokens and the ambiguous phrase "Wish Me Luck" spelled out in typewriter keys, Slemmons refers playfully to the ancient belief in the protective power of jewelry. Other jewelers, including Lisa Gralnick and Daniel Jocz, created contemporary interpretations of sentimental jewelry such as wedding rings, lockets and mourning jewelry. Instead of clamoring to have their work viewed as sculpture, many American jewelers chose to focus on the psychological power of jewelry to communicate meaning.[36]

One of the most compelling explorations of jewelry as a narrative and conceptual medium was Jan Yager's decade-long project, undertaken in 1990, to "beachcomb" the Philadelphia streets and sidewalks surrounding her studio. Her finds—bullet casings, broken glass, syringes and thousands of crack vials—represented the tragedies of poverty, crime, racial injustice and drug abuse. Yager expressed the grief associated with these found objects by setting them in darkly oxidized silver to recall the somber mourning jewelry of the nineteenth century. Over time, she researched local history, including the English colonists' exploitation of indigenous Lenni Lenape people and the Atlantic slave trade that enriched many of Philadelphia's merchants. When she learned that tubular glass beads traded by Europeans in Africa for human "property" were similar in scale and form to the crack vials exchanged in local drug deals, she saw a connection between the bondage of historic slave labor and modern-day drug addiction. The neckpiece *American Collar II*, with its 139 crack vials, 222 crack caps and two syringes arranged in the form of an African Masai beadwork collar, conveys these conceptual linkages between different forms of oppression, past and present.

The Contemporary Jewelry Scene

Since 2000, contemporary jewelry in North America has continued to expand and professionalize. As education in the field has grown increasingly sophisticated, university programs offer instruction in everything from ancient practices of metalsmithing and enameling to new computer-aided design and rapid prototyping, so that jewelers have more choices than ever in selecting materials and processes to convey their ideas. The centrality of academic programs continues to foster an emphasis on intellectually driven jewelry that appeals primarily to art collectors, galleries and museums. Furthermore, in the past decade, major museums have enhanced the status and visibility of such concept-based contemporary jewelry by acquiring, displaying and publishing significant private collections.

Although North American jewelers have always had contact and selective engagement with artists abroad, in recent years international cross-fertilization has become even more important in contemporary practice. Travel, study-abroad programs, artist residencies and the globe-shrinking presence of the Internet have kept American jewelers far more in touch with colleagues elsewhere. The possibilities of global connectedness are manifest in jewelry itself. In her *Continental Drift Brooch*, Sondra Sherman expresses her impulse to "'set the continents free' ... like opening the cages at the zoo."[37] In this work, the high-karat gold continents float freely in water within a complex setting of plastic and metal, so that Asia can jostle against Africa, or Europe might slide over next to South America. The latitude and longitude lines are transformed into the facet lines of a gemstone, and the entire globe is thus represented as a delicate and precious gem containing endless possibilities for change and exploration.

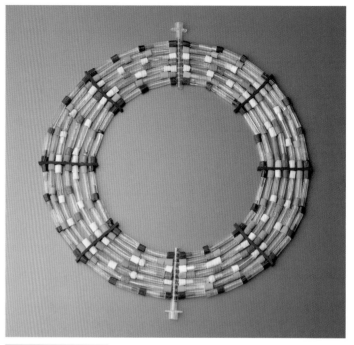

Jan Yager
American Collar II, City Flora/City Flotsam Series,
1996
33 x 31.1 x 0.6 cm
Plastic, rubber, stainless steel, silver, crack vials, crack caps, syringes, cast silver crack cap
Museum of Fine Arts, Boston
The Daphne Farago Collection, 2006.633
Image © 2013 Museum of Fine Arts, Boston

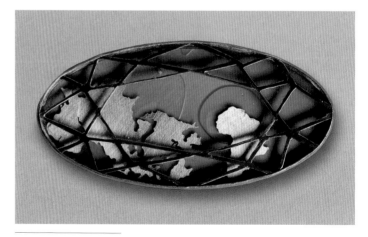

Sondra Sherman
Continental Drift Brooch, 1998
Sterling silver, glass, gold, acetate, water
Philadelphia Museum of Art
Gift of Helen Williams Drutt English in honor of the artist and Madeleine Albright, 2004

Notes

1. For a comprehensive overview, see Lois Sherr Dubin, *North American Indian Jewelry and Adornment: From Prehistory to the Present* (New York: Harry N. Abrams, 1999); for contemporary jewelry of the American Southwest, see Dexter Cirillo, *Southwestern Indian Jewelry* (New York: Abbeville Press, 1992), and Kari Chalker, ed., *Totems to Turquoise: Native North American Jewelry Arts of the Northwest and Southwest* (New York: Harry N. Abrams in association with the American Museum of Natural History, 2004).

2. Curator's statement contained in press release, "Exhibition of Modern Handmade Jewelry Opens at Museum of Modern Art," and list of artists in "Check and Installation List," both in MoMA Archives, exhibition 330.

3. The exhibition catalog was published as a special issue of the Walker's museum journal; see "Modern Jewelry under Fifty Dollars," Everyday Art Quarterly 7 (Spring 1948).

4. The most important survey of Calder's jewelry is Alexander S. C. Rower and Holton Rower, eds., *Calder Jewelry* (New York: Calder Foundation, 2008), an exhibition catalog.

5. On Albers's design philosophy, see Anni Albers, "Designing," *Craft Horizons* 2, no. 2 (May 1943): 7.

6. Moholy-Nagy quoted in *The Jewelry of Margaret De Patta: A Retrospective Exhibition* (Oakland, CA: The Oakland Museum, 1976), 15, an exhibition catalog.

7. On De Patta, see Ursula Ilse-Neuman and Julie M. Muñiz, *Space Light Structure: The Jewelry of Margaret De Patta* (New York: Museum of Arts and Design, 2012), an exhibition catalog; *The Jewelry of Margaret De Patta: A Retrospective Exhibition* (Oakland, CA: The Oakland Museum, 1976), an exhibition catalog; and Robert Cardinale and Hazel Bray, "Margaret De Patta: Structure, Concepts, and Design Sources," *Metalsmith* 3, no. 2 (Spring 1983): 11–15.

8. On MoMA's wartime veterans programs, see "The Arts in Therapy," exhibition file no. 216, MoMA Archives; Meta R. Cobb and Harriet E. Knapp, "Occupational Therapy and the Artist," *Bulletin of the Museum of Modern Art* 10, no. 3 (February 1943): 4–6; and Charles J. Martin, *How to Make Modern Jewelry* (New York: Museum of Modern Art, 1949).

9. On the Handy and Harman workshops, see "Revival Is Sought in Silversmithing: Swedish Baron Here Proposes to Foster Ancient Craft at 25-Day Workshop," *The New York Times*, July 23, 1948; and "American Metalsmithing in the 1940s and '50s," *American Craft* 43, no. 1 (February–March 1983): 86–87.

10. On the connections between Ontario and the SAC, see Anne Barros, *Ornament and Object: Canadian Jewellery and Metal Art, 1946–1996* (Ontario: Boston Mills Press, 1997), 34; see also Anne Barros, "The Metal Arts Guild of Ontario," *Metalsmith* 4, no. 2 (Spring 1984): 43–44.

11. Delrue quoted in Barros, *Ornament and Object*, 27.

12. Barros, *Ornament and Object*, 13–31.

13. On Art Smith, see Barry R. Harwood, *From the Village to Vogue: The Modernist Jewelry of Art Smith* (Brooklyn, NY: Brooklyn Museum, 2008), an exhibition catalog; and James L. De Jongh Arthur, Toni Lesser Wolf, and Yvonne O'Neal, *Arthur Smith: A Jeweler's Retrospective* (Jamaica, NY: Jamaica Arts Center, 1990), an exhibition catalog. For Smith's correspondence with many of his retailers, see Arthur Smith Papers, Brooklyn Museum Archive, SC03, Correspondence 1/1948–2/1982.

14. Kramer quoted in "Surrealistic Jeweler," *The New Yorker*, January 3, 1942, 11–12. For Kramer's vivid descriptions of his own work, see, "Sam Kramer," *Design Quarterly* 33 (1955): 10; and Richard Gehman, "The Doodads Women Wear!" *Saturday Evening Post*, June 18, 1955, 113.

15. Blanche R. Brown, "Ed Wiener to Me," in Ed Wiener, *Jewelry by Ed Wiener* (New York: Fifty 50 Gallery, 1989), 13.

16. See Ruth T. Summers and Bruce W. Pepich, *Ebendorf: The Jewelry of Robert Ebendorf, a Retrospective of Forty Years* (Raleigh: Gallery of Art and Design, North Carolina State University, 2003), an exhibition catalog. On assemblage, see William Chapin Seitz, *The Art of Assemblage* (New York: Museum of Modern Art, 1961), an exhibition catalog; see also *The "Junk" Aesthetic: Assemblage of the 1950s and Early 1960s* (New York: Whitney Museum of American Art, 1989), an exhibition catalog. Woell's reference to "anti-jewelry" quoted from Betty Freudenheim, "An Ambiguous Art: The Jewelry of J. Fred Woell," *American Craft* 49, no. 2 (April–May 1989): 32–35.

17. American Craftsmen's Council, *The Art of Personal Adornment* (New York: Museum of Contemporary Crafts, 1965), an exhibition catalog.

18. For a period survey of body sculpture, see Donald J. Willcox, *Body Jewelry: International Perspectives* (Chicago: Henry Regnery Company, 1973), especially the artist's statement by Fisch, 57. For a survey of Fisch's work, see Arline Fisch et al., *Elegant Fantasy: The Jewelry of Arline Fisch* (San Diego: The San Diego Historical Society, 1999), an exhibition catalog. For Fisch's commentary on her experience in Scandinavia, see *Oral history interview with Arline M. Fisch*, July 29–30, 2001, Archives of American Art, Smithsonian Institution, www.aaa.si.edu/collections/oralhistories/transcripts/fisch01.htm.

19. Philip J. Deloria, *Playing Indian* (New Haven, CT / London: Yale University Press, 1998).

20. Brooks quoted in Ben Mitchell, *The Jewelry of Ken Cory: Play Disguised* (Tacoma, WA: Tacoma Art Museum, 1997), 80.

21. Dubin, *North American Indian Jewelry and Adornment*, 411–416; and Barros, *Ornament and Object*, 29–31.

22. Ellen Berkovitch, "Charles Loloma: Hopi Modernist," *Metalsmith* 26, no. 2 (Summer 2006): 42–49; and Erin Younger, *Loloma: A Retrospective View* (Phoenix, AZ: The Heard Museum, 1978), an exhibition catalog.

23. Mary Ann Scherr interviewed by Mary Douglas, *Oral history interview with Mary Ann Scherr*, April 6–7, 2001, Archives of American Art, Smithsonian Institution, www.aaa.si.edu/collections/oralhistories/transcripts/scherr01.htm.

24. Lechtzin quoted in Ralph Turner, *Contemporary Jewelry: A Critical Assessment, 1945–1975* (New York: Van Nostrand Reinhold Co., 1976), 65.

25. Barros, *Ornament and Object*, 46.

26. Pat Passlof, "Metal Arts in North America," *Craft Horizons* 34, no. 5 (October 1974): 43–45.

27. Lee Nordness, *Objects: USA* (New York: Viking Press, 1970), an exhibition catalog; and Institute of Contemporary Art, Boston, *Jewelry as Sculpture as Jewelry* (Boston: T. O. Metcalf, 1973), an exhibition catalog.

28. Sandra Alfoldy, *Crafting Identity: The Development of Professional Fine Craft in Canada* (Montreal / Kingston: McGill-Queen's University Press, 2005).

29. Linda Munk and May Ebbitt Cutler, "The Jeweller as a Sculptor—and Vice Versa," *Canadian Art*, no. 98 (September/October 1965): 44–48.

30. For a period survey of the trend, see Peter Dormer and Ralph Turner, *The New Jewelry: Trends and Traditions* (London: Thames & Hudson, 1985; reprint, London: Thames and Hudson, 1989), 146–76. Citations are to the reprint edition.

31. Malcolm Knapp, "The Knapp Collection," in *The Jewellery Project: New Departures in British and European Work, 1980–83*, ed. Crafts Council Gallery (London: Crafts Council Gallery, 1983), 4, an exhibition catalog.

32. For a recent catalog raisonné of Schick's work, see Tacey Rosolowski et al., *Sculpture to Wear: The Jewelry of Marjorie Schick* (Stuttgart: Arnoldsche Art Publishers, 2007).

33. Pamela Ritchie quoted in Nancy Tousley and Nancy Dodds, *Body Work: A Selection of Contemporary Canadian Jewelry* (Alberta: Alberta College of Art Gallery, 1985), 23. For Ritchie's more recent work, see Wendy Landry, "Pamela Ritchie: Nova Scotia's Intellectual Gem," *Metalsmith* 32, no. 2 (2012): 22–31.

34. See Lloyd E. Herman and Matthew Kangas, *Tales and Traditions: Storytelling in Twentieth-Century American Craft* (St. Louis, MO: Craft Alliance, 1993); and Lloyd E. Herman, *Brilliant Stories: American Narrative Jewelry* (Washington, DC: International Sculpture Center, 1994). Both are exhibition catalogs.

35. Metcalf quoted in Herman, *Brilliant Narratives*, 15.

36. For several artists' views on rediscovering jewelry's social and emotional meanings, see Bruce Metcalf, "On the Nature of Jewelry," *Metalsmith* 13, no. 1 (Winter 1993): 22–27; Erika Ayala Stefanutti, letter to the editor, *Metalsmith* 14, no. 2 (Spring 1994): 10; Kim Cridler, letter to the editor, *Metalsmith* 14, no. 2 (Spring 1994): 6; and Sondra Sherman, "Jewelers on Jewelry," *Metalsmith* 26, no. 5 (2006): 22–23.

37. Sondra Sherman, email communication with the author, June 21, 2012.

Further Reading

Barros, Anne. *Ornament and Object: Canadian Jewellery and Metal Art, 1946–1996*. Ontario: Boston Mills Press, 1997.

Dubin, Lois Sherr. *North American Indian Jewelry and Adornment: From Prehistory to the Present*. New York: Harry N. Abrams, 1999.

Greenbaum, Toni. *Messengers of Modernism: American Studio Jewelry, 1940–1960*. Edited by Martin Eidelberg. Paris / New York: Montreal Museum of Decorative Arts in association with Flammarion, 1996.

Herman, Lloyd E, guest curator. *Good as Gold: Alternative Materials in American Jewelry*. Washington, DC: Smithsonian Institution Traveling Exhibition Service, 1981.

L'Ecuyer, Kelly H., with contributions by Michelle Tolini Finamore, Yvonne J. Markowitz, and Gerald W. R. Ward. *Jewelry by Artists: In the Studio, 1940–1990*. Boston: MFA Publications, 2010.

Lewin, Susan Grant. *One of a Kind: American Art Jewelry Today*. New York: Harry N. Abrams, 1994.

Minnesota Museum of Art / Renwick Gallery. *The Goldsmith: An Exhibition of Work by Contemporary Artists-Craftsmen of North America*. St. Paul: Minnesota Museum of Art, 1974.

Morrill, Penny Chittim, and Carole A. Berk. *Mexican Silver: 20th Century Handwrought Jewelry & Metalwork*. Atglen, PA: Schiffer, 1994.

Schon, Marbeth. *Form and Function: American Modernist Jewelry, 1940–1970*. Atglen, PA: Schiffer, 2008.

Victoria and Albert Museum. *Masterworks of Contemporary American Jewelry: Sources and Concepts*. London: Victoria and Albert Museum, 1985.

Yarlow, Loretta. *Jewelry as Sculpture as Jewelry*. Boston: Institute of Contemporary Art, 1973.

Latin America.

Valeria Vallarta Siemelink

Introduction

From the strong ritual, mystic, and symbolic function of jewelry in the pre-Columbian era to the shiny opulence that distinguishes the members of drug cartels, Latin Americans have always had a profound and intricate relationship with jewelry. Latin America is an extremely diverse and rich territory that covers over 20 million square kilometers with great variations in political and economic systems. More than 500 million people, a composite of ancestries, ethnic groups and races, speak hundreds of indigenous languages. Each region has witnessed distinct patterns of development. Defining a Latin American identity is difficult. But a common ethos exists between Latin American nations: a hybrid and heterogeneous cultural construction characterized by problems specific to postcolonial societies. The jewelry emerging today portrays an array of idiosyncrasies and styles that reveal the breadth and complexity of the continent's contemporary culture.

Hibridization, a term used by the humanities and social sciences to describe the mixture of races, and frequently borrowed by the cultural realm to discuss the blending and synthesizing of elements belonging to different cultures, is extremely complex in Latin America. The exchanges between the distinct cultures—African, Indian and European—resulted in a new product that expresses the tensions, contradictions and ambiguities of its birth in the New World. The current notion of hybridization, which constitutes one of the key elements in the configuration of a plural, dynamic and constantly evolving identity in Latin America, is multidimensional and continues to have spiritual and aesthetic dimensions. Hybridization accounts for one of the strengths of Latin America's artistic production and lies at the roots of its vitality, originality and constant power to surprise. The establishment of a pattern that combines tendencies from the outside and adapts them to local realities has been the norm since colonization. Today, its contemporary jewelry appears not as a mere imitator of Western movements, but rather as a mechanism that adjusts and transforms prevailing norms.

The mastery of Latin America's goldsmiths and their attitude toward body ornament has fascinated the West for centuries. The emergence of jewelry makers from Latin America into the international field of contemporary jewelry is inevitable in this era of globalization and cultural diversity. After years of relative isolation, a growing connectedness has developed within the Latin American jewelry scene. Its makers now are able to exchange knowledge, ideas and opportunities with their colleagues near and far. Their increasing participation in international events, and the promotion of relevant academic and curatorial projects from the continent, has stimulated the interest of international scholars, curators and critics.

These developments have helped address two matters that, until recently, prevented contemporary jewelry from thriving within Latin America. First, the notion of contemporary jewelry—still a debated topic in the international arena—is becoming clearer for Latin American makers and promoters; there's a commitment to collectively identify and understand the precepts and guidelines and to set their own. Second, these developments provide the international arena with a cultural framework for understanding the contemporary jewelry practices of the continent.

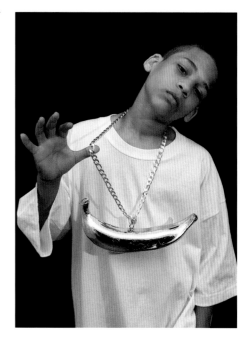

Latin American Modernism

Latin American modernism was a postwar phenomenon that flowered in the early 1920s, stimulated by artists and writers returning home after time spent in Europe; it occurred as a continuation of tendencies interrupted by World War I. The impact of the Mexican Revolution was immense, and the activities of the Mexican muralists in interpreting and disseminating its ideals, in promoting the idea of an art for the people and in helping to realize a cultural nationalism, were felt far beyond Mexico itself. The break with the past was usually affirmed in some form; sometimes this was accompanied by a straightforward celebration of modernity, but more often a reassessment of tradition was involved, as well as a rejection of the colonial period and the Europeanized culture of the nineteenth century in favor of an indigenous cultural tradition. Nationalism, as opposed to internationalism, and the regional versus the central and cosmopolitan, became fundamental issues. Modernity coincided with the desire to explore and define what being Mexican or Bolivian or Argentinean meant.

Indigenismo, a specific movement in Latin American art and literature, began to gain momentum in the early 1930s, manifesting itself in the rediscovery and reevaluation of indigenous American cultures and in the proliferation of Indian-related themes and subjects.[1] The movement, which evolved in Peru, Bolivia and Ecuador, had its deepest implications in Mexico. Artists such as Diego Rivera, David

Jorge Manilla
Ese Hombre, 2007
8 x 5 x 3 cm
Cardboard, dry cactus, corn
paste, silver
Photo by Valeria Vallarta
Siemelink
Courtesy of Otro Diseño

Alfaro Siqueiros and José Clemente Orozco produced an iconographic synthesis of national identity inspired by Aztec and Mayan art, church altarpieces, vernacular decorations, the colors and forms of local pottery, Michoacan lacquer and the experimental achievements of the European avant-garde. This hybrid reorganization of the visual language was backed by changes in the relationships among artists, the state and the working class. Muralism in public buildings; the publication of nationalistic calendars, posters and magazines; and the revitalization of the crafts were the result of a forceful statement of new aesthetic tendencies within the newborn cultural field.

This was the climate that American designer William Spratling found upon his arrival in Mexico in 1929. His close acquaintance with Rivera helped him move swiftly among the cultural circles of Mexico City and become acquainted with their artistic ideals. Soon he transferred to the mining village of Taxco, in the state of Guerrero, where he encouraged the villagers to work the silver they had mined for centuries. Spratling was set to resuscitate the ancient techniques and bring a new dimension to the tired pre-Hispanic sense of aesthetics. Hiring an experienced goldsmith and enrolling other local craftsmen, he created Las Delicias, a workshop that promoted a whole new apprentice system and became a model for others in Mexico. But it would be mainly visual artists, first from Mexico and later from other countries in Latin America, who continued experimenting within the jewelry field in the following decades.

In the late 1940s, the jewelry produced by Spratling, Valentin Vidaurreta, Hector Aguilar and Antonio Pineda was eagerly received by Mexican artists such as Frida Kahlo, Remedios Varo and Lupe Marín, who not only bought and wore it but also became sporadically interested in making jewelry of their own. Kahlo amassed a considerable collection of pre-Hispanic beads, figurines and bells that she combined with silver pieces from Taxco, colorful ribbons and plastic objects. Her ornaments were simple, but they showed a unique attitude toward self-adornment that inspired other visual artists from Latin America to venture into jewelry making.

In the 1940s, Mexican sculptor Juan Soriano worked as a set and wardrobe designer in the local theater scene. Captivated by Kahlo's sense of personal adornment, he created a series of sculptural ornaments made in terra-cotta and ceramics for the play *El Tejedor de Segovia.* Throughout his career, he continued to produce bold jewelry pieces, mostly for friends and family. His last pieces included animal bones and teeth embedded in clay, reminiscent of paleontological findings. Soriano's jewelry work stimulated the interest in body ornaments of fellow artists in Mexico and other Latin American countries. The Uruguayan artist Carmelo Arden Quin, cofounder of the international Madí movement, made wearable objects out of his *formes galbées*, alternations of concave and convex forms in enameled wood, and coplanals, series of polygons forming a single piece that in some cases include movable elements. The Cuban expressionist Luis Martínez Pedro "developed a series of ornaments in the 1950s that reflected his interest in the Caribbean biomorphism and *Santería*, the hybrid Cuban religion."[2] Although none of these artists pursued their interest in jewelry any further, their experiments stimulated other visual artists to consider it as a meaningful and rewarding medium. Collaboration between artists and jewelry makers, and convergence between disciplines that included jewelry making, became common.

One visual artist who might be considered the predecessor of contemporary jewelry in Latin America, Uruguayan Olga María Piria, worked under the tutelage of Joaquín Torres García. She pursued her painting career until 1951, when she met the electronic engineer Carlos Jauregui. While traveling extensively through Europe and northern Africa, the couple became interested in body ornaments. Two years later, they organized a research trip through Argentina, Chile and Brazil, where they visited several jewelry workshops. Back in Montevideo, they set up their own, and Jauregui built an array of innovative tools and machines that allowed him to translate Piria's designs into intricate constructivist ornaments.

Piria's jewelry was mainly executed in either cast or laminated and articulated silver. She translated the essential elements and composition of her paintings in three-dimensional objects, always incorporating symbols into a geometric grid based on the golden section. For Piria, the symbol was a way of synthesizing idea and form while bypassing narrative, which interfered with the unity of the work. She incorporated essential elements of indigenous American art with the basic principles of European constructivism and geometric abstraction. This idea was formally represented by adding highly symbolic pre-Hispanic beads and miniature figurines into complex geometrical silver or wood structures.

Reny Golcman
Mandíbula, 1966
5 x 8.6 cm
Silver, barracuda jaw bone
Photo by Daniella Lesso
Courtesy of the artist

Subversive Jewelry in Postmodern Latin America

The 1960s and '70s witnessed a change in the climate in which Latin American art developed. Prosperity was replaced by an era characterized by political instability and repression under dictatorial regimes. It was a period of violent polemics, but one that also saw a renewal of creativity. Modernism, which had not fully ended in Latin America, overlapped with the radical movements and later with the postmodern.

Brazil engendered a group of daring jewelry makers. The sculptural designs of Caio Mourão and Reny Golcman, among many others, expanded the boundaries of traditional jewelry and challenged its relationship to the body. A painter, sculptor and goldsmith, Mourão broke with the traditional approach to jewelry and redefined the field with his *Anti-jewelry*, purposefully made in a calculatedly crude way. He embraced ancient techniques like fusion, fire cutting and hammering, and worked with materials like bronze, silver and hematite to produce massive ornaments that aimed to criticize jewelry's preciousness in contrast to economic inequality in Brazil. By creating pieces meant to be worn in alternative ways— engagement rings for the "wrong" finger or chains that linked head, neck and waist—Mourão achieved his goal of causing awkwardness in both the wearer and the viewer.

Golcman was a graduate in fine arts and studied under Mourão. She explored taboo subjects like death and sexuality and boldly used socially unacceptable formats and irreverent materials. Her silver *Mutant Jewelry* incorporated fish bones and wild Brazilian seeds that openly suggested feminine sexual organs; the pieces sought to denounce centuries of sexual discrimination, repression and abuse in Brazil and proposed that women comment loudly on the matter by wearing the large and extravagant ornaments to social events.

Two of Brazil's most important postmodern artists, Lygia Clark and Hélio Oiticica, reframed the modernist notions of universal aesthetics in the 1960s by translating them directly onto the body. They manufactured a series of ornament devices such as masks, hoods and cuff links that explored haptic space[3] through tactile, auditory, olfactory and kinetic propositions and created a web of relationships around the body's internal and external spaces. These experiments related a modern European geometric abstract tradition to Brazilian vernacular culture and fused a Western aesthetic canon that privileges vision with Afro-indigenous oral traditions in which knowledge and history are encoded in the body. Clark and Oiticica's manipulable objects, immersive environments and experiential propositions based on wearable works became relevant to contemporary art because of their original development in the context of Brazilian art, and because of the unique universal vocabularies they created and explored.

In Argentina, the opening of avant-garde Galería Folie in Buenos Aires in 1964 marked the start of the current intense experimental period in jewelry. Galería Folie gathered a large group of visual artists led by Victor Grippo, the father of conceptual art in Argentina. Grippo started his career as a painter, then switched to sculpture, producing a series of animated pieces involving complex engines and lighting. He later focused on developing large installations in which he experimented with using the latent energy of organic matter. In 1970, invited by Galería Folie, Grippo began to produce sculptural necklaces, pendants and pocket watches. Although his jewelry production, like that of most of the jewelry makers of that time, was conventionally circumscribed to metals—mostly silver, copper and lead—the aesthetic and functional characteristics of his pieces conveyed all the positive ideological feel of the golden days of the 1970s. Strongly influenced by the work of Brazilians Clark and Oiticica, Grippo gave jewelry a new dimension, displaying his ornaments in a context of highly conceptual installations and encouraging the critical participation of the audience through performance.

Grippo's contemporary, Gyula Kosice, born in Slovakia but a naturalized Argentinean, was an artist, theoretician and poet who became one of the most important figures in kinetic and luminal art. His kinetic sculptures and installations fused wood, metal, glass and resins with water, light, gas and movement. In the early 1960s, Kosice started experimenting with jewelry, at first translating his kinetic wooden sculptures into playful rings and pendants where all the parts were mobile and often interchangeable. Soon he turned to translucent materials such as Lucite and glass, which allowed him to incorporate water or play with light and reflections in his futuristic ornaments. He held his first jewelry exhibition, Bijoux et Sculptures d'Eau, in 1965 at the Galerie Laclochet in Paris. Five years later, Galería Briger in Buenos Aires served as a stage for mobile installations in which dozens of rings and pendants interplayed with light and water. Kosice, like many of his contemporaries, opened ateliers that were able to maintain independence from the jewelry industry and functioned as small academies during the following decades.

Gyula Kosice
Hydrospacial Ring, 1960
3 x 5 x 5 cm
Transparent Plexiglas, green-colored water
Photo by Tine Claerhout
Courtesy of Betty De Stefano,
Collectors Gallery Brussels

From the Void to the Connected

By the early 1980s, the novelty of the subversive artists of the '60s and the '70s had worn off; visual artists, who had provided some of the most interesting material and conceptual proposals in jewelry making, had lost their interest in the field. Most jewelers, living in countries in political and economic turbulence, worked exclusively to satisfy the needs of the commercial jewelry industry. Crafts—and jewelry—occupied a secondary position. No government or private programs existed to encourage experimentation, research or discussion in the field. Jewelers worked in isolation; they were disconnected from events taking place in Europe and the United States, and they had little or no contact with their colleagues in Latin America.

The academic situation was pitiful: training programs were limited and limiting. Jewelers were taught by other artisans and jewelers in family or community workshops, or through apprenticeship programs in large companies needing bench workers. Formal education was only offered in a few crafts schools and technical or gemology institutes in the form of short technical courses. One of the first academies to develop a two-year jewelry program, in 1979, was the Escuela de Artesanía y Diseño (School of Crafts and Design) in Mexico City; other schools, such as the Craft Department of the University of Santiago in Chile and the Escuela de Bellas Artes del Peru (National School of Fine Arts), soon followed. These programs, however, focused exclusively on developing the technical skills of their students and promoting the mastership of traditional silver- and goldsmithing techniques. At the same time, some of the industrial and graphic design institutes of universities, such as the Universidad Nacional Autonoma de Mexico (National Autonomous University), the Universidade de São Paulo (University of São Paulo) in Brazil and the Universidad de Buenos Aires (University of Buenos Aires) in Argentina, started incorporating fashion and jewelry design courses into their curricula. Although these courses had a better theoretical offering than the technical jewelry programs, they were short and sporadic, and all conceptual and experimental aspects of jewelry were disregarded. The ateliers created in the late 1960s by artists such as Mourão, Grippo, Nuria Carulla in Colombia, and Aurelina Soto in Mexico were active for several decades and became the only training centers where students were encouraged to work in a relatively free manner and to think about jewelry beyond its conventional boundaries. Yet the pieces produced in these workshops showed the almost reverent attitude that most Latin American jewelers of the time had for silver—and, to a lesser degree, to other metals. The critique of preciousness, a shift that occurred in Europe in the 1970s and was of tremendous importance for the development of contemporary jewelry, never took place in Latin America, and most of its jewelers seemed unable to view jewelry in nonmetallic terms.

By the end of the 1980s, countries like Argentina, Colombia, Mexico and Cuba saw the birth of a new generation of jewelers with good technical skills and a rich cultural and material repository who felt an urgent need for renewal. Some of these jewelers understood that the educational landscape had to change and they undertook the task of creating new ateliers, encouraging academies and universities to reevaluate their curricula, create innovative study programs and periodically organize workshops and lectures with local and foreign professors. Such was the case of Argentinean Jorge Castañón, a former marine biologist who studied sculpture and carpentry and trained for almost 10 years in various traditional silver- and goldsmithing workshops. By developing impressive technical skills and combining them with a profound understanding of local materials and autochthonous crafting techniques, as well as a powerful and sophisticated aesthetic sensibility, Castañón produced highly expressive pieces that broke the boundaries of jewelry to take on sculptural characteristics. Inspired mostly by natural materials and shapes and concerned with environmental matters, Castañón searched for rare types of wood, preferably discarded or abandoned, weathered by use or nature. Often with the vestiges of its past life preserved—paint flecks, a rusty nail or discoloration caused by fungi—the wood became a protagonist in Castañón's pieces, while rich metals were humbled and used in service to the wood to provide structural support or add color. The work expressed a marked Argentinean identity through a universal language. Aside from his artistic talent, Castañón professed a vocation for teaching that led him to create Taller La Nave in 1990. This small school became a breeding ground for Argentinean talent and a place to discuss local and international developments in the field of jewelry.

Although the last two decades of the twentieth century mostly represented a void in the production of experimental jewelry in Latin America, it may be considered as an era of intense training. Some makers traveled and studied in Europe, becoming familiar with developments in the Western arena of contemporary jewelry. Upon their return home they became

Jorge Castañón
Caja Amarilla (The Yellow Box), 2008
6 x 6 x 1 cm
Found wood, 24-karat gold, sterling silver, steel; constructed
Photo by Maria Eugenia Corries / Jorge Castañón
Courtesy of Otro Diseño

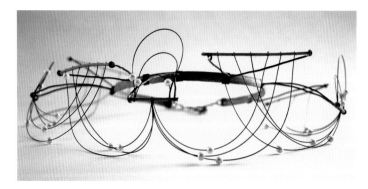

Andrés Quiñones
Gorguera, 2000
Recovered bamboo, silver, freshwater pearls, guitar strings
Photo by Kristian Lutzenkirchen
Courtesy of Otro Diseño

Norman Aboudu
Untitled
Photo by German Santiago
Courtesy of the artist

key figures in shaping the young generation forming the current jewelry landscape by creating schools and designing study programs that incorporated some of the ideas they had encountered abroad. Andrés Quiñones, a sculpture graduate from the Academia de la Esmeralda, for example, studied jewelry making with Aurelina Soto in Mexico City. In 1987, Quiñones enrolled in the Department of Visual Arts at the Escola Massana in Barcelona and traveled through Great Britain and the Netherlands, where he was deeply impressed by the colorful, playful jewelry made of inexpensive or discarded materials. After returning to Mexico, Quiñones engaged in intensive research about the values of traditional jewelry. This resulted in the decision to never buy a single material to create his ornaments. The monstrous social and economic contrasts in his country became a source of reflection for him, and he spent the next two decades collecting discarded materials in the huge waste dumps on the outskirts of Mexico City. The notion of creating luxury items like jewelry from the refuse of Mexico's unequal society fueled the intricately delicate constructions that formed his body of work.

Haitian artist Norman Aboudu grew up in Cuba and studied drawing and sculpture at the Academia Nacional de Bellas Artes San Alejandro (San Alejandro National Academy of Fine Arts) in Havana. His first contact with jewelry was through Brazilian landscape architect and jewelry designer Roberto Burle Marx; working as his assistant, Aboudu became acquainted with the jewelry work of Burle Marx's bother, Haroldo, and some of his peers, including Mourão and the Danish jeweler Kjeld Boesen. In 1981 he traveled to Paris to study at the École BJOP de la Bijouterie-Joaillerie (BJOP Jewelry School). After returning to Cuba, Aboudu continued his career as a visual artist, becoming part of the Cuban art renaissance. Focusing on subjects like politics, migration and marginalization, Aboudu, like many artists of his generation who approached these matters through alternative media, made jewelry his medium of choice. The artist explored the impact of colonialism on the present and the way that modern-day poverty is connected with an unshakable historical process, particularly addressing the tensions created by the illegal immigration of Haitians to the Dominican Republic and of Cubans to the United States. He collected a wide variety of items (textiles, toys, jewelry, cooking utensils, religious paraphernalia, photographs, etc.) that had "migrated" along with their owners from one country to another, then transformed them into ornaments (necklaces, brooches, masks and hair pieces) that incorporated some elements of the host culture. In his small atelier in Cienfuegos, Aboudu started to change the rigid Cuban approach to jewelry making; his teaching was always linked to intense conceptual and material exploration. Artist Marlen Piloto Vázquez, one of Aboudu's students, successfully transferred his approach to the jewelry course at the Academia San Alejandro, one of the first art academies in Latin America to incorporate jewelry into their curricula.

Alexander Bourtteia
Chained, 2007
Silver, lead, sea bean
Photo by Pierre Bouclé
Courtesy of Otro Diseño

The Contemporary Jewelry Scene

By the mid-1990s, the Internet, with its tremendous impact on global culture and commerce, marked a new stage in the development of contemporary jewelry in Latin America. The increased interconnectedness and interdependence of people and countries meant an easier and faster circulation of goods, services, finance, people and ideas across international borders. Jewelry artists from Latin America had the opportunity to travel easily to Europe and the United States to enroll in prestigious jewelry academies.

Between the late 1990s and early 2000s, there was an influx of European artists into Latin America who were as interested in learning about its craft and jewelry traditions as in understanding the past and present of the continent and in nurturing relations with its people. Among these artists were Cape Verdian–Dutch Alcides Fortes, whose impeccable ability to communicate powerfully on an aesthetic level contrasted with a caustic sense of humor in his approach to the crude matters—corruption, social disparity, veiled racism and increasing violence—that suffuse all aspects of life in Mexico. Likewise, the German Beate Eismann successfully merged industrial production and crafting techniques to translate the imagery and symbolism often found in Mexican literature and popular songs into an extensive series of brooches, necklaces and rings. French–South African former watchmaker and visual artist Alexander Bourtteia arrived in Belize in 1998 and became interested in the role that the African diaspora had in contouring the country's biological and cultural landscapes. He applied his precise skills and artistic sensibility to creating minimal but meticulously constructed pieces that narrated the various episodes of African history in that nation. The ideas of these artists, who also engaged in the organization of workshops, conferences and exhibitions that intensified the exchange between local jewelers and jewelers from other Latin American

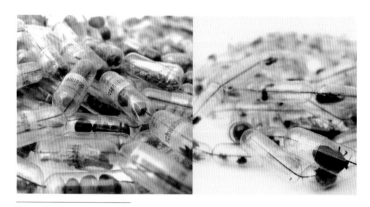

Helena Biermann Angel
Life and Death, 2004
Life (left), 1132 x 0.7 x 0.7 cm;
Death (right), 1445 x 0.7 x 0.7 cm
521 types of seeds, approximately
1500 insects, gelatin capsules
Photo by Ziad Ragheb

Carolina Hornauer Olivares
The Collector (El Coleccionista), 2009
120 x 2 cm
Tinted hair, polki (wool headband covered with hollow silver hemispheres), burnt wood, magnets, iron wire, enameled copper, stone; fabricated, crocheted, textured, cast
Photo by Antonio Corcuera
Courtesy of the artist

Maria Constanza Ochoa
Soft Black and White, 2007
25 x 25 x 3.5 cm
Latex balloons, flour, plastic
Photo by artist
Courtesy of Otro Diseño

countries and from outside the continent, had a deep impact on their local communities.

As the influx of ideas and creative vitality intensified with the physical and virtual mobility of jewelers, the first generation of Latin Americans to take up contemporary jewelry as a vocation emerged in the early years of the new millennium. In 2001 Peu de Reina was formed by Argentinean, Spanish and Portuguese makers who had studied together at the Escola Massana as a collective initiative to organize exchange projects between the three countries. In 2002, Colombian artist Andrés Fonseca founded the Experimental Jewellery Laboratory at the National Autonomous University of Mexico, currently one of the most innovative jewelry academies in Latin America. Claudia Betancourt and Ricardo Pulgar founded Walka Studio in Chile in 2003 as a project aimed at developing creativity and innovation in the field of contemporary craft and jewelry. The couple currently runs a jewelry school; organizes workshops, lectures and exhibitions both in Chile and in neighboring countries; and has gained the continuous support of important organizations such as ProChile and UNESCO. In Brazil, Projeto Nova Joia, founded by Mirla Fernandes, began in 2007 with a series of national exhibitions and later created national and international partnerships to encourage the academic field in Brazil and to promote Brazilian artists in the international arena.

In 2010 the Gray Area Symposium gathered all these organizations and a large group of jewelry artists, researchers and enthusiasts from Latin America and Europe in Mexico City to discuss their own perspectives on contemporary jewelry. The symposium served to make Latin American organizations and individuals aware of the importance of developing a continental connection, and it has encouraged them to commit to the construction of a pan-American notion of contemporary jewelry that addresses regional history, tradition and present-day culture while engaging in the global discussion.

The jewelry art currently produced in Latin America is able to generate both national and transitional communication, delivering a consistent flow of ornaments full of meaning and vitality that—despite being tremendously varied in scope— share and combine some intrinsic elements that give them their particular character. The makers have committed to a career in contemporary jewelry. They come from the most diverse educational backgrounds, many of them from art academies, but also from other fields such as medicine, biology, chemistry, anthropology and architecture. This becomes evident in their choice of materials and themes or the formal and technical execution of their work. These makers have good technical skills, a well-informed sense of aesthetics and the ability to tackle conceptual themes. They show a sensible approach to materials and processes. Their work borrows liberally from various fields, including photography, installation, performance, crafts, fashion and design. Contemporary jewelry continues to develop in close relation to the fine arts.

Being a combination of different styles and influences, contemporary jewelry in Latin America has a hybrid nature. It fuses seemingly diverse references, concepts and materials, both local and foreign, reflecting the historic mix of people and the new dimension the continent has acquired in the age of global mobility. The jewelry conveys the regional and personal identity of its makers, who strive to develop an individual language that allows them to express who they are and explain the culture they come from. The work shows a preoccupation with the continent's historical development and its current socioeconomic and political realities, as well as with personal and emotional subjects. Themes such as gender, family, art, religion, celebration, death, violence and tradition take priority and are negotiated in a highly narrative and expressive manner as well as through abstract or conceptual solutions.

Furthermore, contemporary jewelry seeks to reconcile tradition and modernity. Contemporary jewelers strive to find ways to reach a balance between what they are and where they come from, between the richness of the past and the abundance of the contemporary world. They often focus on pre-Columbian and colonial techniques, the reinterpretation of vernacular jewelry practices, the reinvention of traditional craft techniques and an innovative approach to ancient materials to create body ornaments that play off conventional expectations.

Finally, these jewelers are highly resourceful. Across the continent, many have made an art of improvisation, the intelligent use of native materials and the sensible exploitation of available resources. They demonstrate that recycling and sustainable principles need not be a constraint, but rather a source of differentiation.

Ximena Briceño
Pebbles on the Shore of Eternity, 2010
6 x 14 x 3 cm
Titanium filigree; laser welded, electrochemically anodized
Photo by Johannes Kuhnen
Courtesy of Otro Diseño

Nilton Cunha
The Colour of the Seasons I–III, 2010
Silver, gold, enamel
Photo by Romy Tembuyser
Courtesy of the artist

Notes

1. The term *indigenism* has often been equated with the Western term *primitivism*. However, in Europe primitivism represented the search for the other, and indigenism in Latin America meant just the opposite: the search for the self as part of a Latin American identity. "The implications of this movement, which surpassed modernism, still permeate Latin America's cultural production," as discussed by Michelle Greet in *Beyond National Identity: Pictorial Indigenism as a Modernist Strategy in Andean Art, 1920–1960* (University Park: Penn State University Press, 2009).

2. Samuel B. Cherson, "Lo Latino en el Arte," *Revista Urbe*, February 1975: 30.

3. The word *haptic* refers to the sense of touch, which involves not only the surface of the skin but also the tactile-muscular and tactile-kinesthetic senses, which are inherently spatial. The notion of "haptic space" is not based purely on touch alone, nor on the duality between toucher and touched. It is "an orientation to sensuality as such that includes all senses," according to Iris Marion Young, *Throwing Like a Girl: And Other Essays in Feminist Philosophy and Social Theory* (Bloomington: Indiana University Press, 1990). See page 192.

Further Reading

Davis, Mary L., and Greta Pack. *Mexican Jewelry*. Austin: University of Texas Press, 1963.

Fernández, Sylvia, and Gui Bonsiepe. *Historia del diseño en América Latina y el Caribe*. São Paulo, Brazil: Editora Blucher, 2008.

García Canclini, Néstor. *Arte Popular y Sociedad en América Latina*. Mexico City: Editorial Grijalbo, 1977.

Montecino, Sonia. *Sol viejo, sol vieja: Lo femenino en las representaciones Mapuche*. Santiago, Chile: SERNAM, 1996.

Mosquera, Gerardo. *Caminar con el diablo: Textos sobre arte, internacionalismo y culturas*. Barcelona: Exit Publicaciones, 2010.

Ortiz, Fernando. *Cuban Counterpoint: Tobacco and Sugar*. Havana: J. Montero Editor, 1940.

Paz, Octavio. *Convergences: Essays on Art and Literature*. Oxford: Berg, 1990.

Plazas, Clemencia. "El Caso Mesoamericano." *Gray Area Gris, Mexico City 2010*. Mexico City: Biblioteca Nacional de México, 2010.

Root, Regina A., ed. *The Latin American Fashion Reader*. Oxford: Berg, 2005.

Vallarta, Valeria. *Think Twice: New Latin American Jewellery*. Amsterdam: Otro Diseño, 2008.

Wagner, Renato. *Joia Contemporanea Brasileira*. São Paulo: Câmara Brasileira do Livro, 1980.

Australasia.

Damian Skinner

Introduction

From one perspective, Australia and Aotearoa New Zealand, together known as Australasia, have a great deal in common. Both countries have their origins in the British Empire, with formal settlement beginning in Australia in 1788 with the founding of the colony of New South Wales, and in New Zealand around 1840, when the Treaty of Waitangi was signed between the British crown and the indigenous Māori. The settler colonialism that took place in both countries was founded on the eradication of the indigenous peoples, achieved through various social, cultural and military strategies that reinforced the idea of an empty land waiting to be inhabited by new arrivals. Apart from the shared ties to Britain, many other links unite the two countries. In 1901, when the Australian states entered into a federation, creating modern Australia, New Zealand was invited to join, but decided not to. ANZAC Day, which stands for the Australian and New Zealand Army Corps, is a major day of remembrance in both places, remembering the Gallipoli campaign of World War I. Although a military failure, the heroic actions of Australasian troops became an important part of Australian and New Zealand national identity. Numerous other cultural, political and economic factors, such as the Closer Economic Relations free-trade agreement and the fact that half a million New Zealanders live in Australia, bind the countries together.

From another perspective, Australia and New Zealand are quite different. Australia is a continent. Its Aboriginal peoples, who belong to distinct language and social groups, have been living in the region for many thousands of years. In this hunter-gatherer society, knowledge, rather than property such as adornment or objects, indicated an individual's power and social standing. For example, a design itself (and the associated knowledge) was important, not necessarily its particular manifestation on a body or an object. In contrast, New Zealand is a chain of islands, and the people who would become Māori arrived around 900 years ago. While tribal dialects and differences in social and cultural practices did develop, Māori were still closely related to each other, and produced a large range of highly decorated objects, from architecture to body adornment. These differences were to have a profound effect on the development of the two countries, with European settlers much more willing to acknowledge (even if they didn't respect) Māori as first inhabitants of the land, as opposed to in Australia, where

Helge Larsen and Darani Lewers
Neckring, ca. 1967
9 x 17 x 0.7 cm
Sterling silver; fabricated forms
threaded on wire
Photo by Sotha Bourn
Powerhouse Museum, Sydney.
Gift of Marea Gazzard through
the Australian Government's
Cultural Gifts Program, 2006

the legal fiction of *terra nullius*—land belonging to no one—dismissed the fact of Aborigines as the original residents.

In terms of jewelry, Australia and New Zealand have broadly parallel histories. Indigenous adornment practices were the first forms of jewelry, and colonial jewelry in both countries was heavily indebted to British jewelry trends of the nineteenth century. The mineral wealth of Australia, especially—gold, pearls and opals—was celebrated in jewelry made in the colonies, which tended to follow the European model of naturalistic jewelry, with local flora and fauna replacing English motifs. The Arts and Crafts Movement flourished in Australasia and promoted the recording, cultivating and illustrating of native plants and wildlife, thus offering many opportunities to create local identities for the European settlers. The various movements (modernism, the critique of preciousness, etc.) that make up the history of contemporary jewelry have also been adopted and adapted by Australasian jewelers.

And yet one difficulty in writing a history of Australasian, as opposed to Australian and New Zealand, jewelry, is that these histories are parallel rather than integrated. Although strong political and cultural ties span the Tasman Sea and link the two countries, contemporary jewelry has tended to develop independently in each place, with surprisingly few interactions. New Zealand jewelers have generally proved reluctant to engage with the world at large, and even with their colleagues across the Tasman. In contrast, Australian jewelers have, from very early moments in the history of contemporary jewelry, projected themselves offshore and insistently pursued a place within a larger, international narrative of contemporary jewelry.[1]

Modernist Jewelry in Australasia

The story of modernist jewelry in both countries is a story of immigration. In the 1950s and '60s, a wave of European gold- and silversmiths came to Australasia, bringing with them new ideas about jewelry that would transform the practice from a trade into an art form. It's difficult to talk about this period without ending up with a list of names and dates—beginning with German jeweler Wolf Wennrich, who arrived in Melbourne in 1953, and Dutch jeweler Ida Hudig, who settled in Wellington the same year, and ending, perhaps, with Norwegian jeweler Ragnar Hansen, who came to Australia in 1972, working first at the Sturt workshops in Mittagong, a small country town in New South Wales, before moving to Tasmania. But such a list, while historically accurate, doesn't say much about the modernist jewelry that resulted from this intensive wave of arrivals, and its impact and relationship to the local cultural production.[2]

In the work of Danish jeweler Helge Larsen and his Australian wife and partner Darani Lewers, modernism was abstract and organic, featuring textured, pitted surfaces of silver with the addition of locally sourced natural materials and polished semiprecious stones, "treated as a formal element complementing the metalwork, rather than as a precious point of focus."[3] For British silversmith Tanya Ashken, who settled in Wellington, New Zealand, in 1963, modernist jewelry drew on the aesthetic model of British and European modernist sculpture. Abstract, organic and concerned with an honest engagement with the character and quality of the materials, Ashken's jewelry was small, wearable sculpture that balanced craftsmanship and artistic expression to create formal relationships with a dynamic tension that ensured the abstract didn't become the purely decorative. Wennrich practiced a modernism that, informed by developments in German contemporary jewelry, promoted jewelry as an art form that could, as his work eventually did, leave the body behind. Unlike the dominant varieties of Australasian modernism, which were allied to Scandinavian aesthetics, Wennrich's *Objects* (as he titled them) embraced new materials such as acrylic and tackled themes such as spirituality and war, or the place of humanity in the world—somewhat unusual subjects for modernist jewelry.

The skilled craftsmanship, bold forms, restrained decoration and tasteful natural references of Scandinavian jewelry certainly had a big impact in Australasia. Interestingly, this type of modernism was celebrated as an antidote to the "Australian ugliness" and "featurism," a dishonest dependence on surface elements that spoiled the Australian suburbs.[4] Exhibitions such as Design for Living (1962) and Design in Scandinavia (1968) toured Australia, promoting the message that this style, with its natural materials and organic modernism, was democratic, human and craft-based. In New Zealand, the "Scandinavian urbane" became part of what was known as Pan-Pacific modernism, in which the tenets of international modernism were blended with Pacific style to suit the local conditions.[5]

The pioneering European jewelers who arrived in the 1950s and '60s not only brought skills and ideas about the aesthetics and artistic possibilities of jewelry, but they also became

Tanya Ashken
Pendant, late 1960s
12 x 6.8 x 1.8 cm
Sterling silver, Venus hairstone
rock crystal
Photo by Haru Samishima
Courtesy of the artist

Kobi Bosshard
Pendant, 1977
8.8 x 8 cm
Sterling silver
Artist's collection

Wolf Wennrich
Object, 1974
7.7 x 7.7 x 4.7 cm
Silver, acrylic, steel, brass
Photo by Margund Sallowsky
W. E. McMillan Collection,
Royal Melbourne Institute of
Technology, School of Art and
Design

important teachers. This was especially true in Australia, which had a formal, government-funded education system for contemporary jewelry much earlier than New Zealand, where such courses were not widely available until the 1980s. Working with Danish jeweler Jens Hansen in his workshop or completing an apprenticeship with Swiss jeweler Kobi Bosshard were some of the few ways New Zealanders could, in the late '60s, gain access to ideas and practices of jewelry that moved beyond the conventional.[6] In Australia, European jewelers were central to developing networks and institutions. Helge Larsen taught metalsmithing and design at the University of New South Wales, then established the jewelry course at the Sydney College of the Arts, which was an important institutional platform for the dialogue between jewelry and the fine arts. The Czech silversmith Victor Vodicka, followed by Wolf Wennrich, turned the gold- and silversmithing course at the Royal Melbourne Institute of Technology (now RMIT University) in Melbourne into a leading institution critical in the development of subsequent generations of Australian contemporary jewelers.

The new forms of contemporary jewelry in Australasia were supported by the growth of infrastructure at a public and private level, opening up exhibition opportunities. New Zealand's Queen Elizabeth II Arts Council, established in 1963, organized exhibitions such as New Zealand Crafts 1972, which toured overseas and included the jewelry of Bosshard, Hansen and Ashken. The Crafts Council of Australia, established in 1971, helped organize international exhibitions such as Australian Jewellery (1974), which took Australia to the world, and 10 British Jewellers (1976), which brought the world to Australia.

The Critique of Preciousness

The critique of preciousness was the next development in contemporary jewelry to have a significant impact in Australasia. Introducing new materials to replace the precious substances traditionally used in jewelry production, the critique of preciousness also revolutionized the meaning and potential of jewelry by divorcing the value of the object from the value of the materials used to create it. Jewelry became more democratic, and more alert to the relationship between the object and the body on which it was worn. Although the use of new materials (such as acrylic and aluminum) was the most obvious sign of the effects of the critique of preciousness, it also ushered in a conceptual revolution that matched the formal and material transformations.

Exhibitions like Guaranteed Trash in 1978, held at Fingers cooperative gallery in Auckland, showed how the aesthetic and social possibilities of the critique of preciousness met the social energies and cultural revolution of punk and alternative culture, resulting in jewelry made from a McDonalds milkshake cup, a pink toothbrush with fake toothpaste and diamond, a forty-five record and even a smoked fish on a string.[7] At the opposite end of the cultural scale, the move away from precious materials and conventional meanings in jewelry encouraged New Zealand jewelers to embrace the hippie movement. In 1980, Peter Cape described New Zealand contemporary jewelry as a craft practice with its origins in the talisman and the amulet. Arguing that jewelry lost most of this significance in its dalliance with wealth and status, Cape believed the '70s marked a return to jewelry's origins in such objects of power. He framed this within a rise of social interest in alternative belief systems, "from a preoccupation with one's place in the circle of the Zodiac, through the powers of the Tarot cards, and on to the elegantly diffuse mysteries of the I-Ching," and concluded that "the movement towards talismanic jewellery (as opposed to jewellery which is worn as embellishment, or to demonstrate wealth or taste) has been reflected in studio jewellery in New Zealand over the past ten years."[8]

With such ideas circulating in New Zealand culture at large, it wasn't surprising that contemporary jewelry and contemporary bone and stone carving became closely identified in this period. A pioneering generation of stone carvers, including Theo Schoon, Bill Mathieson and Donn Salt, were joined by younger makers such as John Edgar, while bone carvers such as Owen Mapp and Dave Hegglun made objects and adornment that connected alternative social movements with Māori art.

In Australia there was a similar connection between the freedom of the critique of preciousness and new expressions of national identity. The 1977 exhibition Ten Australian Jewellers marks the transition very well; the predominantly modernist jewelry of the earlier exhibition Australian Jewellery was replaced with more experimental jewelry that suggested a very different idea of Australian culture. Peter Tully's *Australian Fetish Necklace* (1977) is a plastic chain necklace with Perspex and wooden elements representing national symbols. His work represented a movement in Australasian jewelry in which theatrical, flamboyant and hybrid jewelry objects with references to

Owen Mapp
Fern Pendants, 1970s
6.5 x 4.5 x 0.7 cm
Cow bone
Photo by Hanne Eriksen Mapp
Courtesy of the artist

Peter Tully
Australian Fetish Necklace,
1977
37 cm long
Colored acrylic, colored oil paint, gum nuts, metal
National Gallery of Australia, Canberra
Crafts Board of the Australia Council Collection 1980

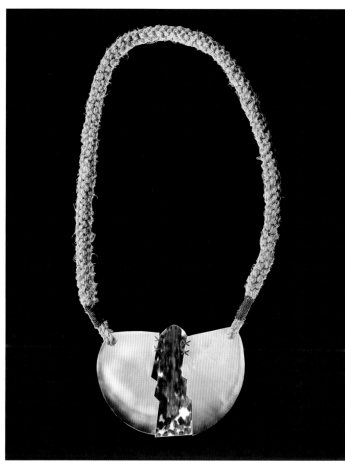

Alan Preston
Breastplate, 1987
3.1 x 58.5 x 20.5 cm
Mother-of-pearl, gold-lipped
oyster shell, tortoiseshell,
'afa (coconut husk fiber), vau
(hibiscus bark fiber)
Photo by Michael Chittenden
Commissioned by the New
Zealand Ministry of Foreign
Affairs
Gift of the Friends of the
Museum of New Zealand Te
Papa Tongarewa, 1993

indigenous adornment helped define a new kind of tribe at home in the city.[9]

Primitivism refers to the appropriation of non-Western art in European art and cultural practices, and this is an important movement in Australasian jewelry. Tully represents one approach, in which a kind of generalized style of ethnic adornment is used to channel Australian identity. But this primitivist turn is most clearly expressed in New Zealand contemporary jewelry of the late 1970s and early '80s. As jewelers internationally explored new materials and new relationships between jewelry and the body, New Zealand jewelers turned their attention to Oceania. They embraced natural materials like shell, stone and fiber, and looked to Māori and Pacific adornment to understand how best to handle such materials—from both a technical and an aesthetic aspect.[10] In the hands of a jeweler like Alan Preston, New Zealand contemporary jewelry became, in works like *Breastplate*, a kind of contemporary Pacific adornment. The materials are similar to those used in older Pacific objects, and the way the materials are joined is a modern and ornamental interpretation of canoe construction techniques. No breastplate in a museum collection is quite like this, but Preston openly declares his relationship to breastplates and the history of adornment found in the Pacific.

As a result of the critique of preciousness, the body was placed at center stage within contemporary jewelry practice. Once jewelers shrugged off their preoccupation with valuable materials and an alliance with privilege, contemporary jewelry became available for an entirely different kind of investigation. The 1982 exhibition Skin Sculpture, which included both New Zealand and Australian jewelers, was really a showcase of "wearable art," and this became an important trend in the 1980s, especially in Australian jewelry. The political potential of this practice was addressed in Worn Issues: Low Cost Jewellery Related to Environmental Issues in Australia, which took place in Sydney in 1984 and challenged the idea of an autonomous jewelry scene that set itself apart from worldly concerns. Although it shared the common reaction against jewelry as a means of storing wealth, it attempted a new direction by changing the means of distribution, rather than only experimenting with new materials. For example, a marketing survey was conducted before the exhibition to ensure the objects met the needs of the intended audience.

The New Jewelry

Contemporary jewelry in Australasia took on two distinct trajectories in the 1980s. Jewelers in both countries found quite different ways to respond to the experimental turn in international jewelry that was named "the new jewelry" in an important book by Peter Dormer and Ralph Turner, published in 1985. Australian jewelers aggressively demonstrated their desire to collapse geography, to escape the tyranny of distance and move beyond the "Australiana" (kangaroos and gum trees) that began to represent a provincial and uninteresting sense of difference. In New Zealand, jewelers absorbed the lessons from international jewelry but articulated a regionalist stance that downplayed connections to Europe in favor of a unique, local approach that emphasized its difference through primitivism. Contemporary jewelry in Australasia became ambitious, making the most of a porous border with fine art and the freedom of critique and experimentation. If adornment became an even more important question in both countries, then the issue of place marked a substantial divergence in attitude and positioning.

This difference can be seen in the two major exhibitions of the 1980s. There's a nice contrast between Bone Stone Shell: New Jewellery New Zealand (1988) and Cross Currents: Jewellery from Australia, Britain, Germany, Holland (1986). Whereas Bone Stone Shell made the most of what was distinctive and different about New Zealand jewelry, such as the use of local, natural materials and references to Pacific adornment, Cross Currents demonstrated that Australian jewelry was as good as anything else happening internationally by actually putting local jewelers alongside their colleagues from other countries.[11]

In the '80s, Australian jewelry was framed through its relationship to European movements, and the Australians included in Cross Currents certainly worked in a way that was highly compatible with the European jewelers selected for the exhibition. As Susanna Heron wrote in her introduction to the British jewelers, "A number of artists and designers were essentially rethinking the idea of jewellery: the methods by which it is worn, the meaning of what is worn, the relationship to the body, materials, techniques and accessibility to the public."[12] Rowena Gough, for example, whose jewelry was featured in Cross Currents, began making works such as *Reptilia* (1986), which unfolds from a rectangular, mechanical-looking "box" into a flexible skin or carapace whose graphite

Rowena Gough
Reptilia, 1986
385 x 47 cm
Japanese kozo paper,
watercolor, graphite
Photo by Ian Tudor
Collection of the artist

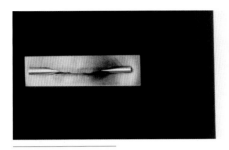

Anne Brennan
"A Subject Is Raised Which
the Liar Wishes Buried"
(object for the mouth, detail
from the series *Something
Altogether Else)*, 1986
Dimensions vary
Gelatin silver photograph, brass
Photo by Michael Kluvanek
Collection of the artist

Margaret West
Bib (protection factor 3.7),
1982
38 x 16 x 0.3 cm
Lead, stainless steel
Photo by artist

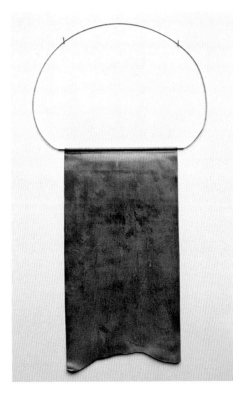

coating leaves gray traces on the wearer. In their embrace of new materials, their relationship to clothing and their intersection with performance, these dramatic works were an investigation of how the jewelry object and body interact when ideas of scale and wearability are challenged. They are clearly related to the so-called "wearables" of Heron and others.

Other Australian jewelers demonstrated the artistic potential of jewelry. Anne Brennan's metal structures were inserted into the wearer's mouth to inhibit speech. These are forms of adornment that constrain and repress the body as well as enhance it, and belong to a feminist project that drew on psychoanalysis and other theories. Margaret West, who taught at the Sydney College of the Arts and had a critical effect on a generation of graduates who moved fluidly among different visual arts, pursued jewelry as a form of fine art. This was not achieved by denying jewelry history and forms in her work (turning it into sculpture), but by developing a poetic language of materials, in which substances such as lead contributed political and metaphorical associations to the work, which might just as often be an installation as a brooch or necklace. Although it would be difficult to wear, *Bib (protection factor 3.7)* doesn't hide its connections to jewelry.[13]

The exhibition Bone Stone Shell also claimed a relationship between New Zealand and European jewelry, but rather than suggest a similarity, the point was to emphasize a difference. "A recent trend in contemporary jewellery has been to use non-precious materials in such a way as to put them in contrast with the inflated value of materials such as gold and diamonds," wrote the curator, John Edgar, in the catalog. "While the monetary value of bone, stone and shell is low, the focus on them here is to establish and proclaim their real aesthetic value in our culture."[14] The point was not to eradicate preciousness from contemporary jewelry, but to refurbish the concept and create a new kind of preciousness that spoke more directly to contemporary forms of identity. Gold and diamonds gave way to abalone and pearl shell, to bone and stone, and these materials became precious to local audiences through the work of contemporary jewelers. The subjects that New Zealand jewelry addressed were diverse, as Roy Mason's mother-of-pearl necklace, bangle and brooch against nuclear testing in the Pacific demonstrates, but the beauty and local resonance of natural materials were often critical to the meaning, as Warwick Freeman's *Paua Bead Necklace* suggests—a string of "pearls" for the proud and culturally aware New Zealander.

The Return to Jewelry

In the 1990s, contemporary jewelers turned away from the experimental nature of "the new jewelry." The idea that contemporary jewelry was a kind of art practice faltered in the face of the obvious lack of interest from the art world: no departments of contemporary jewelry had been established in Australasian art galleries and museums, for example. Contemporary jewelry realigned itself with its craft origins, and jewelers embraced jewelry as an object able to circulate in the everyday world and shape relationships between people. Interestingly, this turn happened at the same time that the ranks of New Zealand contemporary jewelers were swollen by the flood of graduates from the craft design courses that had been established in polytechnics around the country in the 1980s. Formal training, and a greatly expanded infrastructure for contemporary jewelry, however, did not result in the same experimental jewelry promoted by "the new jewelry" movement in the previous decade.

Australian jeweler Susan Cohn is notable for her positioning of contemporary jewelry as a design practice.[15] In a series of exhibitions at the Anna Schwartz Gallery in Melbourne, she systematically investigated the nature and possibilities of jewelry. And Does It Work? (1989) presented ornamental technology, including microphones, headphones and security passes, that were meticulous, functionless copies. Cosmetic Manipulations (1992) explored the relationship between jewelry and self-fashioning. The modernist assumptions of contemporary jewelry—such as authenticity, the original, preciousness—were the target of Way Past Real (1994), which consisted of an installation of her signature donut bracelets, all precisely the same in appearance even though most were anodized gold aluminum, a few were gold-plate and one was pure gold. Reflections on a Safe Future (1995) included the condom pendant *Laliquiana*. With its repurposed Oakley sunglass lenses and Sony technology, this was jewelry of its time in both materials and concept, raising questions about safe sex and personal choice. Catch Me (1998) was a jewelry-specific investigation of necklace components, and Survival Habits (1999) considered the role of jewelry in an uncertain future. Grounded in a design framework, Cohn's practice thinks through the implications and possibilities of the multiple, a process for making democratic jewelry that can reach many people. But this framework also shifts the conversation

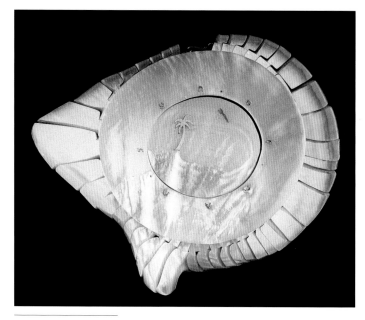

Roy Mason
Sun of man neckpiece, sun of man bangle, sun of man brooch, 1988
Neckpiece diameter, 17 x 18 cm; bangle diameter, 18 cm; brooch diameter, 7 cm
Gold-lipped oyster shell, mother-of-pearl, mercury, silver
Photo by Michael Chittenden
Commissioned by the New Zealand Ministry of Foreign Affairs
Gift of the Friends of the Museum of New Zealand Te Papa Tongarewa, 1993

Warwick Freeman
Paua Bead Necklace, 1986
3 m long
Paua shell, silver, fiber
Commissioned by the New Zealand Ministry of Foreign Affairs
Gift of the Friends of the Museum of New Zealand Te Papa Tongarewa, 1993

around innovation away from the artistic expression that's the default position of contemporary jewelry, and into discussions of technology, social function and user experience.

The social possibilities of contemporary jewelry were also investigated by Australian jeweler Barbara Heath. In 1991 she produced a manifesto that clearly articulated her notion of jewelry as a craft practice. "I will own the role of jeweller within my community. My home will not be separate from my workplace—nor will my work be separate from other aspects of my life—I will construct a whole world out of it." Stating that she wished to be known as a jeweler, rather than as an artist or a designer, she concluded, "I will see jewellery as a vehicle for human interaction and as a jeweller I will be given the voice to be given the hand to serve my clients."[16] Heath often works with found or provided objects, attending to the requirements of the wearer/owner and the objects themselves. As "Jeweler to the Lost," both the title of an exhibition at the Queensland Art Gallery in 2005 and a title she assumed in 1990, Heath makes jewelry that often features very subtle interventions, designed to enhance existing meanings, rather than assume the rights and responsibilities of making an artistic statement.[17]

Settler/Indigenous

Settler societies like Australia and New Zealand, founded on acts of violence that displaced the original inhabitants, raise complex social, political and cultural issues, many of which are about the land and its role in the identities constructed by indigenous peoples and settler populations. Settler culture is concerned with the process of becoming indigenous, and contemporary jewelry has played its part in articulating the relationship between settlers and the land they inhabit. This, for example, is one of the reasons why Australasian jewelry is filled with references to native flora and fauna. While these have been features of both colonial and Arts and Crafts jewelry, contemporary jewelers have proven particularly insightful in working through the implications of jewelry references to nature.

Marian Hosking's *Tall Tree Project* (2005–2007) is a thin silver ribbon that reproduces the surface of a huge Errinundra shining gum tree in Victoria's Gippsland forest. Notably, Hosking avoids the spectacular and iconic in favor of a close-up, jewelry-scale focus on texture and the tactile qualities of the Australian bush—something that, like jewelry, must be experienced on an intimate, personal scale.[18] New Zealand

jeweler Lynn Kelly plays with the preeminent role that nature has in creating New Zealand identity. Her work explores the rich symbolism of botanical specimens recreated in a variety of materials. Plants, like people and cultural practices, travel extensively around the globe, and Kelly productively mines this potential. Her series of brooches and pendants based on specimens of plants collected by Joseph Banks, who visited New Zealand in 1769 as part of James Cook's first voyage, relates to the history and meaning of flowers and plants as decorative elements within jewelry from different periods and places. This series also speaks to the specific cultural processes of identity at work in New Zealand.

A major story in New Zealand jewelry from the 1990s to the present is the emergence of a generation of Māori and Pacific Islander contemporary jewelers who apply the tools of contemporary jewelry to a series of questions tied intimately to the concerns of indigenous people and Pacific Island populations. In 1999, the exhibition 1 Noble Savage, 2 Dusky Maidens presented the work of Pacific Island jewelers Chris Charteris, Sofia Tekela-Smith and Niki Hastings-McFall. Photographed for the cover of the catalog in sepia tones, against a backdrop of tapa cloth, wearing grass skirts and shell necklaces, these jewelers wittily declared what contemporary jewelry might have to offer to contemporary Pacific identity (and vice versa): a playful appropriation of Pacific adornment at once ironic and serious.[19] Clearly these urban, sophisticated jewelers aren't noble savages or dusky maidens, precisely because they claim the stereotype to gain control of the history they represent. Hastings-McFall's lei made from Weed Eater nylon continues the tradition of Pacific adoption of modern materials such as plastic in customary forms while also commenting on the economic condition of Pacific Island peoples in urban New Zealand who disproportionately work in low-wage jobs.

The work of Māori jeweler Areta Wilkinson doesn't seek to copy traditional Māori forms of adornment, which are also currently being made, but rather uses the materials and traditions of contemporary jewelry as it has developed internationally and in Australasia to create jewelry that reflects Māori ideas about the world, the body and the roles and functions of adornment. Wilkinson brings the self-reflexive nature of contemporary jewelry—what distinguishes contemporary from other forms of jewelry—to bear on the world of Māori adornment. In doing so, she can ask questions such as what it means to be Māori in the modern world, and

Marian Hosking
Tall Tree Project (detail), 2006
17 m x 2 cm x 1 mm
Silver cast from pink jeweler's wax
Photo by Claudia Terstappen
Courtesy of the artist

Lynn Kelly
Banks Botanical Specimen Brooch, 2009
10 x 9.5 cm
Sterling silver; oxidized
Photo by artist

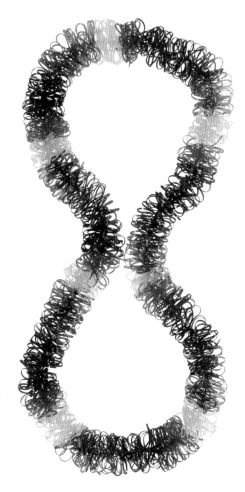

what kind of jewelry will be most able to capture the complexity of tribal identity in the present and future.[20] Her work emerges from the encounter of two things: contemporary jewelry, which she would define as a critical studio craft practice that makes objects grounded in an awareness of the body, and Māori systems of knowledge, which place people in specific relationships to each other and to the world, and which sometimes use objects to mediate these connections.

The Contemporary Jewelry Scene

Since the late 1970s, exhibitions of international jewelry in Australia have introduced local audiences to imaginative and adventurous uses of jewelry (and non-jewelry) forms and materials. Although Australian and New Zealand jewelers are aware of American jewelry, it hasn't had a wide impact beyond those jewelers who choose to engage with the jewelry scene in the United States. The values of American contemporary jewelry certainly haven't shaped Australasian jewelry in the same way as movements and ideas in European jewelry have, a surprise perhaps, given the wider social and cultural impact of America in both Australia and New Zealand. In Australia particularly, there's been a relationship with contemporary jewelry in Japan and Korea, although again this happens more on an individual or institutional level, rather than shaping the fundamental values of the scene.

Australasian jewelry is, in general terms, oriented to Europe, a relationship that has been sustained in a variety of ways. Visitors such as Paul Derrez, a major advocate of Australasian jewelers through Galerie Ra in Amsterdam, and Hermann Jünger and Otto Künzli, both professors at the Akademie der Bildenden Künste München (Academy of Fine Arts, Munich), introduced local jewelers to the seriousness and ambition of contemporary jewelry practice in Europe. Künzli also attracted a number of Australasian jewelers to study in his prestigious jewelry class in Munich, among them Lisa Walker, Sally Marsland and Helen Britton. The link between Munich/ Europe and Melbourne/Australasia has also been sustained by Gallery Funaki, opened by Mari Funaki in 1995. Until her death in 2010, Funaki brought leading European jewelers to Melbourne and created a space for Australasian jewelers to show alongside their international colleagues. In this sense, Gallery Funaki continued to promote the strategy for positioning Australian jewelry that emerged with Cross Currents in the

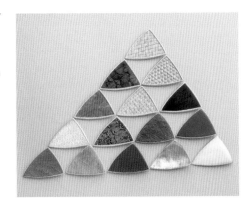

1980s. Local jewelry practice was not best understood through any references to its location in Australia but through its connections to an international field of jewelers.

New Zealand has also, in the past decade, concentrated its focus on Munich, and more widely on European jewelry. Lisa Walker's success as a graduate of Künzli's class has effectively opened up a portal between Munich and New Zealand, creating a renewed sense of the possibilities of New Zealand jewelers working internationally. The government arts funding agency, Creative New Zealand, helps young craftspeople, mostly jewelers, attend TALENTE, one of the exhibitions that make up the SCHMUCK jewelry week in Munich, if their work is selected. This kind of formal funding has been significant in focusing the attention of New Zealand jewelers; in reinforcing the importance of SCHMUCK, the annual exhibition and event; and in buttressing the sense of Munich as perhaps *the* leading contemporary jewelry center in the world.

And yet such northern connections, which echo the original colonial relationship between Australasia and Britain— the imperial center to which local practitioners aspired and followed—are also being challenged by alternative models of international networks. The most sustained example comes through Kevin Murray's curatorial activism, which proposes South-South relations (Australasia looking to other countries of the Southern Hemisphere) rather than the traditional South-North focus. His most recent project, Joyaviva: Live Jewellery Across the Pacific, brings together contemporary jewelers from Australia, New Zealand and Chile around the notion of the charm.[21] This kind of project pursues two related agendas: establishing relationships among countries in the Southern Hemisphere, which usually look north rather than horizontally, and proposing that jewelry practices in peripheral countries may have an important contribution to international debates about contemporary jewelry. The renegotiated idea of the charm at the heart of Joyaviva draws its power from indigenous cultural practices and yet also engages with the relational turn in visual art and its relevance to jewelry, the relationship between jeweler and object as well as between object and wearer, and the possibilities of jewelers interacting with communities in a new, sustained way.

Sally Marsland
Composite Brooch, 1999
6.5 x 4 x 4 cm
Acrylic paint, epoxy resin, powdered graphite, car-body filler
Photo by Tom Haartsen
Françoise van den Bosch Foundation / Stedelijk Museum Amsterdam

Blanche Tilden
The Harder I Work, the Luckier I Get, 2011
0.5 x 1.8 x 56 cm
18-karat gold, mild steel, oxidized sterling silver
Photo by Jeremy Dillon
Courtesy of the artist

Notes

1. This essay is indebted to research and ideas about contemporary jewelry in Australia and New Zealand first developed with Kevin Murray. See Damian Skinner and Kevin Murray, *Place and Adornment: A History of Contemporary Jewellery in Australia and Aotearoa New Zealand* (Auckland: David Bateman, 2013).

2. For a discussion of modernist jewelry in New Zealand, see Damian Skinner, *Kobi Bosshard: Goldsmith* (Auckland: David Bateman, 2012).

3. Judith O'Callaghan, *Helge Larsen & Darani Lewers: A Retrospective* (Melbourne: National Gallery of Victoria, 1986), 12.

4. Robyn Boyd, *The Australian Ugliness* (Melbourne: Cheshire, 1960), 10.

5. Douglas Lloyd Jenkins, *At Home: A Century of New Zealand Design* (Auckland: Godwit, 2004), 123.

6. See Judith Taylor, *The Jeweller's Mark: The Jens Hansen Workshop Story* (Nelson, New Zealand: The Suter, 2000); and Skinner, *Kobi Bosshard*.

7. Suzanne Dale, "Go punk—wear a $2000 carton!," *Sunday News*, May 7, 1978.

8. Peter Cape, Please Touch: *A Survey of the Three-Dimensional Arts in New Zealand* (Auckland: Collins, 1980), 65.

9. See John McPhee, *Peter Tully: Urban Tribalwear and Beyond* (Canberra: National Gallery of Australia, 1991).

10. See Damian Skinner, *Given: Jewellery by Warwick Freeman* (Auckland: Starform, 2004); and Damian Skinner, *Between Tides: Jewellery by Alan Preston* (Auckland: Godwit, 2008).

11. John Edgar, *Bone Stone Shell: New Jewellery New Zealand* (Wellington: Ministry of Foreign Affairs, 1988); Helge Larsen, ed., *Cross Currents: Jewellery from Australia, Britain, Germany, Holland* (Sydney: Powerhouse Museum, 1984).

12. Susanna Heron, "Notes on the Work," in *Cross Currents*, 32.

13. See Cindi Strauss, "Margaret West: Poetic Truths," *Metalsmith* 29, no. 5 (2009): 32–41.

14. Edgar, *Bone Stone Shell*, unpaginated.

15. See Brian Kennedy, Jackie Cooper, and Susan Cohn, *Techno Craft: The Work of Susan Cohn, 1980–2000* (Canberra: National Gallery of Australia, 1999).

16. Barbara Heath, "Manifesto: How are we to survive this habit?" in *There Really Is No New Jewellery.* Conference flier for the Jewellery and Metalsmithing Symposium, School of Art, University of Tasmania, 1991, unpaginated.

17. Barbara Heath, *Barbara Heath: Jeweller to the Lost* (Brisbane: Queensland Art Gallery, 2005).

18. See Claudia Terstappen and Kit Wise, eds., *Marian Hosking: Jewellery* (Sydney: Object, 2007).

19. Chris Charteris, Niki Hastings-McFall, and Sofia Tekela-Smith, *1 Noble Savage, 2 Dusky Maidens* (Auckland: Chris Charteris, Niki Hastings-McFall, Sofia Tekela-Smith, 1999).

20. See Deidre Brown, *Wai: Recollected Works, Areta Wilkinson* (Christchurch: University of Canterbury School of Fine Arts Gallery, 2000).

21. For more information, see the JoyaViva project website at www.joyaviva.net.

Further Reading

Anderson, Patricia. *Contemporary Jewellery: The Australian Experience, 1977–1987*. New South Wales: Millenium, 1988.

———. *Contemporary Jewellery in Australia and New Zealand*. Sydney: Craftsman House, 1998.

Cochrane, Grace. *The Crafts Movement in Australia: A History*. Sydney: University of New South Wales Press, 1992.

Edgar, John. *Bone Stone Shell: New Jewellery New Zealand*. Wellington: Ministry of Foreign Affairs, 1988.

Larsen, Helge, ed. *Cross Currents: Jewellery from Australia, Britain, Germany, Holland*. Sydney: Powerhouse Museum, 1984.

Murray, Kevin. *Craft Unbound: Make the Common Precious*. Sydney: Craftsman House, 2005.

Salt, Donn. *Stone, Bone and Jade: 24 New Zealand Artists*. Auckland: David Bateman, 2005.

Schofield, Anne, and Kevin Fahy. *Australian Jewellery: 19th and Early 20th Century*. Woodbridge, UK: Antique Collectors' Club, 1991.

Skinner, Damian. *Pocket Guide to New Zealand Jewelry*. San Francisco: Velvet Da Vinci, 2010.

———, and Kevin Murray. *Place and Adornment: A History of Contemporary Jewellery in Australia and Aotearoa New Zealand*. Auckland: David Bateman, 2013.

East Asia.

Chang Dong-kwang

Introduction

Korea and Japan historically have a certain degree of homogeneity in philosophy, religion and culture, largely due to the influences of Confucianism and Buddhism, and also to the fact that they share a long tradition of calligraphy with its origins in China. However, they differ in their indigenous faiths. The Japanese follow a native folk religion called Shinto, whereas Koreans turn to a form of shamanism called *Musokshinang*.

Until the start of the modern era in the later nineteenth century, these East Asian nations were united by close political, economic and cultural exchanges. In the modern era, the political landscape changed dramatically, which had a critical impact on the inception and development of contemporary jewelry in each country, introducing some significant differences.

After its forceful annexation by Japan in 1910, Korea was colonized for about 40 years. This brought about an artistic dark age of sorts, as its identity and traditions were lost or severed. Korea regained independence with the end of World War II and established a democratic republic, but in 1950 the Korean War broke out, leaving the country split into two nations. South Korea adopted American educational systems, which in turn laid the foundation for studio craft's subsequent development. The birth of contemporary jewelry in Korea dates to the 1960s when the teaching of metalsmithing was fully implemented in universities, at a time when Korean society stabilized due to economic reconstruction.

Unlike Korea, Japan was eager to embrace modernization. The 1867 Meiji Restoration led Japan to restore imperial rule and embrace Western technologies and cultures, expanding its power. Uninterrupted by invasion and civil war, modern jewelry education was led by the Tokyo National University of Fine Arts and Music (presently called Tokyo University of the Arts), founded in 1887. Art Nouveau and the Mingei Movement, a Japanese form of the Arts and Crafts Movement advocated by Yanagi Soetsu, made an impact beginning in the early twentieth century. As a result, early Japanese jewelry turned to traditional techniques and ardently applied them in its educational system, laying a foundation for contemporary jewelry.

Against this historical backdrop, this chapter explores the development of contemporary jewelry in South Korea and Japan, including how contemporary jewelry in these countries has engaged with international trends in the field.

The Origins of Contemporary Jewelry

After South Korea's sovereignty was reinstated at the end of World War II, Seoul National University, renamed and re-formed from Keijo Imperial University, opened the Department of Applied Arts under the College of Arts in 1946. Under the leadership of Lee Sun-seok, who majored in applied arts at Tokyo Fine Arts School, the department paved the way for contemporary crafts education in Korea. However, after the South rebuilt the nation from the tumult of the Korean War, it wasn't academic institutions but a government-run one, the Korea Handicraft Demonstration Center (KHDC), established in 1958, that brought Korea's craft field back to life. Austin Cox, charged with teaching metalwork and jewelry design, led workshops there that provided contemporary craft education.[1] Until 1960, when KHDC closed, the center served as an outpost for American design and educational standards and techniques. It shifted Korean crafts away from the Japanese models that had informed them previously and played a key role in fostering Korea's early craft and design pioneers, who are tied to the origins of craft (including jewelry) in a contemporary sense.[2] For example, Kwon Gil-choong, who had studied at Seoul National University in the 1950s, worked as a designer at KHDC. The Industrial Design Exhibition in 1960 included about 50 pieces of Kwon's jewelry. Crafted using very basic techniques under primitive workshop conditions, Kwon's jewelry is the first wave of what would become contemporary jewelry, although he stopped working in the field after the 1970s.

While the teaching of Korean jewelry after World War II was led by those who had studied in Japan, and American systems took root after the Korean War, in the 1970s contemporary jewelry in Korea entered a germinal stage. Since then Korean jewelers have strived to both accommodate American and European trends and reconstruct traditional aesthetics.

Postwar Japan's jewelry proved lively, with much activity in associations and groups. The Ur Accessories Association (later renamed the Ur Jewellery Association), established by Hishida Yasuhiko in 1956, was a somewhat old-fashioned organization primarily concerned with interpreting tradition—initially, its exhibitions were themed, and explored decorative styles from around the world, including the ancient Mesopotamian kingdom of Ur, after which the group was named.[3] Employing traditional sword-making techniques like chasing, metal coloring and inlay, the Ur

Jewellery Association maintained an interest in precious metals, unusual gems and traditional techniques, which makes it more a precursor to, rather than an example of, the contemporary jewelry movement as it developed in Japan.

The Japan Jewellery Designers Association (JJDA), founded in 1963 by Hishida Yasuhiko, Iwakura Koji and Hiramatsu Yasuki, led the way in contemporary jewelry by giving it purpose and significance as well as valuing it as a creative means of personal and conceptual expression. The first task was to distinguish jewelry from fashion: "The [JJDA] manifesto stated that JJDA members would stop calling their works accessories, as the word tended to signify they are attachments to hats, purses, and shoes, and thereafter call them pieces of jewellery, as this word implied that the works are artistic creations."[4] Another task was to introduce artistic expression as a key aspect of value. As founder Hishida wrote, "Our work is, of course, not merely to comment on the value, as antiques, of gemstones but to address the question of how we can design pieces to make the most of those stones' beauty. Of course, we may at times not even use gemstones. Our work encompasses the full range of design in precious metals."[5]

During the 1960s, as interest in jewelry changed, creative jewelry became tangible in Japan under the influence of European and Scandinavian designs, "including forms that were warm to the touch or shapes that were easy to use—simple forms that had much in common with modern design."[6] Tokyo National University of Fine Arts and Music and Musashino Art College were especially responsive to the international trends. Hiramatsu Yasuki, who graduated from the Tokyo National University of Fine Arts and Music in 1952, and became a professor there in 1962, represents the shifts that were taking place in the 1960s, as jewelers sought to establish jewelry forms and a vocabulary separate from those of fashion. Primarily working in gold with an aesthetic described as "quiet simplicity, which highlights the inherent characteristic of the metal and enhances the play of light over the surface," Hiramatsu's jewelry bridged Japanese metalsmithing, focused as it was on weapons and hollowware, and the idea of jewelry as an autonomous art practice.[7] The Hiko Mizuno Jewel Design School (now the Hiko Mizuno College of Jewelry), established in 1966, was another institution that played a key role in helping promote contemporary jewelry. By focusing so much on the genre of jewelry and rewriting metalsmithing and creative concepts, the Hiko Mizuno, under the direction of Itoh Kazuhiro, became internationally renowned for producing many innovative and talented jewelers.

Japanese jewelers were well informed about contemporary developments in European jewelry, with exhibitions such as Graham Hughes's International Exhibition of Modern Jewellery 1890–1961, first shown at Goldsmiths' Hall in London in 1961 and reaching Japan in 1965, where it was shown at the Seibu department store. Department store galleries, with their dynamic exhibition programs and catalogs, were an important source of information for jewelers in the 1960s and 1970s. As jeweler Simon Fraser notes, British contemporary jewelry was visible in shows presented by the British Crafts Centre, with jewelers such as Gerda Flöckinger selling regularly in these venues. "This exhibition policy meant shows from all over the world reached Japan and provided diverse information."[8]

New Materials, New Freedoms

The legacy of these developments is perhaps most clearly seen in the first International Jewellery Art Exhibition organized by the JJDA in 1970, which provided a critical opening for Japanese jewelers to pursue the assimilation of fine art practices while encouraging them to view themselves as part of an international field, showing their work alongside colleagues from other parts of the world. This exhibition promoted jewelry as a vehicle for artistic expression and introduced the idea that jewelry's value shouldn't be based on the precious materials from which it was made. As the catalog put it, "The International Jewellery Art Exhibition is not a space to display expensive stones such as diamonds, sapphires, rubies, and emeralds to have them appreciated as decorations, but to demonstrate how an artist's design can enhance the beauty of these stones and precious metals."[9] According to curator Hida Toyojiro, "Here they recognized that jewellery can be an independent art form by virtue of its design. Yet, they still took it for granted that jewellery, even in its independence, had to remain harmonious to the fashion in clothes."[10]

The critique of preciousness and the introduction of new materials opened up two new avenues for Japanese jewelers to explore: references to traditional Japanese forms and materials that could not be achieved using precious materials, and various challenges to conventional jewelry values by the use of unexpected materials such as cement.

In turn, this led to the investigation of the relationship between the jewel and the body and the psychological and spiritual dimensions of adorning the body.[11]

In 1984 an exhibition project involving Fukunaga Shigeki and American gallery owner and collector Helen Drutt became Contemporary Jewelry: The Americas, Australia, Europe and Japan, touring to the National Museum of Modern Art in both Kyoto and Tokyo, and Jewelry International at the Museum of Contemporary Crafts in New York.[12] Introducing Japanese and American audiences to jewelry from their respective countries, as well as to new work from Australia and Europe, the exhibition also resulted in the National Museum of Modern Art acquiring jewelry for its permanent collection, and American collectors becoming more aware of Japanese jewelry. This exhibition cemented the idea of contemporary jewelry as small sculptures, autonomous objects that drew on the abstract forms and rebellious attitudes of Japanese contemporary art in the 1970s, thereby denying "the secondary status traditionally accredited to jewellery which reduced it to mere trinkets for women."[13]

An important moment in the history of contemporary jewelry in Korea was the solo exhibition that Kim Seung Hee held at Midopa Gallery in 1975, after returning from studies in the United States, where she received an MFA from Indiana University in 1973. The exhibition included examples of goldsmithing (rings and necklaces crafted in silver) and metalsmithing (containers and objects). Considering the fact that Korean metalwork was in an embryonic state, it's easy to imagine how strongly the advanced metalsmithing techniques and aesthetic concepts Kim had acquired overseas impacted the local crafts field.[14] Interested in applying the visual language of contemporary jewelry to traditional cultural practices, Kim employed jade, a material with a rich history in Korea, in her jewelry, and reinterpreted the nineteenth-century folk painting called *Minwha*. Her jewelry also responded to contemporary movements in the visual arts. Exploring concepts like drawing in metal and sculpture for the body, she created a series of jewelry objects highly reminiscent of painting and sculpture. She explored the juxtaposition of lines and planes using jewels, and also projected poetic sentiments by adopting realistic shapes while emphasizing the distinct properties of metal and gemstones.

In the late 1970s and early '80s, contemporary jewelry appeared intermittently in exhibitions in Korea as part of the

Kim Seung Hee
Landscape, 2006
4.5 x 7.5 cm
Green zircon, jadeite, green jade, agate, 18-karat gold, sterling silver
Photo by K.C. Studio
Sun Art Center, Korea
Courtesy of the artist

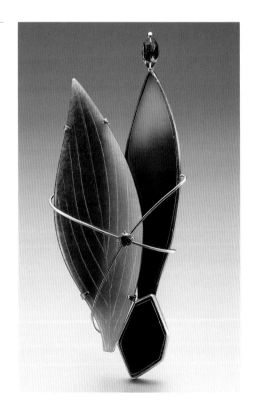

Kim Seung Hee
Landscape, 2006
4 x 7 cm
Blue sapphire, citrine, brown jade, agate, 18-karat gold, sterling silver
Photo by K.C. Studio
Sun Art Center, Korea
Courtesy of the artist

Choo Yae-kyung
Musical Letter, 1987
16 x 16 x 4 cm
Gold, ivory
Courtesy of the artist

metalsmithing practices of craftspeople who had returned from studying abroad. Notably, Choo Yae-kyung, who had studied in Germany and obtained a Master of Goldsmithing qualification in 1978, solidified her status as a jeweler after receiving the grand prize in the art jewelry category of the first Korea Contemporary Jewelry Competition, which was established in 1987. Since then, Choo has continued to create and show contemporary jewelry characterized by formal variations and playful rhythms while experimenting with various materials.

Korean contemporary jewelry entered its renaissance in the 1980s. During this period metalsmithing techniques and more advanced Western concepts were professionally taught in institutions by a new generation of artists who had studied abroad. The specific aesthetic that emerged in the 1970s, involving "the traditional emphasis on materials, precise form, and ornamentation," began to break down as Korean jewelers were exposed to the issues and questions of modernism: "It was inevitable that a clearer understanding of the contemporary became the key issue for Korean students. For this they sought out information and programs primarily in the USA, Germany, and England."[15] There were also specialized crafts galleries opening in succession, as well as active international exchange exhibitions. American Jewelry Now at Walker Hill Art Center in 1986, and the 1988 Contemporary Metal Craft Exhibition, held at the same venue, are considered two of the most important historical exhibitions, offering a unique opportunity to experience the new techniques, materials, forms and themes that were present in contemporary American jewelry.[16]

It wasn't until the late '80s that contemporary jewelry as a self-expressive visual language fully emerged in Korea. Some of the notable names are Woo Jin-soon, who studied at Konstfack in Sweden, graduated in 1980 and returned home in 1981, and Kim Jung-hoo, who studied at SUNY New Paltz in the United States and had her first solo show in 1992. Perhaps unsurprisingly, Woo's early jewelry shared the geometric forms and restrained formal character of Scandinavian design, and, recognizing the values of modernism, her brooches (a favored form) can be seen as miniature sculpture. Her recent work, featuring images of birds, flowers and human figures, goes beyond her earlier interest in simple forms and compositional order and becomes open to narrative and conceptual meanings. Kim was a studio jeweler and the first Korean to use the term *art jewelry* in her exhibition statement. Her jewelry is characterized by its interest in natural, narrative and material beauty. Employing rusty wires, her early work emphasized the changes in metal over time, and the possibilities of formal variations created through compositions of lines and planes. A subsequent series of brooches included colorful gems and gold-gilded human figures, thus invoking sentiment and narrative in the work. Her recent jewelry, which mainly incorporates everyday and found objects, investigates the distinctive properties of the materials and their variability over time.

Kim Jae-young, Hong Kyung-hee and Chae Jung-eun are noteworthy as part of a growing number of contemporary jewelers who studied in Korea rather than traveling abroad for training. Making mostly brooches, Kim, who graduated from Hongik University, Seoul, in 1973, uses traditional materials strongly associated with Asian art, such as jade and bamboo, and the work evokes the tranquil sentiments of Korean ink painting. Her brooches are sculptural and painterly ornaments, blending traditional emotions and contemporary aesthetics. Hong's work includes labor-intensive fabric rings and necklaces, hand-knitted from silver and gold thread, which celebrate the sublime virtue of physical effort. Chae began her career making jewelry with strong ties to body- and fashion-related performance. More recent work includes rings with architectural forms and diverse textures.

The 1990s

In the 1990s, as the number of Korean jewelers returning from study abroad in the United States, Germany, England and elsewhere increased, a new, distinctive group of artist-jewelers emerged, thus leading that decade's jewelry into a period of advancement with intensive experiments in a variety of forms. The foreign-educated jewelers of this generation tried to set jewelry up as an independent genre, emphasizing free expression, experiments with new materials and the exhibition value of their creations.

A number of international exhibitions of contemporary jewelry from Europe and Australia began to balance out the visible presence of American contemporary jewelry within Korea. This included Australia Gold: Contemporary Australian Jewellery and Metalwork at Gallery Bing and Art of Adornment: Australian Contemporary Jewellery at Shinsegae Gallery,

Jin-soon Woo
Left, *Dreamer,* 2008
4.9 x 4.9 x 1.4 cm
Sterling silver, 20-karat gold,
fabricated, oxidized
Private collection
Right, *Happy Bird,* 2008
4.9 x 4.9 x 1.4 cm
Sterling silver, 20-karat gold,
fabricated
Private collection
Courtesy of the artist

Kim Jung-hoo
The Rain Drops VII—Brooch,
2009
9.2 x 9.2 cm
Sterling silver, lapis lazuli
Courtesy of the artist

Kim Jae-Young
Early Bird, 2009
8 x 0.8 x 2 cm
Bamboo, silver, 18-karat gold,
jade, amber
Photo by Myung-Wook Huh
Gallery Hidden Space

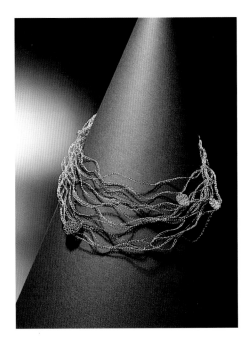

Hong Kyung-hee
Yellow Moon, 2007
17 x 17 x 2 cm
22-karat gold, gold plated on
fine silver, weaving
Photo by Youngil Kim
Courtesy of the artist

Chae Jung-eun
*Three Rings—Six Rings—
GatherRing,* 2000–2009
Each, less than 5 x 5 x 5 cm
Sterling silver, ebony, Picasso
marble; fabricated and cast
Photo by Kwangchung Park

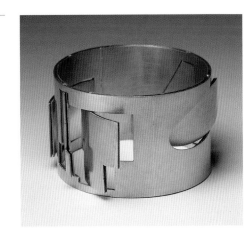

Lee Kwang Sun
M1 Bracelet, 2008
5.5 x 8.5 cm
Tombac, fabricated
Courtesy of the artist

both held in 1994, and Koreanisch-Deutsche Zeitgenössische Schmuck und Gerät Ausstellung, which was displayed at Walker Hill Art Center in 1996.[17]

In terms of Korean contemporary jewelry in the 1990s, it's worth mentioning jewelers Lee Kwang Sun and Lee Dongchun, who both studied at Hochschule Pforzheim in Germany, and Kang Youn-mi, who studied in the United States. Lee Kwang Sun's early work, such as a series of miniature rings, demonstrated an exquisite interest in architectural compositions. Her recent rings have moving parts, enabling wearers to experience the movement of the jewelry tied to the movements of their body. Using alternative materials, she creates organic shapes that express tactile playfulness rather than conceptual seriousness, while also visualizing familiar architectural forms. Lee Dongchun has been recognized internationally as one of Korea's leading jewelers. Focusing on pendants, he references ordinary objects and draws out the possibilities of meaning within them in a way that's conceptual and yet involves simple formal decisions, such as painting the surfaces of his materials. Finally, Kang is interested in painterly expression, or creating a story by putting realistically rendered figures and objects together. For her, a brooch is a canvas for painting and a means of visualizing narratives.

By the early 1990s, Japanese jewelers were actively involved in international movements. Yet this was also the moment in which Japanese jewelry was recognized as distinctive, and a new generation of Japanese jewelers, many of whom studied in Japan rather than abroad, was introduced to an overseas audience. As curator Cindi Strauss writes, "Japanese jewelry artists had steadily been featured in international presentations, but few shows had defined a particularly Japanese style until the 1990s. Beginning with Jewellery Today Japan (1991) and culminating with Contemporary Jewelry: Exploration by Thirty Japanese Artists (1995), at the Museum of Modern Art, Tokyo, Japanese jewelry that was reflective of the artists' cultural origins rather than the trends emanating from Europe was finally documented."[18] If jewelry began as a transplanted Western concept, then by the 1990s it had staked out its own territory in Japan. We might summarize the nature of contemporary Japanese jewelry, first, as conceptual and sculptural expressions for the body; second, as efforts to reinterpret traditional elements in contemporary ways; and third, as cross-genre movements that employed unconventional materials such as ready-mades and found objects.

The first engagement with jewelry as body-related performance art is considered closely connected to the growing association with European universities. Itoh Kazuhiro was the first to work in this manner. Trained in Munich at the Akademie der Bildenden Künste München, and a professor at the Hiko Mizuno College of Jewellery since 1987, Itoh had his first international exhibition at the Electrum Gallery in London in 1977, and his work is concerned with interrogating the nature of jewelry, a strategy that places materials and techniques as secondary in significance, and achieving "the deconstruction of jewellery in material, technique, and style aimed at calling the various accepted merits of jewellery into question."[19] His students work in similar ways, as evidenced in the jewelry of Kobayashi Shinichiro, who graduated in 1995 and uses materials with physical properties that slowly transform, such as charcoal and camphor, to question the notion of permanence and the sensual experience of the jewel. Others who engage with the body as a site for jewelry are Yamada Mizuko, Suo Emiko and Hiraiwa Tomoyo, all graduates of the Tokyo National University of Fine Arts and Music. As Yamada suggests, "The function of jewellery is to adorn the human body. It belongs to the category of craftwork, but I consider it a work of art to be displayed on the body."[20]

The second endeavor, a return to traditional Japanese materials and designs, has been discussed by Hida Toyojiro as a movement particularly located in the early 1990s.

As he wrote in 1991, a number of jewelers were demonstrating a renewed interest in Japanese tradition: "They are now finding such materials as *radon* (mother-of-pearl), *shakudo* (copper and gold alloy), *mokumegane* (woodgrained metal), *urushi* (lacquer) and *washi* (Japanese paper) as well as classic patterns such as *kodai-moyo* (ancient pattern) and *chidori* (bird pattern), which they felt until a few years ago to be outdated and quaint, rich in fresh appeal."[21] For Hida, the main difference was that this interest in Japanese tradition was not a kind of exoticism designed to attract Western attention, but a sincere examination of Japanese cultural heritage.

By 1995, Hida concluded that this return to tradition had not become a dominant aspect of Japanese contemporary jewelry, although he was quick to emphasize that this was "not just a fad, but is a widespread phenomenon that originates

Lee Dongchun
Inhale-Exhale Brooch, 2009
14 x 9 x 3 cm
Thread, latex, iron, paint
Courtesy of Galerie Marzee

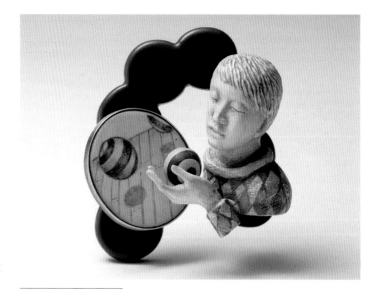

Kang Youn-mi
Bouncing Lesson, 2008
5.3 x 5.8 x 2.5 cm
Sterling silver, copper, wood, enamel, ottchil (traditional Korean lacquer)
Photo by Kwangchun Park
Courtesy of the artist
Private collection

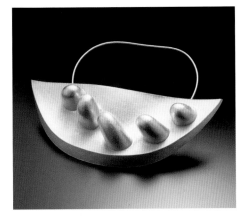

Mizuko Yamada
Breast Ornament, 1994
7.5 x 43 x 35 cm
Silver-plated copper; raised,
soldered
Photo by Hitoshi Nishiyama
Courtesy of the artist

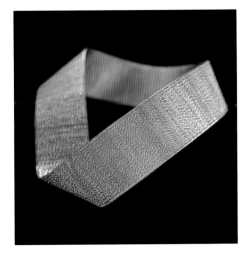

Suo Emiko
Neckpiece, 2003
40 x 27 x 13 cm
Aluminum, gold leaf, copper
Photo by Masatoshi Sosahara
Courtesy of the artist

Hiraiwa Tomoyo
Peace Circle (Bracelet), 2007
12 x 12 x 5 cm
950 silver
Photo by Yoshitaka Uchida

from the artists' innate need to find their own cultural origin."[22] Two of the key players in this movement are Fukuchi Kyoto and Nakamura Minato, who both studied jewelry with Hishida Yasuhiko, the first president of JJDA, while a more recent example is Kaneko Toru. Kyoto's brooches are made from *daifukucho,* a kind of paper used for business account books, and ledger books created for her great-grandfather's drapery firm are referenced in her *Echo of Time Past* brooch (2000). As Cindi Strauss writes, "Fukuchi's *washi* brooches have an ethereal nature, their thin layers show the marks of intervention and history in keeping with the lessons of Hishida and the Japanese jewelry movement of the 1960s and 1970s."[23] The techniques and materials invoke the past, while also allowing for artistic expression. According to Kaneko, who graduated from the Tokyo National University of Fine Arts and Music in 1988, "The theme of my work is how to express the characteristics of various materials including appearances, feel and weight within the field of jewellery," and his shoulder brooches are autonomous structures positioned so they can be viewed from different directions, highlighting the latent qualities of his material.[24]

Employing nonmetal synthetic materials such as hardboard, plastics, urethane, rubber and resin, as well as ready-mades and found objects, the avant-garde jewelers of the cross-genre movement challenged traditional concepts, in part by drawing on the strategies of contemporary art. As Kiyomizu Kyubei put it in his judge's comments for the 1986 International Jewellery Art Exhibition, "In the past, jewellery was mainly under the influence of the fashion in clothes, but these days there seems to be an attitude to assimilate the latest trends in contemporary art."[25] To them, jewelry acted as a conceptual symbol while also being playful, exploring the meanings of signs, like tokens of pop culture. In this sense, it has been suggested that the introduction of men's and unisex jewelry was an anticipated consequence resulting from the emergence of Japanese pop idols and defiant youth culture.[26] Ogura Ritsuko, for example, uses cardboard in her brooches because it's "cheap, non-precious, popular, and nowadays of standard manufacture from factories. There is nothing special about it."[27] Ogura's attitude to her material, despite its humble and everyday nature, is quite different from that of the jewelers who follow the ideas of the Mingei Movement. Inspired by the plastic capsule containers used in coin-operated toy dispensers, Minewaki Mikiko transforms found plastic items, such as toys and consumer objects like disposable cigarette lighters, into jewelry, shifting the meaning of the original and making it available as a tool for artistic expression, while also refiguring the object's relationship to the wearer/body.[28]

These trends were comprehensively addressed in two noteworthy exhibitions: Contemporary Jewellery: Exploration by Thirty Japanese Artists at the National Museum of Modern Art, Tokyo, in 1995, and The Art of Jewellery, which was the 30th anniversary exhibition of the JJDA foundation, hosted at the Museum of Arts & Crafts in Itami.[29] The Itami Contemporary Jewelry Art Competition, launched in 1990, is another institutional factor in the advancement of contemporary jewelry in Japan. With its reinterpretations of traditional techniques and strong manifestations of distinct ethnic flavor and social interest, Japanese contemporary jewelry is actively propelled by individual studio jewelers and those formally educated in specialized academies such as the Hiko Mizuno.

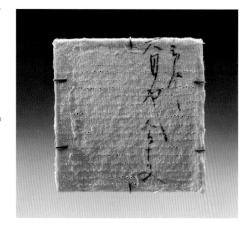

Kyoko Fukuchi
Echo of Time Past, 2000
7.3 x 7.3 x 0.2 cm
Washi paper from daifukucho (a Japanese account book belonging to the artist's family), ink, silver
The Museum of Fine Arts, Houston; Helen Williams Drutt Collection, gift of the Morgan Foundation in honor of Catherine Asher Morgan

The Contemporary Jewelry Scene

The period from 2000 up until the present time in South Korea can be viewed as a transition period. Noticeably, study in the United States has declined while the number of young jewelers who have studied in England and Germany is actively growing. The start of the twenty-first century in Korea was a difficult time, not only in the field of jewelry, but in art as a whole, because the nation's economic turmoil under the International Monetary Fund's rescue program in the late 1990s had ripple effects on all of Korean society. In this inhibited atmosphere, Cheongju International Craft Biennale was born in 1999, providing strong institutional support and international communications around the latest trends and issues of contemporary crafts. In addition, Chiwoo Craft Museum opened in 2005 as a private museum, hosting curated exhibitions that examine the history of contemporary Korean metalwork and the work of young and emerging jewelers.

In reality, however, the Korean crafts field is adrift between a fine art orientation and a design approach. This can be attributed to an intrinsic limit found in the course of development within contemporary jewelry in Korea. The following issues are to be addressed and they remain as tasks for Korean jewelers to resolve; first, disconnection from tradition and the challenge to smoothly absorb traditional techniques into academic courses to interpret them for contemporary

Kaneko Toru
Shoulder Brooches, 1994
Each, 5 x 4.5 x 4.5 cm
Silver
Courtesy of the artist

Ogura Ritsuko
Red Cardboard Brooches,
1994
Left, 11.5 x 4.5 x 2.5 cm; right,
13 x 4.5 x 3 cm
Corrugated cardboard, acrylic,
silver
Photo by Hitoshi Nishiyama

Minewaki Mikiko
Lighters, 2000
2.5 x 2.2 x 1 cm
Plastic disposable lighters
Courtesy of the artist

use; second, artistic delay as the demand for a commercial design approach has overshadowed the value of jewelry as a form of artistic expression; third, an inclination to commercial distribution as jewelry is being traded through commercial galleries and shops rather than being granted artistic meanings through public collections or curatorial exhibitions at museums; and lastly, the segregation between artistic creation and criticism as theories and critical research on jewelry have been discounted as taking second place to creation. Alongside these concerns, artist-jewelers have not fully cast anchor in a desirable system, possibly due to a shortage of specialized magazines, museum curators, public collections and jewelry critics. Nonetheless, fresh ideas and formative expressions are being suggested by Korea's emerging jewelers, and this is why the future of Korean jewelry is promising.

Contemporary jewelry in Japan has proved the epitome of how to deal with the kinds of challenges experienced in Korea. The origin dates back to Tokyo National University of Fine Arts and Music, where traditional aesthetics and techniques succeeded and were pushed further in formal education. The influence of the Mingei Movement, especially, paved the way for such an effort. Thanks to the formation of associations, specialized jewelry schools, magazines and public collections from the 1950s onward, Japanese jewelers were able to keep up with international trends and to improve the status of jewelry as art. A golden epoch began in the late twentieth century in terms of diversity and international exchanges. For example, the Hiko Mizuno College of Jewellery in Tokyo has taken part in the Three-Schools Project, which involves the Rietveld Academy in Amsterdam and the Munich Academy of Fine Arts in Munich, two of the leading schools in Europe.[30] Japanese contemporary jewelry can be said to have achieved a better balance between commercial design and art than has Korean contemporary jewelry, and it undoubtedly stands as one of the leading international trends.

Notes

1. Other instructors at KHDC included Norman R. DeHaan, the center head, Stanley Fistic in charge of industrial ceramic design and Paul Talentino in accessories and training education. Samuel Sherr was the director of the whole project. Kim Jong-gyun, *History of Korean Design* (Seoul: Mijinsa, 2008), 55–57.

2. Some metalwork equipment and facilities used at KHDC were brought from the United States because they weren't possible to manufacture in Korea then. Most of them were transferred to Seoul National University when the center closed.

3. Hitomi Kitamura, *Transfiguration: Japanese Art Jewelry Today* (Tokyo: The National Museum of Modern Art, 2006), 16.

4. Hida Toyojira, *Contemporary Jewellery: Exploration by Thirty Japanese Artists* (Tokyo: The National Museum of Modern Art, 1995), 20.

5. Quoted in Hitomi, *Transfiguration*, 16.

6. Ibid., 16–17.

7. See "Hiramatsu Yasuki," in *Ornament as Art: Avant-Garde Jewelry from the Helen Williams Drutt Collection*, ed. Cindi Strauss (Stuttgart: Arnoldsche Art Publishers, in association with The Museum of Fine Arts, Houston, 2008), 479.

8. Simon Fraser, *Contemporary Japanese Jewellery* (London: Merrell Publishers, Ltd., 2001), 13.

9. Quoted in Hida, *Contemporary Jewellery*, 20.

10. Ibid., 21.

11. Hitomi, *Transfiguration*, 17–18.

12. Helen William Drutt English, "A golden age of goldsmithing: Four decades," in Strauss, *Ornament as Art*, 31–32.

13. Hida, *Contemporary Jewellery*, 21.

14. For recollections about the exhibition, refer to Kim Seung-hee, "Drawings in Metal," in *Joy of Creation* (Seoul: Sukjoo Arts and Cultural Foundation, DATE), 125–126; *The Metal Arts of Seung Hee Kim* (Paju, South Korea: Nabizang, 2006), 177; *Forms of Happy Life* (Seoul: Chiwoo Craft Museum, 2005), 51, an exhibition catalog.

15. Jamie Bennett, "Contemporary Korean Jewellery," in *Zeitgenössische Schmuckkunst in Korea*, ed. Jong Sun Goo (Pforzheim, Germany: Schmuckmuseum, 1994), unpaginated.

16. American Jewelry Now is considered one of the most sensational exhibitions in the history of contemporary Korean jewelry. Curated by American Craft Museum, it featured the work of 57 leading jewelers. Refer to Paul J. Smith, *American Jewelry Now* (Seoul: Walker Hill Art Center, 1986), 5, an exhibition catalog. Hosted by Hongik Metal Craft Association, the '88 Contemporary Metal Craft Exhibition featured the work of 24 metalwork professors from 18 American universities. Sarah Bodine and Michel Dunas, "New Directions in American Metalsmithing: The 1980s," *Monthly Crafts* 1, no. 4 (June 1988): 4–22 and plates on 28–75.

17. The exhibition at Gallery Bing was co-curated by Asia Link and Royal Melbourne Institute of Technology (RMIT). The exhibition at Shinsegae Art Gallery was curated by the Queen Victoria Museum and Art Gallery as part of Asian-traveling exhibitions. Peter Timms, "Playing with Gold," in *Australia Gold: Contemporary Australian Jewellery and Metalwork* (Melbourne: Asia Link and RMIT, 1994), n.p.; Glenda King, "Australian Jewellery," in *Art of Adornment: Australian Contemporary Jewellery* (Launceston, UK: The Queen Victoria Museum and Art Gallery, 1994), 9–16, an exhibition catalog. The exhibition was hosted by Korea Jewelry Design Association in collaboration with Jens-Rüdiger Lirenzen from the Pforzheim University and curated by Ralph Turner. Ralph Turner, "Eine Frage des Stellenwert," in *Koreanisch-Deutsche Zeitgenössische Schmuck und Gerät Ausstellung* (Seoul: Walker Hill Art Center, 1996), n.p., an exhibition catalog; and Jens-Rüdiger Lirenzen, "Zeitgenössische Schmuck und Gerätgestaltung in Deutschland," in *Koreanisch-Deutsche Zeitgenössische Schmuck*, n.p.

18. Cindi Strauss, "A brief history of contemporary jewelry, 1960–2006," in Strauss, *Ornament as Art*, 25.

19. Hida, *Contemporary Jewellery*, 23.

20. Ibid., 164.

21. Ibid., 22.

22. Ibid., 22–23.

23. Cindi Strauss, "Fukuchi Kyoto," in Strauss, *Ornament as Art*, 140.

24. Hida, *Contemporary Jewellery*, 158.

25. Ibid., 20.

26. Hida Toyojiro, "Circumventing Modernism: Japanese Jewellery of the 1990s," in *Contemporary Japanese Jewellery* (London: Merrell Publishers and Crafts Council, 2001), 22–23.

27. Cindi Strauss, "Ogura Ritsuko," in Strauss, *Ornament as Art*, 234.

28. Hitomi, *Transfiguration*, 145.

29. Helen W. Drutt English and Peter Dormer, *Jewelry of Our Time: Art, Ornament and Obsession* (London: Thames and Hudson, 1995), 344.

30. Ellen Maurer Zilioli, "Construction site jewellery," in *The Fat Booty of Madness*, ed. Florian Hufnagl (Stuttgart: Arnoldsche Art Publishers, 2008), 63–64.

Further Reading

8th Itami City Contemporary Craft Exhibition: Jewellery. Itami, Japan: The Museum of Arts and Crafts, Itami, 1997. An exhibition catalog.

Chang, Dong-kwang, ed. *The Breath of Nature: The Invitational Exhibition of Cheongju International Craft Biennale 2001.* Cheongju, South Korea: The Organizing Committee of Cheongju International Craft Biennale, 2001. An exhibition catalog.

———. *Korea Fantasia: A Stratum of Modern Korean Metal Work.* Seoul: Chiwoo Craft Museum, 2006. An exhibition catalog.

———. *Metal Arts of Seung Hee Kim.* Paju, South Korea: Nabizang, 2006.

———, ed. *Yoo Lizzy: A Retrospective of 40 Years of Metal Works.* Paju, South Korea: Nabizang, 2009.

Fraser, Simon. *Contemporary Japanese Jewellery.* London: Merrell Publishers and Crafts Council, 2001.

Hida, Toyojira. *Contemporary Jewellery: Exploration by Thirty Japanese Artists.* Tokyo: The National Museum of Modern Art, 1995.

Hitomi, Kitamura. *Transfiguration: Japanese Art Jewelry Today.* Tokyo: The National Museum of Modern Art, 2006.

Koreanisch-Deutsche Zeitgenössische Schmuck und Gerät Ausstellung. Seoul: Walker Hill Art Center, 1996. An exhibition catalog.

Strauss, Cindi, ed. *Ornament as Art: Avant-Garde Jewelry from the Helen Williams Drutt Collection.* Stuttgart: Arnoldsche Art Publishers, in association with The Museum of Fine Arts, Houston, 2008.

Sugihara, Nobuhiko, et al., ed. *Masterpieces of Contemporary Japanese Crafts: Commemorative Exhibition for the Opening of the Crafts Gallery.* Tokyo: The National Museum of Modern Art, 1977. An exhibition catalog.

Southern Africa.

Sarah Rhodes

Introduction

Africa is a vast continent made up of 54 diverse and varied countries. Its jewelry is as varied as the cultures, traditions, materials and skills of the peoples who live there. In northern African countries, jewelry produced from patterned and ornate metals has traditionally been a male activity. Ancient Egyptian jewelry was primarily made from gold. Often highly decorated with flowers, birds and insects, it provided the inspiration for the curved lines and stylized decoration of the Art Nouveau period in Europe and America. In East Africa, body alteration and scarification have long been an outlet for artistic expression.[1] In recent years, these have been appropriated by exponents of body modification and tattooing in the West, as has the South African Zulu women's practice of stretching the earlobes with large, flat plugs. The women of the Surma and Mursi peoples of Ethiopia still follow the ancient tradition of wearing lip plates, which are inserted into the lips of teenage girls. Traditionally, married women of the South African Ndebele would gradually stretch their necks with brass or copper neck rings, which they believed to have strong ritual powers as a sign of wealth.

This essay focuses on contemporary jewelry in South Africa, Botswana and Namibia. These countries share geographical borders and their histories are heavily enmeshed, yet even discussing just these three countries involves difficulties. Contemporary jewelry is all but nonexistent in Botswana and has no long-standing tradition in Namibia. Because of this, with the exception of exhibition catalogs and a handful of magazine articles, there's been very little documentation of the subject. Discussing the legacy of colonialism and apartheid in an objective and sensitive way has also thrown up challenges, particularly in relation to post-apartheid South Africa, where ethnic classification and definitions are highly political and culturally charged.

Conventional jewelry, supported by the highly sophisticated and established mining sector built on southern Africa's mineral and metal wealth, has become the region's most visible practice of jewelry. South Africa, and Botswana and Namibia to a lesser extent, have developing creative economies. Jewelry design and manufacture is being strengthened by initiatives from governments and the private sector, as well as through the education systems.

For example, although Botswana has been mining diamonds since their discovery a year after its independence in 1967, the country has little in the way of jewelry design and

David Atho Moatisi
The Stripes, 2010
No dimensions given
18-karat white gold, diamonds
Photo by Cyrus Kets
Diamond Trading Company
Botswana—Shining Light Diamond
Design Awards Collection
Sponsored by Eurostar Botswana
(Pty) Ltd.

manufacture. The lack of jewelers and jewelry tradition can be attributed to Botswana's youth as an independent country, its small population, its lack of manufacturing infrastructure and its relatively young education system. Botswana has few jewelers, based mainly in the capital city Gaborone, usually of Indian descent, who make jewelry in the European tradition.

Since the 2009 establishment of the Diamond Technology Park, a sorting and grading facility in Gaborone, and the recent relocation there of the De Beers diamond sales office, the capital of Botswana has transformed into a major rough-diamond hub, and the jewelry industry as a whole in that nation is set to grow. Botswana is one of the only countries in the world that's able to cut, market and sell its own conflict-free diamonds. To capitalize on the fact that the diamond industry is Botswana's most important growth sector, the government has established the country's first jewelry design and manufacture course at the newly built Oodi College of Applied Arts and Technology.[2] The creation of this course and Botswana's participation in the De Beers annual Southern Africa Shining Light Awards jewelry competition will foster jewelry design and could be the starting point for contemporary studio-based jewelry. The precious nature of the competition materials (gold, diamonds and silver) means that the jewelry designs are heavily influenced by a historic European tradition of jewelry style and manufacture. However, Botswana's landscapes and flora are referenced in the jewelers' work. The winner of the first competition in 2009, Katja Nilsson, designed a necklace in the shape of a baobab. Subsequent winner David Atho Moatisi's *The Stripes* (2010) neckpiece is made from white gold set with black and white diamonds evocative of zebra stripes, drawing on Botswana's abundant wildlife.

South Africa is one of the foremost producers of the world's precious metals and minerals, but its jewelry industry is very small and underdeveloped in comparison to that of Europe, Australasia, Asia and America.[3] The decades of oppression and isolation of the apartheid era (1948–1994) and the stringent metals and mineral regulations instituted by the government stunted its growth.[4] South Africa's colonial and apartheid history left its contemporary artists and craftsmen cut off from the rest of the world for many years, resulting in a sector that's only recently begun to flourish. European settlers brought their jewelry traditions to South Africa in the nineteenth century. The practice of using fine metals and precious stones to produce traditional pieces of fine jewelry continues today, with strong South African brands such as Charles Greig Jewellers, founded in Johannesburg in 1899, flourishing. This contrasts with contemporary jewelry, which has emerged over the past three decades, partly due to the opening up of South Africa to the rest of the world after apartheid and to the establishment of jewelry design and manufacture courses in colleges and universities.

Because of the size of its population (with 50 million inhabitants, South Africa is roughly 25 times as large as Namibia and Botswana) and history, South Africa is the only country within southern Africa with a wide variety of contemporary jewelers. The boundaries between art, craft and design are blurred in post-apartheid South Africa, and jewelry is no exception, falling across all three categories, ranging from traditional Xhosa and Zulu beadwork and conventional diamond engagement rings to one-off studio jewelry. The development of contemporary jewelry has been influenced by its definition both within education and in the wider context. Currently, the government positions the jewelry sector under the auspices of the Department of Mining and Minerals rather than in the Department of Arts and Culture, which is problematic for contemporary jewelers. They work in a complex social, political and economic context.

Modernist Jewelry in South Africa

South Africa's motto, "Unity in Diversity," accurately describes a country with 11 official languages and a wide mix of cultures. Conversely, South African contemporary jewelry has a predominantly European aesthetic. This developed in the 1950s and '60s when Europeans, mainly Germans, provided jewelry instruction in the form of apprenticeships and were also involved in setting up the first jewelry course at Universiteit Stellenbosch (Stellenbosch University) in 1968. After training, apprentices would take their trade test to qualify as jewelers, then work for established businesses or set up their own workshops.

Erich Frey and Kurt Jobst were two of the most prominent jewelers from the 1950s and 1960s. They provided apprenticeships and training and set the stage for today's contemporary jewelers. Frey immigrated from Germany, where he'd already undergone a traditional jewelry apprenticeship, to South Africa in 1952. Frey made "a unique contribution to the establishment of a South African identity in the manufacturing

Kurt Jobst
Ring, n.d.
No dimensions given
18-karat green gold with
baroque pearls and granulation
Photo courtesy of Tarquinius
Jobst Billiet

Dieter Dill
Crossroads, 1992
4 x 3 x 3 cm
18-karat yellow gold; lost wax
casting
Photo by artist

silver and goldsmith fraternity. His use of semiprecious stones and organic material (ivory, bone, and wood) represents a landmark moment in the history of local precious metal design."[5] Frey's jewelry designs were inspired by the South African landscape and plant life, and he referenced his interest in Etruscan art and Danish design in his work. His appreciation of Danish jewelry extended to importing the more affordable commercial work of Georg Jensen to sell in his shop in Pretoria. Frey had contact with other South African artists of the time, among them Walter Batiss, Alexis Preller, Cecil Skotnes, Danie de Jager and Karin Skawran, all of whom had unique styles difficult to describe by the artistic movements of the twentieth century. Jeweler contemporaries with whom Frey associated included Jobst, Kurt Donau, Egon Günther and Dieter Dill. Each of these jewelers was primarily concerned with creating original works of art rather than mass producing and commercial selling. Their attention to detail, design and quality of craftsmanship shines through their work even today.

Kurt Jobst, like Frey, also completed his jewelry apprenticeship in Germany, in the Bauhaus tradition. He moved to South Africa in 1935 after the political climate in his homeland became unbearable to his liberal views. He opened his own workshop in Johannesburg, where he undertook all design work and directed every stage of production. The South African writer Nadine Gordimer describes Jobst's passion for his work and "pride in the noble impersonal tradition of craftsmanship, which he worked all his life to be worthy of."[6] His work crossed the boundary and scale of jewelry with the production of platters, goblets and wrought-iron fire grates. Over the years his workshop took on a scale and proportion unique in South Africa at the time, with several staff trained by him. He died unexpectedly in 1971 in a road accident while returning from Swaziland, where he was planning to move his workshop and set up a jewelry training school for the Swazi government.

Education in South Africa

The greatest influence in jewelry during the 1970s and '80s continued to come from Germans. This is mainly because South-West Africa (now Namibia) gained independence, prompting many of the Germans settled there to immigrate to South Africa to start a new life. The establishment of jewelry training courses in the late 1960s, '70s and '90s continued the development of jewelry in South Africa. Stellenbosch University's jewelry course was established by German jewelers in 1968. Starting in 1971, Dieter Dill led it for more than 20 years, basing it on European educational systems, notably Hochschule Pforzheim (Pforzheim School of Applied Arts), Akademie der Bildenden Künste München (Academy of Fine Arts, Munich) and the Central School of Art and Design, London. The jewelry course is located in the Fine Art Department, which has a big impact on the work produced. The basic philosophy of the course was to establish an extensive technical knowledge of jewelry combined with an artistic sensibility. It included a theoretical, scientific element coupled with a creative, practice-orientated strand, which continues today.

Stellenbosch University's jewelry course has played a large part in forming contemporary jewelers in South Africa and beyond. During his long tenure at the university, Dill trained and mentored numerous well-known jewelers, including Johan van Aswegen, who teaches at the Rhode Island School of Design, and Errico Cassar, who was also taught by Hermann Jünger and went on to run the course after Dill. Carine Terreblanche, the current head of the jewelry course and a practicing jeweler, was herself taught by both Dill and Cassar. She describes the course as "a creative workshop where ideas are developed by expressive means in tune with trends in the contemporary design world while at the same time reflecting its African and South African influences and identities" and believes that "contemporary jewelry, with its indisputable ability to provoke, critique, record, transmit and generate new meanings, qualities and ideas is able to engage individuals in a deep and personal way, and also to forge common bonds among groups—something of great importance in post-apartheid South Africa."[7]

The Natal Technikon (now the Durban University of Technology [DUT]) jewelry course began a decade after the Stellenbosch University course, in 1978. Its current course leader and practicing jeweler, Chris de Beer, was trained at Stellenbosch by Dill and has run the department at DUT for more than 20 years. Many of his former students have gone on to become established jewelers and jewelry teachers around the country. Practicing jeweler Vassiliki Konstandakellis is head of the jewelry department at the Cape Peninsula University of Technology. Verna Jooste is also a lecturer and technician at Stellenbosch University and her work questions the notion of preciousness of jewels and metals, as well as

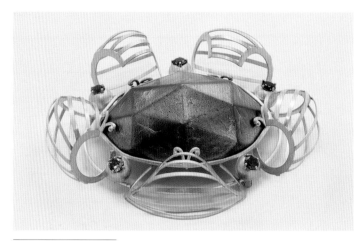

Errico Cassar
Untitled, 2012
2 x 7.5 x 6.5 cm
18-karat gold, tourmalines, fire opals, enamel, gold foil; sifted, kiln fired, carborundum stone ground, sanded, claw set
Photo by Rikus de Wet
Courtesy of the artist

Chris de Beer
Tyre Rings, 2003
Largest, 3 cm (diameter) x 3.5
cm (height)
White-wall tires, sterling silver;
carved
Photo by artist

Esmarié du Plooy
*Choker from Eucalyptus
Seedpods,* 1994
40 x 2 cm
Individual eucalyptus seedpods
cast in sterling silver, assembled
onto handmade link-on-link
chain, oxidized
Photo by Anna Richerby
Private collection
Courtesy of the artist

the value placed on religious symbols. Her work has included beaded images of famous Johannesburg landmarks and a rosary made of toys. Esmarié du Plooy is inspired by the flora and fauna of the Western Cape and casts natural objects such as seedpods in silver to produce tactile surface patterns and shapes on her jewelry. She is head of Jewellery Manufacture at the College of Cape Town.

The European link was further strengthened in the 1990s by international companies such as De Beers, AngloGold and Anglo Platinum. In an effort to provide a skilled workforce for their mining interests, these businesses helped establish vocational jewelry training centers based on the European model of jewelry education. The Cape Peninsula University of Technology jewelry design and manufacture course was established in 1993 by John Skotnes (originally apprenticed to Kurt Donau), prompted by the jewelry industry, which wanted the college to train middle managers. The course has grown over the years and produces a wide range of jewelry designers, makers and stakeholders in the jewelry sector, not just for industry. Some, such as Ute Winzker, have gone on to establish their own jewelry workshops. Others, such as Theresa Burger and Ilze Oberholzer, have established successful jewelry careers in other countries.

The Legacy of Apartheid

The legacy of the apartheid era and its segregated, imbalanced education system has left the creative industries predominantly the preserve of white designers. Although there are prominent young black fashion designers now emerging in South Africa, the jewelry scene still lacks black jewelry designers. While the expense of materials and setting up a jewelry workshop is prohibitively costly to those from disadvantaged backgrounds, the education system is the main factor. When young, impoverished black students are able to access a university education, they prefer to study a more traditional profession such as law or medicine. However, this is slowly starting to change, particularly within the *technikons*, or institutes of technology. Durban University of Technology reports an increase in the number of previously marginalized students enrolling in courses. In addition, the post-apartheid government has put an emphasis on the jewelry industry as a vehicle for job creation and growth. As a result, the last few years have seen the establishment of inclusive jewelry schools in South Africa's townships, introducing contemporary jewelry to black youth who were historically left on the fringes. National jewelry design competitions and an increase in exhibitions are starting to bring contemporary jewelry to a wider South African audience.

The Thuthuka Jewellery Development Programme, a nongovernmental organization working in partnership with the Department of Arts and Culture and various jewelry education institutions, was established in 2007. It combines focused one-to-one jewelry skills development mentoring with entrepreneurial business basics. This annual competition establishes a credible benchmark and encourages young jewelers to aspire and excel. It culminates in an exhibition at the University of Johannesburg, with the winners awarded jewelry tools and materials. The founder, Carola Ross, states that it supports future jewelers to follow their passion and reshape an unequivocally contemporary South African aesthetic. The program facilitates rural and urban jewelers to work together, developing traditional and contemporary techniques to create unique work in both jewelry and affiliated sectors.[8]

Vukani-Ubuntu is a community-based organization established in 1999 to provide sustainable development through training, job creation and entrepreneurial development in the jewelry industry. It's the largest mineral-beneficiation organization in the jewelry sector in South Africa. Vukani-Ubuntu is also the largest trainer and skills developer of emerging black jewelers in the industry, providing access to the formal sector to many previously underprivileged individuals, and therefore contributing to black economic empowerment and poverty alleviation in South Africa. The project provides incubator studios for its trainees to progress in the market and set up as jewelers in their own businesses. While the emphasis is on mass-market jewelry, Visha Naidoo, former head of the Atteridgeville Jewellery Project (established by Vukani-Ubuntu), won the top prize at Jewellex 2011, Africa's premier jewelry and watch expo, with her one-off design for a neckpiece for the Pravda Vodka Royal Collection.

Thomas Mosala
Dragon Fly, 2011
3 x 2.6 x 7 cm
Sterling silver; soldered, pierced
Photo by David Ross
Courtesy of Thuthuka Jewellery
Development Programme
(www.jewelleryafrica.co.za)

**Malcom Betts for LOSA
Gold Jewels**
*Vukani-Ubuntu Wood/Gold
Ring,* 2004
Outside diameter, 2.5 cm,
width 1 cm
African black wood with
22-karat gold inlay
Photo by Z. Svoboda, Vukani-
Ubuntu / LOSA Collection

Contemporary Jewelry and Identity

During apartheid South Africans were very isolated in the access they had to the rest of the world, particularly with regard to culture, which was heavily censored. Post-apartheid, the creative industries have opened up to the rest of the world. This has led current jewelers to question the term *jewelry*

Beverley Price
Original Product jewelry,
since 1996
13 cm in diameter
Mixed media
Photo by artist

and make works from diverse materials, as well as question "African-ness" and identity. South African contemporary jewelry produced over the past few years engages with current themes and discourse.

Beverley Price uses the graphic designs of South African brands of household goods and foods, which evoke a sense of nostalgia and are instantly recognizable to South Africans, to produce colorful necklaces. The labels for Black Cat peanut butter, Marmite and Rooibos tea used in her necklace and bracelet transport South Africans back to the kitchens of their childhood. Even the folded and stamped metal frames evoke the zinc metalworkers of rural South Africa who used to hand make tin baths and buckets by the side of the road. Price describes herself as "working across the paradigms of goldsmithing, fine art, craft and design with the intention of stimulating the long-term development of a hybrid style of South African jewelry that melds South African indigenous adornment and Western jewelry practices, as well as to promote a debate and a growing visual discourse in the form of art jewelry and a recognisably fine South African design."[9]

Marlene de Beer's work concerns her Afrikaner heritage and South Africa's past. It involves the revisiting of memories, forming part of a personal attempt at understanding and reinterpreting past and present situations as a personal resistance to colonization and oppression, and an attempt at reconstructing a fragmented personal and cultural identity.[10] She combines a mixture of materials and approaches to produce necklaces, pendants, medals and artworks that, through self-reflection, explore identity. De Beer believes that identity is uniquely embedded within social, cultural and personal experiences. Her jewelry visually references both her Afrikaner background, with the choice of a traditional cameo, and the multicultural nature of KwaZulu-Natal, through the use of glass seed beads.

Other jewelers explore materials through their work, moving from the traditional metals of gold and silver into found objects and recycled materials. Geraldine Fenn views her work as small sculptures with a sense of humor and fun. She juxtaposes established jewelry structures of silver ring shanks with colorful, quirky plastic toys, challenging the convention of jewelry made from precious metals. Philippa Green from Cape Town combines seemingly worthless clear thermoplastic with expensive diamonds and precious metals to produce cuffs and bangles that she describes as wearable art.

Marlene de Beer
Cameo, 2011
4 x 2.5 cm
Slip-cast stoneware cameo
set in silver pendant with white
glass bead detail
Photo by Chris de Beer

Other contemporary jewelers are concerned with social and cultural notions. Popular culture and the idea of cuteness provide Eric Loubser with inspiration for his jewelry, which questions religion and consumerism, issues he views as the more troubling aspects of life. His miniature, self-enclosed worlds of small sculptures inside biosphere-like glass domes contrast serious social and personal commentary. Nanette Veldsman (née Nel), another graduate from Stellenbosch and current lecturer there, pushes the boundaries of contemporary jewelry and fine art practice. Her hot pink silicone brooches reference experimental materials, Ashanti talismans and the commercialized diamond industry, questioning the body-object relationship. She deconstructs traditional symbols of South African identity, which becomes a complex interrogation of her ethnicity, nationality and gender. *Verkeerd-om Protea* (2007), a pink silicone and silver brooch, is part of a collection that exploits the materiality of silicone and plays with the concept of secrets. The back of the brooch contains the detail, known only to the wearer, while the front challenges the viewer with the erotic overtones of its rubbery flower petals.

Namibian contemporary jeweler Frieda Lühl trained in Germany and at Stellenbosch University in South Africa. Using traditional jewelry techniques such as engraving, repoussé, enameling and mokume gane, she references Africa by incorporating local materials such as ostrich eggshell and Namibian gemstones, beach pebbles and shells. Lühl is part of a Namibian jewelry collective of young goldsmiths exploring what contemporary Namibian jewelry might be. Their first exhibition, 5 of a Kind, was held in 2011 at the Omba Gallery in Windhoek. Attila Giersch, Heike Lukaschik, Sylvia von Kuehne and Stefan Dietz, along with Lühl, are a small but innovative group. The aim of their first exhibition was to rethink traditional African materials—horn, wood, palm nuts, etc.—making use of them in original ways, with an individual approach. Lukaschik juxtaposes jewelry materials with long-established African crafting methods, incorporating basket-weaving techniques into silver wire.

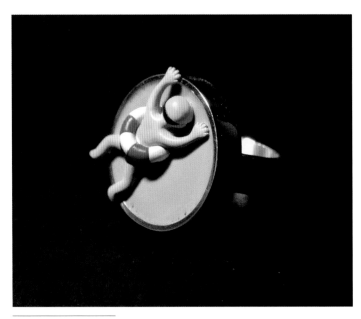

Geraldine Fenn
Untitled, 2007
3 x 2.4 x 2 cm
Sterling silver, resin, plastic
found object
Courtesy of the artist

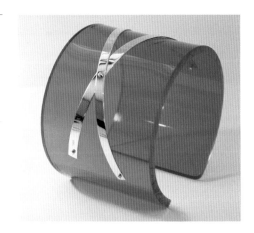

Philippa Green
*Amber Lucite Cuff with
Sterling Silver Strips,* n.d.
6.5 x 5 x 6.5 cm
Lucite, sterling silver
Photo by artist

Jewelers Working with African Artisans

Historically, artists and designers have looked to Africa for inspiration for their work, but more recently there's been an emergence of European jewelers working directly with African artisans, typically instigated by nongovernment organizations.[11]

Eric Loubser
Boom, 2008
5 x 6 x 6 cm
Sterling silver, glass, modeling
grass, found object, adhesive,
piercing
Photo by artist

Nanette Veldsman
Protea I & II, 2007
9 x 9 x 4 cm
Silicone, silver, onyx, gold leaf
Photo courtesy of the artist

Frieda Lühl
Untitled, n.d.
Pendant, 6 x 7 x 1 cm
Sponge coral, beach pebble,
ostrich eggshell, silver;
collected, fabricated, set
Photo by artist

This can be attributed to the popularity of craft and the handmade as an antidote to the mass-produced, homogenized goods spread by globalization. It also reflects the prominent rise of sustainability issues in design, both environmental and social, and the growth of "design for development."[12]

The San[13] of the Kalahari in Botswana have been part of two notable designer jewelry projects in recent years. In 2007 the Evangelischer Entwicklungsdienst (Church Development Service), an association of Protestant churches in Germany also known as EED, initiated a collaboration between Gantsi Craft Trust, a grassroots San craft project, and the French/Ivorian fashion designer Mickaël Kra. From workshops held with the San, Kra produced a range of jewelry, *Pearls of the Kalahari,* made from ostrich eggshell beads, leather, porcupine quills and glass beads. All the collaborators spoke of an exchange of ideas and skills, and the San hoped the project would assist in presenting a new image of themselves to the rest of the world. Kra credits the collaboration with inspiring his future design work, while the Church Development Service believed that it provided a lever toward socioeconomic advancement for the San.[14] This was also the aim of UK-based gem specialist Anna Haber, who in 2010 brought together jewelry designer Sabine Roemer and the San from Gantsi Craft to produce the *Jewels of the Kalahari* fashion jewelry collection. The jewelry, which sold in London boutiques, combined ostrich eggshell beads with silk ribbon and silver. Haber's goal was to create awareness of the San and build a sustainable business to generate a consistent income and ongoing work for the San.

European jewelers are working along similar lines in other parts of Africa, too. French product designer Florie Salnot designed a jewelry range with women in the Saharawi refugee camps of Algeria using plastic bottles. The aim was to make the non-precious valuable and draw economic gain for the women from waste. Salnot developed a unique, fully sustainable technique using hot sand from the desert to shape strips of plastic bottles that the women form into jewelry pieces to sell in Europe. In contrast to Salnot's direct use of the desert environment to make her jewelry and the recycling of plastic, British-based Maya Antoun draws on the ancient jewelry technique of filigree and, working in collaboration with artisans in Sudan and the Democratic Republic of Congo, produces jewelry that she describes as exploring the reality of globalization and hybrid cultural ethnicity. London-based

Antoun was born in the Sudan and her work is influenced by her multiethnic background. She brings the labor-intensive and slowly disappearing technique of filigree into a different context through her collaborations with Sudanese fashion designer Omer Asim. A traditional handcraft from Africa is transported to the modern catwalk. Salnot graduated from the Royal College of Art in 2010, the same year that Antoun graduated from Central Saint Martins College of Art and Design, which is indicative of the cross-cultural and interdisciplinary methodologies of current postgraduate design studies in the UK.

The history of jewelry apprenticeship, teaching and learning between Europe and South Africa, like cross-cultural and cross-discipline collaborations, goes in both directions. Several South African and Namibian jewelers have chosen to practice and teach in Europe. This two-way migration of jewelry skills and expertise calls into question the idea of African-ness as a fixed notion of identity and instead introduces multiplicity and hybridity. Well-known jeweler Daniel Kruger is originally from Cape Town, where he trained in the early 1970s before studying with Hermann Jünger at the Akademie der Bildenden Künste München (Academy of Fine Arts, Munich). Now a resident of Berlin and head of the jewelry program at Burg Giebichenstein Kunsthochschule Halle (University of Art and Design, in Halle, Germany), Kruger has a prominent jewelry practice and teaching career spanning Europe, South Africa and the United States. His jewelry is one of the best examples of primitivism in contemporary jewelry, fed by subtle and distinctive references to traditional crafts, material choices and the flora and fauna that make adornment in Africa distinctive.

Africa has long provided the inspiration and reference point for artists and jewelers in the West. In more recent times, researching and working side by side with Ashanti jewelers in Ghana, the Swiss jeweler Johanna Dahm has explored the ancient technique of lost-wax casting.[15] This range of jewelry, though stemming from low-tech origins, is sophisticated and has a contemporary sensibility that speaks softly of Africa. Continuing this exchange of skills and knowledge, Dahm, in 2011, taught the jewelry students at Stellenbosch University the low-tech, lost-wax casting techniques of the Ashanti, bringing West African jewelry knowledge to South Africa, echoing the continent's history and cross-cultural exchanges.

Florie Salnot
Plastic Gold Necklace, 2011
6 x 20 x 40 cm
Plastic bottle
Photo by Anne Schuhmann
Courtesy of Sandblast
(sandblast-arts.org)

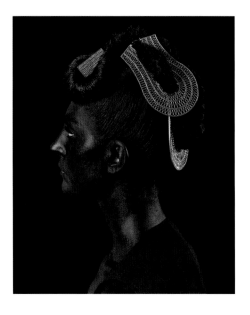

Maya Antoun
Untitled, 2011
Dimensions vary
Silver gilt, filigree
Photo by Jon Cartwright
Maya Antoun for Omer Asim

Daniel Kruger
Untitled, 2010
Length, 63.5 cm
Silver; forged, constructed,
pierced
Photo by Udo W. Beier
Courtesy of the artist

The Contemporary Jewelry Scene

The post-apartheid changes to the country, coupled with the rise of the Internet and globalization, have allowed South African contemporary jewelers to participate fully in international exhibitions. Errico Cassar, Daniel Kruger, Beverley Price, Chris de Beer and Carine Terreblanche have all successfully taken part in the well-established SCHMUCK jewelry competition held annually at the Internationale Handwerksmesse in Munich. In 2011 South African jewelers' profiles were raised internationally with two major exhibitions of work. Dichotomies of Objects: Contemporary South African Studio Jewelry from the Stellenbosch Area toured in the United States and eKapa: Contemporary Jewellery from Cape Town showed at the Bluecoat Display Centre in Liverpool, providing an opportunity for 12 jewelers from Cape Town, working in diverse materials, to showcase their work in the UK. Dichotomies in Objects illustrates the conceptual orientation of Stellenbosch University's jewelry department and represents a current of radical avant-garde practice in South African jewelry today. "A strong awareness of contemporary global jewelry practice informs the exhibition, and lends it a competitive and cosmopolitan feel. Often provocative in content or radically experimental in form, the emphasis is not on functionality but on expanding the frontiers of the applied arts in the South African context."[16]

The Fine Ounce Goldsmith Collective formed in 2011. It consists of seven jewelers based in Cape Town who have the aim of raising awareness of the process of designing and making unique jewelry and promoting the status of individually handcrafted pieces over mass-produced goods. Their work asks, "Can the terms *jewelry* and *art* ever be synonymous, or do they meet? If so, where?" These jewelers—Adi Cloete, Frieda Lühl, Giselle Petty, Heidi Liebenberg, Adeline Joubert, Maike Valcarcel and Jane McIlleron—exhibited together in the show 56 Rings in Cape Town and have plans to expand their collective further.

Over the past 10 years, South Africa has seen a rise in design as a result of a number of factors, which has also influenced contemporary jewelry development. First and foremost is the growth in design media. Before 2000, there were only a few lifestyle magazines available, prior to a huge increase in the variety of publications aimed specifically at the design market. The rise of the mobile phone opened up the African continent and made people aware of technology and its possibilities.[17] The escalation of arts and craft initiatives in the country, particularly those backed by the government, raised the profile of design and the creative industries throughout the country. This has also influenced the development of contemporary jewelry.

In 2005, the Design Indaba conference in Cape Town formed the country's first national, annual platform for contemporary jewelry at the Design Indaba Expo, which runs concurrently with the world-renowned design conference. Curated by established contemporary South African jewelers such as Geraldine Fenn, the exhibition Emerging Creatives introduces new jewelers to a national and international audience. The exhibition is sponsored by the Department of Arts and Culture and provides valuable exposure for young jewelers.

This focus on design isn't always supportive of the contemporary jewelry scene that is flourishing in South Africa. The Jewellery Council of South Africa is the only organization that provides support solely for jewelers, but it's geared toward commercial jewelry and the jewelry industry rather than contemporary jewelers. That there's little or no research output in this area and a lack of dedicated periodicals, magazines or journals are indications of the small size of the contemporary jewelry scene in South Africa. This is compounded by the lack of retail outlets for contemporary jewelers to sell their work, with only two shops, both in Johannesburg, specializing in contemporary jewelry handmade in South Africa. Tinsel stocks work by roughly 20 jewelers. Veronica Anderson Jewellery works with a different retail model, giving the jewelers she represents three or four themes per year for which they produce work. In other parts of the country there are galleries and shops that stock contemporary South African jewelry alongside other art, craft and design. Most notable are Africa Nova in Cape Town, The Dorp Street Gallery in Stellenbosch and the Artisan Contemporary Gallery in Durban. However, the universities and *technikons* continue to train jewelers who go on to win awards and exhibit both nationally and internationally. With the help of dynamic design platforms such as the Emerging Creatives exhibition, South African contemporary jewelry will continue to develop.

Nic Bladen
Fynbos Tiara, 2012
No dimensions given
Sterling silver
Photo by artist

Notes

1. Angela Fisher, *Africa Adorned* (London: Collins Harvill, 1984), 17.

2. The curriculum, workshops and studios for the Jewelry Design and Manufacture course have been in development for more than six years. The Certificate level is scheduled to begin in 2012–2013, followed by Advanced at a later date.

3. A Manufacturing Association survey in 2000 found that there were roughly 400 qualified jewelers, which, in a country of 50 million people, shows how small the sector really is.

4. Starting in 2008, all jewelers, regardless of the size of their business, had to apply for a gold license involving a lengthy set of conditions, including a demonstration of Black Economic Empowerment compliance. Due to cost, fulfilling the requirements has proved so difficult for sole traders, particularly designer/maker contemporary jewelers, that some have closed.

5. Fred van Staden, "South African Goldsmiths: Eric Frey, Stephen Colegate, Maia Holm, Maurice Pitol." *South African Journal of Cultural History*, July 2011. www.sagoldsmiths.blogspot.com/2011/07/south-african-goldsmiths-erich-frey.html.

6. Quoted in Dieter Jobst and Arno Jobst, *Kurt Jobst: Goldsmith and Silversmith, Art Metal Worker* (Johannesburg: Gerrit Bakker, 1979), 45.

7. M. Tibbs, ed., *Dichotomies in Objects: Contemporary South African Studio Jewelry from the Stellenbosch Area* (Stellenbosch: Department of Visual Arts, Stellenbosch University, 2010), 13, an exhibition catalog.

8. Carola Ross, *The Thuthuka Jewelry Development Programme* (Pretoria: Department of Arts and Culture, South African Government, 2010), 7, a project leaflet.

9. From her presentation at Design Indaba Inspire, 2005.

10. Marlene de Beer, "Memory-Based Expressions of the Self: Demonstration/Expression of Identity Through the Art of Making," in *Making Connections: Self-Study & Social Action*, ed. Kathleen Pithouse, Claudia Mitchell and Relebohile Moletsane (New York: Peter Lang Publishing, 2009), 77.

11. The American nonprofit organization Aid to Artisans is one of the most prominent organizations pairing designers from the United States and Europe with developing world artisans. Since 2007, they've worked with Italian design house Artecnica to produce the *Design w/Conscience* range of products.

12. The concept is not new (writers Victor Papanek and Gui Bonsiepe explored it), but in recent times it has highlighted the important role of design in sustainable economic development.

13. The issue of name is a contentious one and it is recognized that there's no single term used by all San groups (from Botswana, Namibia and South Africa) to call themselves. San, Bushmen, Basarwa and First People of the Kalahari are used interchangeably.

14. Vornese, F. and Annette Braun. *Mickael Kra: Jewellery Between Paris Glamour and African Tradition.* Germany: Arnoldsche, 2006.

15. Johanna Dahm, *Lost and Found: Asanti Trail to Rings* (Sulgen, Switzerland: Niggli Verlag, 1999).

16. Tibbs, *Dichotomies in Objects*, 9.

17. A. Viljoen, *Growing a Design Nation: 40 Years of South African Design Excellence* (CITY, South Africa: South African Bureau of Standards, 2010).

Further Reading

Clarke, Duncan. *African Hats and Jewelry*. London: Grange Books, 1998.

Fisher, Angela. *Africa Adorned*. London: Collins Harvill, 1984.

Jennings, Helen. *New African Fashion*. Munich: Prestel, 2011.

Jobst, Dieter, and Arno Jobst. *Kurt Jobst: Goldsmith and Silversmith, Art Metal Worker*. Johannesburg: Gerrit Bakker, 1979.

Jones, Linda Jeanne. *eKapa: Contemporary Jewellery from Cape Town*. Liverpool, UK: Bluecoat Display Centre, 2011. An exhibition catalog.

Kalman, Lauren. "South Africa: Unearthing Artistic Talent in the Land of Mining." *Metalsmith* 29, no. 3 (2010): 20–23.

Nettleton, Anitra C. E., Julia Charlton, and Fiona Rankin-Smith. *Engaging Modernities: Transformations of the Commonplace*. Johannesburg: University of the Witwatersrand Galleries, 2003.

Ross, Carola. *The Thuthuka Jewellery Development Programme*. Pretoria: Department of Arts and Culture, South African Government, 2010. A project leaflet.

Tibbs, M., ed. *Dichotomies in Objects: Contemporary South African Studio Jewelry from the Stellenbosch Area*. Stellenbosch: Department of Visual Arts, Stellenbosch University, 2010. An exhibition catalog.

Van der Star, Rene. *Ethnic Jewellery: From Africa, Asia and Pacific Islands*. Amsterdam: Pepin Press, 2002.

Van Staden, Fred. "South African Goldsmiths: Eric Frey, Stephen Colegate, Maia Holm, Maurice Pitol." *South African Journal of Cultural History*, July 2011. www.sagoldsmiths.blogspot.com/2011/07/south-african-goldsmiths-erich-frey.html.

3.

Contemporary Thinking for Contemporary Jewelry.

Damian Skinner

Unlike Part 1 and Part 2, in which contemporary jewelry is precisely defined and distinguished from jewelry and adornment, Part 3 takes a broader approach. While contemporary jewelry as a special kind of object and practice remains in view, some of these essays deal with conventional jewelry (gemstones, for example, or fine jewelry made in precious materials), or things like accessories or tattoos and body piercing, which more traditionally belong to fashion, design or sociology. How does contemporary thinking in other disciplines help us rethink the field of contemporary jewelry? How is contemporary jewelry being renewed by new ways of thinking about old problems or opportunities?

The present moment has been labeled the third wave of craft, with the first wave being the Arts and Crafts Movement, in which craft was formulated as an antidote to the industrial revolution, and the second wave being the studio craft movement, in which craft became a vehicle for originality and artistic expression. Like much contemporary art, third wave craft seeks to create and foster social relations, networks and communities through the processes of craft. Within the third wave, the high levels of skill involved in studio craft are a liability, a barrier to participation and engagement. The spirit of third wave craft is best expressed in the do-it-yourself (DIY) movement and in craftivism—craft skills engaged in the service of politics, community engagement and social networks. DIY craft, for example, is like studio craft stripped of its romantic associations. DIY craft doesn't believe in truth in the sense that animates studio craft—no truth to materials, for example. It also seeks to collapse distinctions between artist, craftsperson, designer and small-business owner.

The distinctive values of third wave craft reveal the limitations of our current models of writing about craft and contemporary jewelry. Craft discussions generally seek to validate the objects and practices they talk about. They favor celebration rather than critical perspectives and are quick to define the objects and processes of craft in an oppositional manner (e.g., not fine art, not design). This type of discussion tends to promote a victim culture in which craft needs to be protected, its traditions and heritage nurtured.

But a growing chorus of voices, including some of the authors of Part 3 of this book, argues that contemporary jewelry should give up trying to be a form of fine art and instead embrace the field of design. There is, of course, no right answer—just a lot of interesting possibilities, each of which involves gains and losses. The authors in Part 3 lay out different issues that might challenge the established ideas about contemporary jewelry, and identify some of the opportunities of the present and future.

The first four essays in Part 3 explore different ways in which jewelry-like objects and practices are operating in a dynamic way in the culture at large. The neurological effects of gemstones (discussed by Barbara Maria Stafford), the cultural life of jewelry (Marcia Pointon), the contemporary jewelry possibilities of accessories and modern technology (Elizabeth Fischer) and the socially charged practices of body modification (Philippe Liotard)—these aren't directly related to contemporary jewelry, but each topic offers a series of histories and ideas that can be used to think differently about the contemporary jewelry field. The next three essays tackle various "others" that contemporary jewelers have been struggling with throughout the twentieth century: conventional jewelry (Suzanne Ramljak), fine art (Julie Ewington) and design (Mònica Gaspar). The final three essays explore the implications of possibilities facing contemporary jewelry, as different ideas or movements, such as relational aesthetics (Helen Carnac) or DIY (Barb Smith), offer new ways to think about contemporary jewelry as a political practice (Kevin Murray).

These essays don't present a comprehensive picture of the challenges and opportunities that contemporary jewelry is facing a decade into the twenty-first century. They represent some of the issues that seem most pertinent for contemporary jewelry to come to terms with, such as DIY, critical design and the relational turn. Other essays seek to bring new perspectives to old questions, asking again what distinguishes contemporary from conventional jewelry, or how contemporary art and contemporary jewelry both relate to the temporality of their names, or how best to understand and take advantage of contemporary jewelry's social significance.

Laura Potter
You Are Not Special, 2010
7 x 5 x 0.5 cm
Cotton, linen, reclaimed metal
brooch, cross stitch
Photo by Matt Ward
Collection of the artist

The Jewel Game: Gems, Fascination and the Neuroscience of Visual Attention.

Barbara Maria Stafford

Each time our gaze strikes the surface of any material or substance, a small miracle occurs. That which was nothing before becomes something for a few moments, and then nothing again once our gaze is averted. Looking at jewels makes us aware that we are aware, integrating the mind with the body at a particular instant in time while simultaneously incorporating the nonhuman world into our innermost being. Flow, the cognitive psychologist Mihaly Csikszentmihalyi remarks, is that mental state when we are so involved in an activity that nothing else seems to matter.[1] Objects in this scenario are scaffolds to support moments of reflection. The present is extended indefinitely, prolonged until it's broken or interrupted.

This observation takes me back to one of the earliest memories of my mother, in which I'm a little girl sitting at her knee in a darkened room in Fort Monroe, Virginia. It's 1947 and we're peering into a leather jewel box. She and I have recently immigrated to the United States from war-torn Vienna with my stepfather. During the often-repeated ritual of opening and closing this box—a veritable memory palace—I relive her past experiences as if they are mine in an intense intimacy that will never come again. We sit alone. She weeps and speaks quietly in German of things I can't understand as she fingers a brandy-colored topaz necklace or a square-cut aquamarine ring or a floral spray of diamonds. Seeing and doing was undergoing. Old joys and pains were repurposed through pondering and paying close attention.

My mother now lies demented in a nursing home. When she speaks it's a muttered mixture of English and German and, increasingly, strange words of her own devising. On my visits, I bring bright baubles and jingling trinkets and always try to wear something she unfailingly desires: a brass belt with inlaid glass stones, a rope of resin beads, a metal cuff. She reaches out, smiling broadly, and strips me of my jewelry. Miraculously, jewels still attract her attention and remain somehow comprehensible in a cognitively darkened world where all other meaning has fallen away.

Why, when all else mentally speaking is gone, do we still notice bright, shiny, translucent gems? I argue it's because they so fundamentally engage our awareness that whatever's left of self-consciousness comes to the fore as a momentary but total involvement in the present. Individuals live in isolated spheres of incredible cognitive richness that get triggered by special objects. This raises a corresponding neuroscientific question: How does the brain work, say, to visually locate a coral necklace in the tangled depths of a jewel box, or to discern a broken bead of yellow amber on a cluttered table in a darkened room?

While Rudyard Kipling's metaphysical spy story, *Kim*, is about many things in colonial India, it's also fundamentally about the strenuous training of visual perception. Significantly, jewels and gems play a critical role in this acute education of the senses.

Consider this passage evoking the dim curiosity shop in Simla, run by the top British spy master, Lurgan Sahib, where the young boy Kim has gone to sharpen his visual acuity and so, too, become a spy. Kim muses that while his native Lahore Museum was larger, the shop had "more wonders— ghost daggers and prayer-wheels from Tibet; turquoise and raw amber necklaces; green jade bangles; curiously packed incense-sticks in jars crusted over with raw garnets; the devil masks of Buddha and little portable lacquer altars; Russian samovars with turquoises on the lid; egg-shell china sets in quaint octagonal cane boxes; yellow ivory crucifixes . . ."[2] But while "a thousand other oddments were cased, or piled, or merely thrown into the room," they were mere distractions to be ignored compared to the real work of understanding what to pay attention to.

This evocative passage captures in a nutshell an ancient worldview rooted in magic, technology and optical illusion. But Kipling's gem-studded descriptions also allow us to see jewels as present-day examples of embodied cognition, tokens of mental rehearsal and springboards for hypnagogic imagining. The ability to discern the difference between truth

and deception is one of the leitmotifs of the novel. As part of the training occurring within the dim confines of the curio shop, Sahib shows Kim how to discriminate "sick" balas rubies or "blued" turquoises from undoctored sapphires and fine pearls. This exercise serves as a prelude to the Jewel Game.

Not unlike contemporary virtual reality tools—electronic gloves, stereoscopic goggles—scintillant gems could act as conjuring devices summoning up alternative realities. The marvel-filled shop in Simla is both the venue and the inspiration for the start of the Jewel Game. As part of his initiation into the clandestine double-life "game" of British espionage in India, Kim and his opponent, the Hindu boy protégé of Sahib, must pore over a handful of stones cast onto a copper tray by the master of the game. After these trifling odds and ends are placed under wraps again, the battle of the competing attentional skills begins.

The Jewel Game is simple but the skill set required of the players is not. The two competitors must recall and describe precisely how variously patterned stones looked: their mineral composition, flaws, colors, cracks, chips, size, shape, inscriptions, age, veining and imagery. The winner has the most commanding technique, the most perfect recall. To put it scientifically, the Jewel Game is an attentional and detectional experiment requiring subjects to find and identify singular forms in a complex visual field. This test of perceptual and recollection skills seems to suggest that only a highly focused awareness is capable of attaining the real. What becomes clear, however, is that this power of luminous spatial arrays to attract and transport us owes less to mysticism and more to a fundamental discriminatory task of the primate visual system: the basic human need to search a cluttered visual scene for objects of interest.

By asking what holds vision (as in, what fascinates)—despite the nonstop conflicting information bombarding all of our senses during the course of everyday life—I want to shed light on integrative consciousness.[3] Noticing signifies cognitive receptivity, the careful absorption in mindful seeing.[4] Conversely, we should remember that engrossing gems have long protracted our attention spans, combating perpetual and endless distraction.[5] Observing or watching brings something to the center of our attention to the exclusion of all else.

The theory of fascination, founded on the power of suggestion and the supposed ability of natural or engraved gems to attract or repel cosmic influences, is thus newly relevant. The belief in the occult ability of individual colored stones to confer their virtues on the wearer and to transmit them at a distance through the force of concentrated vision raises key neuroscientific questions about consciousness

Unidentified photographer
Crystal Ball in the Hall of Gems and Minerals,
pre-1958
Smithsonian Institution Archives: Image # 2009-2187

Unidentified photographer
View of the Lahore Museum in Pakistan, ca. 1890
Alinari Archives via Getty Images

and the functions of our attentional networks. Like the art lover who succumbs to his discoveries and becomes an ardent collector, the "gem watcher" can become a practicing gem wearer.[6]

The production of fascination, or the artificial compelling of "awareness, concentration, consciousness and noticing" has a venerable history inseparable from the rise of optical technologies.[7] It's common to crystal ball scrying and divination rituals based upon staring into sacred wells, glass mirrors, globules of quicksilver, polished steel, level water and pools of ink to spot or discover something important that is otherwise invisible.[8] These ambiguous glossy surfaces serve "to attract the attention of the gazer and to fix the eye until, gradually, the optic nerve becomes so fatigued that it finally ceases to transmit to the sensorium the impression made from without and begins to respond to the reflex action proceeding from the brain of the gazer."[9] In short, as George Frederick Kunz, an early cultural historian of gems, remarks, the vertiginous effect of prolonged gazing is that the internal impression appears to be externally projected, seeming to originate outside the beholder's body.

Sparkling stones were long believed to mirror what computer scientist Jaron Lanier calls a "biorealistic" universe of wonders.[10] That is, their watery depths and brilliant surfaces were much more than reflectors of their surroundings. Old legends tell of the unsettling effects wrought by ominous and luminous stones, patterned minerals, sacred charms, symbolic signets, astrological tokens and prophylactic talismans on highly sensitive nervous systems.[11]

Gems and jewels thus exceed both their ancient role as magical artifacts as well as their contemporary incarnation as consumer products—expensive rocks bought or sold "because they are pretty," fashionable ornaments directed at arousing our drives and desires. Instead, we should view them primarily as controlling phenomenological experiences commandeering our visual attention.[12] Launching viewers into spatial exploration, these beautifully colored sighting and eye-tracking stones prove what neuroscientists studying the more than three dozen visual areas of the brain are showing, namely that to see is to attend.[13]

This hypnotic power of gems reveals the brain-mind's selection of physical features, such as shape, from the flow of distracting sensory events. But it also helps illuminate the enigma of the evolutionary purpose of color vision. Kipling's evocation of the riveting emotional as well as chromatic cues moving the eyes and grabbing the notice of the players ("all red and blue and green flashes" or "the vicious blue-white

Dorling Kindersley
A Collection of Colourful Gemstones, n.d.
Courtesy of Dorling Kindersley / Getty Images

spurt" of a diamond) makes the case for the essential role played by brightness and color in fixing the attention in a complex environment. Recall the high-arousal conditions operating in Lurgan Sahib's shadowy and dappled curio shop—an establishment, we are told, more cluttered than the Lahore Museum. Like a shock threat, each precious object flashes in the gloom.

Kim's attempt to combine and separate complex sensory signals coming from motley objects in the world is an externalization of the more general problem of visual sense. Vision's mechanisms are coded along a number of separable dimensions: color, orientation, shape, brightness, direction of movement. These features must be synthesized to form a single object, bound together and fixated by attention. While debate continues to swirl around the question of whether we first behold an object or its characteristics, jewels and jewelry suggest the primacy of the qualities (size, hue, faceting, brilliance) over the recombined representation.

Gems and jewels, then, create an interactive environment composed of affecting things. Because their purpose is to be noticed, to command interest, they enable us to be in someone else's mind. By scrutinizing them, we make someone's activity the center, object or topic of our attention. As portable devices for creating an intense kind of

connectedness and communication, efficacious gems shed light on the neuroscientific problems of attention, memory and reflection. They also tell us a lot about visual illusion. Seeing can block thinking, just as thinking can block seeing.

The primal belief in performative substances that lure and allure—such as carved or engraved talismans, spell-averting or procuring amulets, shimmery hypnotic moonstones, animated eye stones and binding love charms—surprisingly intersects with contemporary questions about how we orient our conscious and unconscious mental processing toward sensory stimuli, activate ideas from memory and maintain ourselves in an alert or contemplative state.[14] Gemstones have always been extensions of our senses, bodies and minds. Today, however, we can also understand them as tools for focused thinking, for demonstrating the connection between attention and consciousness.

Günay Mutlu
Yellow Diamond in the Dark, n.d.
© Günay Mutlu / Getty Images

Notes

1. Mihaly Csikszentmihalyi, *Flow: The Psychology of Optimal Experience* (New York: Harper & Row, 1990).

2. Rudyard Kipling, *Kim* (New York: The Modern Library, 2004), 153.

3. See my "Crystal and Smoke: Putting Image Back in Mind," in *A Field Guide to a New Meta-Field: Bridging the Humanities Neuroscience Divide,* ed. Barbara Maria Stafford (Chicago / London: University of Chicago Press, 2011), 49–58.

4. For more extensive explorations of the phenomenon of attention, see my *Echo Objects: The Cognitive Work of Images* (Chicago / London: University of Chicago Press, 2007), chapter 6; and *A Field Guide to a New Meta-Field*, introduction.

5. For a summary of recent research on mobile technologies ushering in an age of distraction, see Cathy N. Davidson, *Now You See It: How the Brain Science of Attention Will Transform the Way We Live, Work, and Learn* (New York: Viking Press, 2011).

6. Robert Wyndham, *Enjoying Gems: The Lure and Lore of Jewel Stones* (Brattleboro, VT: Stephen Greene Press, 1971), 13.

7. M. R. Bennett and P. M. S. Hacker, "Attention, Awareness and Cortical Function: Helmholtz to Raichle," in *History of Cognitive Neuroscience* (Oxford: Wiley-Blackwell, 2008), 44.

8. See my *Visual Analogy: Consciousness as the Art of Connecting* (Cambridge, MA / London: MIT Press, 1999), especially chapter 3, "The Magic of Amorous Attraction."

9. George Frederick Kunz, *The Curious Lore of Precious Stones* (Philadelphia / London: J.B. Lippincott Company, 1913), 176.

10. Jaron Lanier, *You Are Not a Gadget: A Manifesto* (New York: Alfred A. Knopf, 2010).

11. Isidore Kozminsky, *The Magic and Science of Jewels and Stones* (New York / London: G. P. Putnam's Sons, 1922), 18–71.

12. Colin McGinn, *Mindsight: Image, Dream, Meaning* (Cambridge, MA: Harvard University Press, 2004), 68.

13. Steven Yantis, "To See Is to Attend," *Science 299* (January 3, 2003): 54–55.

14. Paul E. Desautels, *The Gem Kingdom* (New York: A Ridge Press Book Random House, 1976), 12–30.

Further Reading

Bennett, M. R., and P. M. S. Hacker. "Attention, Awareness and Cortical Function: Helmholtz to Raichle." In *History of Cognitive Neuroscience.* Oxford: Wiley-Blackwell, 2008.

Csikszentmihalyi, Mihaly. *Flow: The Psychology of Optimal Experience.*
New York: Harper & Row, 1990.

Gazzaniga, Michael S. *The New Cognitive Neurosciences.* Cambridge, MA / London: MIT Press, 2000.

Kosslyn, Stephen M., and Olivier Koenig. *Wet Mind: The New Cognitive Neuroscience.* New York: Macmillan International, 1992.

Kunz, George Frederick. *The Curious Lore of Precious Stones.* Philadelphia / London: J. B. Lippincott Company, 1913.

McGinn, Colin. *Mindsight: Image, Dream, Meaning.* Cambridge, MA: Harvard University Press, 2004.

Posner, Michael I., Charles R. R. Snyder, and Brian J. Davidson. "Attention and the Detection of Signals." *Journal of Experimental Psychology* 109, no. 2 (June 1980): 160–174.

Stafford, Barbara Maria. *Echo Objects: The Cognitive Work of Images.* Chicago / London: University of Chicago Press, 2007.

———. *A Field Guide to a New Meta-Field: Bridging the Humanities-Neuroscience Divide.* Chicago / London: University of Chicago Press, 2011.

———. *Visual Analogy: Consciousness as the Art of Connecting.* Cambridge, MA / London: MIT Press, 1999.

The Cultural Meanings of Jewelry.

Marcia Pointon

"AHHH My beauty…past compare, these jewels bright I wear! … Tell me was I ever Margarita? Is it I? Come, reply!…Mirror, mirror tell me truly!" Lovers of Hergé's series of classic comic books featuring Tintin and his grumpy friend Captain Haddock will recognize this as the fragment of libretto (from "L'air des Bijoux" in Gounod's *Faust*) sung by Bianca Castafiore in several of the adventures. The Milanese diva is the owner of the Castafiore emerald, the theft of which is the centerpiece of the book of that title; Bianca is stout and matronly, and wears a lot of prominent jewelry.[1] This vignette of the aging and no-longer-beautiful celebrity anxiously examining her reflection in the mirror and carrying along priceless items of jewelry on her travels is a hybrid that encapsulates many of the cultural relations that jewelry and its ownership exemplify: the unchanging beauty of gemstones in contrast to the depredations of old age (against which they also serve as a defense); anxiety and loss; the way that jewelry can comprise extreme wealth in a small, readily transportable artifact; vulgarity, in-your-face taste and self-dramatization; self-delusion, desire and cupidity; the naming of jewels; and social disruption— the thief responsible for lifting the emerald turns out not to be the Roma gypsies who are the suspects, but a magpie, and we are thus reminded that speculations surrounding the possible thieves of famous jewels may underscore assumptions about class and race.

Hergé (Georges Prosper Remi)
The Castafiore Emerald, 1963
© Hergé / Moulinsart 2012

In autumn 2011, the jewelry of Elizabeth Taylor attracted record visitors prior to its auction. As with other famous assemblages of jewelry (the Duchess of Windsor's, sold in Geneva in 1987, went for $50 million), there are certain pieces that, like the Castafiore emerald, are understood to embody the life story of the owner and are named accordingly.[2] The Taylor-Burton Diamond, referencing Taylor's fifth marriage, to Richard Burton, is one such. Jewelry acquires value from this kind of provenance. In the early eighteenth century, the Duchess of Marlborough wrote memoranda about her jewelry, specifically registering, for example, "the fine large pear [i.e., pearl] drops that were the queen of Bohemia's."[3] The Lennox jewel was acquired by Queen Victoria in 1842 for her private jewelry collection. A locket commissioned by the Countess of Lennox, almost certainly in memory of her husband, who died in battle in 1571, it had been one of the most prized objects in the collection of the eighteenth-century connoisseur Horace Walpole.

Named jewelry, then, works as a sort of archive or register; bodies that have owned, worn and touched the artifacts leave a phantom imprint. Clothing does something similar, but this is readily accounted for by the fact that garments shape themselves to accommodate the particularities of an individual body. Jewelry, however, is always to some degree or other hard and resistant: while materials vary (with diamonds the hardest mineral of all), the setting with jewels mounted in it doesn't normally shape itself to the body but is superimposed onto it. Furthermore, jewelry can be readily dismantled and the more valuable the stones it contains, the more susceptible it is to rapid transformation by thieves. In contrast, Vermeer and Rembrandt paintings get stolen but no one can turn them into raw material for resale, nor do they carry with them an aura of their previous owners.

To name something is to claim ownership in a public act of affirmation: it's a social gesture as well as a kind of descriptor or cataloging device allowing that item to be distinguished from others in a collection. The names survive even if the events or alliances that gave rise to the names do not. Moreover, giving a precious stone a name overwrites its complex origins, often erasing a history of theft, bribery, murder and corruption and thereby presenting the gem as pure value, aesthetic and financial. The egg-shaped Orlov diamond, for example, with its 189.60 carats cut into approximately 180 facets, originated in India, where it was looted in the eighteenth century by a French, or perhaps Afghan, soldier. In a sequence of events involving a double murder, the stone eventually reached Amsterdam, where Count Orlov, a Russian nobleman who had orchestrated

Unidentified maker
The Darnley or Lennox jewel, ca. 1571–1578
6.6 x 5.2 cm
Gold, enamel (émail en ronde bosse, émail basse-taille), Burmese rubies, Indian emerald, cobalt blue glass
Supplied by Royal Collection Trust / © HM Queen Elizabeth II, 2012

the assasination of Catherine the Great's husband, Peter III, purchased it. Orlov had been Catherine's lover, but he'd been cast aside and hoped to buy himself back into her favor with the gift of this immense stone. Catherine accepted the gift but didn't welcome him back into her arms. The Orlov diamond was mounted in the Imperial Sceptre, which is displayed in the Treasures of the Diamond Fund at the Kremlin.[4]

To attach your name to a precious stone is to advertise your power to acquire something of immense value. Thus, when London jeweler Laurence Graff paid more than $46 million for a rare pink diamond, he immediately renamed it the Graff Pink.[5] When he bought it, the 24.78-carat pink diamond was mounted in a ring, but this was of no interest to observers and presumably not to its new owner, either.

Jewelry is a tautological term. With an etymology that goes back to the Middle Ages, it refers to what is made by a jeweler, or to ornaments sold by a jeweler. Likewise, a jeweler is one who sells jewelry. Jewelry is also a collection of jewels, and has traditionally referred especially to items in which precious stones were mounted.[6] While jewelry made of non-precious materials may have immense personal value as a receptacle for memory, as a nonverbal record of an event or as possessing a talismanic quality that its owner believes will be magically effective, it is precious stones mounted in

jewelry that produce this unique configuration whereby the setting (with all its artistry and craftsmanship) may be simply overridden by the compelling value of the gemstone. One explanation for this is that the mount originates in a period and has a particular style and may therefore be regarded as unfashionable, whereas the stone never changes.

This oscillation between the timeless and the time-bound has been a source of great fascination. Only in static collections like treasuries—the best example is perhaps that of the Habsburg Empire now in the care of the Kunsthistorisches Museum in Vienna—are we likely to find precious stones in their original settings. The idea of a private collection of jewelry is always relative. Collectors of paintings, wine or corkscrews don't appear publicly with them on their bodies. But jewelry occupies an uncertain ground between personal adornment, work of art and financial investment, and at the end of the day (as the sale of Elizabeth Taylor's jewelry demonstrates) it is financial value that triumphs. The collection is dispersed, the stones may be renamed and remounted, and they will in all likelihood disappear from sight. Inherited heirlooms are by definition supposed to remain unaltered (the owner has custody for his or her lifetime only) but the line between heirloom and personal jewelry often gets blurred, not least in royal collections.[7]

William M. Vander Weyde
World's Great Diamonds: Nassau / Grand Duke of Tuscany / Orlov, n.d.
16.5 x 21.6 cm
Negative, gelatin on glass
Courtesy of George Eastman House, International Museum of Photography and Film

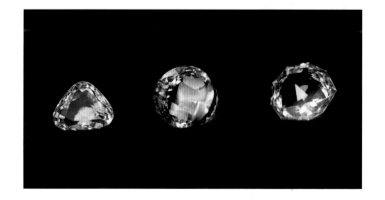

We might consider jewelry in two categories: the useful and the affective. When we think of jewelry today, it tends to be personal adornment that comes to mind. The rapper Nelly, posing in lots of bling, demonstrates the use of jewelry as affirmation of the wearer's status and ability to purchase expensive consumer goods, and draws attention by its glitter to his fine physique. Owning glittering jewels has never, however, been a prerequisite to benefiting from them. When the stars at the Oscar awards photographed for tabloid magazines appear in diamonds loaned by Bulgari, De Beers, Harry Winston and others, both parties profit by the advertisement.[8] This wouldn't have surprised Mary Delany, a bluestocking who became famous for her correspondence, flower drawings and collages. In 1729, she attended court "in all my best array, borrowed my Lady Sunderland's jewels, and made a tearing show."[9] What matters in these instances is that the stones are not only real, but are known to be so. The imprimatur of Lady Sunderland (whose jewels would certainly have been recognizable), or of famed American jewelry company Harry Winston, guarantees their authenticity and thus their enhancement of the wearer. Valuable jewelry worn in public is useful to the wearer insofar as it reminds people of the wearer's purchasing power (direct or indirectly through gifts), but it is also affective in that it arouses feelings in viewers—whether of awe, envy, admiration or a subliminal desire to emulate.

Authentic jewels were described by the sociologist Georg Simmel as "super-individual." He argued that "the appearance of the 'genuine' consists in the fact that it represents, in every respect, more than its mere outward appearance, more than this appearance shares with a fake."[10] So the important thing with fake jewelry is for no one to know it's fake. In the eighteenth century, when jewelry was often the only capital over which women had control, it wasn't uncommon for fakes to be substituted for genuine, even mixing authentic and imitation in the same setting, perhaps because a gambling debt needed to be paid. Today we are told, "Replicas take away the worry." Rapper Jay-Z proposed to singer Beyoncé with an 18-carat flawless diamond ring worth an estimated $5 million, but also gave her an imitation version to wear in public.[11]

The idea of jewelry functioning exclusively as adornment is relatively new. Throughout the early modern period (ca. 1600–1800) and on through the nineteenth century, any man with claims to gentility would have had his own personal seal or set of seals, which were often attached by a ribbon and displayed prominently rather than being tucked inside his breeches. Unlike Nelly's bling, seals had a practical use:

Bryce Duffy
Nelly, 2004
© Bryce Duffy/CORBIS OUTLINE

their imprint in warm wax, sealing an envelope, guaranteed the identity of the correspondent. The gentleman would also have had a cane with an elaborate and expensive head.[12] A lady of the house in an elite family would have owned a chatelaine; this ornamental clasp was worn at the waist during the day with useful things like keys, a watch, scissors, household notebook, seals and penknives attached to it. But the object itself was often of gold or silver and highly embellished. It worked as an ornament, a useful device and a status symbol.

There's something forlorn about pawnbrokers' shop windows, with their displays of jewelry that was once carefully chosen and personally valued and that has, of necessity rather than desire, been exchanged for cash. Small, worn on the body, handled and often valuable, jewelry connects people separated by circumstance and history. In particular, lockets, the combination of miniature portraits and jewelry that can be worn around the neck or kept hidden close to the body, resonate across time and space. When Mozart was on a long professional tour in 1789, he took with him such an object, writing to his wife, "My dearest, most beloved little wife! — Remember that each night before going to bed I talk to your portrait for a good half an hour and do so again when I wake up."[13] Lockets sometimes contained the hair of a loved one,

Unidentified maker
Chatelaine, early nineteenth century
53.5 x 35 x 2 cm
Cut steel
© Victoria and Albert Museum, London / V &A Images

whether living or dead, thus enshrining a bodily trace in the manner of a relic.

Although the fashion for lockets declined at the end of the nineteenth century, the importance of jewelry as bearer of family memories did not. Among items collected in the Jewish Museum Berlin are many small-scale personal possessions, witnessing not only to the convenience of jewelry as portable wealth in times of trouble but also to the value placed on jewelry as freighted with memory. Jacob Simon and his family, emigrating from Bingen on the Rhine to Chile just before the outbreak of World War II, took the jewelry that had belonged to his mother, who had died in 1928 or 1930. Now back in Germany and displayed in a case under the title *Objects of Memory*, the jewelry serves as a correlative for the unspeakable losses suffered by refugees.

Many jewelry designs imitate natural forms such as flowers and foliage or small creatures. These visual references, devised though craft skills in materials that endure, bring together notions of timelessness, freedom and personal identity in an object that draws the eye and demands both scrutiny and touch. They cannot answer Bianca Castafiore's question "Is it I?" but they can offer the illusion of a beauty that's not subject to the destruction of time. As jeweler Humphrey Butler declared in an advertisement, "Jewellery! Because Great Sex Doesn't Last Forever!"[14]

Notes

1. Hergé published the original *Les Bijoux de la Castafiore* as a strip between 1961 and 1962, and in book form in 1963. www.tintinologist.org/guides/books/21castafiore.html.

2. Avril Groom, "Watches and Jewellery," *Financial Times*, November 12, 2011.

3. Althorp Papers, British Library Add MS. 75402 quoted in Marcia Pointon, "Material Manoeuvres: Sarah Churchill and the Power of Artefacts," *Art History* 32, no. 3 (June 2009): 495.

4. DeeDee Cunningham, *The Diamond Compendium* (London: NGA Press, 2011), 648–650.

5. Acquired November 2010. www.graffdiamonds.com/_html/index.php?sectionid=2&pgid=590.

6. This tradition has been challenged by designers employing inexpensive materials such as plastics in the twentieth and twenty first centuries.

7. Queen Marie Antoinette, for one, disregarded this distinction and appropriated items from the Crown Jewels for her personal use.

8. The names of the lenders are cited in the photo captions. "Bling around the Collar" and "Dripping with Ice," *People*, March 15, 2004, 57–58.

9. Mrs. Pendarves (later Mary Delany) to Mrs. Anne Granville, March 4, 1728/29, in *The Autobiography and Correspondence of Mary Granville, Mrs. Delany,* 3 vols., ed. Lady Llanover (London: R. Bentley, 1861–2), 191. For this and other examples, see Marcia Pointon, *Brilliant Effects: A Cultural History of Gem Stones and Jewellery* (New Haven, CT / London: Yale University Press, 2009), 24–5.

10. Georg Simmel, "Exkurs über den Schmuck," in *Soziologie: Untersuchungen über die Formen der Vergsellschaftung* (Writings of Sociology), in *Georg Simmel: Gesamamtausgabe,* ed. O. Rammstedt, Band xi (Frankfurt-am-Main, Germany: Suhrkamp, 1992), 412–21, quoted in Pointon, *Brilliant Effects*, 4.

11. Miranda Bryant, "More Londoners Are Faking It to Keep Hold of Their Jewellery," *Evening Standard*, October 24, 2011.

12. The Bond Street jeweler, Asprey, still sells canes with fancy heads as part of its range of gifts.

13. Wolfgang Amadeus Mozart to his wife, April 16, 1789, in *Mozart: A Life in Letters,* eds. Cliff Eisen and Stewart Spencer (Harmondsworth, UK: Penguin, 2006), 166.

14. *Vanity Fair,* January 2008, 63.

Further Reading

Balfour, Ian. *Famous Diamonds.* 3rd edition. London: Christie, Manson & Woods Ltd., 1997.

Culme, John, and Nicholas Rayner. *The Jewels of the Duchess of Windsor.* London: Thames & Hudson in association with Sotheby's, 1987.

Epstein, Edward Jay. *The Diamond Invention.* London: Hutchinson, 1982.

Fales, Martha Gandy. *Jewelry in America, 1600–1900.* Woodbridge, UK: Antique Collectors' Club, 1995.

Howarth, Stephen. *The Koh-i-Noor Diamond: The History and the Legend.* London: Quartet Books, 1980.

Papi, Stefano. *The Jewels of the Romanovs: Family and Court.* London: Thames & Hudson, 2010.

Pointon, Marcia. *Brilliant Effects: A Cultural History of Gem Stones and Jewellery.* New Haven, CT / London: Yale University Press, 2009.

Scarisbrick, Diana. *Jewellery in Britain, 1066–1837: A Documentary, Social, Literary and Artistic Survey.* Norwich, UK: Michael Russell, 1994.

Taylor, Elizabeth. *My Love Affair with Jewelry.* New York: Simon & Schuster, 2002.

Tolliver, Gabriel A., and Reggie Ossé. *Bling: The Hip-hop Jewellery Handbook.* London: Bloomsbury, 2006.

Yogev, Gedalia. *Diamonds and Coral: Anglo-Dutch Jews and Eighteenth-Century Trade.* Teaneck, NJ: Holmes & Meier, 1978.

The Accessorized Ape.

Elizabeth Fischer

In the 1961 film *Breakfast at Tiffany's*, Holly Golightly introduces her neighbor Paul Varjak, a penniless writer, to Tiffany's. Paul looks for a present for Holly, and the salesman suggests a relatively affordable sterling silver telephone dialer: "Strictly as a novelty, you understand, for the lady and gentleman who has everything." It's highly plausible that in 1961 Tiffany's would sell not only jewelry but also small items closely related to the human body. However, to catch the eye of those who already have all the high-end jewelry they want and the means to buy it, the telephone dialer must be endowed with preciousness. This is achieved not because it's made of silver, but through its nature as something absolutely state of the art and modern. It bestows on the user the status of someone who can afford the most up-to-the-minute object.

The silver telephone dialer answers all the requirements of jewelry: it's small, precious, an article of value, a status symbol, an object "worn by people as decorative and symbolic additions to their outward appearance."[1] The telephone dialer is an ornament for the household or office. It's as closely linked to the user's body as jewelry is, for it extends the finger, replicating its function. Finally, it's an object perfectly in tune with its times, a "novelty," like any fashionable item. Does the similarity between jewelry and the dialer place them in the same category? Does a telephone dialer, which is an accessory, become a piece of jewelry when it's made of silver? Does a piece of jewelry become an accessory when it's not made of precious stones and metals?

Commonly, jewelry isn't considered functional, whereas accessories always have utility. However, they're similar in many ways: both are in close—even intimate—connection with the body; both act as a primary means to express at once individual and social identity; both become intensely personal items; today, both are considered desirable, even "must-haves"; both have become contemporary conversation pieces. Jewelry and accessories have developed into highly functional items in terms of society and consumption, identity and emotions. This similarity is a twentieth-century development in the relationship of jewelry and accessories to dress and the body.

Almost up to World War I, only the face and hands were visible in Western dress. The rest of the body was completely covered by garments. Even heads were covered with hats and framed by collars and veils, while hands were enhanced by lace cuffs or sheathed in mitts and gloves. Save for rings on the fingers, jewelry was never directly in contact with the body. Rather, it was worn over clothing. In aristocratic dress, jewels were often sewn onto the material, integrated in the outfit's decoration. Gemstones and precious metals were the preserve of the noble, rich and powerful. Assembled as jewels, they spoke of power, lineage, patrimony and wealth.

Starting in the nineteenth century, the trappings of the new wealthy businessmen and industrialists increasingly rivaled the prized jewels worn by the aristocracy. A growing affluent middle class aspired to new forms of jewelry. To meet demand, jewelry was produced industrially from cheaper materials. It also gradually succumbed to the vagaries of fashion and became less tied to special occasions and their required formal wear. Jewelry enhanced the cleavage and arms bared by evening gowns. It was just one ornament among many others in female dress, where woven patterns were bedecked with embroidery and lace. Jewelry imparted movement and sparkle to an otherwise stiff corseted silhouette, a function usually overlooked in histories of fashion or jewelry.[2]

The upheaval of World War I ushered in a new era in dress, more notably for women. Dresses shortened, while evening wear completely revealed the arms and the back. Jewels were no longer sewn onto the material, and clothing became less ornamented. The new streamlined silhouettes changed the relationship between jewelry and dress. *Vogue* stated in 1921: "Sparkling jewellery is undoubtedly an absolute necessity for modern fashion."[3] In 1926, Gabrielle Chanel perfected the little black dress, considered one of the starting points of modern fashion. It could be worn

Anoush Abrar and Aimée Hoving
Fashion Series: Mama, 2010
© Anoush Abrar & Aimée Hoving

from morning to evening, suited to any occasion simply by dressing it up or down with jewelry.

Although Chanel designed costume jewelry meant for pairing with unadorned outfits, she herself didn't hesitate to wear several different necklaces (or brooch and necklace) over a decorative collar or a cardigan with a striped motif. Moreover, she boldly mixed precious and costume jewelry, thus putting the focus on aesthetic function as signifier of taste rather than indicator of rank, fortune and status. Ornament and beauty weren't equated with preciousness anymore. Jewelry, especially costume jewelry, entered the category of accessories that included shoes, gloves, hats, fans, canes, parasols, etc. In this way, as chief adornment of modern dress, jewelry, far from being *accessory*, was deemed absolutely *necessary*.

Chanel freed jewelry from its centuries-old bond with a woman's dependence on a man, as either legitimate spouse or kept woman. In combining fake and real jewels, she consciously charted the way for women to appropriate jewelry as a personal and chosen expression of taste and statement of identity, just like any other accessory.[4] Chanel thus heralded current female consumer practices. More and more women live independent lives and careers and are affluent enough to buy pricy jewelry for themselves. Furthermore, they don't think twice about wearing it with jeans or inexpensive garments.

The hippie revolution brought two major changes in Western dress. The body was suddenly very much revealed, and men adopted some feminine traits: colorful and patterned clothing, textile ornamentation (embroidery, frills), long hair and jewelry hitherto reserved for women, such as necklaces, bracelets and earrings. The masculine adoption of jewelry further confirmed its transfer to the field of accessories. Jewelry for men is a rich area for future market and design development, in close connection with the design of electronic devices.

Today, other parts of the body have become even more exposed: waist, midriff, lower back, buttocks, legs. It isn't just a question of more skin exposure. Synthetic fabrics and jerseys—elastic, thin, sometimes more or less transparent, clinging and mercilessly figure-hugging—delineate every limb and muscle, especially because clothing is rarely lined and underwear is minimal. The body now isn't so much clothed as adorned, adorned with accessories and…adorned in visibility. This has ushered in new types of ornaments, applied directly to the skin. Tattooing and piercing have existed since antiquity, but for centuries were used as discriminating signs, for specific groups at the margins of society. They became particularly visible with the punk movement, as signs of rebellion against the establishment, before being taken up by the mainstream. The fashion industry used this type of

A Young Lady on the High Classical School of Ornament From Punch, July 16, 1859
General Research Division, The New York Public Library, Astor, Lenox and Tilden Foundations

A YOUNG LADY ON THE HIGH CLASSICAL SCHOOL OF ORNAMENT

skin decoration to create shock waves on the catwalk and in advertisements. With its adoption as an ornament by younger generations, piercing no longer has rebellious connotations. It's used to highlight specific parts of the body and add a kinetic dimension.[5] The studs and other items used for piercing exactly fit the definition of jewelry, though they're not yet considered as such.

In the 1990s, jewelry was used in spectacular ways to highlight fashion in catwalk shows. Fashion designers relied on hair and makeup artists, stylists, accessory and jewelry designers, and music and set designers to augment the visual impact of their shows. "The emergence of jewellery in this period was different because it pinpointed a relationship with the body rather than the space surrounding it. Indeed, often the style of the jewellery came to summarize the style of the designer in a kind of pictorial shorthand."[6] In shows and advertisements, jewelry has become a way of expanding the brand's message. For the past 30 years, accessories have brought in the most income for high and low brands. In the hierarchical relationship between clothing, considered essential, and accessories, considered secondary, sales have tipped in favor of accessories. Jewelry is now in the fore, indispensable in the performance of fashion on the catwalk and in the street.[7]

Today, both young men and women have wholly adopted this culture of the accessory, wearing caps, earrings, chains, bracelets, sporting bags and indispensable electronic devices. These last have become vital to the "supermodern" human being—always on the move, always connected, living with an overabundance of space, information and individualization, as defined by the anthropologist Marc Augé.[8]

Younger generations have embraced the mobile phone as an extension of their identity. It's kept permanently close at hand, if not in hand. They go to extreme lengths to personalize it with jingles, pictures and applications. It's the depository of their social selves, harboring all their contacts and exchange of messages.[9] As electronic devices become more sophisticated, they also become the repository of knowledge, obtainable in seconds flat with the swipe of a finger.

The "ornaments" custom made for these technological tools prove how precious they are to their users: patterned covers, trinkets to dangle from them, incrustations of Swarovski crystals, if not real diamonds. Some items become one with the person. (Watches are almost never taken off, even in the pool or the shower.) The mobile phone is kept by the bedside, and in the pocket or bag all day. It's the last thing to go on the dresser before bed, and the first item to be donned or consulted. The day's outfit is now paired with

---

Cecil Beaton
Coco Chanel in London, ca. 1938
© Condé Nast Archive / Corbis

fine white cables that link earpieces to portable electronic appliances. These cables are the ubiquitous twenty-first-century necklace, taking no account of gender, class or age.

We use a piece of electronic equipment to get in touch with the wide, wide world of our friends and acquaintances, to hear our favorite tunes and use selected applications, to receive information, to consult and share the documents stored in our personal cloud, another invisible (or rather, immaterial) extension of the self. However, to access this permanent connection, there's always the need for a real tool, a vehicle, which remains undisputedly material. So, too, has jewelry always been about human relationships and communicating social position and identity. It remains precious both materially and emotionally, small in size, and close to the body. Accessories, including jewelry as it has evolved in the twentieth century, have taken over the function jewelry used to have. Jewelry still has that purpose; however, it has also become an expression of personal identity, taste and beliefs.

Jewelry designers are now free to explore much wider avenues than preciousness and social rituals. Using the body as a catalyst rather than a location, they question our relationship to materials, to objects and to the body. Naomi Filmer's *Breathing Volume* sculptures focus on the mouth, chin and neck, describing the association between a volume of space and the body, the space through which a person passes and the space that passes through a person as the breath goes in and out.[10] As a jewelry designer, Filmer focuses her main area of exploration on the body in its relationship to materials and objects, as a conversation between flesh, body and object, which encompasses sensations, aesthetic definitions, attitudes, postures and points of communication. Standing at the nexus of art, fashion and design, her work highlights the intrinsic preciousness of the contemporary body. More straightforwardly, Philipp Eberle's *Wind of Chains* headphone set highlights issues of communication, posture and aesthetics surrounding the ubiquitous earpiece cables.

The modern avatar of the silver telephone dialer, as extension of the finger, is the stylus used instead of thumb and finger on the portable screen. We're still material girls and boys, and accessories are our best friends, however much part of our world now revolves in a virtual and immaterial dimension. New needs can be answered by the qualities of jewelry, while a wide range of objects, from accessories to prosthetics, benefit from the design, development and manufacture of jewelry. "Eyeglasses have been transformed from medical necessity to fashion accessory. This revolution

---

Naomi Filmer
BREATHING VOLUME: absorb, 2009
35 x 30 x 40 cm
Resins and polymers; hand fabricated
Photo by Jeremy Forster
Han Heffken Foundation

Naomi Filmer
Orchid Neck-Piece for Anne-Valerie Hash, 2008
23 x 20 x 20 cm
Silver plate on copper electroforming over synthetics
Photo by Jeremy Forster
Anne-Valerie Hash Archive

has come about through embracing the design culture of the fashion industry."[11] In the same way, design sensibilities might be applied to hearing and communication aids, even to inner prostheses like the pacemaker. In making these objects appealing, design helps foster a positive relationship with disabilities and their outward signs and effects. A hearing aid doesn't actually have to *look* like a hearing aid. Its design can refer to other items for the ear: earrings, earphones, Jawbone Bluetooth headsets that fit in or around the ear or the tasseled earplugs worn by Holly Golightly when her neighbor knocks at the door. In this way, jewelry and its makers offer new insights on the relationship of objects with the body, challenging traditional boundaries.

The bodies of today engage us in our social life, are the standard bearers of our identity and are still the main seat of emotions, sensations and actions. The bionic bodies so often imagined for the future should retain the same capacities, augmented by extensions made of materials. In this sense, the body is absolutely precious, as highlighted in Filmer's works. Without the body, adornment and accessories are meaningless. As long as objects are meaningful vectors in our relationships with others and our environment, and the more materials are intricately incorporated into the body and the person, the realm of jewelry will have a part to play in society and in individuals' lives.

Philipp Eberle
Wind of Chains, 2010
20 x 45 cm
Headphones, jewelry components
Photo by Sabine Hartel
Courtesy of the artist

Notes

1. Marjan Unger, "*Freedom Has Its Limitations. Jewellery Today, Seen from a Dutch Perspective*" (lecture, Pinakothek der Moderne, Munich, during SCHMUCK 2012). http://die-neue-sammlung.de/archive/event/2012/marjan-unger-freedom-has-its-limitations-jewelry-now/?L=1.

2. Elizabeth Fischer, "Jewellery and Fashion in the Nineteenth Century," in *The Fashion History Reader: Global Perspectives,* eds. Giorgio Riello and Peter McNeil (London / New York: Routledge, 2010), 311–313.

3. Jean Castarède, *Histoire du luxe en France: Des origines à nos jours* (Paris: Éditions Eyrolles, 2007), 309–310.

4. For more on the subject of Chanel's influence on the norms of femininity, see Martha Banta, "Coco, Zelda, Sara, Daisy, and Nicole: Accessories for New Ways of Being a Woman," in *Accessorizing the Body, Habits of Being I,* eds. Christina Giorcelli and Paula Rabinowitz (Minneapolis / London: University of Minnesota Press, 2011), 82–107.

5. Karmen MacKendrick, "Technoflesh or, 'Didn't That Hurt?'" *Fashion Theory* 2, no. 1 (March 1998): 3–24.

6. Caroline Evans, *Fashion at the Edge: Spectacle, Modernity, and Deathliness*, 2nd ed. (New Haven, CT / London: Yale University Press, 2007), 231–233. Maia Adams, *Fashion Jewellery: Catwalk and Couture* (London: Laurence King Publishing, 2012) offers an overview of an entire generation of contemporary jewelry designers creating fashion jewelry.

7. Suzy Menkes, "Baubles, Bangles and Bags: Who Cares about the Clothes?" *International Herald Tribune*, October 6, 2002.

8. See Marc Augé, *Non-Places: Introduction to an Anthropology of Supermodernity* (London: Verso, 1995), 35–36; Andrew Bolton, *The Supermodern Wardrobe* (London: V&A, 2002), 7.

9. Corinne Martin, "Le telephone portable, un objet incorporé?" in *Objet, Bijou et Corps, In-corporer*, eds. Monique Manoha and Alexandre Klein (Paris: L'Harmattan, 2008), 85–96, texts from the fourth Biennale du Bijou Contemporain de Nîmes held in the fall of 2005.

10. Interview with Naomi Filmer, http://arttube.boijmans.nl/en/video/AoF-NF-en. The sculptures were shown in the exhibition *The Art of Fashion, Installing Allusions* at the Museum Boijmans van Beunigen, The Art of Fashion, Installing Allusions (Rotterdam: Museum Boijmans van Beunigen, 2009), an exhibition catalog.

11. Graham Pullin, *Design Meets Disability* (Cambridge, MA: MIT Press, 2009), 16–23, 38.

Further Reading

Brand, Jan, and José Teunissen, eds. *Fashion & Accessories*. Arnhem, The Netherlands: ArtEZ Press, 2007.

Cappellieri, Alba, ed. *Jewelry Now: Art, Fashion, Design*. Milan: Electa, 2011.

Farren, Anne, and Andrew Hutchinson. "Cyborgs, New Technology, and the Body: The Changing Nature of Garments." *Fashion Theory* 8, no. 4, (2004): 461–476.

Finessi, Beppe, ed. *Ultrabody*. Mantua, Italy: Corraini, 2012.

Museum Bellerive, Zurich, and MUDAC, Lausanne. *Body Extensions*. Stuttgart: Arnoldsche Art Publishers, 2004.

Neri, Leyla Belkaïd, ed. *Access to Accessory*. Geneva: Haute école d'arts appliqués HES Geneva, 2005.

Pieter T'Jonck, ed. *SuperBodies*. Exhibition catalog for the third edition of the Triennial for Contemporary Art, Fashion, and Design in Hasselt, Belgium, 2012.

Pullin, Graham. *Design Meets Disability*. Cambridge, MA: MIT Press, 2009.

Serres, Michel. *Petite Poucette*. Paris: Le Pommier, 2012

Tisseron, Serge. *Petites mythologies d'aujourd'hui*. Paris: Aubier, 2000.

Vincent, Susan J. *The Anatomy of Fashion: Dressing the Body from the Renaissance to Today*. Oxford, UK: Berg, 2009.

Warnier, Jean-Pierre. *Construire la culture matérielle: L'homme qui pensait avec ses doigts*. Paris: Presses Universitaires de France, 1999.

Body Modification from Punks to Body Hackers: Piercings and Tattoos in Postmodern Societies.

Philippe Liotard

Police in Indonesia's most conservative province raided a punk-rock concert and detained 65 fans, shaving their heads, forcing them to bathe, and stripping away body piercings, dog-collar necklaces and chains because of the perceived threat to Islamic values.[1]

This news item demonstrates that, in some places in 2011, you still couldn't make changes to your body without consequences. What's interesting about this case is the violence of the authorities against people who just have a different look. This violence can be understood as an answer for insulting—via the body—the symbolic (and thus political) order. Forty years earlier, in Great Britain, punks barged with a bang into the lives of a very reserved British society. They spit on English conventions by donning a revolting yet carefully studied appearance. Their opposition to mainstream society was a kind of ethic. And even if the rebellion began with music, the do-it-yourself philosophy of the punks involved the body very early on. The punk movement of the mid-'70s created a new way of wearing jewelry and tattoos and is the starting point for many transformations in contemporary appearance.

This movement is often caricatured, but we can analyze its effects on contemporary style. For punks, the body was a tool as powerful as music. They made the raised middle finger and the stuck-out tongue commonplace. They had Mohawked, spiked and colored hair. They wore tattoos on visible and previously unused parts of the body—neck, head, hands—focusing on aggressive patterns such as rats, spiders and spiderwebs, skulls, daggers, crosses, and skeletons and bones. While these icons had existed as tattoos before, they hadn't been as visible. These "ornaments" announced the punks' rejection of social order and normalized bodies.

This new style, identified by Dick Hebdige, a sociologist who studied subcultures, in 1979, became a way to fight the adult world without uttering a word.[2] Punks invented a strong "fuck you" style. The significant strength of their new look came from a kind of everyday-life obscenity.

What's also of interest in the punk movement is the fact that men's bodies, as well as women's, hijacked the ordinary uses of clothes and jewels. Chains, safety pins, dog collars and leashes became elements of punk ornamentation, along with fishnet stockings, miniskirts worn with Doc Martens, and studded perfecto jackets. Punks gleefully paraded in torn, stained and gaudy clothes, marrying colors against all the canons of good taste. Men and women shared the same accessories: ears or cheeks drilled with safety pins, exaggerated makeup, rings placed in the ear and nose and linked by a chain.

In this way, punks produced significant differences from other youth styles, mixing colors and altering the meaning of looks. They opened many possibilities in the underground contemporary construction of appearances. With their altered rebel bodies, punks quickly gave birth to a charged self-image. Their very own promoters conspired with the media they despised and turned them into symbols of decadence, then exported their body aesthetics across the world.

During that time, genital and breast piercings became popular in BDSM (bondage/discipline/sadism/masochism) and gay cultures. Genitals and nipples offered a new space for intimate ornamentations, under the influence of Gauntlet, the first piercing shop, opened in 1975 by Jim Ward in Los Angeles. During the '80s these practices remained discreet. However, they were about to burst out and join the fashion world in the '90s, in particular with the public use of piercings by the fashion designer Jean Paul Gaultier.

In the same period, some of this transgressive use of body modification took an aesthetic turn. On the West Coast of the United States, some tattoo artists introduced Pacific stylings in their inking of skin. Tattoos weren't just a way of showing an antisocial character, but a method of defending an aesthetic vision inspired by a "tribal" style. Two complementary uses of tattoos coexisted. The first

Peggy Photo (née Morrison)
Ron Athey, 1982
Courtesy of the artist

one displayed a nonconformist and antisocial posture exaggerated in punk style; the second explored aesthetic perspectives that aimed at the embellishment of the body. These two purposes for the same practice must be kept in mind in order to understand how body modifications reveal the tensions between the normalization and the transgression of the appearance.

Initially marginal practices stemming from the underground and subcultures, the practices of piercing and tattooing came out of the closet, becoming popularized and gathering wider and wider social groups. Within less than 20 years (from the early '80s to the end of the '90s), they became commonplace adornments involved in identity and gender constructions through that double movement of transgression and normalization.

Punks initiated an aesthetic based on the deconstruction of white American gender norms. Before the '80s, being tattooed or pierced (except for the ears of women) was a kind of claimed marginality. But gradually, we can observe a valued use of tattoo and piercing that tends to be part of femininity and masculinity codes. For example, in the mid-1990s, American heterosexual pornography erased pubic hair on women and chest hair on men and showed tattoos and piercings, even on intimate parts. A new way of marking the

body became visible. Pornography made body hair unwanted and tattoos desirable: tattoos on the pubic area and tramp stamps (tattoos directly above the buttocks) were seen as feminine, and big tribal tattoos on the shoulder and chest were a sign of manhood and virility.

By the first decade of the twenty-first century, female porn stars with piercings of the nipple, clitoral hood, and labia began to appear. A new category of porn actress emerged, the so-called Suicide Girls, heavily pierced and tattooed models who established a new fantasy niche. (Previously, actresses wore just one or two tattoos or piercings, whereas Suicide Girls sported many.) As far as male models were concerned, nipple or genital piercings (for example, Prince Albert rings on the glans) were exposed only in homosexual pornography. But generally, mainstream pornography offered visibility to transgressive and intimate ornamentation practices, strengthening gender stereotypes. Women can be genitally pierced as long as the jewel remains discreet. If not, they cross the line into BDSM style. In men, the groin and torso are shaved, but genital piercings aren't acceptable.

These observations might seem surprising. Nonetheless, pornography prefigures the common uses of piercings and tattoos of today's teenagers. The body-artist/performer Ron Athey says it was hardly conceivable for him, during

Denis Rideau
Portrait of Gwendoline
Courtesy of the artist

Manoly Magdala
Self-Portrait, 2009
Chamor piercings by Tribal Act (Paris),
transdermal implants by Lukas Zpira, shirt by Holy Mane
Photo by artist

the '80s, to imagine that a navel piercing might someday become a stylish accessory for respectable girls, or that a nipple piercing could be fashionable.[3] Now, piercing and tattoos are the tools of an ordinary look. They're used both for matching the standards of appearance and for producing a "unique" appearance.

The democratization of the Internet brought with it a continuous flow of images. Common tattoos and piercings are shown on teenagers' blogs. It proves that they've become more socially acceptable for young people, certainly because of the increasing number of celebrities who publicly sport their tattoos or piercings. This self-presentation in the media conforms rather scrupulously to gender roles. Women's piercings are often worn around the lips, in the tongue or on the wing of the nose. For men it's on the eyebrow and in the cartilage of the ear. Some mixed practices exist, such as the labret or the ears. However, even if some parts can be pierced by either girls or boys, a distinction remains with regard to color, size, material or the motif or design of the jewel worn. For teenagers, wearing piercings is significant if it fits within the gender codes.

After leaving the subcultures and reaching mainstream groups, piercings and tattoos tended to reinforce gender norms. Their popularization can be seen as a way to underline hegemonic masculinity or stereotypic feminity.[4] If we look at the more common tattoos, we can identify gendered patterns or gendered areas of placement on the body. This is the same with the jewelry. In the '80s, punks used everyday objects (nails, safety pins) to create new "jewels." "Modern primitives" (popularized by the special 1989 issue of RE/Search[5]), straight-edge punks and posthuman mutants have all experimented with many materials—wood, surgical steel, titanium. What followed is a wide range of new, specialized jewelry for the nostril, navel, breast and so on.

Some people, however, get involved in experimental and innovative practices that continue to blur respectable appearances and disturb the codes of the look. The democratization of practices of body ornamentation (which are made "in the flesh") doesn't necessarily mean that gender standards are called into question. Nevertheless, avant-garde experimentations in body modifications create new applications for tattoos and piercings that blur some of the gender borders. Large tattoos on the arm, back or leg are traditionally worn by men and are viewed as an affirmation of masculinity. However, all through the '90s, women began to wear full sleeves—tattoos on the entire arm—and even on the whole back without being seen as bad girls. The aesthetic turn addresses the body of women as well as the body

Claire Artemyz
LUKAS—Head with Implanted Spikes, 2010
Courtesy of the artist

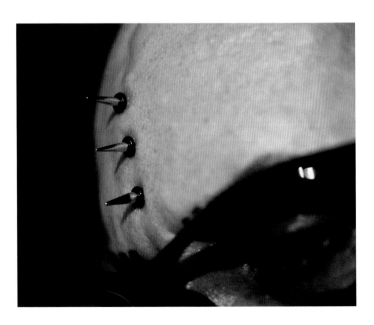

of men. Wearing large jewelry on stretched pierced lobes bypasses the usual categorization between the appearance of men and women. Beyond a certain diameter, jewelry simply breaks the standards of Occidental suitability.

Another practice that appeared in the mid-1990s consisted of inserting a foreign object under the skin.[6] The object itself isn't meant to be seen; rather, its form creates a kind of sculpture. Subdermic and transdermic implants are one of the most recent inventions of the "do it yourself" body. These evolutions of appearances paint a broad stroke of possibilities, spreading from the most common of tattoos and piercings to the most unlikely "bodmods."[7] As far as jewelry is concerned, almost everything can be used almost anywhere, from the tongue to the navel. The multiplicity of uses, the mix of different practices (tattoo, piercing, scarification, implants) expands, day after day, the boundaries of the imagination.

A couple of limits still remain: the ability of the body to accept foreign bodies or unusual treatments, and the normative force of society. But new materials and new techniques spur the imagination to invent new ways of changing appearance again and again. Nonetheless, cutting-edge body modifications are generally male practices. Among them, heavy transdermal implants or metal prosthetic teeth cause their owners to look straight out of a post-apocalyptic

movie. The *Mad Max* style has crossed the boundary of fiction to reach into real life, mixing flesh and steel. Postmodern punks wear metallic Mohawks or subdermic implants.

In 2001 I wrote that "creating a hybrid ideal of the body is a game for the privileged."[8] Now, the DIY body spreads from the homeless to the trendy middle class. The metallic-spike-Mohawked, postmodern punk goes on shaking up conventions by creating a revolting yet artfully crafted appearance. It's not a revolution, but certainly an evolution, a sort of mutation made possible by a kind of self-correction of the body seen as a draft.

But beyond the look, "body hacking" [9] continues down another road. It tries to cross the border from metallic and silicone implants to multiapplication technological implants, going from flesh/object to biology/technology hybridizations. As the body-hacktivist Lukas Zpira says, "Things of virtual nature are replaced by more palpable objects, familiar and recognizable. We are no longer in the imaginary world but rather one of desire."[10]

Lukas Zpira
Untitled, 2008
Courtesy of Lukas Zpira / www.blowyourmind-production.com

Yann Levy
Studio Portrait of Jean-Luc Verna
Courtesy of the artist

Notes

1. "Police shave the heads of punks in Aceh, Indonesia, and force them to bathe," *The Telegraph*, December 14, 2011.

2. For more about the punk movement, see Dick Hebdige, *Subculture: The Meaning of Style* (London: Methuen & Co, 1979).

3. Ron Athey, "L'encre et le métal," *Quasimodo (Modifications corporelles)*, no. 7 (2003): 113–120.

4. As defined by R. W. Connell in *Which way is up? Essays on sex, class and culture*. (Sydney: Allen and Unwin, 1983).

5. V. Vale & A. Juno, eds., *RE/Search: Modern Primitives* (San Francisco: RE/Search, 1989).

6. Invented by Steve Haworth in Phoenix, Arizona.

7. Mike Featherstone, ed., *Body Modification*. London: SAGE Publications, 2000.

8. Philippe Liotard, "The body jigsaw," *Unesco the Courier*, July-August 2001, 22–24.

9. This expression has been created by Lukas Zpira to explain his approach to body modification.

10. Laurent Courau, "You Can't Say You Didn't Know—ITW by Laurent Courau," September 7, 2010, online interview. http://laspirale.org/texte.php?id=307 (English version: http://lukaszpira.wordpress.com/interviews).

Further Reading

Featherstone, Mike, ed. *Body Modification*. London: SAGE Publications, 2000.

Holland, Samantha. *Alternative Femininities: Body, Age and Identity*. Oxford, UK: Berg, 2004.

La Spirale: An Ezine For the Digital Mutants. *Theme: Tatouage*. http://www.laspirale.org/theme.php?id=41.

Muggleton, David, and Rupert Weinzierl, eds. *The Post-Subcultures Reader*. Oxford, UK: Berg, 2004.

Pitts, Victoria. *In the Flesh: The Cultural Politics of Body Modification*. New York: Palgrave MacMillan, 2003.

A Touchy Affair: On Contemporary and Commercial Jewelry.

Suzanne Ramljak

The relationship between art and commerce is a tricky one. While both spheres have their distinct means and ends, they're also interlinked in many ways. The aim of art has been variously defined to encompass everything from overcoming personality (T. S. Eliot) to breaking the frozen sea within (Kafka).[1] The goal of business is invariably tied to monetary gain. Nonetheless, these two endeavors often converge in pursuit of their objectives. Ultimately, no creative practice can survive without capital, and every business needs structure and vision to thrive.

A similar interaction exists between the artistic and the commercial realms of jewelry. The dense terrain of contemporary jewelry harbors several coexisting subcultures, each with its own producers, consumers, networks and values. In zoological terms, one could say that all jewelry is of the same species, within which are numerous breeds marked by pronounced formal and behavioral traits. There is no fixed terminology for these jewelry subsets, but the two sectors considered here are widely known as contemporary jewelry and commercial jewelry. A comparison of these strains serves to highlight similarities and differences in their material, style, content and function.

It's useful to first establish the common denominators in all jewelry practice. On the most basic level, every jeweler— whether an academically trained studio artist or a manufacturer of mass-produced lines—is involved in creating ornament for the body. The human form is the jeweler's domain, whether explicitly or implicitly. Each jewelry type, excepting the pin, is directly affixed to the skin, rubbing on flesh and circling an appendage. As such, jewelry's contours and scale must defer to our anatomy. In addition to size, jewelry has to contend with weight and the pull of gravity on the object and the wearer. While most jewelry accommodates the body's limits, certain works place demands on the human frame and impinge on physical comfort. This factor of "wearer friendliness" proves to be a key distinction between much contemporary jewelry and commercial work.

Jewelry makers also share a heritage of craftsmanship and technical knowledge that provides mutual ground for the profession. As producers, they're involved with the acquisition of tools and materials to realize their creations. Although the current palette of jewelry materials is vast, across the board there's growing concern for sustainability, ethical sourcing and environmental soundness. Within the art jeweler community, the strongest voice for such accountability is Ethical Metalsmiths, launched by studio artists to educate about mining issues and encourage advocacy.[2] In the corporate arena, the cause is championed by the "No Dirty Gold" campaign that supports the rights of communities affected by mining operations. Major jewelry retailers like

Cartier, Fortunoff, Tiffany & Co. and Zales have adopted the initiative's Golden Rules, which include supply-chain transparency, choosing responsibly sourced materials and reducing environmental impact.[3] Regardless of motives or aesthetic disputes, jewelers big and small are rallying around such ethical causes.

The rift between hand-wrought and machine-made factions—once a defining factor between art and industry—is also gradually closing, with new technologies entering the jeweler's studio and CAD/CAM becoming standard in academic curricula. Many leading studio jewelers are enlisting computer technology to propagate their ideas in a more accessible manner. Ted Noten's vending machine installation, *Be nice to a girl—buy her a ring!*, borrows this handy format for dispensing products to offer an affordable line of rapid-prototyped rings.[4] Like other populist jewelry productions, Noten's ornamental snack machine fulfills a tenet of his jewelry manifesto, *In Celebration of the Street*, which declares, "Jewellery must be owned by the public if it wants to touch the public."[5]

Just as jewelry artists are making forays into the wider marketplace, so too are we witnessing large-scale manufacturers touting the artisanal status of their mass-produced items. These mergers of art and commerce are joined by new hybrids of production and consumption. A

Atelier Ted Noten
Be Nice to a Girl—Buy Her a Ring!, 2008
Dimensions vary
Vending machine, 3-D printed rings in glass-filled nylon
Atelier Ted Noten / Red Light Design / Droog Design / Amsterdam,
The Netherlands
Photos by Atelier Ted Noten / www.tednoten.com

growing desire for customization has generated a trend known as *prosumerism*—a cross between producer and consumer behaviors. For art jewelers this tendency finds expression in interactive kits or projects, which give buyers leeway to make choices and individualize their products. Such jewelers as Arthur Hash, Benjamin Lignel and Thomas Mann are helping put creative power in the hands of people, involving them in making, not just wearing, jewelry. Customization is also taking hold in the commercial jewelry industry. Stuller, a leading manufacturer and supplier in the field, offers retailers CounterSketch Studio software, which promises to allow "anyone in your store to express their creativity and take custom design jobs from start to finish, while your customers participate in a personalized jewelry-buying experience."[6]

Along with sustainability, computer technology and customization, art and commercial jewelry often share stylistic similarities and overlapping trends. Fashion jewelry, by its very nature, involves the renewal of past styles to maintain an ever-changing supply of goods. Such fashion merchandising relies on the public's historical amnesia to ensure that borrowed modes will seem fresh. Jewelry artists also draw upon the past, enlisting forms and motifs from history, but they move at a meandering pace and aren't compelled to spur and fulfill appetites for the latest look. Even today, when contemporary jewelry is undergoing an ornamental revival, this engagement with history entails deconstruction or abstraction of stylistic conventions and a critical attitude toward social norms.

The divergent stances between art and commercial jewelry can be most clearly seen with regard to its luxury status and the value of precious materials. While all jewelry falls into the market category of hedonic versus utilitarian consumption, its cultural value and social function exceeds its materials and price tag. The commercial industry's fixation on intrinsic worth and monetary value does not define the art jeweler's practice, which often tests conventional definitions of value. Whereas commercial jewelry is made *for* money, much contemporary jewelry is instead made *about* money and mainstream values. Indeed, a number of jewelers, foremost Kathy Buszkiewicz, have focused their jewelry on the relative nature of all values, and how we come to accept prescribed valuations.

In our pluralist era without clear hierarchies, there's no dominant or driving sector of cultural influence. High art, fashion, street life and pop culture all draw energy and inspiration from each other. The circuitous life cycle of hip-hop jewelry demonstrates such multidirectional flow of effect and appropriation. This ostentatious genre of body ornament was spawned by young musicians, who usurped generic conservative jewelry—gold chains, small diamonds, charms

Kathy Buszkiewicz
Vanitati Sacrificium: Eternity, Fancy and *Macho*, 2001
Eternity, 0.6 x 2.5 x 2.5 cm; *Fancy*, 2.5 x 2.5 x 2.5 cm; *Macho*, 2.9 x 2.5 x 2.5 cm
18-karat gold, U.S. currency, cubic zirconia
Photo by artist
Private collection

and pendants—and turbocharged its scale and inconography. Pumped up and pimped out, bling-bling jewelry came to communicate machismo, danger and the newly minted buying power of successful hip-hop artists. As hip-hop music gathered market force, a neutered bling style was sold to the masses as a flashy shell of its former acerbic self. After going through this cycle, these blinged-out baubles landed back in the high-end inventory of fine jewelry stores from whence they hailed.

A similar recycling of street aesthetics is found in the jewelry field's engagement with graffiti art. Like hip-hop, its musical equivalent, graffiti emerged as an expressive outlet for urban youth. With rebellious origins and vandalistic intentions, it slowly infiltrated the commercial sphere, entering the vocabulary of common culture and ultimately showing in art galleries. Jewelers of all stripes were not immune to graffiti's graphic pull. *Pop Rock Daddy* by Daniel Jocz was part of his *Ruff* series inspired by Dutch seventeenth-century stiff lace collars. This neckpiece of aluminum, chrome and auto-body lacquer is layered with airbrushed imagery lifted from custom motorcycle art, pop culture and the vivid graphics of graffiti taggers. Like real graffiti, Jocz's aggressive riff on traditional ornament is brash, unsettling and threatening with its spiky chrome "thorns" aimed at the wearer's neck.

When graffiti is translated into high-end commercial jewelry, a much tamer necklace is born. Tiffany & Co. celebrates Paloma Picasso as its star designer, describing her as "universally acclaimed for her bold jewelry designs," and creating "sumptuous pieces [that] have a strong, dynamic presence."[7] In Picasso's own *Graffiti* jewelry collection, words like *peace, love* and *kiss* are rendered in cursive script and wrought in precious materials, including white gold and diamonds. In scale, tone and message, this dainty adornment couldn't be farther from the gutsy street art it feigns to convey.

A sharp analysis of these contending culture tiers is found in Clement Greenberg's seminal essay "Avant-Garde and Kitsch" of 1939. For Greenberg, kitsch is the "simulacra of genuine culture" that "provides vicarious experience for the insensitive with far greater immediacy."[8] Greenberg cited Pablo Picasso as the epitome of avant-garde art in contrast to the then-popular social realism of Ilya Repin. "Where Picasso paints cause," Greenberg wrote, "Repin paints effect." Repin "predigests art for the spectator and spares him effort, provides him with a shortcut to the pleasure of art that detours what is necessarily difficult in genuine art."[9] Ironically, 70 years later the great Picasso's daughter, Paloma, personifies the very syndrome that Greenberg bemoaned: overprocessed

Daniel Jocz
Pop Rock Daddy, 2007
45.7 x 30.5 x 25.4 cm
Aluminum, copper, auto-body lacquer, chrome
Photo by artist
Ornamentum Gallery

commercialized fare with a pretense of making a true cultural contribution.

While the interplay of kitsch and avant-garde pertains to all visual arts, jewelry is unique in the fact that it's worn on the body and circulates in the larger world. In spite of its intimacy and personal associations, jewelry remains a form of public art. As it travels on the wearer into social space, it transmits signals to strangers. As a worn experience and broadcast device, jewelry also has allegiance with performance art. The question then becomes: What happens when different types of jewelry are worn, or performed, in the communal realm?

Daisy Chain, a double-sided neckpiece by Keith A. Lewis, provides a model in which to consider jewelry's social dynamic, as well as the contrast between contemporary and fashion jewelry modes. One side of the necklace seems innocent, with benignly pretty flowers like those on costume jewelry, while the reverse features close-cropped photos of anuses. Depending on which side faces out, wearers can either fade into the social landscape or fiercely announce themselves to others in proximity. "Wearing the piece becomes a sort of playground dare," states Lewis. This and his other works "assert the primacy of sexual desire," according to the artist, and act as "a sexual emissary to be worn on the body and in public."[10] Such jewelry ends up performing the wearer's body itself, situating its desires up front and center.

A prime measure of contemporary jewelry, and of all high art, is how much it asks of the viewer. Does the piece require us to work, to *appreciate* it in both senses of the word? In this regard, it's helpful to recall Marcel Duchamp's claim that it's the viewer who completes the artwork. This is in stark contrast to commercial jewelry, which conversely promises to complete the wearer, as in a recent advertisement that states: "Every woman knows that it's the fashion jewelry that completes the look, and Lord & Taylor is here to help."[11] Jewelry as finishing touch is diametrically opposed to jewelry as starting trigger for active appreciation.

The degree of work involved in artistic experience brings us back to Clement Greenberg's analysis of kitsch. Greenberg acknowledged that the laboring classes lack "enough leisure, energy, and comfort to train for the enjoyment of Picasso."[12] Rather than working for one's cultural pleasure, it's easier, and more affordable, to opt for less demanding diversions. Discomfort is an acquired taste, as is much contemporary jewelry. But feeling uncomfortable ignites self-consciousness and elicits a state of heightened alert. Once the uneasiness wanes, viewers and wearers can settle back down with a newfound awareness. And sometimes being uneasy in the world is the only way to achieve comfort within one's own skin.

Keith A. Lewis
Daisy Chain, obverse and reverse, 2001
Diameter, 20 cm
Sterling silver, 18-karat gold, magazine photos, watch crystals
Photo by Doug Yaple

Notes

1. "The role of art is not to express the personality but to overcome it." —T. S. Eliot; "A book should be an ice-axe to break the frozen sea within us." —Franz Kafka

2. Founded in 2004 by artists Susan Kingsley and Christina Miller, Ethical Metalsmiths seeks to "channel information about mining issues and encourage jewelers to become informed advocates for social and environmental responsibility." (Statement of purpose from About Us section of www.ethicalmetalsmiths.org.)

3. Issued by the "No Dirty Gold" campaign, and posted on www.nodirtygold.org, The Golden Rules are proposed as "social, human rights, and environmental criteria for more responsible mining of gold and other precious metals."

4. Ted Noten's *Be nice to a girl—buy her a ring!* was part of Red Light Design at experimentadesign, Amsterdam (September 18–November 2, 2008), a cooperative effort among Droog Design, the city of Amsterdam, and jewelry designers.

5. Ted Noten and Gert Staal, *Ted Noten: CH2=C(CH3) C(=O)OCH3 enclosures and other TN's* (Rotterdam: 010 Publishers, 2006), 115.

6. Promotional copy for CounterSketch Studio 2.6, on www.gemvision.com.

7. "Tiffany designer Paloma Picasso is universally acclaimed for her bold jewelry designs. Her eye for color is brilliant and her sumptuous pieces have a strong, dynamic presence," from Paloma Picasso designer page at www.tiffany.com.

8. Clement Greenberg, "Avant-Garde and Kitsch" in *Art and Culture: Critical Essays* (Boston: Beacon Press, 1971), 10 and 15.

9. Greenberg, "Avant-Garde and Kitsch," 15.

10. Keith Lewis, Artist Statement, "Curated Exhibition in Print—Contemporary Enamel," *Metalsmith* 23, no. 4 (August, 2003): 33.

11. From Lord & Taylor online advertisement, January 18, 2012.

12. Greenberg, "Avant-Garde and Kitsch," 18.

Further Reading

Cohn, Susan, ed., and **Deyan Sudjic**. *Unexpected Pleasures: The Art and Design of Contemporary Jewelry*. Milan / Geneva / New York: Skira Rizzoli, 2012.

Farneti Cera, Deanna. *Jewels of Fantasy: Costume Jewelry of the 20th Century*. New York: Harry N. Abrams, 1992.

Noten, Ted, and Gert Staal, eds. *Ted Noten. CH2=C(CH3) C(=O)OCH3 enclosures and other TN's*. Rotterdam: 010 Publishers, 2006.

Ramljak, Suzanne. "View: Prosumer Jewelry." *Metalsmith* 28, no. 5 (October 2008): 16–17.

Strauss, Cindi. *Ornament as Art: Avant-Garde Jewelry from the Helen Williams Drutt Collection*. Stuttgart: Arnoldsche Art Publishers, 2007.

Woolton, Carol. *Fashion for Jewels: 100 Years of Styles and Icons*. London: Prestel Publishing, 2010.

Now and Then: Thinking about the Contemporary in Art and Jewelry.

Julie Ewington

Is the *contemporary* in contemporary jewelry the same as the *contemporary* in contemporary art? This is an immensely complex question. One immediate answer is affirmative: all cultural practices are, inevitably, sustained by fundamental social matrices and issues, and the historical conditions governing the character, social location and experience of contemporary art extend to other creative fields, such as jewelry. As jeweler Lisa Walker asserted, "The strange world of contemporary jewelry would fit perfectly into contemporary art, some day they'll finally realize this."[1] Looking across cultural practices in any context is immensely rewarding: artistic manifestations clearly participate in energetic neighborly conversations, and not remotely enough work has been undertaken to place jewelry in its historical and cultural settings.[2]

Jewelry is a marvelous terrain for considerations about the contemporaneity of culture, partly because of its extraordinary longevity and enduring appeal; it may be the oldest continuous form of art making practiced in the great majority of human cultures.[3] Despite the enormous diversity of materials used across various societies and the development over time of new technologies, jewelry has remained remarkably constant in its forms and purposes. It is literally circumscribed by its affinity with human bodies, and, in its turn, circumscribes them; it marks us, threads our hair and pierces our bodies. The infinitely various ways that jewelry adorns the body are open to complex significations, but, in a nutshell, jewelry marks affiliations, status and social locations; in dialogue with social groupings, it allows for the expression of personal individuality; it acts as nonverbal signs, whether in nonliterate cultures or today's mass metropolitan societies; and it serves as a form of portable and inalienable wealth. Jewelry is supplementary—that is, it eventually derives not from physical necessity but from the sheer propensity for delight. Its necessity is of a different order.

In many ways, too, because jewelry's social uses are clearly identifiable (though prone to slippage between them), it offers an exceptionally rich set of histories and practices for examining dialogue between continuity and change. It's simultaneously graspable and slippery. Importantly, contemporary jewelers are acutely aware of what art historian Terry Smith calls "the stronger sense of contemporaneity at work" today: "The coexistence of distinct temporalities, of different ways of being in relation to time, experienced in the midst of a growing sense that many kinds of time are running out, is the third, deepest sense of the contemporary: what it is to be with time, to be contemporary."[4]

The currently perplexing theoretical issue—whether the period of contemporary art has extended roughly since the 1960s and become irrefutably dominant since the 1990s—is particularly relevant for jewelry. In this period a remarkable group of artist-jewelers flourished and became internationally renowned under the self-proclaimed banner of the contemporary jewelry movement.[5] Committed to innovation, using non-precious materials, privileging experimentation over status and monetary value, often focused on jewelry's capacity to signify and exceptionally reflexive about shared values and interests, these jewelers have dedicated themselves to the interrogative capabilities of their practice. Fundamentally cosmopolitan, their jewelry nevertheless often exemplifies the deep affiliations with local traditions, social contexts and practices that is one hallmark of contemporary art. For while (and because) many pieces pass through centuries of multiple uses and social locations, illuminating them through this endurance, jewelry can directly challenge contemporaneity by drilling into the past.

Crucially, some contemporary jewelry indexes continuity through time. In Australia, indigenous Tasmanian jeweler Lola Greeno and her peers are practitioners of an ancient form of jewelry. They continue to make exquisite shell necklaces called *maireeners*.[6] Worn by their ancestors for thousands of years and recorded in the earliest European images of Tasmanian people, these ur-necklaces are long, continuous strands. Greeno uses the same (now diminishing) natural resources, techniques and knowledge as her forebears. In the past two decades these beautiful contemporary necklaces have been

Lisa Walker
Necklace, 2010
50 x 35 x 2 cm
Plastic, spray paint, thread
Courtesy of the artist
Collection of National Gallery of Victoria, Australia (pending)

collected by museums, where they affirm Tasmanian Aboriginal culture, refuting previous claims of its extinction over nearly two centuries of colonization.[7] Once ceremonial gifts marking family and community alliances, the necklaces are now sold in museum shops and galleries and are worn by individuals aware of their cultural significance. Always acknowledging subtle variations in each maker's style, maireeners today are identical to those made thousands of years ago: they encapsulate the argument against a simple notion of "the contemporary" as an interpretive frame.

Another equally emphatic answer to the original question would be negative, looking to conventional demarcations between art and jewelry—jewelry as a subset of craft—and insisting on the specificity of each cultural practice (jewelry, painting and post-1980s video installation, for example). This argument appeals to the nuanced histories of each form, emphasizing the particularities of each context. But while it's extremely valuable to attend to each practice's local histories, eventually medium-based approaches become blinkered, and in some cases fatally limiting.

Take the work of Karl Fritsch, for example. He romps through the genealogies of traditional European jewelry, placing precious gems in settings that simultaneously mock various notions of value while reaffirming, by remaking, the very forms and histories

he seems to parody. Fritsch said, "What I find really fascinating, and one of the reasons why it's so interesting to make jewellery, is the moment of recognition when something that comes across cute and pretty has on second glimpse an almost obscene grotesqueness."[8] He makes purposeful perversions of conventional forms and materials, especially extraordinary gem-set rings. Working within a broadly accessible jewelry vernacular, Fritsch makes intelligent appraisals of established forms of beauty that have struck a chord with audiences today who are skeptical of jewelry's traditional functions of securing social status and displaying wealth. A form of internal critique, Fritsch's jewelry suggests how craft is firmly embedded within specific histories and contexts.

Taken on their own, neither of these approaches suffices. To unpack intricate relationships between such rich and freighted terms as *the contemporary*, art and jewelry require more thought. Fritsch's jewelry, as we have seen, would be unintelligible without a knowledge of European jewelry, but it derives its fullest meaning from the ways it deploys and challenges that history in the contemporary context. At any rate, the question this essay addresses provokes multiple answers, not all of them reconcilable. I will counter with others: Can contemporary art be defined? May contemporary jewelry be defined? And are these unitary practices, or are they so

Lola Greeno
Green Maireener Necklace, 2007
180 x 1.5 cm
Green maireener shells threaded with double-strength quilting thread
Queensland Art Gallery
Purchased 2008, Queensland Art Gallery Foundation Grant
Acc. 2008.087

Karl Fritsch
Rings, 2007–2008
Dimensions vary
Silver, gold, rubies, sapphires, diamonds
Photos by the artist
Gallery Funaki

profusely diverse, so ungraspable, that arguments suggesting they be defined as contemporary exist, in actuality, precisely to make sense of multiple coexisting artistic expressions? In the current global cultural arena, whether works and enterprises are encountered actually or virtually, one recognizes an extraordinary plethora of art that is simultaneously rich, strange, evidently incommensurable and often overwhelming.[9]

So, what implications does the notion of the contemporary have for jewelers? Walker's recent work is emblematic of this rich immediacy, in the second of art historian Smith's senses of the contemporary. Her inspired fooling about in the here and now, collaging and assembling found elements from various sources, is, however, splendidly strategic. In fact, in cultural theorist Meaghan Morris's immortal phrase, it is "semiotically delinquent." Walker's profligate energies and enthusiasms seem diametrically opposed to Greeno's. Taking great pleasure in quotidian materials and objects, Walker too makes necklaces, though from entirely different materials. Above all, she's attuned to the nuances of her sources: Walker's work is deliberately interrogative of contemporary notions of value.[10]

I now want to look at temporal and historical markers in jewelry from Australia and New Zealand, reading works as contemporary interventions into jewelry's long histories that problematize both past and present. If Greeno's maireeners are

contemporary affirmations of continuity and survival, then other works actively interrogate the historical past. Jewelers today are exceptionally well informed about art and jewelry of the past. Yet while many were trained by late modernists, through the period of postmodernism, and are acutely aware of their own locations in historical time, not all jewelers riffing on historical themes are postmodernists. On the contrary, their interests and affiliations are more deliberate, more selective.

Blanche Tilden plays with the forms of industrial modernity in impeccable works assembled from purpose-made glass and metal components. Often these are long sinuous chains invoking the imagery of mass production: one thinks of factory production, assembly lines, bike chains, even the way these processes and objects match the exact passing of mechanical time. Yet the effect or emotional impact of these shiny, perfectly manufactured elements is far more ambiguous. While they seem removed from human intervention, each part is lovingly crafted, and something of their emotionally remote perfection speaks of nostalgia for a mechanically ordered view of the universe. With Tilden's long poetic meditation in metal and glass, which speaks to the fundamental role of machines in modernity, her chains literally articulate circularity.

Crucially, wearers of Tilden's chains comment on their emotional attachment to them.[11] Carrying affection and offering

Blanche Tilden
Robyn McKenzie Wearing Nightrider Necklace, 2002
Diameter, 26 cm; height, 20 cm
Borosilicate glass, aluminum; flameworked, anodized
Photo by Marcus Scholz
Private collection of Robyn McKenzie

protection has been one of jewelry's main functions across time and cultures, one that Greeno's maireeners and Tilden's chains share. Situating Greeno and Tilden in the same frame reveals the usefulness of the notion of "the co-temporary" as part of "the contemporary."[12] Greeno and Tilden exhibit in the same time and space in Australia. This points to the key problem of using the term *contemporary* as a form of periodization: these two jewelers have fundamentally different relationships not only to historical periods but, arguably, also to the broader sense of how human history is registered in time and place.

In Margaret West's recent work, simple emblematic brooches are reduced in form and means; paradoxically, as in the best modernist art, reduction makes the work richer. Intervening into slices of stone, West suggests a strictly modernist affiliation with the idea that the material should speak, embodying its own truth. Indeed, West privileges the beauty and the density of each stone—basalt, granite, often marble— its obduracy speaking to the depth of geological time, and, by implication, to the ineffable magnificence of the universe. (All this in less than 2 inches [5.1 cm] squared.)[13] But something in this work is far older than modernism. West inscribes into stones. This recalls ancient writing, so that many brooches are like thoughts pinned to a coat, like wearing a brief poem. She sets human time into the complex temporalities of the natural

world, dramatizing these long engagements. Now unrepentantly hybrid rather than pure in the modernist sense, West's brooches remind us that her other practice is poetry. (One recent poem is titled "The Tacit Truth of Stone."[14])

Warwick Freeman has also recently played with stone, but to different ends. Take the suite of stone pendants titled *Handles* (2009). In a pronounced case of Duchampian naughtiness, a group of pendants is ranged along a shelf, like so many diminutive lingams, but the forms are borrowed from modern resin screwdriver handles and each mimics the original size of the handle. The sleek modern design of the original mass-manufactured tools is part of their appeal: they are pleasing objects. Translated into stone they're not only comically outrageous, but they also turn back time. Modern manufacture gives way to a new stone age in Freeman's hands, recalling the American painter Barnett Newman's 1952 diatribe against New York's Museum of Modern Art as a haven for Bauhaus screwdriver designers.[15] Freeman's handles are, eventually, a contemporary rumination on the passing of time and, inevitably, changes in making.

If the idea that all cultural practices today are necessarily contemporary—that everything made at this time, regardless of origin, social context, style and material, or even artistic intent, somehow belongs together—if this idea is, at its core,

Margaret West
Petal, passing, 2009
10 x 7.5 x 0.5 cm
Basalt, paint, silver
Photo by artist

both irrefutable and trivially true, then this proposition is, finally, radically problematic. It permits a far more interesting idea: that co-temporal objects pose valuable questions about how to interpret practices that appear to be irreducibly different, precisely because they keep those questions open, fluid and active. Given our unprecedented access to information about artistic practices across the globe, including jewelry, the best response to the question heading this essay might be to say, "No, not exactly, but yes, almost"—and then to keep passing the problem along a (sometimes discontinuous?) line of propositions and cases, until, much enriched, we find ourselves back at the beginning. The richness of this problem, and this metaphor, will always return me to jewelry.

Warwick Freeman
Handles, 2008
80 mm tall (largest)
Pendants: quartz, jasper, nephrite, basalt, conglomerate, petrified wood
Photo by Roy Tremain

Notes

1. See Lisa Walker, "revelations no 4," in *Lisa Walker Wearable*, Liesbeth den Besten et al. (Munich / Wellington: Braunbooks, 2011), 62.

2. See Marcia Pointon, *Brilliant Effects: A Cultural History of Gem Stones and Jewellery* (New Haven, CT / London: Yale University Press, 2009) for an exemplary historical study.

3. Kate Ravilious, "Oldest Jewelry Found in Morocco Cave," *National Geographic News*, June 7, 2007, http://news.nationalgeographic.com/news/2007/06/070607-oldest-beads.html.

4. See Terry Smith, *What Is Contemporary Art?* (Chicago: University of Chicago Press, 2009), 3–4, 241–71.

5. See Terry Smith, *Contemporary Art: World Currents* (London: Laurence King Publishing, 2011); and Terry Smith, Okwui Enwezor and Nancy Condee, eds., *Antinomies of Art and Culture: Modernity, Postmodernity, Contemporaneity* (London: Duke University Press, 2008), especially Smith's introduction.

6. Francis E. Parker, "An Unbroken Strand: Palawa Shell Necklaces" in *Floating Life: Contemporary Aboriginal Fibre Art* (Brisbane: Queensland Art Gallery, 2009), 75–76 and 144; Greg Lehman, "Lola Greeno," in *Beyond the Pale: Contemporary Indigenous Art: 2000 Adelaide Biennial of Australian Art, Art Gallery of South Australia* (Adelaide: Art Gallery of South Australia, 2000), 29–32.

7. See Lyndall Ryan, *Tasmanian Aborigines: A History Since 1803* (Sydney: Allen & Unwin, 2012) concerning the "history wars" that started at least as early as her original 1981 book on the colonization of Tasmania and its indigenous inhabitants.

8. Karl Fritsch, *Returning to the Jewel Is a Return from Exile: Robert Baines, Karl Fritsch, Gerd Rothmann* (North Melbourne: Australian Scholarly Publishing, 2010), 38.

9. See Terry Smith's discussion of Hal Foster's original question, "Are there plausible ways to narrate the now myriad practices of contemporary art over the last 20 years?", in *Contemporary Art: World Currents*, 252.

10. See Liesbeth den Besten et al., *Lisa Walker Wearable* (Munich / Wellington: Braunbooks Publications, 2011).

11. See Merryn Gates et al., *Blanche Tilden: True* (Nacogdoches, TX: SFA Press, 2010).

12. See Smith, *What Is Contemporary Art?*

13. See Margaret West's website, www.margaretwest.com.au, for texts by the artist on her work.

14. Margaret West, "The Tacit Truth of Stone," in *Margaret West, Leaf and Stone* (Sydney: Brandl & Schlesinger, 2012), 80.

15. See Julie Ewington, *Owner's Manual: Jewellery by Warwick Freeman* (Auckland: Starform, 1995); Damian Skinner, *Given: Jewellery by Warwick Freeman* (Auckland: Starform, 2003); Barnett Newman, "Open Letter to William A. M. Burden, President of the Museum of Modern Art" (1953) and "Remarks at the Fourth Annual Woodstock Arts Conference" (1952), in *Selected Writings and Interviews*, ed. John O'Neill (Berkeley and Los Angeles: University of California Press, 1992), 38, 245.

Further Reading

Anderson, Patricia. *Contemporary Jewellery in Australia and New Zealand*. Sydney: Craftsman House, 1998.

Birnbaum, Daniel, et al. *Defining Contemporary Art: 25 Years in 200 Pivotal Artworks*. London: Phaidon Press Ltd., 2011.

Cohn, Susan, ed., and Deyan Sudjic. *Unexpected Pleasures: The Art and Design of Contemporary Jewelry*. Milan / Geneva / New York: Skira Rizzoli, 2012.

den Besten, Liesbeth. *On Jewellery: A Compendium of International Contemporary Art Jewellery*. Stuttgart: Arnoldsche Art Publishers, 2011.

Dormer, Peter, and Ralph Turner. *The New Jewelry: Trends and Traditions*. London: Thames and Hudson, 1985.

English, Helen W. Drutt, and Peter Dormer. *Jewelry of Our Time: Art, Ornament and Obsession*. London: Thames and Hudson, 1995.

Ewington, Julie. "In Time." In *The Second Asia Pacific Triennial of Contemporary Art*, edited by Caroline Turner and Rhana Devenport, 19–20. Brisbane: Queensland Art Gallery, 1996.

Fabian, Johannes. *Time and the Other: How Anthropology Makes Its Object*. New York: Columbia University Press, 1983.

Smith, Terry. *What Is Contemporary Art?* Chicago: University of Chicago Press, 2009.

Smith, Terry, Okwui Enwezor, and Nancy Condee, eds. *Antinomies of Art and Culture: Modernity, Postmodernity, Contemporaneity*. London: Duke University Press, 2008, especially Smith's introduction.

Turner, Ralph. *Contemporary Jewelry*. New York: Van Nostrand Reinhold Co., 1976.

Turner, Ralph. *Jewelry in Europe and America: New Times, New Thinking*. London: Thames and Hudson, 1996.

Jewelry in the Expanded Field: Between Applied Social Art and Critical Design.

Mònica Gaspar

In catalog forewords, portfolios, or conference statements, one often encounters the assertion that jewelry is an art form. And yet most correspondences between visual art and contemporary jewelry are in fact visual, established through similar strategies of photography and the relation of images on the page, rather than through the content or intentions of the objects and practices themselves. For jeweler Jivan Astfalck, understanding jewelry as an art practice means not relying on aesthetic criteria (this piece of jewelry looks like that piece of art) but instead identifying the "integrity of its enquiry."[1] This requires a content-based rather than material-based or merely skill-driven approach. The urgency behind the desire to have contemporary jewelry welcomed as an art form has distracted attention from other important issues—for example, dealing with contemporary jewelry's legacy as applied art, or (re)defining its relationship with design and fashion.

It's true that conceptual and critical approaches to jewelry wouldn't have been possible without the integration of jewelry education into a fine-art context. Since the mid-1950s in Europe, a time when terms like *emotional design* or *conceptual design* didn't yet exist, the practice of creating functional objects in an expressive and conceptual manner has been hosted by craft departments in art schools. Studio jewelry naturally evolved as an expressive, postmodern object under the auspices of art—importantly, not the kind of art celebrated by the art world, but rather an art of the objet d'art, dealing with all the suspicions of decoration and lack of conceptual drive that are the legacy of this history.

By the beginning of the twenty-first century, a moment in which a "return of beauty" was proclaimed, ornament and conceptualism were no longer seen as opposites in the fields of art and design. Several exhibitions confirm this shift, for instance La Beauté at Palais d'Avignon (Avignon, France, 2000) and Regarding Beauty: A View of the Late Twentieth Century at the Smithsonian Institution (Washington DC, 1999). Artists such as Fischli/Weiss, Mariko Mori, Matthew Barney and Pipilotti Rist, to mention a few examples, became interested in the subject of beauty, and in ornament in particular, working with different media, from photography to object-based installation and performance. Aesthetic experience flowed everywhere, reaching from high to low culture, from economics to entertainment, politics and fashion. This meant that absolutely everything could be a subject of aesthetics, and therefore a matter of design. The art critic Hal Foster has described this period as the era of total design, while the philosopher Yves Michaud has referred to it as the age of aesthetics.[2]

In recent years, the role of the designer as author has gained a new currency in discussions about the boundaries between art and design, which in turn has transformed the perception of design as a cultural player. A growing number of designers and artists are, together, questioning the conventions of contemporary product culture. They work outside of market constraints and opt for a speculative practice beyond that of mere problem solving. They have been trained as artists, craft practitioners or product designers. Their work is self-reflective, critically engaged with the present, and adopts serious, playful or poetic formats. The results exist as one-offs or limited editions, or remain ambiguously perched between artwork, prototype and finished product, often presented in a specialized (art) gallery.

Such practices, taking place in a territory of "in-betweenness," are developing their own vocabulary, beyond an exhausted art-versus-design rhetoric. *Conceptual design*, a term used by Renny Ramakers and Gijs Bakker, the founders of Droog Design, and *critical design*, a term used by theorist and interaction designer Anthony Dunne, refer to design that has a reflective and speculative nature and is able to pose questions and tell stories, proving that a product can "make you think" or that design can be expressive.[3] A flourishing milieu of galleries, fairs and institutions celebrate the contemporary objet d'art and develop their own terminology to describe it. The historical term *studio craft*, popular in English-

Maarten Baas
Stacked Dining Chairs, 2006
80 x 40 x 45 cm
Clay, steel
Photo by Maarten van Houten, www.maartenvanhouten.nl / Baas & den Herder BV

Karl Fritsch
Ring, 2007
6 x 4 x 4 cm
Gold
Courtesy of the artist

speaking countries, still refers to the artistic exploration of traditional craft techniques as studio-based practice, producing one-off pieces and limited editions. This has been challenged by the relatively new phenomena known as design art, a term coined in the trade of limited-edition furniture, and which has expanded as a marketing tool in the context of auction houses specializing in twentieth-century antiques.

A return of the term *applied* has recently opened up a reflective space where art, craft and design not only reevaluate their making processes but also meet social sciences, anthropology and psychology in order to critically investigate the making of, and living with, things. Dunne has identified a new designer attitude, which he describes as that of an applied conceptual artist, someone who socializes artistic practice and introduces a critical perspective in the context of product culture.[4] *Applied social art* is the term the installation artist Mladen Miljanovic uses to define some of his work, when his participatory practice aims to have a therapeutic effect on the communities he involves (mainly veterans of the Bosnian war).[5] The value of the term *applied* is that it refers immediately to the personal sphere. It's performative and functional in the sense that it suggests an action (to apply something somewhere) as much as a reaction (it has been applied).[6] Because the unstable condition of

being applied requires an agent and a goal external from itself, it remains both pragmatic as well as utopian in nature. Its ability to generate actions makes it a social and cordial art.

Contemporary jewelry belongs to this discussion and reflects this problem in an exemplary way. The attributes of the applied include participation and interaction, which naturally relate to the communicative nature of jewelry. Contemporary jewelry develops at the intersection of artistic and design professions, in order to generate speculative, critical, poetical or utopian work that engages with everyday life and the personal sphere, beyond the quest for the white cube. This is precisely what the return of the applied seeks to capture.

Contemporary jewelry is slowly being recognized as part of this new cultural landscape, and measured with the same critical expectations and aesthetic standards as other products. For instance, Maarten Baas with his *Clay Furniture* and Karl Fritsch with his jewelry both engage in intense material and technical research, testing through the playful shapes of their objects the difference between amateurism and professionalism, while reflecting on the meaning of manufacture today. The Campana brothers, with their *Paraíba Chair* (formerly the *Multidão Chair*), and Lisa Walker, with her *Newtown Necklace*, both offer a comment on the emotional attachment to things and a critical view of consumer culture

Fernando and Humberto Campana
Paraíba Chair, 2012
Cotton dolls, stainless steel
Photo © Luis Calazans
Courtesy of Estudio Campana

Lisa Walker
Newtown Necklace, 2010
50 x 35 x 2.5 cm
Wool, stuffing, thread
Photo by artist
Collection of the Françoise van den Bosch Foundation

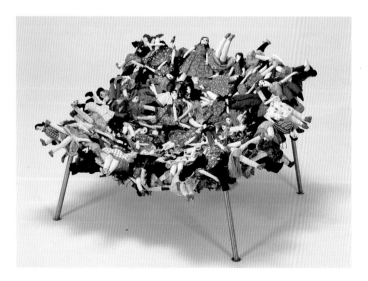

and its gluttony, blurring the boundary between trash and treasure. Robert Stadler's furniture that appears to be melting, recalling the tradition of the surrealist object, and Pia Aleborg's *Take Your Seat* brooches ask questions about luxury, gender issues and the tension with tradition.

In a time when current contemporary aesthetic practices are borrowing strategies, sites and players not only from art and design but also from many other disciplines, jewelry makers have a chance to prove that contemporary jewelry is one of the most exciting forms of contemporary object culture, fluctuating between the public and private spheres of everyday life, art, design, fashion, social sciences, religion, precision engineering and philosophy.

What contemporary jewelry has to offer in the expanded field of art and design is not only objects but also a specialized knowledge, a particular way of looking at things and posing questions. The act itself of wearing, and the kind of knowledge embedded there, has become a central question and field of investigation. Walker's work exemplifies the jewelry-like character of almost anything when she provocatively proves that everything can become "wearable," and in so doing comments on value, consumption habits and emotional attachment to things. Gemma Draper explores the area of user-centered experiences when she creates mysterious objects that have appropriated familiar gestures, such as holding a pen or texting a message on the mobile phone. How can we explore the thousands of ways in which people nowadays create identity through the owning, using and wearing of objects? How might we understand how meaning and value are produced in these choices? Contemporary jewelry artists and designers are already offering some answers to such essential questions.

At the same time, the understanding of personal adornment as a cultural technique is taken into consideration within academic communities, such as the one initiated at the University of Applied Sciences Trier in Germany, which is paving the way for a theory of jewelry with the aim of investigating why people adorn themselves and what jewelry does to them.[7] Contemporary jewelry has consolidated its place in higher education (BA and MA courses) in art and design colleges all over the world. An interdisciplinary learning context, and engagement with a more reflective practice, is providing a fertile background for new generations to develop exciting work. Since the mid-1990s, jewelers have positioned themselves in the field of design and fashion with a critical edge, or they have developed conceptual work for a specialized circuit within the arts. Pushing the boundaries

Robert Stadler
Pools and Pouf, 2004
Largest, 94 x 245 x 90 cm
Black leather, plywood, synthetic fabric
Photo © Robert Stadler
Courtesy of Carpenter's Workshop Gallery

Pia Aleborg
Take Your Seat, 2001
20 x 15 x 7 cm
Reindeer skin, horsehair, rivets, plywood
Photo by Anna-Mia Brolund
Courtesy of the artist

of the jewelry field, these practitioners don't stay only within academic communities but also use their potential to reach new audiences, setting up their own studios and businesses that challenge the way jewelry is traditionally communicated and displayed. Internet platforms and social networks are having an unprecedented impact on the debate culture around contemporary jewelry. These are positive changes that affect the way jewelry is made, perceived and talked about, consolidating and further expanding the emotional, social and political impact of jewelry in people's lives.

Notes

1. Jivan Astfalck, "Jewelry as a Fine Art Practice," in *New Directions in Jewelry*, ed. Catherine Grant (London: Black Dog Publishers, 2005), 19.

2. Hal Foster, *Design and Crime (And Other Diatribes)* (Brooklyn: Verso, 2003); Yves Michaud, *L'art à l'état gazeux: Essai sur le triomphe de l'esthétique* (Paris: Hachette, 2004).

3. Renny Ramakers and Gijs Bakker, eds., *Droog Design: Spirit of the Nineties* (Rotterdam: 010 Publishers, 1998); Anthony Dunne, *Hertzian Tales: Electronic Products, Aesthetic Experience, and Critical Design* (Cambridge, MA: MIT Press, 1999).

4. Dunne, *Hertzian Tales.*

5. Tina Lipsky, *Conversation between Mladen Miljanovic and Tina Lipsky* (Vienna: MUMOK, 2010).

6. Mònica Gaspar, "The Return of the Applied," in *Metadomestic*, ed. Mònica Gaspar (Linz: Landesgalerie, 2011), an exhibition catalog.

7. Wilhelm Lindemann, ed., *Thinking Jewellery: On the Way towards a Theory of Jewellery* (Stuttgart: Arnoldsche Art Publishers, 2011).

Further Reading

Astfalk, Jivan. "Jewelry as a Fine Art Practice." In *New Directions in Jewelry*, edited by Catherine Grant. London: Black Dog Publishers, 2005.

Dunne, Anthony. *Hertzian Tales: Electronic Products, Aesthetic Experience, and Critical Design*. Cambridge, MA: MIT Press, 1999.

Ericson, Magnus, and Ramia Mazé, eds. *Design Act: Socially and Politically Engaged Design Today—Critical Roles and Emerging Tactics*. Stockholm: Iaspis/Sternberg Press, 2011.

Foster, Hal. *Design and Crime (And Other Diatribes)*. London / New York: Verso, 2001.

Gaspar, Mònica. "The Return of the Applied." In *Metadomestic* exhibition catalog, edited by Mònica Gaspar. Linz: Landesgalerie, 2011.

Huber, Jörg, Burkhard Meltzer, Heike Munder, and Tido von Oppeln, eds. *It's Not a Garden Table: Art and Design in the Expanded Field*. Zurich: JRP/Ringier, 2011.

Lindemann, Wilhelm, ed. *Thinking Jewellery: On the Way towards a Theory of Jewellery*. Stuttgart: Arnoldsche Art Publishers, 2011.

Lovell, Sophie. *Limited Edition: Prototypes, One-Offs and Design Art Furniture*. Basel: Birkhäuser, 2009.

Press, Mike. Design, culture, craft, crime and research. http://mikepress.wordpress.com.

Ramakers, Renny, and Gijs Bakker, eds. *Droog Design: Spirit of the Nineties*. Rotterdam: 010 Publishers, 1998.

Thinking Process: On Contemporary Jewelry and the Relational Turn.

Helen Carnac

As defined by art curator Nicolas Bourriaud, relational aesthetics is "an art taking as its theoretical horizon the realm of human interactions and its social context, rather than the assertion of an independent and private symbolic space."[1] Contemporary jewelry has an inherent connectedness to human interaction, through processes of making, materials, issues of wearing, gift giving or marking significant events and occasions. It would therefore seem to be deeply connected to relational aesthetics. As Caroline Broadhead writes, "Objects that are used in close relationship to an individual can indicate a personal history, declare a relationship to others and raise issues of identity and status. What is worn is a source of constant fascination and curiosity, demonstrating the continual two-way process of expression by one person and the impression it makes upon others."[2] And yet, as a subset of craft, contemporary jewelry can also be individualistic and autonomous. One only has to think of the mythology behind studio craft, in which the heroic, highly skilled and autocratic maker toils alone in the studio. The resulting object, an outcome of the maker's singular artistic sensibility, moves from studio to gallery, encountering a limited audience, indeed often a single user or wearer, before finally ending up in a museum, preserved for posterity precisely because it's beyond use.

I'm struck by the artist Jeremy Deller's observation of British life in the 1980s slipping away from a manufacturing economy to one of leisure and entertainment.[3] This is shown in his 2010 film, *So Many Ways to Hurt You (The Life and Times of Adrian Street)*, which begins with an image of a coal miner (Street's father) alongside his son, a pro wrestler dressed in what an exhibition brochure describes as "glam-rock semi-transvestite fashion."[4] Street, who one generation previously would have worked at the coalface, had chosen to pursue a career in light entertainment. For me, this also seems like a poignant evocation of the current contemporary jewelry world, which, I'd like to propose, has become a matter of entertainment for a very select group. Contemporary jewelry is mostly made to be displayed in exhibitions, photographed and written about, collected and put into museum vitrines—watched but not worn. Its relevance would appear to be confined to its own relatively small world and its discourses.

If this is indeed the case, can contemporary jewelry be relational in any way or form? Has the contemporary jewelry world noticed what's going on elsewhere? And how successfully is contemporary jewelry negotiating new modes of craft and design practice that embrace collaborative making and audience engagement without dismissing the made object? Is contemporary jewelry necessarily a project and product of the self? And if it does embrace a more relational model, will something get lost in the process of change?

Kevin Murray recently wrote about the jewelers Susan Cohn and Robert Baines and their respective, very different positions about jewelry practice. As Murray put it, "For Baines, the ultimate scene is at the bench, where the lone artist faces their own demons and angels in the task of bearing testament to the millennia of metalsmithing traditions. While for Cohn, the main arena is the street, where jewelry provides a currency for purchasing identities and pleasures. The position of each seems appropriate to their own domain."[5] Both of these modes continue to remain relevant, but should they stay separate domains? Perhaps, as Murray goes on to suggest, it's the opening up of relationships between the two, and between contemporary jewelry and other fields, that needs to be encouraged.

In the fields of design and craft, significant shifts in thinking about relational models have taken place over the past five years. In movements such as Slow Craft, the imperative has been to use longer thinking processes, which might involve open-ended design strategies, and long cycles of designing that consider process, provenance,

Dennis Hutchinson
Adrian Street and His Father, 1973
Courtesy of Mirrorpix

locality, reflection and working with others. The making of objects comes from positions of deep knowledge of material and processes, with a heightened awareness of detailed material manipulation, social practices and locale. The process of doing something is a living thing that might not be pinned down—it comes into being over time and isn't static. The made object isn't necessarily the end point but is nonetheless important.

Perhaps in the contemporary jewelry field it would be helpful if there were an opening up to the "total environments" that Sarah Pink speaks of: "Human beings are continuously and actively involved in the processes through which not only culture, but also the total environments in which they live are constituted, experienced and change continually over time."[6] The anthropologist Tim Ingold has also developed the concept of a "sentient ecology," proposing that human beings engage with and are part of the world, not through the dualistic workings of mind and body, culture and nature, but as a "singular locus of creative growth within a continually unfolding field of relationships."[7] It could be useful to think about Ingold's ideas and the importance of the knowledge we have in our own environments, and how this can be shared and developed in a larger world.

Of course, this desire for an open-ended process means that the craftspeople and designers who could fit under the moniker Slow Craft are sometimes ambivalent about terms such as *relational aesthetics* and the art historical discussions that they represent (including the term *Slow Craft*) precisely because of an interest in a lived experience, where work (and ideas) develop and evolve in a way that cannot necessarily be predicted or predicated by an art-historical movement. Though we may be concerned with some of the same principles articulated in Bourriaud's relational aesthetics, if we align our practices with such narratives, do they become a static product of cultural canons?

There's evidence that makers and designers are responding to the "relational turn," and embracing an expanded view that doesn't stop at making work, but also seeks to address issues beyond the studio: the reuse of material, industrial heritage, why we have and make stuff and where it's all going, all grounded in a consideration of, and a desire to work with, others.

The ceramic artist and practice-based researcher Neil Brownsword makes work that's deeply connected to the ceramic industry in Stoke-on-Trent (UK). Having apprenticed at Wedgwood at age 16, he went on to study

Steve Speller
Neil Brownsword at Bournes Bank Burslem, Stoke-on-Trent,
2007
Courtesy of Helen Carnac

Thinking Process

through the BA, MA and PhD levels, continuing to live and work in Stoke-on-Trent. "This (apprentice) experience was to prove profoundly important. His career as an artist can be read as an extended and varied meditation on the area in which he grew up and on the decline of its pottery industry over the past 20 years. His work also interrogates the nature of skill and its uncertain and contingent relationship with creativity."[8]

Rebecca Earley is a textile designer and researcher. Through ideas borne of her 10-year-long Top 100 recycled shirts project, she now works with the Textile Environmental Design group,[9] at a public policy level with the Swedish government and with fashion companies such as Gucci, enabling new strategies for the reuse of textiles in industry. Similarly, the United States-based Ethical Metalsmiths have raised awareness in the goldsmithing field, bringing attention to destructive mining and refining processes, and asking individuals to consider their own responsibilities, particularly where there's no regulation, to ensure they work with others in mind.[10]

What's compelling about these examples is that their original interest came through and from the act of making things, which they continue to do at a consistently high level of skill, all while being thoroughly entangled with the histories and processes of what they do, where they're located and what this may mean for others.

And what about contemporary jewelry? During the Association for Contemporary Jewellery's conference Carry the Can, held in London in July, 2006, James Evans presented a series of stories, recollections and thoughts about jewelry as case studies in *La Mort De Joaillier (The Death of the Jeweller)*. An active jeweler in the 1980s, Evans designed and made commissioned work in what might be thought of as a conventional studio model. However, in the following years, working as an historian, he became intrigued by what had happened to his works and decided to trace their life histories. Over an extended period, Evans tracked down his jewelry and recorded the oral stories of those who have lived with it. Transcending time and place, the result was a series of poignant evocations of how the things around us continue to accrue meaning, shape relationships and change in relationship to those around us. Evans talked about the role a brooch had played in the life of a man and his three successive wives, through life, divorce and death. Evans's project suggests that we still underestimate the power of jewelry as a symbolic object that mediates relationships in the world, and if we were more often reminded of such strong stories, we would remember

Mah Rana
From Meanings and Attachments, 2001–ongoing
Digital photography and film, text, audio
Photo by artist

Polly: *"My silver necklace was given to me by Ivan, when our daughter Eloise was born. He had actually bought it two months before, when we were on holiday in Corsica—he'd managed to keep it a secret. I wear it most of the time and Eloise loves to point out to me that it represents her birth."*

James Evans reading excerpts from *La Mort du Joaillier: tales from beyond the grave,* during the Under the Counter Exhibition. Smiths Row, Bury St Edmunds, UK, 2010
Photo by David Gates

the importance of making jewelry to wear. Projects such as Mah Rana's *Meanings and Attachments*, which documents people and their jewelry, offer intelligent ways to think about this. They encourage making and wearing because they're about jewelry, not contemporary jewelry.[11]

In 2007, Elizabeth Callinicos developed a participatory project called *Mirror, Mirror*, which took place at the Ars Ornata Europeana symposium in Manchester (UK). Callinicos asked the audience to take an envelope containing a highly polished, mirrored stainless steel object, to own it and interact with it for a few hours in the context of the symposium, and then to return it to her. The artist sought to bring a collective response to a series of near identical starting points. What she was met with both intrigued and unsettled her—the discontent from some of the audience at being "gifted" a piece that demanded a return and the dissent from those who wouldn't return their piece contrasted with the willingness of others to interact with the work and hand it back.

Again, in all the above examples, research and understanding have come through practice and from the making of objects in relationship to people. In Callinicos' case, what's striking is the setting up of a collective experience where individuals, asked to make a response to an ensemble, ultimately reveal their ability to remain part of the collective or to demand single ownership of a part of it.

In Jeremy Deller's work, jewelry makes an appearance. The artist passes commentary on a set of discrete objects in *The Battle of Orgreave (An Injury to One Is an Injury to All)* (2001) which documents, through film and objects, the restaging of a violent conflict that took place during the 1984–85 miners' strike in the UK. One exhibit, a denim jacket adorned with badges, caught my eye. These small intimate "strike" badges capture the importance of jewelry. Striking miners collected them as tokens of visiting and joining different picket lines, but they were also the trophies of undercover police, who used them as evidence in their investigations and to track the miners' protest activities. I acknowledge that this example is grounded in an event of national conflict, but I hope we'll see a return to provocative acts in jewelry making that can maintain a social, real-life and outward-facing view—that remind us of the importance of wearing jewelry. If we can remember what's important while discarding what's not, we may yet see something more connected to life, place and people than the contemporary jewelry we have come to know.

Elizabeth Callinicos
Mirror, Mirror, 2007
15 x 7.3 x 0.05 cm
Laser-cut stainless steel
Photo by David Gates

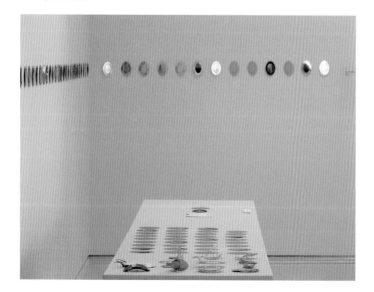

Notes

1. Nicolas Bourriaud, *Relational Aesthetics* (Dijon, France: Les Presses du Réel, 1998), 14.

2. Caroline Broadhead, "A Part/Apart," in *New Directions in Jewellery*, ed. Catherine Grant (London: Black Dog Publishing, 2005), 25.

3. Jeremy Deller: Joy in People (exhibition at Hayward Gallery, London, February 22–May 13, 2012).

4. *Jeremy Deller: Joy in People* (London: Hayward Gallery, 2012), exhibition guide.

5. Kevin Murray, "Is contemporary jewellery alive or dead?—the prognosis," *Craft Unbound*, September 4, 2011. www.craftunbound.net/medium/jewellery/is-contemporary-jewellery-alive-or-deadthe-prognosis.

6. Sarah Pink, *Doing Sensory Ethnography* (London: SAGE Publications, 2009), 29.

7. Tim Ingold, quoted in Amanda Ravetz and Jane Webb, "Migratory Practices: Introduction to an Impossible Place?" *Craft + Design Enquiry* 1 (2009): 13.

8. Tanya Harrod, "The memory-work: recent ceramics by Neil Brownsword," in *Neil Brownsword: Collaging History*, by Neil Brownsword, T. Harrod, and D. Barker (Stoke on-Trent: The Potteries Museum & Art Gallery, 2005), 4.

9. www.tedresearch.net.

10. www.ethicalmetalsmiths.org.

11. http://meaningsandattachments.tumblr.com.

Further Reading

Baudrillard, Jean. *The Consumer Society: Myths and Structures* (published in association with *Theory, Culture & Society*). London: SAGE Publications, 1970.

Carnac, Helen. *A Shared View: Stitching Together Ideas in Time*. CITY: Greenlab, 2012.

Carnac, Helen. *Taking Time: Craft and the Slow Revolution*. Birmingham, UK: Craftspace, 2009.

Carnac, Helen, and Ruth Rushby. *Process Works*. New Haven, CT: Site Projects, 2007.

Chapman, Jonathan, and Nick Gant. *Designers, Visionaries + Other Stories: A Collection of Sustainable Design Essays*. Oxford: Routledge, 2007.

Gauntlett, David. *Making is Connecting*. Cambridge, UK: Polity Press, 2011.

Ingold, Tim. *Lines: A Brief History*. Oxford: Routledge, 2007.

Manzini, Ezio. *The Material of Invention: Materials and Design*. Cambridge, MA: MIT Press, 1989.

Papanek, Victor. *Design for the Real World: Human Ecology and Social Change*. London: Thames & Hudson, 1985.

Partington, Matthew, and Linda Sandino. *Oral History in the Visual Arts*. Oxford: Berg, 2012.

Ravetz, Amanda, Alice Kettle, and Helen Felcey, eds. *Collaboration through Craft*. Oxford: Berg, 2013.

Thackara, John. *In the Bubble: Designing in a Complex World*. Cambridge, MA: MIT Press, 2005.

The Political Challenge to Contemporary Jewelry.

Kevin Murray

What does politics have to do with jewelry? At its most obvious, jewelry operates as a status symbol. It's a way in which wealth can be put on display. This is in part to justify affleuence and in part to provide a spectacle that others can enjoy. A unique example of this is the Piscatory Ring worn by the pope.[1] This ring is cast in gold for each pope and destroyed upon his death. It's traditionally used as a signet to seal official documents, and visitors pay respect to the pontiff by kneeling and kissing his ring. The uniqueness of the ring to each pope is a materialization of his singular status.

Beyond the individual, jewelry is also a means of regulating social status. In feudal society, sumptuary laws ensured that those seeking to climb the social ladder couldn't usurp markers of status. In 1533, under the rule of Henry VIII, An Acte for Reformacyon of Excesse in Apparayle was passed to regulate the display of luxury items such as pearls. This was partly in response to a growing merchant class that could afford to purchase goods previously associated exclusively with the aristocracy.[2] The use of jewelry to control rank was more recently practiced in the military. In 1760, rank in the British Army was signified by the pattern of lace on the cuff. Badges were introduced in 1810, to be worn on epaulettes. Such insignia are bestowed and removed in solemn rituals that induct the individual into a formal military role.

Jewelry, traditionally, is a means of upholding rank. It's thus a force of resistance to modern politics, which focuses on the redistribution of wealth. As part of the process of democratization and the emergence of the middle class following industrialization, movements from communism to Occupy Wall Street have targeted the uneven distribution of resources in society. Jewelry was therefore largely irrelevant to the utopian states, such as Soviet Russia and Maoist China, that emerged in the twentieth century. At most, adornment was reduced to the wearing of mass-produced badges in honor of socialist heroes. There was no substantial adaptation of jewelry to suit common needs, as happened with consumer goods such as cars or suits. But while jewelry upheld rank, it wasn't always according to the hierarchy of preciousness. There were variants of nationalism that sought to invert the value of materials. In 1813, the Prussian royal family asked citizens to donate their gold jewelry to support the uprising against Napoleon. In return, they sported iron brooches and rings inscribed with *Gold gab ich für Eisen (I gave gold for iron)*. Gold was transformed from a proof of status to a sign of shame.

Given the public nature of jewelry, it has the capacity to align its wearer to a specific cause. It thus can be a means of mobilizing opinion. In 1788, the English Quaker Josiah Wedgwood commissioned a cameo brooch depicting a slave seeking freedom, which was shipped to Benjamin Franklin in the United States, where it was to be worn as a bracelet or hair ornament.[3] Later, during the time of the Suffragette movement, the group's colors of purple, white and green were used in jewelry to profess solidarity with the cause. In 1909 a military-style medal was created to commemorate those Suffragettes who participated in a hunger strike.[4]

Today, some professional female politicians use contemporary jewelry to exercise power. Galerie Marzee worked with female members of the European Parliament in a project that uses contemporary jewelry as a public commitment to a common Euro-identity.[5] Madeleine Albright's book *Read My Pins* presents jewelry as a useful device for cutting through intransigent political positions by appealing to a personal response. She associates jewelry with a particularly feminine approach to politics: "The world has had its share of power ties; the time seemed right for the mute eloquence of pins with attitude."[6] Most of the brooches she mentions are anonymous illustrative jewelry sourced from stores. They're democratic "pins of the people" rather than prestigious art pieces.

As a core mission in the contemporary jewelry movement, the critique of preciousness has a strong

political dimension. Dutch jewelers have used the traditional association with prestige as a target for conceptual pieces, such as in the 1977 *Queens* series of necklaces by Gijs Bakker that, made from laminated photographs of royal jewels, mock their pretension. This move fell within the mission of modernist design to make beauty and function accessible to anyone. But the critique of preciousness is not necessarily political. Besides democracy, it's also associated with artistic freedom. According to this argument, the value of the work should be read according to its creative input rather than the materials themselves. The critique of preciousness was thus a necessary component of the development of a contemporary jewelry market.

Within this critique, a number of individuals made political statements with their work. This included David Poston's eloquent manacle of forged mild steel inlaid with silver, *Diamonds, Gold and Slavery Are Forever* (1975), which signaled his decision to avoid gold because of its association with South Africa's apartheid regime. This political voice seems a natural part of any art form, which enables artistic voice.

There are times when an adornment goes viral, reproducing itself without any obvious direction. The AIDS

Ribbon was developed in 1991 by the Visual AIDS Artists Caucus in New York. This red ribbon pinned to clothing quickly became synonymous with the call to recognize the impact of the disease. It drew on the tradition established during the Gulf War of tying yellow ribbons around trees and street poles to honor those away at war. The initial batch included 3,000 ribbons, manufactured in a simple three-step process. These were then delivered to the Tony Awards, which ensured celebrity endorsement, and the trend quickly took off. Over the next years, 1.5 million were made. A key element in this design was the condition that no individual be seen as its creator and that it be kept copyright free, never used for profit. Mike Carson, editor of *Entertainment Weekly,* outlined its success: "People come up to me and ask me how to get one," Mr. Carson said. "I laugh and say, 'Go to Woolworth's.' But I'm glad they ask. At the deli two months ago, this woman said: 'Why do you wear that?' And I was able to explain. It feels good to say the word AIDS out loud, not in a shameful way, not in a hushed tone, but as something we all think about and share with the rest of the world."[7] As a testimonial object, the AIDS Ribbon brought into public circulation what was otherwise a subject of shame.

Gijs Bakker
Alexandra Necklace, 1977
Diameter, 40.4 cm
Color photo, PVC
Photo by Rien Bazen
Courtesy of the artist

David Poston
Diamonds, Gold, and Slavery Are Forever, 1975
Iron
National Museums Scotland, Edinburgh

In 2003, a coalition of nongovernmental organizations developed a campaign titled "Make Poverty History" (MPH) in order to mobilize public opinion. Their target was the G8 Gleneagles Summit, due to happen in 2005. They hoped that a unified popular protest would pressure world leaders to focus on poverty reduction. Like the AIDS Ribbon, the MPH wristband was promoted as a public-domain adornment, encouraging people to make their own and wear it creatively. The campaign climaxed in 2005 during three "white band days." It's estimated that 8 million people participated.

Despite the democratic associations of the critique of preciousness, contemporary jewelers rarely seem to touch on the topic of distributed power. But some examples can be found in Australia, which is otherwise on the periphery of the movement. Susan Cohn's *I protest: LOVE NO WAR (3)* (2004) renders the photograph of a street scene into a mosaic of badges, each bearing the words *LOVE NO WAR*. Cohn had worked with badges previously, including a provocation during the Biennale of Sydney, where she distributed badges with the words *Craft is a hand job*. She also created a series of badges, each of which represented a segment of the word *Melbourne*. But in this case, the work rested as a complete set on the art gallery wall. Its dissemination was only implied. The scene itself reflected this ambiguity. The image of a female suicide bomber sits above an antiwar message, unsettling the natural tendency to approve female agency. The effect of the work as art is more to raise questions than galvanize action.

Alternative uses of politics have come from relational jewelry. Roseanne Bartley's *Culturing the Body* (2002) distributed metal and red thread tags, each stamped with a word then charged in political discourse, such as *un-Australian* and *queue jumper*. These words had emerged in response to the 2001 *Tampa* incident where a conservative government won an election after scapegoating 438 rescued refugees onboard the MS *Tampa* as un-Australian, and refusing them entry to Australian waters. Those wearing Bartley's tags were asked to note the responses they received while wearing them. The act of wearing these words in public countered their use in scapegoating those who were absent and thus unable to defend themselves.

Jewelry can also be political by circumventing the dominant systems for the monetary exchange of goods. Vicki Mason's 2010 *Broaching Change Project* aimed to reintroduce the issue of republic into the public discourse in Australia. In order to bypass clogged media venues, she devised three brooches based on common garden plants—

Susan Cohn
I protest: LOVE NO WAR (3), 2004
179.5 x 119.6 x 8 cm
Badge units, mixed media
Photo by Shannon McGarth
Courtesy of the artist

wattle, oregano and rose. In so doing, Mason tied the republic to the growing interest in communal gardens. The brooches were given away as door prizes at the exhibition Signs of Change, with the proviso that anyone who received one had to give it away to the next person who expressed interest in it. The journeys can be tracked on a blog where recipients comment on their period as temporary owners. Mason's project demonstrates how jewelry can be used to transmit political messages under the radar of official media.

The opposition between politics and aesthetics has been of concern for jeweler Bruce Metcalf. He argues that if you want to effect political change, you're better off being a politician than a jeweler. "If I have a responsibility, it is to exercise my gift. It is to function as an autonomous artist who serves only my own vision. In the long run, this is my only hope to have a real effect on the world."[8] This challenges the nature of contemporary jewelry. Metcalf has presented the imposition of a collective political agenda as a threat to artistic freedom. Indeed, it can be argued that politics is relatively incidental to studio jewelry. At most, it becomes a gesture in irony, not intended to make any substantial change in the world.

However, it's another matter for jewelry that draws from the street. The relational paradigm does have the potential to tap a popular energy similar to that found in public demonstrations. The critical framework for this is more likely to come from design than from visual art. In design, the focus is on use rather than representation. How well does this jewelry help create solidarity among people with similar political interests?

Design reconnects contemporary jewelry to the original democratic aspirations of the critique of preciousness. The originality of the jeweler isn't found in the object but in the methodology of its distribution. Politics thus offers an important challenge to contemporary jewelry, harking back to its origins. Can we imagine a future where contemporary jewelry is worn by the multitude?

Roseanne Bartley
Culturing the Body (Materialising the Unaustralian), 2000-2002
7-10 cm x 1-1.5 cm
Sterling silver, silk thread; embossed, oxidized
Photo by artist

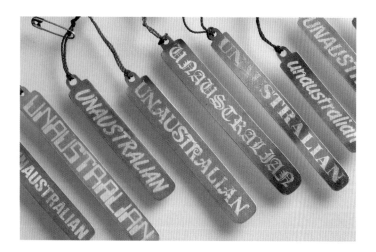

Notes

1. Dieter Philippi, *The Piscatory Ring (Anulus piscatoris) of Pope Benedict XVI*, www.dieter-philippi.de/en/ecclesiastical-fineries/ring-of-the-fisherman-piscatory-ring.

2. Leah Kirtio, "'The Inordinate Excess in Apparel': Sumptuary Legislation in Tudor England," *Constellations* 3, no. 1 (2012): 17–29.

3. Paul Scott, "Willows, Windmills and Wild Roses: Recycling and Remediation," in *Thing Tang Trash: Upcycling in Contemporary Ceramics*, eds. Jorun Veiteberg and Heidi Bjørgan (Bergen, Norway: Bergen National Academy of the Arts and Art Museums, 2011), 43; and *Africans in America Part 2/"Am I Not a Man and a Brother?"*, Africans in America Resource Bank, www.pbsorg/wgbh/aia/part2/2h67.html.

4. Ivor Hughes, "Suffragette Jewelry, Or Is It?" *New England Antiques Journal*, www.antiquesjournal.com/Pages04/Monthly_pages/march09/jewelry.html.

5. Pat Cox, *Jewellery: The Choice of the Europarliament* (Nijmegen, The Netherlands: Galerie Marzee, 2004).

6. Madeleine Albright, *Read My Pins* (New York: Harper, 2009).

7. Jesse Green, "The Year of the Ribbon," *New York Times*, March 5, 1992.

8. Bruce Metcalf, "Concerning Ethics in Jewelry," www.brucemetcalf.com/blog/?p=97.

Further Reading

Albright, Madeleine. *Read My Pins: Stories from a Diplomat's Jewel Box*. New York: Harper, 2009.

Craig, Gabriel. *JewelReCulture Vol. 1: Austerity Measures*. www.conceptualmetalsmithing.com/2010/07/jewelreculture-vol-1-austerity-measures.html.

Green, Jesse. "The Year of the Ribbon," *New York Times*, March 5, 1992. www.nytimes.com/1992/05/03/style/the-year-of-the-ribbon.html.

Hardt, Michael, and Antonio Negri. *Empire*. Cambridge, MA: Harvard University Press, 2001.

Hodkinson, Stuart. "Inside The Murky World of the UK's Make Poverty History Campaign." *Znet*. www.zcommunications.org/inside-the-murky-world-of-the-uks-make-poverty-history-campaign-by-stuart-hodkinson.

Kirtio, Leah. "'The Inordinate Excess in Apparel': Sumptuary Legislation in Tudor England." *Constellations* 3, no. 1 (DATE): 17–29.

Scarisbrick, Diana. *Rings: Jewelry of Power, Love and Loyalty*. London: Thames & Hudson, 2007.

Van den Hout, Marie-José, ed. *Jewellery: The Choice of the Europarliament*. Nijmegen, The Netherlands: Galerie Marzee, 2004.

Victoire de Castellane: Fleurs d'excès. Paris: Gagosian Gallery, 2011.

Žižek, Slavoj. "The King Is a Thing." *New Formations* 13 (Spring 1991): 19–37.

DIY in Theory and Practice.

Barb Smith

Short for do it yourself, DIY is the acronym for a group of making practices that encompass everything from farming, canning and hacking to crafting and art as social practice. The concept is broad and familiar. Its intentions and results are distinctively expressed in cities, garages, academia and rural America. The outcomes aren't so divergent in practice, but DIY is a problematic concept, which is increasingly evident when considering DIY in relation to craft. Any attempt at a definition of DIY is met with ambiguity. Contemporary politics, economics, pop culture and community building comprise a DIY ethos that renders its objects almost invisible. DIY, as a lifestyle choice, is a way of *being* in the world. As such, it's best discussed not in terms of its objects but as a cultural movement that began to thrive as postmodernism ended.

This essay considers what DIY might mean to us now, in theory, and what DIY is actually doing, as a practice, by identifying the gap between intent and outcome. A lifestyle, or way of being, as expressed through the format of jewelry, is a difficult topic. What is DIY in relation to jewelry? What's the difference between the claims made when DIY discussions are applied to jewelry and how such "DIY jewelry" works in practice?

An essay on DIY jewelry involves writing from a place between individual experience and shared meaning.

Something *made* is always a time capsule. All artists pull what they can from their culture, place or time. They analyze this sample, make, and then give something back. Understanding the conditions that bred the aesthetics, politics and lifestyle of the DIY craft movement doesn't begin with the format of jewelry, but rather with an examination of a network of historical, cultural, social, technological and economic developments over at least the past 30 years. Writers and makers alike have suggested that DIY practitioners are subversive, media-literate semioticians undertaking a third-wave feminist remix of domestic craft practices. "DIY craft as a movement emerged as part of community activism, with a lineage that can be traced back to the 1980s and the punk movement, 'zine activity and into the early 1990s with the Riot Grrrl movement."[1]

Casual and cool, political and subversive, romantic and wholesome, DIY is hard to define. This adds to its mystique. A rudimentary definition might regard DIY as a social phenomenon that utilizes the Internet to express a noncritical postproduction ethos of a craft community responding *to* the shortcomings of studio craft and the hierarchies of academia. The *we* in DIY linguistics consumes *you and I* by establishing an assumed common value system. Of course *we* are all interested in sustainability,

economic reform, social responsibility and self-sufficiency—in theory. How do these ideals manifest in practice? Inherently activist, DIY is craft as a verb, a state of being, an action constructing its identity in opposition to the academy and other institutions perceived as stewards of Craft as a noun. DIY places emphasis on the doing, not the done. The *we* of collective experience and community building has become a defining feature of DIY culture. Pronouns define the experience of readers, writers, makers and wearers; they're illustrations of community and the framework of DIY in theory. After the emphasis on the gulf between craft as a verb and Craft as a noun, it's actually the pronouns that are really worth dissecting.

What's at stake in understanding how pronouns operate, and how this process can attach to worn objects, is demonstrated in the American political arena.

In a television interview on Wednesday, Mr. Obama was asked why he wasn't wearing an American flag on his suit. "Is this a fashion statement? Those have been on politicians since Sept. 12, 2001," a reporter from KCRG-TV in Cedar Rapids said.

"The truth is that right after 9/11 I had a pin," Mr. Obama replied. "Shortly after 9/11, particularly because as we're

Venetia Dale
Dollar General, 2007
6.4 x 3.8 cm
Found flag pin in plastic bag, brass safety pin
Photo by Adam Krauth
Courtesy of the artist

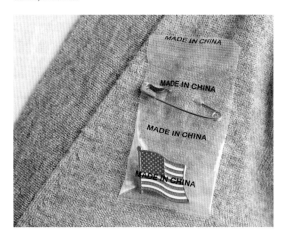

talking about the Iraq war, that became a substitute for, I think, true patriotism, which is speaking out on issues that are of importance to our national security.

"I decided I won't wear that pin on my chest," he added. "Instead I'm gonna try to tell the American people what I believe what will make this country great and hopefully that will be a testimony to my patriotism."[2]

In a post-9/11 world, the American flag is a signifier for solidarity and unequivocal patriotism. Due to its proliferation, "[the flag's] status as an icon of the kitsch aspects of American patriotic culture has become ... overdetermined."[3] Pinning something to your chest is perhaps the simplest and most compelling gesture of adornment. The wearer identifies with a constructed set of notions found within a given community. The point Obama makes is that the flag pin has become a passive representation of shirtsleeve ideology. Might the same thing be said about DIY?

Returning to pronouns, it's been said that politics always begins with the naming of the enemy. "All politics mobilizes the we in tandem with another word, they...politics feeds on identities. Identities start fights."[4] In the context of this essay, the *we* is the I and you of DIY. *They* refers to academic studio craft, the entity that DIY has most clearly defined itself against. "Today, studio craft is recognized as valuing skill, connoisseurship and tradition, and its social structure seems to generate the need for educational and professional hierarchies. In contrast, DIY craft emerges from a culture that does not seek professional validation within traditional art methodology but rather is motivated by joining with others socially in shared, creative activity."[5]

The Society for Contemporary Craft's exhibition DIY: A Revolution in Handicrafts presents a mainstreamed, institutionalized DIY that has an ineffectual relationship with contemporary political issues. The exhibition provides an important benchmark: by 2010, DIY had "evolved and matured...with little crossover into or support from the established craft world...[and was operating]...at the margins of the mainstream contemporary craft field."[6] The jewelry of Cranbrook graduates Seth Papac and Sarah Kate Burgess, and SIU-Edwardsville graduate Robert Longyear, are collections of quasi-altered found objects and narrative assemblages. Considering the use of found objects, the jewelry has more in common conceptually with Arte Povera than with DIY. This work relies on an established art stratagem: juxtaposition of lowbrow materials and highbrow format. Any relationship between 2010 DIY and 1990 DIY is purely aesthetic; it *appears* to be naive and deskilled,

Lisa Walker
Brooch, 2001
10 x 3 x 1.5 cm
Silver, lacquer, plastic, green-lipped mussel shell painted green and discarded at sea by Michael Smither and Gian McGregor
Collection of the artist

Seth Papac
Maria, 2009
122 x 31 x 11 cm
22-karat gold, 18-karat gold, silver, brass, steel, rubber, plastic, nylon, found objects
Photo by Travis Roozee
Courtesy of the artist

roughly approximated and juxtaposed with jarring transitions between elements. The jewelry is a signifier of taste and design, not ideology. The highly stylized results actually disagree with the framework of the exhibition: "Essential elements of this movement are through its association with social and political commentary, while at the same time emphasizing the development of strong, local communities, and environmentally responsible living."[7] Where are the "essential elements" of DIY in these jewelers' work? What the exhibition actually capitalizes on is aesthetic-as-trend: found objects gain the appeal of European jewelry.

The DIY aesthetic, which was first developed with specific political intent, has become an empty sign for critical action. The appropriation and commodification of the DIY aesthetic results in an outcome that is antithetical to the principles DIY is believed to represent. This process is not limited to craft.

"Indivisible" is a word that brings together Starbucks partners, our suppliers and the American people…One hundred percent of the materials are from right here in the U.S.A. The red, white and blue cord is manufactured in Rhode Island, and the brass crimps come from Florida. The zinc alloy bead is made in a woman-owned manufacturing plant in Los Angeles where the wristband is also being assembled."[8]

When it began selling wristbands with a charm stamped with the word *indivisible*, Starbucks married "social responsibility with the most important issue of the year—jobs creation—in a…way that seamlessly integrates into the culture of the company and values of the customer base."[9] The grassroots micro-lending plan initiated by Starbucks CEO Howard Schultz is a blend of capitalism and social responsibility, an honorific expenditure defining what is "right."[10] The message is timely; the bracelets have become the official, if unaffiliated, fashion statement of Occupy Wall Street. Their location by the register incites an impulse buy; the description implies ownership and pride over the mode of production. When the 99 percent buy and wear an "Indivisible" bracelet made by the 1 percent, they exemplify contemporary conspicuous consumption that doesn't simply display a particular social status, but a socially *aware* status.[11]

The "Indivisible" bracelet is an affordable, socially visible good that commercializes altruism and is more about the catharsis of the wearer than initiating critical action. Jewelry as campaign badge, moral compass or souvenir of

The Spill Smiths
1,500 Brooches, 2010
Each, 4 x 5 cm
Laser-cut acrylic
Photo by Ryan Holandes
Courtesy of Gabriel Craig

experience becomes an exercise in social thinking instead of true collaborative action. But what happens if another layer is added? Is the message or outcome different if the jewelry is handmade? When considering DIY's emphasis on craft as a verb, how does a state of being or an action translate into a product?

By placing the emphasis on the action, DIY is presented as inherently activist, feminist, democratic and anti-capitalist. As a physical representation of these ideas, DIY jewelry is more often a form of tokenism and evidence of virtue. Empathy and emulation become the focus of the Spill Smiths project, based at the Savannah College of Art and Design, "a two-part awareness project created in response to the 2010 gulf oil spill."[12] This project, part exhibition and part retail store, conjures many questions about intention and outcome. How does consciousness raising translate into action? Who benefits? What's the relationship between art and charity? As DIY is institutionalized, do makers simply highlight that they have the privilege to deny their privilege? Why be critical of the altruistic? Is making something by hand really a radical act?

DIY craft, as exemplified by Faythe Levine's documentary *Handmade Nation*, embraced the inherently political nature of craft. But a craft fair or the Spill Smiths project "looks not like an alternative to but precisely the norm of advanced capitalism, with its relentless entrepreneurialism in which even improvised, local cultural networks of exchange become forums for commerce."[13] Modern-day industry and economies, even craft economies, are, in theorist Guy Debord's phrase, fundamentally spectaclist and hierarchic.[14] The Spill Smith brooches create a feedback loop in which the economy develops for itself; the catalyst for community is product. The spectacle of its consumption creates a social relation among people.

The moral imperative of jewelry becomes the handmade as gift evidence. Walking away from the exhibition, one can feel better without thinking about what the oil spill actually means. "[This] message of citizenship is also one of consumer-citizenship…a kind of prepackaged sentiment… and that it is enough."[15] The doing, the community building organized around a craft action, illustrates the DIY ethos. The done, in the form of a handmade brooch, is a souvenir of social awareness.

Why is it difficult to try to address a brooch, which is trying to address an idea, which it doesn't actually address? Take this essay. To write about DIY jewelry, I had to move through a discussion of cultural, social and economic conditions, technology, activism, values and lifestyle before

Written by Cinnamon Cooper and Amy Carlton of the D.I.Y. Trunk Show, illustrated by Kate Bingaman-Burt
Craftifesto, 2008
Courtesy of Faythe Levine, *Handmade Nation: The Rise of D.I.Y. Art, Craft, and Design*

I even got around to addressing a physical object. After discussing theory, research and content, I might never get around to addressing the actual piece at all. What is the brooch doing and why can't I talk about it? Is the brooch acting critically? Is it possible that a brooch can't tell me a great deal about media theory or Baudrillard's ideas of hypperreality? Is it also possible that a brooch can't tell me a great deal about the social, environmental and economic impact of an oil spill in the Gulf of Mexico?

One decade into the twenty-first century, craft as a verb and Craft as a noun are ideologically divided. If craft wants to participate in the production of culture in meaningful and progressive ways, this is problematic. As DIY is branded, marketed and institutionalized, its momentum as a cultural, social, political and craft movement simultaneously slows. It has lost what was once so startling and unusual about the "de-skilled" aesthetic. DIY, as a craft movement, has vanished into the concept. As an academic examining my responsibility to the field and to the broader culture, I'm left working with the words *craft* and *DIY*. Considering lifestyle, these two words are like two shades of the same color. DIY craft, jewelry included, is the conceptual ghost of what craft has always been about: making things by hand. That value system is *ours*.

Notes

1. Dennis Stevens, "DIY: Revolution 3.0-Beta," *American Craft*, October/November, 2009, www.americancraftmag.org/article.php?id=8837.

2. Jeff Zeleny, "Obama's Lapels," *New York Times*, October 4, 2007. http://thecaucus.blogs.nytimes.com/2007/10/04/obamas-lapels.

3. Marita Sturken, *Tourists of History: Memory, Kitsch, and Consumerism from Oklahoma City to Ground Zero* (Durham, NC: Duke University Press, 2007), 56.

4. Peter Schjeldahl, "*Of Ourselves and of Our Origins: Subjects of Art*" (lecture, School of Visual Arts, New York, February 4, 2011). http://vimeo.com/26294782.

5. Stevens, "DIY: Revolution 3.0-Beta."

6. Society for Contemporary Craft, "DIY: A Revolution in Handicrafts." www.contemporarycraft.org/The_Store/DIY_2.html.

7. Society for Contemporary Craft.,"DIY: A Revolution in Handicrafts."

8. Starbucks, "Help U.S. Jobs, Get an Indivisible Wristband." www.starbucks.com/blog/help-u-s-jobs-get-an-indivisible-wristband.

9. Dominic Basulto, "Starbucks: Venti Plans for Micro Loans," *Big Think*, October 20, 2011. http://bigthink.com/ideas/40761.

10. Thorstein Veblen, *The Theory of the Leisure Class* (New York: Penguin, 1979), 119.

11. "Since the consumption of these more excellent goods is an evidence of wealth, it becomes honorific; and conversely, the failure to consume in due quantity and quality becomes a mark of inferiority and demerit … Conspicuous consumption of valuable goods is a means of reputability to the gentleman of leisure … On pain of forfeiting their good name and their self-respect in case of failure, they must conform to the accepted code, at least in appearance." From Veblen, *The Theory of the Leisure Class*, 74–84.

12. thespillsmiths.org. http://thespillsmiths.blogspot.com/p/spill-smiths.html.

13. Julia Bryan-Wilson, "Sewing Notions," *Artforum* (February 2011): 74.

14. "The society based on modern industry is not accidentally or superficially spectacular, it is *fundamentally spectaclist*. In the spectacle— the visual reflection of the ruling economic order— goals are nothing, development is everything. The spectacle aims at nothing other than itself." From Guy Debord, *The Society of the Spectacle*, trans. Donald Nicholson-Smith (New York: Zone, 1995), 10.

15. Sturken, *Tourists of History*, 135.

Further Reading

Adamson, Glenn. "Craftier Than Thou." *American Craft*, April/May 2011.

http://americancraftmag.org/article.php?id=12081.

Auerbach, Lisa Anne. "d.d.i.y. Don't Do It Yourself." *Journal of Aesthetics & Protest*, no. 6. www.joaap.org/6/lovetowe/lisa.html.

Dawkins, Nicole. "Do-It-Yourself: The Precarious Work and Postfeminist Politics of Handmaking (in) Detroit." *Utopian Studies* 22, no. 2 (2011): 261–284.

Hanish, Carol. *The Personal Is Political: The Women's Liberation Movement Classic with a New Explanatory Introduction.* www.carolhanisch.org/CHwritings/PIP.html.

Levine, Faythe, and Cortney Heimerl. *Handmade Nation: The Rise of DIY, Art, Craft, and Design.* New York: Princeton Architectural Press, 2008.

Metcalf, Bruce. *DIY, Websites and Energy: The New Alternative Crafts.*

www.brucemetcalf.com/pages/essays/diy_websites_energy.html.

Stevens, Dennis. "Validity Is in the Eye of the Beholder: Mapping Craft Communities of Practice." *Extra/Ordinary: Craft and Contemporary Art.* Edited by Maria Elena Buszek, 43–58. Durham, NC / London: Duke University Press, 2011.

Contributors.

Helen Carnac is an artist, maker and curator who lives and works in London. Central to her practice as a maker and a thinker are drawing, mark-making and the explicit connections among material, process and maker. Carnac often works in interdisciplinary environments. She's a founding member of the collaborative making project Intelligent Trouble, as well as a fellow of the Royal Society of Arts.

In 2006 Carnac was co-chair for the UK's Association for Contemporary Jewellery's conference Carry the Can. In 2009 she was awarded a UK cultural leadership fellowship and curated the UK national touring exhibition Taking Time: Craft and the Slow Revolution, which opened at Birmingham Museum and Art Gallery. Carnac's current and recent projects include guest professor, Kunsthochschule Berlin-Weissensee (Berlin, 2011); an artist collective called Walking, Talking, Making (2010); Marking Place (Sint Lucas, Antwerp, 2011); Intelligent Trouble (The Institute of Making, King's College London, 2011); The Tool at Hand (Milwaukee Art Museum and touring, 2011–2012); Drawing, Permanence and Place (Kunstverein, Coburg, and touring, 2012); and Side by Side (Siobhan Davies Dance, London, 2012).

Liesbeth den Besten is an art historian who earned her degree at the University of Amsterdam in 1985. She has worked as an independent writer, advisor, lecturer and curator in the field of contemporary crafts and design, with a special interest in contemporary art jewelry. She has been the chairman of the Françoise van den Bosch Foundation since 2000. She is a member of Think Tank, A European Initiative for the Applied Arts. She teaches at the Gerrit Rietveld Academie's jewelry department in Amsterdam.

Her books include *On Jewellery: A Compendium of International Contemporary Art Jewellery* (Arnoldsche, 2011); *Sterke verhalen, Hedendaagse sieraden uit Nederland: Cerita-cerita Besar, Perhiasan masa kini dari Belanda* (Erasmus Huis, 2006), a catalog accompanying a touring exhibition about narrative Dutch jewelry made at the request of the Dutch cultural institute in Jakarta; and

De nieuwe keten van de burgemeester (Stedelijk Museum Amsterdam, 2001), a catalog accompanying the exhibition showing the results of a design project for mayoral chains of office.

Chang Dong-kwang is an art critic, part-time professor at Seoul National University and independent curator. He completed a doctoral course in art criticism from the graduate school of Hong-Ik University in Seoul. Over the past few years, his research interests have been object aesthetics in contemporary crafts and the paradigm shift of crafts exhibitions since 1945.

Chang's publications include *Listening to the Sounds of History at the River of Life* (Meditation, 2003), co-authored with Jung Young-mok; *The Metal Arts of Seung-hee Kim* (Nabizang, 2006); *Yoo Lizzy, A Retrospective of 40 Years of Metal Works* (Nabizang, 2010); and *Spirit of Jang-in* (Powerhouse Museum, 2011), co-authored with Min-jung Kim and Lee Gwi-young. He has curated a number of exhibitions, including Indoor Scenery with Candlesticks (Gallery Bing, 1990); Fuji-Seoul, It's Horizontal and Vertical (Ilmin Museum of Art, Seoul, 1997); World Contemporary Craft Now (Cheongju International Craft Biennale, 1999); The Breath of Nature (Cheongju International Craft Biennale, 2001); Esprit of Bojagi: Abstract Space and Fabric Arts (Arko Art Center, Seoul, 2002); Korea Fantasia: A Stratum of Modern Korean Metalwork (Chiwoo Craft Museum, Seoul, 2006); and Delta: the Junction of Different Eyes (Daegu Textile Art Documenta, 2008).

Julie Ewington is a writer, curator and broadcaster. Since 2001, she has been the head of Australian Art and now curatorial manager of Australian Art at the Queensland Art Gallery | Gallery of Modern Art, leading a department embracing indigenous and non-indigenous art from European colonization to the present. A specialist in Australian contemporary art across all media, with a longstanding interest in contemporary jewelry, she has also written extensively on contemporary art from Southeast Asia and worked in a curatorial role on the Asia-Pacific Triennial of Contemporary Art series from 1996 to 2012.

Previously an art historian in Australian universities, Ewington has worked as a curator since 1989. Her major projects include The Art of Fiona Hall (2005); Scott Redford: Introducing Reinhardt Dammn (2010); and two surveys, Contemporary Australia: Optimism (2008) and Contemporary Australia: Women (2012), all at the Queensland Art Gallery. Her key publications include *Interstices: Works by Margaret West from 1981–1992* (Canberra School of Art, 1992); *Owner's Manual: Jewellery by Warwick Freeman* (Starform, 1995); *Brought to Light: Australian Art 1850–1965* and *Brought to Light II: Australian Art 1966–2006* (both Queensland Art Gallery, 1998 and 2007, respectively); *Fiona Hall* (Piper Press, 2005); and the forthcoming *Del Kathryn Barton* (Piper Press, 2013).

Elizabeth Fischer is in charge of the Jewellery Design Department at the Geneva University of Art and Design (HEAD—Genève). She is an art historian who lectures in the cultural history of dress and apparel and contributes to exhibitions on dress and jewelry. She is currently engaged in a research project on ornament, dress and the body in relation to design.

Some of her published work includes "Fashion and Jewellery in the Nineteenth Century" (in *The Fashion History Reader*, Routledge, 2010); "Avvisovi che se voi vedessi come costoro vanno vestiti… Le costume et son image dans la perception de l'étranger: autour du Triomphe de la Mort de Palerme," in *Entre l'Empire et la mer : traditions locales et échanges artistiques (Moyen Age-Renaissance)*, sous la dir. de Mauro Natale et Serena Romano, actes du colloque de 3e Cycle Romand de Lettres, Lausanne-Genève, 22/23 mars, 19/20 avril, 24/25 mai 2002, Viella, Rome 2007, p. 265-279; "Les nouveaux habits du Moyen Age. Le rôle du costume médiéval dans la peinture d'histoire suisse au XIXe siècle" (in *Art + Architecture en Suisse*, Société d'histoire de l'art en Suisse SHAS, no. 4 [2006]: 51–57); "Le costume ne fait pas le modèle" (in *Charles Gleyre, le génie de l'invention*, Musée cantonal des Beaux-Arts, 2006); and "Robe ou culottes courtes: l'habit fait-il le sexe?" (in *Filles et garcons: Socialisation différenciée?*, Les Presses universitaires de Grenoble, 2006).

Mònica Gaspar holds an MA in art history from the University of Barcelona and a degree in cultural studies from Zurich University of the Arts. She works internationally as a curator, writer, lecturer and consultant, researching on design and craft as critical practices and aspects of agency and participation in the arts and contemporary jewelry. Currently, she lectures at the Jewellery Design Department of Geneva University of Art and Design (HEAD—Genève) and is a member of Think Tank, A European Initiative for the Applied Arts.

Gaspar's curatorial projects include Neue Masche. A New Hook. Rethinking Needlework (Zurich: Museum Bellerive, 2011) and Metadomestic (Linz: Landesgalerie, 2011; Middlesbrough Institute of Modern Art, 2012), both of which explored the impact of "the applied" in the discourses of design and art. Jewelry-related exhibitions include curating the SCHMUCK show (Internationale Handwerksmesse, Munich, 2010); Nomad Room (CCB: Centro Cultural de Belém, Lisbon, 2005); and the first public collection of contemporary jewelry in Spain at the Museum of Applied Arts, Barcelona, in 2001. Her books include *Peter Bauhuis. Abecedarium: Jewel, Vessel, Implement* (Arnoldsche, 2012), co-authored with Peter Bauhuis and Pravu Mazumdar; *Anima Animus. Tord Boontje and Emma Woffenden: A Shadow Play* (Ebeltoft Glasmuseum, 2009); and *Manon Van Kouswijk, Lepidoptera Domestica* (Fonds BKVB, 2006).

Elyse Zorn Karlin is a jewelry historian and co-director of The Association for the Study of Jewelry and Related Arts (ASJRA). In that position she also serves as executive editor of the association's magazine, *Adornment,* and runs its annual conference. Her areas of specialty are the Arts and Crafts and Art Nouveau periods and jewelry of the American first ladies.

Karlin is the author of *Jewelry and Metalwork in the Arts and Crafts Tradition* (Schiffer Publishing, 1993/2007); the co-author of *Imperishable Beauty: Art Nouveau Jewelry* (MFA Publications, 2008); and the editor of the catalog *International Art Jewelry: 1895–1925* (Elyse Zorn Karlin, 2011). Her curatorial projects include Jewelers of the Hudson Valley (The Forbes Galleries, 2011); International Art Jewelry: 1895–1925 (The Forbes Galleries, 2011–2012); The Finer Things: Jewelry and Accessories from the 1890s–1930s

(Stan Hywet House Hall and Gardens, Ohio, 2012); and Out of This World! Jewelry in the Space Age (The Forbes Galleries, 2013).

Kelly Hays L'Ecuyer is the Ellyn McColgan Curator of Decorative Arts and Sculpture, Art of the Americas, at the Museum of Fine Arts, Boston. A graduate of Cornell University and the American and New England Studies Program at Boston University, she joined the MFA staff in 2001. She oversees collections of American decorative arts and sculpture in all media, with a focus on nineteenth- and twentieth-century art, craft and design.

For the 2010 opening of the MFA's Art of the Americas wing, she co-curated galleries for nineteenth- and twentieth-century art and was a contributing author to *American Decorative Arts and Sculpture (MFA Highlights)* (MFA Publications, 2006) and *A New World Imagined: Art of the Americas* (MFA Publications, 2010). She helped organize the exhibition The Maker's Hand: American Studio Furniture, 1940–1990 (MFA, 2003) and co-authored the accompanying catalog. After spearheading the acquisition of the Daphne Farago Collection of jewelry for the MFA in 2006, she presented an exhibition of the collection in 2007. Her book *Jewelry by Artists: In the Studio, 1940–2000* (MFA Publications, 2010) won awards from the Association of Art Museum Curators and the American Library Association.

Benjamin Lignel first trained in philosophy and literature, then in art history, at New York University, and furniture design, at the Royal College of Art in London. He devotes most of his time to creating jewelry, but recently he has also been engaged in curatorial and writing endeavors.

Lignel is a co-founder of La Garantie: Association pour le Bijou, a French association with a mission to study and promote jewelry. In this capacity, he co-curated Also Known as Jewellery* (2009), an exhibition of French contemporary jewelry that toured seven cities, and helped program and organize the 44th Schmucksymposium Zimmerhof (Bad Rappenau, 2012) in Germany. He began contributing essays and op-eds to magazines and publications in 2006, and became a member of Think Tank, A European Initiative for the Applied Arts in 2009.

Philippe Liotard is a sociologist at the Université Claude Bernard Lyon 1 in France. He was one of the creators of *Quasimodo*, a journal of sociopolitical analysis about the body. His research interests include body modifications (from piercing and tattoos to prostheses), gender, identity, sports and the relationship between body and culture.

Liotard has published many articles and book chapters about contemporary jewelry, transgendered bodies, disabilities and sexuality. "Modifications Corporelles" (*Quasimodo* No. 7, 2003) discusses contemporary body modifications. One of his most recent papers was written with Sandrine Jamain-Samson about the hypersexualization of female bodies; it's called "La 'Lolita' et la 'Sex bomb,' figures de socialisation des jeunes filles. L'hypersexualisation en question" (in *Sociologie et sociétés: Pour une sociologie de la mode et du vêtement*, Les Presses de l'Université de Montréal, 2011).

Kevin Murray is an adjunct professor at Royal Melbourne Institute of Technology University (RMIT University) and visiting professor at Australian Catholic University. His PhD was in the area of narrative psychology. From 2000 to 2007, he was the director of Craft Victoria, where he developed the Scarf Festival and the South Project, a four-year exchange program involving Melbourne, Wellington, Santiago and Johannesburg. He is currently a vice president of the World Craft Council Asia Pacific Region, an online editor for the *Journal of Modern Craft*, and a coordinator of Southern Perspectives, a south-south intellectual network. He is the coordinator of Sangam: The Australia India Design Platform as part of the Ethical Design Laboratory at RMIT Centre for Design.

His curated exhibitions include Joyaviva: Live Jewellery Across the Pacific (RMIT Gallery, Melbourne, 2012); Signs of Change: Jewellery Designed for a Better World (FORM Centre for Design, Perth, 2010); Guild Unlimited: Ten Jewellers Make Insignia for Potential Guilds (Craft Victoria, Melbourne, 2001); and Water Medicine: Precious Works for an Arid Continent (Curtin University Gallery, Perth, 1997). His books include *Craft Unbound: Make the Common Precious* (Thames & Hudson, 2005) and *Place and Adornment: A History of Contemporary Jewellery in Australasia* (Bateman Publishing, 2013), co-authored with Damian Skinner.

Marcia Pointon was a professor of art history at the University of Sussex and, starting in 1992, Pilkington Chair of art history at the University of Manchester. She is now a professor emeritus in art history at the University of Manchester and an honorable research fellow at The Courtauld Institute of Art, and works as an independent scholar and research consultant.

She is the author of many books, including *Hanging the Head: Portraiture and Social Formation in Eighteenth-Century England* (Yale University Press, 1993) and *Strategies for Showing: Women, Possession and Representation in English Visual Culture, 1665–1800* (Oxford University Press, 1997). Her book *Brilliant Effects: A Cultural History of Gem Stones and Jewellery* (Yale University Press, 2009), won the Historians of British Art Book Prize in 2011. Her new book, *Portrayal and the Search for Identity*, was published by Reaktion Books in November, 2012.

Suzanne Ramljak, a writer, art historian and curator, is editor of *Metalsmith* magazine and curator of exhibitions at the American Federation of Arts. She was formerly editor of *Sculpture* and of *Glass Quarterly* magazines, as well as associate editor of *American Ceramics* magazine.

Ramljak is the author of *Crafting a Legacy: Contemporary American Crafts in the Philadelphia Museum of Art* (Rutgers University Press, 2002) and *Elie Nadelman: Classical Folk* (American Federation of Arts, 2001), and has contributed to numerous other publications, including *Objects and Meaning: New Perspectives on Art and Craft* (Scarecrow Press, 2005) and *One of a Kind: American Art Jewelry Today* (Abrams, 1994). She has lectured widely on contemporary art and served as guest curator for several exhibitions, among them Playtime: Toys for Adults (Brookfield Craft Center, 2006); Different Tempers: Jewelry and Blacksmithing (Center for Craft, Creativity & Design, 2009); and Body Language: Contemporary Art Jewelry (Wayne Art Center, 2013). Ramljak is completing a forthcoming book and exhibition on protective ornament, *On Body and Soul: Contemporary Amulets to Armor* (Schiffer Publishing, 2014).

Sarah Rhodes is a jeweler, designer and researcher at Central Saint Martins College of Art and Design in London, from which she received an MA in design: jewellery. She also has a post-graduate certificate in art and design education and a BA in three-dimensional design in ceramics. Rhodes' work is concerned with ethical practices and social sustainability. Based in Africa for many years, she is developing her practice-based PhD research into collaborative work between established designers and grassroots African craft producers, challenging current preconceptions of the designer's role in the developing world.

Rhodes' jewelry has been exhibited internationally in southern Africa, India and the UK, including the London Design Festival and Sotheby's. Her consultancy work includes developing the curriculum for Botswana's first jewelry design and manufacture course and designing the spring/summer 2009 jewelry collection for the fair trade jewelry company, Made.

Valeria Vallarta Siemelink is a Mexican architect with degrees in museum studies and art history. She currently lives in the Netherlands, where she works as an independent curator, and is the co-founder and president of the Otro Diseño Foundation for Cultural Cooperation and Development. In 1993 she was awarded the National Prize for the Arts by Forndo Nacional para la Cultura y las Artes (National Trust for the Arts and Culture) for her curatorial work at museums such as the National Museum of Art and the Museum of Modern Art in Mexico City. Her field of interest focuses on contemporary art, design and jewelry, as well as gender, identity and migration studies; she has a particular interest in the cultural production of the Latin American and Caribbean regions.

Siemelink's recent exhibitions include Think Twice (Museum of Arts and Design, New York, 2010); Ultrabarroco (Ex Teresa Arte Actual, Mexico City, 2010); and Walking the Gray Area (Galería Emilia Cohen, Mexico City, 2010). She is currently working on a new major exhibition called Disposable Women. Her publications include her thesis, "Living without the Privileges of Sight: A Natural History Museum for Visually Disabled Audiences," completed at the National University of Mexico in 1993, and *Objects and Meaning in Latin America's Cultural Production* (National University of Mexico, 2007). She's currently editing a book on contemporary jewelry from Latin America.

Damian Skinner is an art historian, curator of applied art and design at the Auckland Museum and former editor of Art Jewelry Forum. He was a Newton International Fellow at the Museum of Archaeology and Anthropology, University of Cambridge, from 2012 to 2013. His research interests include contemporary jewelry, New Zealand studio craft, indigenous art and the relationship between art and politics in settler colonial societies.

Skinner's books include *The Carver and the Artist: Maori Art in the Twentieth Century* (Auckland University Press, 2008), which was based on his PhD thesis; *Cone Ten Down: Studio Pottery in New Zealand, 1945–1980* (Bateman Publishing, 2009), co-authored with Moyra Elliott; *Alan Preston: Between Tides* (Godwit, 2008); *Kobi Bosshard: Goldsmith* (Bateman Publishing, 2012); *Pocket Guide to New Zealand Jewelry* (Velvet da Vinci, 2010); and *Place and Adornment: A History of Contemporary Jewellery in Australasia* (Bateman Publishing, 2013), co-authored with Kevin Murray.

Barbara Smith received her MA in Photography and Related Media from Purdue University and her MFA in Metal from the State University of New York at New Paltz. She's currently a Visiting Assistant Professor in Craft and Material Studies at Virginia Commonwealth University.

Her work has been exhibited in shows at Sienna Gallery; Houston Center for Contemporary Craft; Center of Contemporary Art (CoCA) in Seattle; AG Gallery in New York; Museum of Contemporary Craft; School of the Art Institute of Chicago; The Museum of Fine Arts, Houston; and Dorsky Gallery Curatorial Programs in New York. She was awarded a 2011 New York Foundation for the Arts Fellowship in Crafts/Sculpture and attended the Skowhegan School of Painting and Sculpture in 2012. Her writing has been featured in the *Shawangunk Review, Metalsmith* magazine, Art Jewelry Forum, and *The Journal of Modern Craft* online.

Barbara Maria Stafford is an independent writer, curator and speaker. She is critic-at-large in the College of Architecture at the Georgia Institute of Technology, where she initiated an art/science salon by curating two exhibitions, The Salon for Vision (2011) and The Neuro-Salon (2012), and organizing their accompanying conferences. See www.barbaramariastafford.com.

Stafford's work has consistently explored the intersections between the visual arts and the physical and biological sciences from the early modern to the contemporary era. Her current research charts the revolutionary ways the neurosciences are changing views of the human and animal sensorium, shaping fundamental assumptions about perception, sensation, emotion, mental imagery and subjectivity. The author of 10 books, her publications *Echo Objects: The Cognitive Work of Images* (University of Chicago Press, 2007) and *A Field Guide to a New Meta-Field: Bridging the Humanities-Neurosciences Divide* (University of Chicago Press, 2011) investigate emerging cross-disciplinary entanglements.

Namita Gupta Wiggers is director and chief curator at the Museum of Contemporary Craft in partnership with Pacific Northwest College of Art. Through curatorial practice, Wiggers considers how craft and design function as subjects and verbs, as simultaneously distinct and intersecting practices, and how the exhibition operates as a site and space for cultural inquiry. Wiggers pursued doctoral studies in art history at the University of Chicago, where she earned her MA. She holds BAs in art history and English from Rice University. She is co-founder of the Critical Craft Forum and serves on the board of trustees of the American Craft Council.

Wiggers's publications include *Generations: Betty Feves* (Museum of Contemporary Craft, 2012); *Ken Shores: Clay Has the Last Word* (Museum of Contemporary Craft, 2010); and *Unpacking the Collection: Selections from the Museum of Contemporary Craft* (Museum of Contemporary Craft, 2008). She edited Garth Clark's *How Envy Killed the Crafts Movement: An Autopsy in Two Parts* (Museum of Contemporary Craft, 2009) and contributed essays for *Hand + Made: The Performative Impulse in Art and Craft* (Houston: Contemporary Arts Museum, 2010). She presented the keynote lecture at Schmucksymposium Zimmerhof in 2012. Her articles on jewelry include "Curatorial Conundrums: Exhibiting Contemporary Art Jewelry in a Museum Environment" (on the Art Jewelry Forum website, 2010) and "Mining History: Ornamentalism Revisited" (*Metalsmith*, 2009), co-authored with Lena Vigna.

Acknowledgments.

Many people have made this book possible. I'd like to thank Mike Holmes, who was the first to hear about the idea on a plane to Mexico, and Susan Cummins, who worked out how to make it happen. Both were critical in helping me develop the concept of this book and in encouraging me to believe that it was possible to pull it off. Without them, this book wouldn't exist. I am extremely grateful to the board of Art Jewelry Forum, which gave me permission to commit AJF to an expensive, multiyear publishing project. I'd like to acknowledge Sally von Bargen and Marion Fulk, who were the financial officers during this project, and Joy Martin, who paid all the bills. Also, a special thanks to Sienna Patti, the third member of the AJF Publications Committee, who, along with Susan Cummins, kept me in line in the most elegant way possible and has been an important sounding board as the project developed.

Marthe Le Van was responsible for introducing me to Lark Crafts and managing the initial stages of the project. Nathalie Mornu, who became my editor just before the text began to roll in, has been both wise and calm throughout the carnage. Without her, this book would be a very different—and I can't help thinking, lesser—publication. I would also like to acknowledge Jeanne Gardner and Susie Silbert, who have done a fantastic job managing the image acquisition and permissions process for this book. Aaron McKirdy, the graphic designer, managed to find a way to make an overly complex structure seem straightforward and devised a layout that, when I saw it, was exactly what I didn't know I had been looking for. Thanks are also due to Carol Morse Barnao for her art production.

There would, of course, be no book without the authors who agreed to take part. My biggest thanks go to Mònica Gaspar, Benjamin Lignel, Kevin Murray and Namita Gupta Wiggers, who took part in the round table that became Part 1 of the book. Four days of intense jewelry conversations, followed by a couple of years of Skype conferences and emails, have left their imprints all over this project. Liesbeth den Besten, Chang Dong-kwang, Elyse Zorn Karlin, Kelly Hays L'Ecuyer, Sarah Rhodes and Valeria Vallarta Siemelink performed the unenviable task of shrinking entire regional contemporary jewelry histories into 5,000-word essays. They made it seem so effortless that I often forgot to feel sorry (and apologetic) for the awfulness of the task. Finally, the authors in Part 3 of the book—Helen Carnac, Julie Ewington, Elizabeth Fischer, Mònica Gaspar, Philippe Liotard, Kevin Murray, Marcia Pointon, Suzanne Ramljak, Barbara Smith and Barbara Maria Stafford—deserve my thanks for agreeing to write about their, and my, interests, and how these different themes and issues offer challenges and opportunities for contemporary jewelry. As an editor, it is an amazing privilege to work with such smart people, and to see your initial ideas for a book fleshed out through writing that is dynamic, urgent and authoritative.

A number of people have read various sections and drafts of this manuscript in various states of completion, and I am grateful for their comments and suggestions: Jivan Astfalck, Susan Cummins, Marion Fulk, Mònica Gaspar, Benjamin Lignel, Kevin Murray, Sienna Patti, Sondra Sherman, Margaret West and Namita Gupta Wiggers.

A huge number of people have contributed their time, expertise and permissions in terms of locating and acquiring the images for this book. As well as all those people acknowledged in the image captions, I would like to thank the following individuals and institutions: Mark Adams; Elisabeth R. Agro (Philadelphia Museum of Art); Ellen Alers (Smithsonian Institution Archives); Alternatives Gallery; Anne-Valerie Hash Archive; art gallery Putti; Artists Rights Society, New York; Jivan Astfalck; Atelier Ted Noten; Volker Atrops; Atta Gallery; Roseanne Bartley; Susan Beech; Daniel Bell (The Royal Collection); Jennifer Belt (Art Resource); Martha Bielawski; Tarquinius Jobst Billiet; Alexander Blank; Jo Bloxham; Kate Bonansinga; Anne Brennan; Esther Brinkmann; Caroline Broadhead; Anne Bromer; Lola Brooks; Doug Bucci; Christophe Burger; Liesbet Bussche; Anna Cable (Te Runanga o Ngai Tahu, Auckland Museum); Cecile Camberlin (Moulinsart); Ana Cardim; Helen Carnac; Khadija Carroll; Pierre Cavalan;

Jacqui Chan; Chi ha Paura ...?; Susan Cohn; Octavia Cook; Beverly Cory; Michael Couper (Fingers Jewellery, Auckland); Gabriel Craig; Susan Cummins; Linda-Anne D'Anjou (Montreal Museum of Fine Arts); Sarah Davis (Siegelson, New York); Peter Deckers; Liesbeth den Besten; Betty De Stefano (Collectors Gallery Brussels); Die Neue Sammelung—The International Design Museum Munich; Iris Eichenberg; Ethical Metalsmiths; Eurostar Botswana; Cristina Filipe; Naomi Filmer; Karin Findeis; Jantje Fleischhut (OP VOORRAAD); Marta Fodor (The Museum of Fine Arts, Boston); Brian Foulkes; Françoise van den Bosch Foundation; Warwick Freeman; Galerie Marzee; Galerie S O; Galerie Spektrum, Munich; Gallery Funaki; George Eastman House, International Museum of Photography and Film; Getty Images; Rowena Gough; Lisa Gralnick; Cheryl Grandfield-Dodd; Graziella Grasetto; Fiona Grimer (Victoria and Albert Museum); Carole Guinard (Musée de design et d'arts appliqués contemporains, Lausanne); Judy Gunning (Queensland Art Gallery); Gésine Hackenberg; Han Heffken Foundation; Kirsten Haydon; Iwona Hetherington (Powerhouse Museum); Leonor Hipolito; Ellen Holdorf (Museum of Arts and Design); Mike Holmes; Eveline Holsappel; Peter Hoogeboom; Marion Hosking; Thaïs Hourbette (Carpenters Workshop Gallery); Rock Hushka; J. Gold & Co.; Arno and Dieter Jobst; Karin Johansson; Lisa Juen; Lauren Kalman; Susan Kaplan; Nathan Kerr (Oakland Museum of California); Veronica Keyes (Museum of Fine Arts, Houston); Erica Kim (Georg Jensen USA); Anya Kivarkis; Klimt02 Gallery; Melanie Knight (Mirrorpix); Kieron Kramer; Otto Künzli; Auli Laitinen; Kelly Hays L'Ecuyer; Anne Lennox (W.E. McMillan Collection, Royal Melbourne Institute of Technology, School of Art and Design); Lesley Craze Gallery; Faythe Levine; Andy Lim (Darling Publications); Georgia Loloma; William Loohuis (Museum CODA Apeldoorn); Rebecca Loud (Museum of New Zealand Te Papa Tongarewa); Lure Jewelry, Dunedin; Suska Mackert; Benjamin Macklowe (Macklowe Gallery); Jorge Manilla; Owen Mapp; Suzanne Martinez (Lang Antiques); Robyn McKenzie; Timothy McMahon; Nanna Melland; Bruce Metcalf; Metropolitan Museum of Art; Amandine Meunier; MIMA Institute of Modern Art; Thoko Modisakeng (DeBeers Group); Marc Monzó; Museum Het Kruithuis, Netherlands; Museum of Contemporary Craft in partnership with Pacific Northwest College of Art; Museum of Fine Arts, Houston; Museum voor Moderne Kunst Arnhem; National Gallery of Victoria; Sonya Newell-Smith (Tadema Gallery); Nick Nicholson (National Gallery of Australia, Canberra); Tatsuro Nishimura; Objet Rare; Ornamentum Gallery; Otro Diseño; Yuka Oyama; Xavier Padrós; Helena and Lasse Pahlman; Seth Papac; Diana Pardue (Heard Museum, Phoenix); Sienna Patti; Ruudt Peters; Susan Pietzsch; Caroline Pisciotti (Estudio Campana); Laura Potter; Suzanne Pressman (Three Graces Gallery); Kellie Riggs; Talia Roland-Kalb; Carola Ross (Thuthuka Jewellery Development Program); Rotasa Collection; David Roux-Fouillet; Marie-Claude Saia (Montreal Museum of Fine Arts); Isabel Schmidt-Mappes (Schmuckmuseum Pforzheim); Constanze Schreiber; Anna Schwartz; Katie Scott (Gallery Funaki); Michael Shulman (Magnum Photos); Susie Silbert; Smithsonian American Art Museum; Ulrike Solbrig; Paul Somerson (Chicago Silver); Bettina Speckner; The Spill Smiths; Gisbert Stach; Stedelijk Museum Amsterdam; Lisa Stockhammer-Mial (Three Graces Gallery); Cindi Strauss, Lorraine Stuart and Marty Stein (Museum of Fine Arts, Houston); Zdenek Svoboda and Demos Takoulas (Vukani-Ubuntu Development Project); Rachel Timmins; Giema Tsakuginow (Philadelphia Museum of Art); Marie-José van den Hout (Galerie Marzee); Wil van Gils (Stedelijik Museum 's-Hertogenbosch); Manon van Kouswijk; Luci Veilleux; Caroline Volcovici; Kate Wagle; Walka Studio; Lisa Walker; Anna Wallis; Susannah Wells (Smithsonian Institution Archives); Margaret West; Areta Wilkinson; Sarah Williams (The Museum of London); Margaret Wilson (The National Museum of Scotland, Edinburgh); Yale University Art Gallery; and Christoph Zellweger.

I'd like to acknowledge the funders and sponsors of this book. The Rotasa Foundation and Art Jewelry Forum provided the initial funding that made it possible to begin this project, and a major grant from the Windgate Foundation enabled us to complete it to a high standard. I am profoundly grateful for the support—in a financial sense, but mostly in terms of the vote of confidence that it represents.

Finally, I'd like to thank and recognize all the contemporary jewelers, both those who are represented in the pages of this book and those who are not, who have made objects and developed practices of such richness over the past 70 years. This publication is a small gesture of respect for their achievement and what it has meant to me and the many others who have had the privilege and pleasure of viewing, owning and wearing contemporary jewelry.

Index.

Credits.

Copy editor

Nathalie Mornu

Book design

Aaron McKirdy

Art director

Carol Morse Barnao

Photo research

Jeanne Gardner

Susie Silbert

Editorial assistance

Dawn Dillingham

Hannah Doyle

Kevin Kopp